LATIN AMERICA

STUDIES OF THE AMERICAS

Edited by James Dunkerley
Institute for the Study of the Americas
University of London
School of Advanced Study

Titles in this series published by Palgrave Macmillan:

*Cuba's Military 1990–2005: Revolutionary Soldiers during
Counter-Revolutionary Times*
By Hal Klepak

The Judicialization of Politics in Latin America
Edited by Rachel Sieder, Alan Angell, and Line Schjolden

Latin America: A New Interpretation
By Laurence Whitehead

Latin America: A New Interpretation

Laurence Whitehead

LATIN AMERICA
© Laurence Whitehead, 2006.

All rights reserved. No part of this book may be used or reproduced in any manner whatsoever without written permission except in the case of brief quotations embodied in critical articles or reviews.

First published in 2006 by
PALGRAVE MACMILLAN™
175 Fifth Avenue, New York, N.Y. 10010 and
Houndmills, Basingstoke, Hampshire, England RG21 6XS
Companies and representatives throughout the world.

PALGRAVE MACMILLAN is the global academic imprint of the Palgrave Macmillan division of St. Martin's Press, LLC and of Palgrave Macmillan Ltd. Macmillan® is a registered trademark in the United States, United Kingdom and other countries. Palgrave is a registered trademark in the European Union and other countries.

ISBN 1–4039–7131–5

Library of Congress Cataloging-in-Publication Data is available from the Library of Congress.

A catalogue record for this book is available from the British Library.

Design by Newgen Imaging Systems (P) Ltd., Chennai, India.

First edition: January 2006

10 9 8 7 6 5 4 3 2 1

Printed in the United States of America.

Contents

Acknowledgments

This book of essays would never have seen the light of day but for the steady encouragement and warm support of James Dunkerley, who persisted when most others would have lost patience. I am also indebted to the London Institute of Latin American Studies in another sense. As coeditor of the *Journal of Latin American Studies* between 1988 and 2000, I worked regularly with the Institute's team (especially with James's predecessor, Victor Bulmer-Thomas), who made me feel that ILAS was a home from home. Several of the longer (and better footnoted) essays were inspired by my experience of editing a Journal that is, after all, dedicated to "characterizing Latin America." Attentive readers may note the heavy reliance of these chapters on the many carefully documented and precisely focused Journal articles to support my own more sweeping and speculative interpretations.

These essays were written during the 1990s, with various disparate audiences in mind. It was the challenge posed by S. N. Eisenstadt, at a very stimulating workshop in Martin Luther's old stamping ground of Erfurt, that provoked me into writing the first version of the "Mausoleum" paper (Chapter 1 here), and that guided my efforts to redraft all the pieces so that they more explicitly focus on what was always my underlying preoccupation: how to characterize this large region, and to differentiate it from all others. The central tenets of his argument are therefore given due attention in the conclusion.

Another critical debt is to Alexandra Barahona de Brito, who deployed her own very considerable expertise (both editorial and substantive) to help turn a relatively disjointed collection of essays into a more integrated volume. (Certain passages owe so much to her advice that her name ought to appear as their author, but since they also express my own views she advised me to claim them.) Guillermo O'Donnell also played a catalytic role, always prompting me to aim a little higher.

As always, my college provided me with the ideal environment for study and writing, and allowed me to indulge in a type of work, which is quite tangential to its dominant antispeculative ethos. It also provided me with the administrative and secretarial support of Sarah McGuigan, without whom I would be lost. The love and support of my family was, as always, indispensable. They tolerated my bouts of distractedness, and in return I coaxed the spiders out of the house. At short notice my sister, Miriam Wood, came to the rescue over the index. None of the above has any responsibility for the oddities and flights of fancy here. They are all my own.

LAURENCE WHITEHEAD
Nuffield College, Oxford, April 1, 2005

Acronyms

APRA	*Alianza Popular Revolucionaria Peruana* (Popular Peruvian Revolutionary Alliance)
ARENA	*Alianza Republicana Nacionalista* (Nationalist Republican Alliance)—El Salvador
BONOSOL	*Bono Solidario* (Solidarity Bonus)—Bolivia
CANTV	*Compañía Anónima Nacional Teléfonos de Venezuela* (National Telephone Company of Venezuela)
CARICOM	Caribbean Common Market
CBF	*Corporación Boliviana de Fomento* (Bolivian Development Corporation)
CFE	*Comisión Federal de Electricidad* (Federal Electricity Commission)—Mexico
CIEPLAN	*Corporación de Investigación Económica para América Latina* (Research Corporation for Latin America)—Chile
CNG	*Conselho Nacional de Geografia* (National Council of Geography)—Brazil
CODELCO	*Corporación del Cobre—Chile* (Copper Corporation)—Chile
COMIBOL	*Corporación Minera de Bolívia* (Bolivian Mining Corporation)
CORFO	*Corporación de Fomento de Chile* (Chilean Development Corporation)
CPPD	*Concertación de Partidos por la Democracia* (Concertation of Parties for Democracy)—Chile
CTC	*Telefónica de Chile* (Chilean Telephone Company)
CVF	*Corporación Venezolana de Fomento* (Venezuelan Development Corporation)
CVRD	*Companhia Vale do Rio Doce* (Vale do Rio Doce Company)—Brazil
DASP	*Departamento Administrativo do Serviço Público* (Administrative Department of the Civil Service)—Brazil

DDR	*Deutsche Demokratische Republik* (German Democratic Republic)
ECLAC	Economic Commission for Latin America (also cited as CEPAL—*Comisión Económica para América Latina*)
EDC	*Electricidad de Caracas*—Venezuela
EDESUR	*Empresa Distribuidora Sur Sociedad Anónima* (South Distribution Company)—Chile
ENARSA	*Energía Argentina SA* (Argentine Energy Company)
ENDESA	*Empresa Nacional de Electricidad* (National Electricity Company)—Chile
ENE	*Escuela Nacional de Economía* (National Economics School)—Mexico
ENTEL	*Empresa Nacional de Telecomunicaciones* (National Telecommunications Company)—Argentina
EU	European Union
FMLN	*Frente Farabundo Marti de Liberación Nacional* (Farabundo Martí National Liberation Front— now *Partido de Liberación Nacional* (National Liberation Party, PLN)—El Salvador
FOBAPROA	*Fondo Bancario de Protección al Ahorro* (Bank Fund for Savings Protection)—Mexico
FUSADES	*Fundación Salvadoreña Para el Desarrollo Económico y Social* (Salvadorean Foundation for Economic and Social Development)
GATT	General Agreement on Trade and Tariffs
GDP	Gross Domestic Product
HDI	Human Development Index (of the UNDP)
IBGE	*Instituto Brasileiro de Geografia e Estatística* (Brazilian Institute of Geography and Statistics)
ICE	*Instituto Costarricense de Electricidad* (Costa Rican Electricity Institute)
IDB	Inter-American Development Bank (also cited as BID—*Banco Interamericano para el Desarrollo*)
IDEA	Institute for Democracy and Electoral Assistance— Sweden
IIK	*Institut für Iberoamerica-Kunde* (Institute for Ibero-American Studies)—Hamburg, Germany
ILO	International Labour Organisation
IMF	International Monetary Fund
INS	Immigration and Naturalisation Service (now Immigration and Customs Enforcement)—USA

ITAM	*Instituto Tecnológico Autónomo de México* (Autonomous Technological Institute of Mexico)
IUDOP	*Instituto Universitario de Opinión Pública* (University Institute of Public Opinion)— El Salvador
KMT	*Kuomintang* (Taiwan)
MERCOSUR	*Mercado Común del Sur* (Southern Common Market)—Argentina, Brazil, Paraguay and Uruguay
MIT	Massachusetts Institute of Technology—USA
NAFTA	North American Free Trade Agreement
OAS	Organization of American States
OECD	Organization for Economic Cooperation and Development
OXFAM	Oxford Committee for Famine Relief
PAN	*Partido Autonomista Nacional* (National Autonomist Party)—Mexico
PDC	*Partido Demócrata Cristiano* (Christian Democratic Party)—Chile
PDVSA	*Petroleos de Venezuela* (Venezuelan Petroleum)
PEMEX	*Petroleos Mexicanos* (Mexican Petroleum)
PETROBRÁS	*Petróleo Brasileiro SA* (Brazilian Petroleum)
PNC	*Policia Nacional Civil* (National Civil Police)— El Salvador
PRD	*Partido Revolucionario Democrático* (Democratic Revolutionary Party)—Mexico
PRI	*Partido Revolucionario Institucional* (Institutional Revolutionary Party)—Mexico
PRTC	Puerto Rico Telephone Company
PT	*Partido dos Trabalhadores* (Workers Party)—Brazil
SINPAS	*Sistema Nacional de Previdencia y Asistencia Social* (National System of Welfare and Social Assistance)—Mexico
SPP	*Secretaría de Programación y Presupuesto* (Secretariat for Planning and Budget)—Mexico
TELESP	*Telecomunicações de São Paulo* (São Paulo Telecommunications)
TELMEX	*Teléfonos de México* (Mexican Telephone Company)
UCA	*Universidad Centroamericana* (Central American University)—El Salvador
UCV	*Universidad Central de Venezuela* (Central University of Venezuela)

UN	United Nations
UNAM	*Universidad Nacional Autónoma de México* (National Autonomous University of Mexico)
UNDP	United Nations Development Programme
USAID	United States Agency for International Development
USIP	United States Institute of Peace
WB	World Bank
WOLA	Washington Office in Latin America
YPF	*Yacimientos Petrolíferos Fiscales* (Fiscal Petroleum Deposits)—Argentina
YPFB	*Yacimientos Petrolíferos Fiscales Bolivianos* (Bolivian Fiscal Petroleum Deposits)

Introduction: Latin America in Comparative Perspective

I. Introduction

This volume consists of a collection of many previously dispersed articles and chapters on Latin America's relative distinctiveness as compared to other "large regions." As a comparativist with genuine interest in the rest of the world as well as my chosen region, I am unable to endorse any of the various "essentialist" characterizations of the subcontinent that can be found in the literature. It has multiple, overlapping, identities. There is not just one "Latin American civilization," as Huntington would have it.[1] It is not controlled by its inescapably Hispanic Catholic traditions as Wiarda posited.[2] And contrary to Haya de la Torre, there is not just one "Indo-America," but many fragmented indigenous legacies.[3] Many regionally distinctive features are variants or offshoots of patterns developed elsewhere, particularly Europe and North America, even if the local adaptations also differ from their external inspirations in all sorts of easily neglected ways.

But this still leaves room for some more positive assertions about shared characteristics or recurrent features of social behavior and understanding in this vast, uneven, and rapidly changing culture zone. The structures and influences binding the region together may be insufficient to generate a homogenous product (in the way that, for example, the US culture zone homogenizes tastes and attitudes, not just within the United States but more generally). But over 500 years of Christianization; of saturation with Spanish and Portuguese linguistic practices; after almost two centuries of constitutional nationalism; given the transforming economic effects of foreign investments, immigration, and technology transfer; and given even the most contemporary influences of today's *telenovelas*—all these have nevertheless produced powerful cumulative effects accentuating some critical commonalities, and squeezing out many alternative possibilities that can be observed in other parts of the world. This book attempts to decipher such underlying tendencies and regularities, and to locate their genealogies and prospects.

So, to what extent can we generalize about "Latin America?" Area studies specialists are acutely aware of the region's heterogeneity, and the many divisions and exceptions that must qualify any summative statement. Yet, that itself is a generalization permitting comparison and contrast with elsewhere. "North America," for example, is often presented as relatively homogeneous and characterized by a configuration of rather stable and distinctive features (law, market, institutions, and culture) that differentiate the United States and Canada from the twenty republics to the south. (Samuel Huntington has even postulated the existence of two rival "civilizations" in the Americas, and has recently tried to suggest that Anglo-Protestant civilization may be under threat of encroachment from Latino advance.[4]) Social scientists rarely hesitate to generalize about the United States and its evident "exceptionalism"—"the first new nation" as it is often called—although for many analytical purposes the heterogeneity of U.S. society, and the existence of Utah or Greenwich Village would also point to the dangers of over-generalization there too.

It may be that there is less scope for bold region-wide assertions about Latin America than about North America, but there is still a level of analysis at which commonalities may be explored, and the characteristics supposedly distinctive to this large region may be evaluated. To attempt this is not to "essentialize" a regional tradition, or to deny the possibility of change and even convergence as extra-regional or universal processes operate upon it. A dispassionate exploration of common characteristics should always entertain the possibility that on close inspection these may prove illusory or that where they are confirmed within the region they are *also* present elsewhere. This volume contains a succession of such explorations—incomplete exercises, each reflecting my own personal interests and competences. Not until the conclusion do I directly attempt to answer the opening question.

Much obviously depends on the domain under investigation. If the focus is the effects of two centuries of liberal constitutionalism then the appropriate universe of cases includes North Central and *South America*, and how far the first differs from the rest. If the issue is the legacy of five centuries of indoctrination in the Catholic faith, then Latin America should be bracketed with southern Europe, and again the main question would be one cluster or two?. If the question is how European colonial rule impacted upon pre-Conquest social formations, then comparison and contrast with parts of Asia may be more appropriate. But overarching generalizations about Latin America typically encompass all these domains, and many others (the legacy of slavery, Iberian linguistic and cultural traditions, the consequences of natural resource abundance, and the telluric force of the subcontinent's often untamed nature, for example). One way to advance in this tricky terrain would be briefly to review some broad comparisons between Latin America and other large world regions—not only Europe and North America, but also Asia, Africa, the Islamic world, and Australia.

These are holistic and "configurative" assessments in that they attempt to sum up the overall and interconnected characteristics that may distinguish one large region from all others.[5] Such assessments are inherently stylized, shorthand, and ideal-typical. They aim to capture recurrent tendencies rather than to establish immutable contrasts. For example, Latin America may share some important features in common with other parts of the Iberian cultural community, and share others with the "Third World," and still others with all areas of "recent settlement." A configurative approach points to the particular combination of all these components that is unique to the region, and that will therefore condition the precise form of its relations with the rest of the world. So the claim is not that everything that happens in Latin America is fully determined by single components of the regional configuration (such as by its postulated bias to modernity,[6] or its proclivity for "top down" reforms—both quite widespread characteristics of the contemporary, more globalized international system); rather, this type of assessment is intended to direct attention to the particular patterns of interaction with the outside world that can be expected of this large region given its overall configuration of characteristics. Such patterns can fall short of full determination, but still be highly recurrent and distinctive. Thus, the aim of the comparison is to highlight respects in which Latin America as a whole can be usefully differentiated from the rest of the world despite its internal diversities.[7] This introduction considers those other five regions in reverse order, leaving Europe to the last and devoting most attention to that source of influence and contrast.

II. Latin America Compared to Other Large World Regions

If Latin America is heterogeneous and currently vulnerable to negative stereotyping, the same is all the more true of the *Islamic world*. The point here is not to provide an overall summary of the collective characteristics of this community,[8] but rather to isolate a few crucial respects in which they can be used as a contrast with Latin America.

Looking beyond the obvious (and hopefully temporary) fact that much of Islam is currently viewed with fear and distrust by many in the Western democracies, we can hope to isolate some deeper features of this tradition (or civilization) that differentiate it from *nuestra América*. One might cite the authority of the Koran and the mosque, reverence toward certain very distinctive literary and artistic traditions, military and political humiliation by the Israelis, difficulties with some key tenets of Western liberalism (such as separation of Church and State), a secular judiciary, and attitudes toward women, among others. Since the fall of the Ottoman Empire the Islamic world has lost its last great political center of authority, and there seems to be an unsatisfied desire for the creation of a substitute politico-religious leadership. Latin America self-evidently differs from the Islamic world on all these (and quite a few other) dimensions.

For the purposes of this book, one particular unifying feature of Islam can be counter-posed to Latin America: its vision of the past. Whatever differences may separate the diverse strands of Islam, they are united by a shared emphasis on the ultimate authority of a seventh-century Arabian prophet, an authority that reaches across the public and private realms, and that regulates attitudes toward the economy and the state as well as socialization and culture. By contrast, despite the prevalence of Christianity, Latin Americans recognize no comparable unified traditional authority, and assume a considerable separation between the distinctive spheres of social life. The European Conquest cut off subsequent Latin American communities from all the great pre-Conquest sources of authority that were indigenous to the Americas and it established a separation of roles between distant alternative European centers of power (the Iberian courts, the Vatican, and after independence, the cities of London, Paris, or New York).

In summary, Islam still turns to Mecca and the Koran for unity and direction whereas Latin America is oriented toward a multiplicity of external sources of inspiration, all characterized by role differentiation. Moreover, since Independence Latin American elites have characteristically justified their reforms and innovations by reference to what they present as the most modern of international practices. In a wide range of domains they often criticize the status quo from the standpoint of real or imagined better models developed in the most advanced metropolitan centers. (As various chapters in this book show, such models are not necessarily stable or appropriate, but they can provide strategic elites with a powerful array of justifications for the imposition of their preferred reforms.) For this reason, this volume refers to a Latin American "bias toward modernity" (in fact toward multiple and overlapping versions of modernity) as well as to the tendency to promote innovations "from above and without." The Islamic world has traditional and internalized norms that counteract any such tendencies. Relatively speaking, at least Latin America lacks such counterweights.

SubSaharan Africa is also diverse, and more so than Latin America on some key criteria such as language, religion, ethnicity, and political traditions. In contrast to Islam, and in common with Latin America, its elites may also be unambivalently keen to assimilate models and practices from former colonial and metropolitan sources. But in this case, direct colonial rule remains a living memory and postcolonial elites are far more incipient, while the authority and social embeddedness of the new African states is generally much less firmly established. What this comparison highlights about Latin America is the exceptional precocity of modern state formation (and autonomous state organization) in Latin America, and its centuries long traditions of elite formation and socialization, free from direct imposition and external control. Compare, for example, the oldest universities of Latin America (which date back to the sixteenth century and so precede all the U.S. Ivy League colleges) to the twentieth-century origins of educational establishments in Africa. Latin American elites and their professional cadres may look to Europe and North America for examples to emulate, but they do so from a highly elaborated and deeply entrenched local standpoint. They are not *parvenus* to the European tradition. No doubt Africa shares with Latin America many of the structural characteristics that can be summed up by the term "peripheral development." Acute social inequalities and the widespread absence of basic security from violence, hunger, or disease, weaken the social foundations required for constructive reform in both; but outright state failure and unbridled conflict for the control of natural resources are more characteristic of Africa, and barring some notable exceptions, almost entirely absent in the case of twentieth-century Latin America.

Latin America may also be compared to the long-established centers of civilization in *Asia*, as in China, Japan, India, or Korea. In these cases, there are obviously deep connections to many aspects of an ancient and non-Western past—in this sense some of the comments already made about the weight of Islamic traditions may apply with even greater force. But in addition, all these nations experienced foreign occupation, war, and massive dislocation of traditional institutions during the twentieth century on a scale unknown in Latin America since the 1820s. Empires and dynasties were overthrown, foreign armies held sway and withdrew, political boundaries were forcefully redrawn on a massive scale, and if some well-established elites survived or adapted, others of great distinction were eradicated. State organization may often be far more effective than in Africa or the Islamic world, but if so this has been a product of intense effort and bold experimentation. The incremental nature of state formation and restructuring within secure boundaries that has characterized Latin America is a luxury that has been unavailable to the dynamic—often "developmental"—state of East Asia. Millennial Asian religious and civilizational experiences, often linked to traditional zones of dense agrarian settlement that favor close social integration, contrast with Latin America's many areas of more recent and less crowded settlement, and with the safety valve provided by land abundance, even to those Andean and Meso-American peoples with similar pre-Conquest histories. And Latin America's post-Conquest and post-Independence deference to foreign models, together with the accompanying insistence on their appropriation by long-established vested interests, is difficult to replicate in much of Asia, where local pride demands that indigenous traditions should also be respected and used to control the functional imitation of external practices. In short, Latin America is far more wholly integrated into Western traditions and assumptions. Its unbroken independence may have allowed considerable latitude over the terms and contents of its foreign borrowings, but "our America" always searches for variation within a trans-Atlantic worldview, rather than seriously imagining any alternative civilizational traditions or alternatives. On this argument Latin America is essentially located in what Alain Rouquié has referred to as Europe's "Far West."[9]

Latin America as part of the "New World" can also be compared to other large areas of *recent settlement*, not only the United States and Canada, but also Australia and New Zealand. Economic historians have done substantial work on this topic, mostly from the standpoint of explaining why countries mostly settled by English speakers and governed under Anglo-Saxon legal and institutional provisions may have achieved greater and more durable economic success than the various republics of Iberian origin.[10] A common conclusion has been that "institutions matter," although different starting points and contracting economic endowments and opportunities complicate the discussion. For the purposes of this volume it is not just relative economic performance that requires comparison, vital though that undoubtedly is. The attempt here is to specify in what respect Latin American societies *as a whole* can be compared with or differentiated from those of other large regions. From this perspective, internally generated economic dynamism and effective state organization constitute two important—and possibly linked—components in a broader configuration. Other potentially distinguishing critical features might include social cohesion or integration and the stability (or volatility) of collective self-understanding. Of these latter two dimensions it is possible to identify some rather marked contrasts between the Latin American republics and the English-speaking areas of recent settlement. For a start, of course, the recent nature of settlement is more evident in much of the latter than in most of the former. The original inhabitants of Mexico and the Andes have not been overwhelmed and marginalized to anything like the same extent as in North America and Australasia. Together with the legacies of slavery (especially in Brazil and the larger Caribbean islands) this greatly complicates processes of social integration and generates conflicting visions of collective identity. Even where such tensions are diminished, however, there are other indicators of Latin America's distinctively compartmentalized and contested social configurations.

The extremes of income and asset inequality that can be found as readily in Argentina and Chile as in Brazil or Peru provide telling evidence of this. These acute material inequalities are accompanied by subjective divisions (over conceptions of social justice, the discriminatory workings of public institutions, the substantive content of claims to citizenship, and the desirability of systemic change), which add up to a very different public discourse and pattern of expectations in the Latin American republics from the individualist discourse prevalent in the Anglophone countries of recent settlement. At least in the "collective imagination"—if not always in the observed practices—of these latter societies, individual rights are taken as guaranteed, social actors are assumed to have internalized the logic of existing institutional rules, and the resulting model is held to be guided by the preferences of the median voter and of the sovereign consumer. In this setting, most foundational issues are off the agenda, modernity is a given ("we *are* the modern world"), and major historical alternatives lie outside the collective imaginary. The institutional framework is therefore an unquestionable given, and issues of reform can be posed in essentially utilitarian terms. The idea of importing wholesale reform blueprints from other, more successful, societies is not seriously entertained, and ruling elites are basically quite cohesive, patriotic, and fairly well controlled by mass opinion. Of course these generalizations can all be criticized at the margins, but *grosso modo* they serve to highlight features that differentiate the Latin American region from other countries of recent settlement.

III. Latin America and Europe

Finally, when we turn to a comparison between Latin America and *Europe* a rather fuller and more historically oriented perspective is required. This is because the relationship between these two large regions has endured for so long and been so intense and reciprocal that a merely external comparison (like those sketched above) would miss a fundamental point. It is only a partial exaggeration when Alain Rouquié refers to Latin America as Europe's "Far West." At any rate, even in an extremely summary overview an attempt should be made to unravel some of the major interactions and shared perceptions (as well the growing divergences and entrenched misperceptions) on both sides of the European Latin American relationship.

Since the "New World" first emerged in the European mind—the world that opened up to seafarers once the Admiral had raised the royal standard with its F and Y insignia on the small island called Guanahani, or Lucayos, or Watling Island in the Bahamas on Friday, October 12, 1492, chroniclers, intellectuals, and academics have attempted to make sense of what is now "Latin America." The history of the encounter between Europe and that New World has been told and retold from so many angles, with such varied emphasis and objectives, that one might suppose that there is now little new to be said.[11] But that is to overlook Collingwood's "familiar fact that every generation finds itself interested in, and therefore able to study historically, tracts and aspects of the past which to its fathers were dry bones, signifying nothing."[12]

Since the French second empire, the subcontinent has been referred to as "Latin" America for a good reason. It has especially long-standing and intimate ties, not so much with Europe as a whole as with the Catholic Romance language countries of South-West Europe, with strong cultural affinities with Spain and Portugal as well as France and Italy. In addition to language, religious, and family ties, consider the historical origins of such characteristic regional institutions as the *latifundio*, the *plaza pública*, and the republican constitution—not to mention legal traditions. Similarly, in the political realm, the Latin American countries are all in a rather direct sense "children of the French Revolution" with corresponding conceptions of popular sovereignty, individual rights, the Napoleonic role of the nation-state and the left-right ideological spectrum. When the Christian Democratic and Socialist Internationals expanded their activities in Latin America they encountered numerous apparently familiar landmarks, as did Europe's Jacobin Left. And in the economic realm, Latin America developed with an overwhelmingly outward—coastal and indeed centrifugal—orientation, that lasted from the Conquest until about 1930. During that period of more than four centuries, the economic focus was not so much outward as "Europe-ward," first on the Iberian Peninsula, then Britain and, to a lesser extent, France, Germany, and

Italy. It was only because the Europeans destroyed their own presence through internecine conflict that Latin America fell so completely under U.S. influence during the middle half of the twentieth century. As this unrivalled U.S. supremacy has gradually waned since the 1950s, both globally and regionally, so Latin America's historical orientation toward Europe was again revived.[13]

There is a marked contrast here between Latin America and other areas of the so-called Third World. As already mentioned, the retreat of Western influence in the Middle East has uncovered quite different historical orientations, which remained subterranean during the brief interlude of Christian ascendancy. The decolonization of Asia and Africa also gave rise to the expression of a wide range of local traditions that were at least partly a repudiation of European models. It is only in Latin America that contemporary aspirations for national autonomy (or, in this case, resistance to Great Power hegemonies) actually involve reaching out to the new Europe that was reconstructed after two great wars.

The idea of a specifically "Latin" America originated as an external construction, intended to aggregate the non-Anglophone states and societies of the western hemisphere for the purpose of generating a manageable picture of the world and its subdivisions. As such the defining conditions were negative and derived from without. Over time, this collective identity has acquired a certain internal acceptance, notably in the cultural sphere (the boom in the Latin American novel, music, and cinematography are examples), and also in some public policy arenas (positively, when there is diplomatic advantage in banding together, and also negatively, as in the Latin America-wide debt crisis). But the region contains many competitive interests and rival elites, and this particular collective identity has been contested as much as it has been affirmed (e.g., by postulating a Brazilian, or Mexican, or indeed an Indo-American alternative). The region is in any case blurred at the edges (most references to it overlook Puerto Rico, not to mention Miami, and are equivocal about Haiti). So we have an externally derived classification that is only partially and selectively internalized within the subcontinent.

This makes it essential to stress that characterizing Latin America *tout compris* should not obstruct the parallel enterprise of characterizing individual republics or subregions within the large region. On the contrary, these two cognitive enterprises should be seen as complementary— just as we can *both* track family resemblance and individual difference in our interpersonal relations. The "large region" characteristics singled out for particular attention in this volume include a strong outward orientation (particularly among competitive elites who aspire to enhance their authority by presenting themselves as bearers of internationally approved standards of "modernity"); and the recurrent difficulty in stabilizing a unique version or model of modern practice, so that alternative projects continually jostle and overlap, without achieving completion or consensus, and the landscape is littered with residues of superseded innovations.

IV. Configurative Characteristics

Stated in this form, these are very broad-gauge suggestions that need to be grounded both historically and with reference to specific social domains. The chapters in this book tackle this task from a variety of angles. This section addresses the *longue durée* background to the region's distinctiveness, under six general headings: demography, the resource base, built environment, ecological exchange, the "collective imagination," and political practices. The aim here is not to elaborate on any of these vast and complex topics, but rather to remind the reader of their interconnectedness, and of the most basic ways in which they link this large world region with others—especially with Europe— and also increasingly for the twentieth century onwards with North America. The distinctive nature of Latin America's external linkages goes far toward illuminating the factors differentiating it from other large regions. The first four topics—demography, resource base, built environment, and ecological exchange—all help to explain both the strength and the pattern of Latin America's typical external orientation. In particular, they draw attention to the subcontinent's intense, protracted, and troubled reciprocal relationship with Europe, which has long provided a critical reference point for its competitive projects of modernization and reform. The last two topics—the "collective imagination" and political practices—help to explain why stable consensus behind such initiatives is so elusive.

Demography

If we start with *demography*, over the centuries the population of Latin America has been subject to intense Europeanization. This is, needless to say, an observation that has to be formulated with care. There has been a resurgence of indigenous movements in many countries (including Ecuador), and Europeans were of course responsible for the African slave trade. The demographic origins of the present population of the New World are extremely heterogeneous. Nevertheless, if we consider the dominant languages, religions, educational influences, or markers of elite status, the weight of European influences (some direct, some filtered through North America) is very striking. This is a population more subject to Europeanization than, say, the peoples of Africa, Asia, or the Middle East. The flows across the Atlantic are complex and varied. They range from *golondrinas* to Jesuits, from poets to financiers, and they can be two-way flows. The very words "Latin America" are eloquent about this deeply rooted relationship, signaling the preeminence of the Romance languages and the foundational claims of the Florentine businessmen (among them Amerigo Vespucci) who coined the term "the New World."

In many parts of Latin America the European orientation of dominant elites gave rise, during the early twentieth century, to strenuous policies of selective immigration intended to "whiten" the demographic composition of the society, and thereby reinforce defenses against the negative characteristics they attributed to many of their own people. Here is a striking *longue durée* illustration in support of the claimed outward orientation of ruling strata, and the transformative nature of some of their projects for "modernizing" from above. But the history of these projects also highlights their lack of consensus and the incompleteness of their application. These initiatives were often strongly resisted by the popular classes they were directed against, and to varying degrees they could be thwarted, diverted, or halted midway, with the result that rather than transforming the whole society they added new segments and new elements of heterogeneity. The "non-white" population typically retained enough of its traditions and distinctive outlook to push back the newcomers and to absorb their influence without being swamped by it.

Over the past quarter century, Latin America's distinctive demography has again contributed to the repositioning of the region in the world economy. From being a magnet for immigration, the subcontinent has become a large source of out-migration—above all to North America, but also increasingly to Western Europe. This is changing the economic and social balance in the region, generating huge new flows of family remittances from the developed world, undermining some old elites, and stimulating new patterns of outward-oriented innovation.

The Resource Base

There was always a powerful resource base underpinning these demographic flows, which also underlies the recurrent if intermittent episodes of trans-Atlantic convergence. The precious metals of the colonial period financed European expansion, and the primary exports of the nineteenth and early twentieth centuries provided vital inputs to European industrialization. From the Second World War

Latin American resources supplied the Western alliance with strategic inputs from a secure hinterland. Here, too, the relationship was always a two-way—albeit asymmetrical—exchange. Europeans supplied the shipping, the ports, the credit, and in the nineteenth century, the railroads. After 1914, Europe had far less to offer Latin America, a not inconsiderable factor in explaining the subcontinental switch toward inward-looking development. After the end of the Cold War, however, resource flows from Europe revived, notably in such areas as telecommunications and banking, and now all the main vehicle manufacturers of Europe are integrating Latin America into their global strategies. Despite technology shifts, and although different parts of the European and Latin American economies may rise or fall, the long-term habit of intense resource exchange undergirds the social imbrication of the two regions.

In the twentieth century, of course, this economic orientation toward Europe was displaced, partly by a shift to inward-looking development, and partly by the rise of the U.S. as the principal market, and source of credit and technical innovation. Curiously enough, even in the twenty-first century it seems that Latin America's insertion in world markets may still be shaped by its distinctive resource base, this time with China as the new outlet for its agricultural and subsoil commodities. In this area, as elsewhere, the subcontinent displays a highly distinctive profile that reinforces the traditional outward orientation of its elites, and their need to monitor and catch up with developments in the various more dynamic centers of global economic innovation. An economy (or rather, a cluster of rival and loosely linked economies) geared to external stimuli will require compartmentalized expertise to adapt to shifting international opportunities and fashions. Rival groups of experts will promote alternative projects derived from their particular sources of training, and their distinctive international linkages. Each sectoral initiative (deepwater oil prospecting, pension privatization, genetically modified grain production, to name just a few) can be forcefully promoted in the name of external necessity, but each will also threaten the interests of other long-standing local economic groups. So long as the resource base remains abundant and varied, and the international commodity lottery continues to fluctuate, successive initiatives of this kind will clash against each other. Only a much more integrated and cohesive domestic economy can bring this cyclical pattern to a close, and the scale of resource abundance in the region has delayed this prospect.

As a large region with many still underpopulated areas, this natural resource abundance interacts with a human resource base characterized—much more so than in other regions of recent settlement—by extremes of inequality and lack of social cohesion. So a related aspect of Latin America's distinctiveness is the role of the still under-exploited resource base as an escape valve, or as a source of hope of social mobility for some of those trapped at the bottom of the social pyramid. As illustrated by this volume, and by chapters four and five in particular, this in turn reinforces competition between alternative development strategies none of which have yet proved to be durably hegemonic.

The Built Environment

The built environment provides one highly visible demonstration of this region's social imbrication with Europe. The cities of late medieval Europe were seldom entirely new foundations conceived on paper before they were inscribed on the landscape. By contrast, many Latin American cities originated as a concept, or invention, just as the new world itself was "invented" before it was occupied. When Bartolomé Columbus laid out the urban design for Calle las Damas in 1496 there was nothing archaic about the Santo Domingo governor's palace, the harbormaster's dwelling, or what became the first cobbled street in the Americas. The layout expressed what were then most modern Spanish ideas about architecture, town planning, urban settlement, and about the place of education: in 1538, the convent became St. Thomas Aquinas University, the first in Latin America, abutting what were also the first church and cathedral of the New World. The enterprise foreshadowed in miniature the hundreds, and eventually thousands, of *plazas públicas* and preplanned urban settlements that Iberian settlers would replicate across the entire subcontinent. Indeed, in 1573, Philip II promulgated ordinances specifying the scale of all plazas—between 200 and 300 feet wide and between 300 and 800 feet long—and the configuration of the associated public buildings, including the rectangular street plan of all Spanish New World cities. In more recent centuries, European architectural influences have continued to mark the layout of Latin American cities, from the influence of Baron Haussman's Paris on the construction of the *avenidas* of Buenos Aires and Mexico City to the transcription of Le Corbusier's theories into the geometry of Brasilia (a topic elaborated on in the first chapter).

Although in this respect influence has flowed from East to West, here too there was always a two-way process of exchange, with some Latin American constructions also inspiring European builders. But the "New World," unlike the old, contained such an abundance of apparently unoccupied space that it was feasible to conjure up settlements of every derivation—Swiss chalets, Mennonite communities, Jesuit missions, refuges for escaped slaves, and much more. All these buildings and many other diverse structures could be found in separate enclaves scattered across a vast territory with luxury condos overlooking precarious *favelas*. They provide a physical expression of the social dispersion and lack of cohesion that obstructs the stabilization of consensual outcomes.

Ecological Exchange

Beyond the cities, recent historians have examined more closely the impact of European occupation on the countryside of Latin America, and modern ecological historians have uncovered a much more far-reaching process of trans-Atlantic exchange and reciprocal influence than was hitherto imagined. Elinor Melville, for example, has demonstrated how the introduction of old world grazing animals into the semiarid central highlands of Mexico transformed the physical environment, marginalized the indigenous majority population, and gave rise to the *latifundios* that have so engaged the curiosity of successive generations of agrarian historians.[14] Ecological history portrays a very wide range of reciprocal influences. The potato brought from the Andes made possible an upsurge of peasant subsistence agriculture in Ireland that reached its tragic culmination with the famine of the mid-nineteenth century, when that mono-crop failed. The European livestock that colonized the Argentine *pampas* provided much of the protein that had been missing from the diet of British workers at the onset of the industrial revolution. The Caribbean sugar monoculture created wealth and international dependency on an unparalleled scale, and did much to drive the slave trade. Thus is the flourishing discipline of environmental history uncovering unsuspected chains of causation and interdependence that link Latin America to the world system, and that assign it a very distinctive place there.

From the standpoint of Western rationality and European science the ecology of Latin America seemed to present a *terra incognita*, a rich diversity of life-forms that were awaiting incorporation into systems of classification and analysis already fully elaborated from without. Thus, for example, Eduardo Lourenço has portrayed Latin America as the continent where an "excess" of nature reduced the scope for "culture," and as a latecomer to a preexisting European system of scientific classification that from the outset (and indeed, he suggests, even now) views the continent's natural endowments from the outside.[15]

This was not, of course, the way the pre-Conquest inhabitants of the Americas viewed their natural environment, but whatever systems of classification they had independently produced were swamped by the importation of European concepts. Even in terms of apprehending their own unique biological and physical patrimony, the Latin Americans had to start from an outward orientation. Over time, local investigations and discoveries have challenged and enriched international scientific understanding of nature, and there remains immense scope for this process to be extended, notably in relation to Amazonian studies but also in many other settings. From the standpoint of this volume, the significant point here is the continued prevalence of external sources of expertise and validation in the assessment of Latin America's natural endowments. The modern standards used to estimate biodiversity, the number of hectares dedicated to the cultivation of the coca leaf, natural gas reserves, or the region's contribution to global warming, all obey a Western technological rationality mostly funded and directed from without. Of course, Latin American experts share this scientific outlook, and make valuable contributions to this research but they seldom lead or control it. All too often they are local subcontractors for initiatives mostly driven from without (hitherto from Europe, currently mostly from North America), and not necessarily structured to prioritize Latin America's distinctive interests.

The "Collective Imagination"

With a heavily Europeanized population, strong resource flows between Europe and Latin America, cultural imbrication and ecological interdependence, it is hardly surprising that the two peoples should also share a considerable repertoire of common ideas and assumptions. From the earliest period of European exploration the new world stirred the imagination of the old. Sir Thomas More's *Utopia* was imagined in response to the first reports of seamen returning from the Americas. For several centuries the elites of Latin America aspired to be educated in accordance with the highest achievements of European culture. They not only studied in Europe but also tried to replicate European institutions of learning in their own continent. Not only humanists, but also scientists like Darwin and Humboldt set out from Europe to understand the whole world by observing the new. Latin American writers and artists captured the imagination of European readers in part because they were so steeped in European culture. The exchange of ideas and experiences has intensified with the massification of communications. Sub-Comandante Marcos sometimes seemed to command a larger audience in Paris and Barcelona than in Chiapas or Oaxaca. Latin Americans of all kinds are keen to teach in Europe as well as to learn from her. Osvaldo Brand has even claimed that it was Latin Americans who invented the quantity theory of money.[16]

But if Europe, and more recently the United States, occupy such a preeminent position in the collective imagination of successive generations of Latin American elites, it is also noteworthy that Latin America has an integral place in the European imagination and in its self-understanding. This is obviously truer of Spain and Portugal than of the rest of Europe, but it extends well beyond the Iberian Peninsula. Latin America also occupies a significant—traditionally negative—role in the collective imagination of Protestant North America. In both Europe and the United States these images are currently being reactivated and transformed by the experience of *en masse* immigration from the subcontinent. So it would be a mistake to think of either Europe or the United States acting externally on Latin America to the exclusion of the influences of empathy and mutual projection that also shape the relationship.

However, if we couch the exchange of values and symbols in these terms it is immediately apparent that this is not a relationship between equals. Whereas for Latin Americans the examples of Europe and the United States remain a constant source of orientation, these metropolitan partners are far more fickle. They may intermittently attend to what they regard as positive trends in Latin America, but their attention span is short, and they are easily distracted by the claims of other regions, or discouraged by setbacks. Latin American opinion was not traditionally free to disregard how their region was perceived in Europe and is not currently free to neglect the collective perceptions of their region of the United States or, say, the Organisation for Economic Cooperation and Development (OECD). This is in part because of the continuing international vulnerability of the subcontinent, but also because domestic mass opinion remains sensitive to international criticism. In each separate country of the region, and also domestically in the struggles between rival elites, there is much to be gained or lost by positioning oneself relative to competitors on a scale of external influence and approval. Here again we can see something distinctive about Latin America. The external orientation, and the rivalry for recognition as interpreters of "best modern practice" are stronger than elsewhere, and that affects the way collective perceptions shape regional responses to new experiments. Social security reforms that throw existing entitlements into turmoil can, for example, be pushed through in Latin America in the name of modernity when much more cautious reforms in Europe or the United States meet far more unified resistance.

Political Practices

The example of social security reform directs attention to the area of political practices. Many of the strands of the past political history linking

Europe to the Latin American region were far from liberal. Indeed they included colonialism, absolutism, mercantilism and, in the twentieth century, Great Power rivalries that even involved espionage and subversion. But the liberal strand cannot be disdained, and indeed is now certain to be revalued, given the paternity of the French Revolution and its constitutional legacies. Aguilar Rivera recently reconsidered Latin America's early nineteenth-century constitutional experiments, viewed not as failed exceptions to liberal doctrine but rather as integral components of a liberal political tradition that spanned both sides of the Atlantic and that is only now coming to full fruition.[17] Within this framework it is the Americas as a whole that constitute the Atlantic liberal community. But this reading of liberalism runs up against a very strong alternative tradition, according to which the mainstream is provided by the United States alone, and both the European and the Latin American variants are seen as less successful, or secondary. The establishment of reasonably solid constitutional democracies throughout Europe, and even now in much of Latin America, invites Aguilar Rivera's reappraisal of this perspective. This is only one possible reading of political history, which raises issues that the previous generation would have viewed as Collingwood's "dry bones, signifying nothing."[18]

But those old debates about popular sovereignty, the separation of powers, the federal versus central attributes of government, the constitutional responsibilities of courts, and the legally binding character of international treaties are old no more. Both in Europe and in Latin America they have become young and vibrant again. From the perspective of the *longue durée*, such liberal political theory is anchored in a much deeper flow of shared experience and understanding. For that reason we should expect Europeans and Latin Americans to listen to each other with heightened attention. But still, as illustrated by the example of social security reform mentioned above, and as apparent in other chapters in this book, Latin America's current experience of liberal democracy and neoliberal economic reform differs significantly from that of the old world. Currently, the strongest source of external influence on the region's ideas about liberal economics and about democratic politics must be North American, rather than Western European. But whichever of these happens to predominate at a particular conjuncture, the region's distinctive configuration of societal characteristics and political traditions can be relied upon to filter and redirect the way such external models are in practice locally received, understood, and implemented. This configurative influence virtually ensures that the results will substantially diverge from what a straight reading of universal liberal theory would anticipate.

V. Themes and Organization

This introduction has barely skimmed the surface of the problem of how to characterize Latin America's "distinctiveness." Subsequent chapters tackle various aspects of the question in more detail. The first chapter deals with the orientation toward modernity. The essential claim is that the European Conquest so overwhelmed the preexisting subjectivities that Latin America was transformed into a cultural zone unusually dominated by successive projects of "modernity." But it argues that many of these projects have initially been driven "from above and without," that they have mutated substantially in the course of their adoption, and may therefore only be partially digested rather than fully assimilated and wholeheartedly taken over by the local societies (a contrast with, say, the bland uncontested modernity of Australia). Consequently, there is always foot-dragging and resistance and the landscape is littered with successive incomplete or superseded modernist projects.

The second chapter looks at the high ambitions and low performance in much of the history of state organization in Latin America, with particular emphasis on the period 1930–1980, which was the high point of "inward looking" and "state-led" development. During this period (more than either before 1930 or after 1980) most of the drive to "modernity" was increasingly channeled (still from above and in a sense "without") through the state structures, which expanded, assumed even greater responsibilities, and eventually lost their initial capacity for transformation. The chapter attempts to map that dynamic and to draw conclusions about the various dimensions of "stateness" in Latin America as compared with "the State" in abstract.

The third, fourth, and fifth chapters all examine the relative lack of social control over the development of elite "expertise." The third chapter reflects on the "politics of expertise" in Latin America considering both the strengths and the weaknesses of a system that greatly empowers a narrow stratum of (real or supposed) possessors of exclusive knowledge about how to "solve" society's most pressing problems. In contrast to most of the literature, which focuses solely on economic expertise, this chapter casts the net wide also treating military, engineering, legal, and medical expertise as comparable with economic know-how. It is possible that in a future, more democratic and pluralist Latin America, these claimants to overriding authority may all be subjected to increased peer group and societal answerability. The fourth chapter, on the more specific subject of economic expertise in Mexico, highlights the persisting impediments to democratic accountability in this area. The fifth chapter examines the unstable structure of recent privatization experiments, focusing on the partial theories that guided Latin America' privatization processes in the 1990s, and the lopsided results that therefore ensued. It provides a contemporary case study of the latest variant of "modernizing" innovation to encounter predictable societal resistance.

Chapter six explores the paradox of persisting extremes of social inequality in a large region now almost uniformly governed according to (loosely) democratic political procedures, and reviews the impediments to social consensus arising from the, often precarious, nature of democratic citizenship in the region and from the continued prevalence of multiple forms of citizen insecurity. The underlying assertion is that political democracy presumes some universalism not merely of procedures but also of outcomes. If this is accepted as the latest template of "modernity" it remains far from fully assimilated in Latin American practice. The conclusion draws together these themes by reference to long-standing debates about the balance between continuities in Latin American history and the recurrent desire for systematic change.

What this introduction has tried to establish is that there is a worthwhile question to be addressed concerning distinctive societal configurations that are more prominent in Latin America as a whole than elsewhere. This has been shown by reference to a succession of large region comparisons, each of which highlights certain features of the overall Latin American experience that are different from the dominant patterns found elsewhere. Obviously that exercise leaves a great deal of scope for diversity and variability within Latin America and it draws attention to broad differences that are relative rather than absolute in character. There is inevitably a component of personal judgment and indeed subjective emphasis in any such exercise. It is intended to reintroduce some neglected issues into the study of the regional experience, and also to encourage further work by others (who will doubtless aim to correct my distortions).

Although this introduction operates at a very high level of abstraction it invokes "configurations" rather than "civilizations," and thereby tries to avoid unnecessarily stereotyping a culture zone with distinctive patterns of elite competition arising from a combination of centuries of unbroken local development, poor social integration, the absence of a consensual and unified past, and the recurrent tendency to assume that best practices need to be imported from elsewhere in order to overcome deep-seated local deficiencies. But there is no single unified "modernizing" elite, and the actually existing, highly fragmented, and competitive elites may also have to contend with the distrust and rival claims that are intermittently expressed by wider and less organized sectors of society. The latter have good reason to act on their own behalf to shape policy changes that could otherwise seriously disregard their interests. Indeed, under democratic conditions broad strata in deeply unequal societies have every incentive to mobilize and intervene when change is afoot, both to assert their precarious citizenship rights and to ensure that their views—often quite divergent from dominant orthodoxies—are not simply disregarded or bypassed. In any case, there is no single and exclusive source of best practice that can be invoked. Instead there are multiple and competitive versions of "modernity" on offer. So this is a region with a bias toward modernity, with competitive elites that possess considerable autonomy and resources for experimenting with innovations, but also with divided and distrustful societies that seem to face persistent difficulties in internalizing and stabilizing any particular model of reform.

Of course, it makes a huge difference whether someone else's idea of modernity is forcibly imposed (as through military occupation or colonial rule) or whether alternative models are selectively introduced by locally established elites, who may identify more with the sources of the models adopted than with their "stubborn and backward" local "subjects," and who have leeway to pick and mix, to influence the timing of change, and to adjust all innovations to their own power requirements. Latin America differs profoundly from Asia, Africa, and the Middle East in that, with limited exceptions, it has experienced almost two centuries of independent, postcolonial rule. It also differs in that its sixteenth- to eighteenth-century experience of colonialism had such a devastating impact on the pre-Conquest population that it broke lines of continuity with the indigenous past, and dislocated the possibilities of an imagined reconnection with the region's social premodern roots and traditions.[19] Latin America could better be classed with areas of massive "recent settlement" like North America and Australia, the "new nations" of the Anglophone world, except that in these latter cases it was not someone else's idea of modernity that was on offer, but "one's own." These are societies that—rightly or not—consider themselves to be integrally modern, where the pre-Conquest heritage was more or less comprehensively obliterated, where relatively greater social integration limits both the scope and the need for ruling elites to turn elsewhere for models of reform, where the range of alternative "modernities" that can be considered is far narrower, and where a consensus has been established that "we are already modern" (the "first new nation," the "lucky country").

From this comparative perspective, Latin America's historic orientation toward external models is therefore quite distinctive. The first question is how these alternatives are perceived and appropriated by local elites, which is not necessarily how they are understood or intended from the outside. (One could, for example, review the last half-century of Latin America's distinctive pattern of interactions with the International Monetary Fund (IMF) as exemplar of these *desencuentros.*) The second question is the extent to which any particular modernizing initiative is appropriated, adapted, and internalized not only by its initial promoters but also by the wider—and more heterogeneous—society at large. Where this occurs one would expect to encounter a more stable, but more hybrid, variant of modernity. In Latin American conditions, however, at least relative to elsewhere, there is considerable scope not only for unilateral top-down experiments, but also for broad-based distrust and even resistance to such initiatives. Equally, however, given the presence of competitive elites with access to diverse external sources of support, and given what are often weak mechanisms for building consensus, many projects initially launched with strong momentum fail to stay the course or to live up to their promise, and this expectation tends to become self-fulfilling. This may be because such projects are poorly conceived in the first place, but even sound projects are liable to be deflected from their intended course, and projects that make sense in abstract are simply unappealing because they are not locally owned. To follow up on this hypothesis, the first chapter views Latin America as a "mausoleum of modernities."

Chapter 1

Latin America as a "Mausoleum of Modernities"*

I. Introduction

The aim of this chapter is to highlight some basic and interlocking features of Latin American social organization and experience that help us to locate the subcontinent in comparison with Europe, North America (the "West") and also other major world regions ("non-West"). This undertaking is a response to the challenge to take seriously the notion of "multiple modernities," and work out what it implies about the history of certain specific societies, in contrast with others. The challenge is both theoretical—to clarify the utility and limitations of the "multiple modernities" perspective; and regional—to shed fresh light on the distinctive characteristics and trajectories of historical development in the region subjected to empirical enquiry.

My area of study includes the twenty republics of South and Central America that secured their political independence in the nineteenth century as a result of the Napoleonic wars. It therefore includes Cuba, the Dominican Republic, and Haiti, but not Puerto Rico or the wide range of smaller Caribbean states and entities that remained under colonial rule into the mid-twentieth century. Even with these temporal and spatial limitations the scope of the enquiry is vast, selective, and nearly all taken from increasingly high quality secondary sources. In principle, all the theoretical claims and interpretative suggestions are open to confirmation or modification in the light of the historical evidence. A broad comparative essay of this kind is productive if it draws attention to aspects of historical reality that might otherwise be overlooked or remain underappreciated in their full dimensions, and if it stimulates new empirically grounded enquiries.

Such an exercise clearly involves a high level of aggregation and abstraction, and requires summary discussion of patterns of behavior in a wide variety of domains—including political and economic organization, but also cultural and intellectual activities, and underlying beliefs or assumptions about the world. The object is to emphasize two key features of post-independence Latin American experience that tend to differentiate this region from others, and help to account for its distinctive preoccupations, including its recent and distinctive experiences of economic and political liberalization.

The two features selected for emphasis are, first, the region's general orientation toward "modernity," often conceived in terms of catch-up with, or importation of, the latest models of organization approved in the reputedly "most advanced" regions of the outside world; and, second, the unevenness and incompleteness with which successive models of this kind are assimilated. The combination of these two features, it is argued, leads to a characteristic pattern of reforms promoted "from above and without" followed by various locally understood responses that may be summed up as defensive absorption and deflection. According to this stylized interpretation the typical modernizing initiative is thereby stabilized and internalized, but in a form that differs markedly from the promises and expectations of the first phase. By the time this has occurred, the latest external models of good practice have usually evolved with the result that new programs of modernization from above and without are brought forward to remedy the dissatisfactions arising from the previous cycle. In consequence, it is argued that Latin America can be differentiated from other world regions by the extent to which its social landscape is "littered" with the results of successive drives for "modernity," each of which crystallized a tangible and substantive result before being supplanted or cast adrift. If there is any substance to this thesis, it should be possible to identify a wide array of such no longer fashionable monuments to once desired futures (a "littered landscape"). More clearly than elsewhere, Latin America should display the characteristics of a "mausoleum of modernities."

The *limited* and *relative* status of these claims must be underscored from the outset. The aim cannot be to rewrite Latin American history; rather the hope is that by scrutinizing the region through the optic of "multiple modernities" one can highlight certain recurrent patterns and orientations that are somewhat more prevalent here than elsewhere. One can also group together certain tangible realities—such as those pertaining to the built environment or cycles of political reform—that would otherwise be studied in isolated fragments when they might be better understood as repetitive expressions of an underlying orientation toward modernity.

Two other points should be made at this juncture. First, and clearly, the "modernities" in question are always both multiple and fragmentary. They never achieve total ascendancy in the "collective imagination" and they always jostle against one another. What distinguishes the Latin American case is precisely this instability, this contested-ness, this continuous cross pressuring arising from the perceived gap between really existing conditions and the various standards of modernity by which they are constantly judged and found wanting. Second, the claim that reforms are carried out "from above and without" can be regarded as a "dependency" perspective, denying the endogenous nature of change, and even as Eurocentric or colonialist. The point, however, is that what matters here is not the view of the analyst as much as the perspective of opinion formers and policymakers in Latin America, their mentalities, and recurrent patterns of response: whether or not the outside world is actually "modern" in the sense evoked here, what matters is that it is perceived as validating one or another pattern of modern ideas or practices that Latin American innovators therefore seek to make their own. To be effective in the region, any reform project needs this kind of external validation, given the weakness of "tradition" as a source of justification.

The chapter proceeds as follows. The introduction outlines the approach, and situates this type of enquiry within the comparative literature, noting its methodological implications and limitations. The second section expands on the distinctiveness of the region's general orientation toward modernity, and on the specific manner in which such impulses have been absorbed. The third section proposes a cyclical view of successive waves of modernization, each followed by an analytically distinct successor before the first cycle can be completed. (This "interrupted cycle" perspective can be derived from the two main distinctive features of Latin America's approach to modernity outlined in section two.) The fourth section assembles a variety of examples of the "littered landscape" that can be presented as evidence in support of the cyclical perspective on reform. One good place to search for evidence of this imaginative construction of successive and superseded modernities is the built environment, so this receives special attention. The fifth examines the strong liberalization drive of the 1990s to explore how far it differs from earlier, less complete, cycles of reform. The conclusion reverts to questions of comparative social theory more generally.

Since this chapter makes use of the word "modernity" and works within the standpoint of the "multiple modernities" literature some preliminary comments on the terminology are required. It follows Charles Taylor's proposal that we should understand by modernity, *inter alia*, "the emergence of a market-industrial economy, of a bureaucratically organized state, of modes of popular rule," and that on this understanding we should expect its progress to be "wave like." It broadly accepts his view that the processes of marketization and state formation are "in a sense irresistible. Whoever fails to take them on, or some good functional equivalent, will fall so far behind in the power stakes as to be taken over, and forced to undergo these changes anyway. There are good reasons in the relation of forces for the onward march of modernity so defined."[1] It also endorses his general standpoint on popular rule, which is viewed as both integral to modernity and as the route through which people threatened by the disruptions of modernization may acquire resources to defend or recast their traditions. "It would be better to speak of alternative modernities, as the cultures which emerge in the world to carry the institutional changes turn out to differ in important ways from each other. Thus a Japanese modernity, an Indian modernity and various modulations of Islamic modernity will probably enter alongside the gamut of western societies which are also far from being totally uniform."[2] This formulation conveys what is meant here by "multiple modernities" and poses the key question addressed in this chapter: where in the gamut of Western societies does the Latin American experience fit?

Arguments of this type are highly synthetic, and involve very broad comparisons between large regions viewed over long historical periods. There is no substitute for close and careful examination of more specific materials but when informed by such detailed casework they may indicate an overall interpretative framework within which they can be developed. The relationship between interpretation and evidence is particularly fraught when operating at this level of abstraction as the analytical categories employed (in this case "modernity") are open to multiple interpretations,[3] and the distinctions made are likely to be tendency statements rather than clear-cut dichotomies. Thus, for example, the fourth section of the chapter cites a range of examples of Latin America's "littered landscape" of now superseded modernizing initiatives. But if Oscar Niemeyer's Brasilia provides one vivid illustration of this thesis, it must be weighed against Pierre-Charles L'Enfant's District of Columbia. The Manaus Opera House (1896) and the *Teatro Nacional* of San José (1897) may provide the most eloquent testimonies to the imaginative hold that European cultural models once had over the minds of modernizing elites in far-flung corners of the subcontinent, but of course that hold was not merely regional.[4] So although the illustrations in section four below may be striking, on their own they cannot provide decisive confirmation of the general argument. It needs to be established that such relics of past futures are more characteristic of Latin America than of other regions; that they were more clearly superseded and discarded under the impact of subsequent disconnected modernizing impulses.

Such judgments are typically elusive and debatable. The first possible justification for an exercise of this type is not that it forecloses such debate, but that it suggests otherwise unexplored areas of regional enquiry. The second is that it invites parallel reflections in other settings. Since the initial hypothesis is that these patterns of cyclical and incomplete modernization are more characteristic of Latin America than elsewhere, it can be falsified *either* by showing that their importance in the subcontinent is being overstated *or* that they are also prevalent in other regions. This chapter, then, may provoke non-Latin Americanists into demonstrating the presence of similarly "littered landscapes" on their terrain. A third possibility, which would also justify the exercise, would be that the interpretation only holds for some *subregions* of Latin America or for some specific period of time that needs to be more precisely specified. Whichever of these possible vindications is adopted, the exercise has the merit of connecting the regional experience with the dominant preoccupations of the general literature on comparative historical sociology.[5] The scope and limitations of this type of enquiry have been hotly debated in the sociological journals.[6] So a final justification of this exercise is that it provides a further, regionally informed opportunity to establish the advantages and limitations of the grand sociological approach to comparative history.

II. Latin America's Distinctive Relation to "Modernity"

The postmedieval expansion of Europe obviously took very different forms in different places. These ranged from the settlement of previously uninhabited territories, through varying kinds of exchange and acculturation, to indirect rule, outright conquest, and even wholesale extermination of subject peoples. Of course, in Latin America and the Caribbean (and especially in the densely settled highlands of Meso-America and the Central Andes) the essential form was conquest, although with some admixture of the other elements. The Conquest was followed by three centuries of colonial rule, involving: intense christianization; the parceling out of land and of those who worked on it, together with other natural resources, between the conquerors and their descendents; and the development of an intense trans-Atlantic trade, which included large-scale importation of slaves from Africa, and the export of bullion and other primary products from a network of Latin American ports and administrative centers.

The important point for our purposes is that this wholesale post-Conquest reorganization (reinforced by demographic collapse of the indigenous population under the onslaught of European origin disease vectors) rendered completely unfeasible any serious notion of an overall return to a pre-European past.[7] This was a qualitatively different unfeasibility from that applying to, say, the Mughal Empire or the Kingdom of the Zulus. The razing of Tenochtitlán in 1521 and the sacking of Cuzco were part of what allowed the entire substitution of Spanish Catholic civilization to take place. The preexisting architecture, social structure, and even historical memories were to be so comprehensively suppressed that an eventual reversal became impossible. There is an evident analogy here with the preceding expulsion of Islam from the Iberian Peninsula. Three centuries of colonial rule followed this work of eradication, in contrast to the initially more tentative, and generally lighter and briefer, periods of imperial subordination experienced elsewhere.[8] Moreover, Iberian colonization of the Americas took place in a vast subcontinent most of which was lightly populated or indeed almost uninhabited. Far from being the India (or Asia) initially sought by the *conquistadores*, America was indeed a "New World" wide open to the transformative impact of European settlement.

For the past half millennium the dominant agenda of resource seizure and land occupation, political organization, economic rationalization, and cultural innovation has been led by a succession of elites whose worldviews are traceable to, and still overwhelmingly influenced by, the evolving mental universe of the "West" (originally Iberia, then western Europe, and now predominantly the United States). All roads lead to Rome as far as the Christian heritage is concerned (none to Canterbury, none to Constantinople, and of course none to Mecca or the Ganges). Similar considerations apply to the ultimately Roman foundations of Latin American judicial institutions and its legal professions, and to the entire intellectual baggage accompanying reliance on Spanish and Portuguese linguistic codes. Here, then, we find a key element differentiating Latin America from, for example, most Asian, African, and Middle Eastern experiences of European expansion. In this region, no traditional civilization (or divergent worldview such as Islam) remained sufficiently intact to offer an alternative. Even the often deeply traditional Catholic Church of Latin America is still directed from Europe and in its way subjected to the consequences of European social progress. A wide variety of responses to Iberian colonialism remained possible, of course, but they all involved acquiescence to much of its essential legacy. Insofar as Americans of any social extraction wished to displace control either by Bourbon administrators

or *peninsulares* they had to position themselves as alternative intermediaries with a modern world whose basic features they would have to
understand and, to a substantial extent, accept.[9] By the time the
French Revolution disrupted Iberian colonial rule, the range of historical possibilities opening up within the confines of this inescapably
Western post-Conquest orientation were becoming so wide that it
might seem that almost nothing was excluded.

"Multiple modernities" may therefore be thought to embrace all
possible historical trajectories and so to explain none. After all, the
Spanish Bourbons of the late eighteenth century were influenced by
the European Enlightenment as well, and made strenuous efforts to
"modernize" their colonial regimes (expelling the Jesuits, rationalizing administration, and promoting scientific investigations in the
Americas, most notably the enquiries of Alexander von Humboldt).
The American Creoles who nurtured an increasingly anti-peninsular
patriotism were equally likely to be influenced by other vigorous
aspects of European modernity—Freemasonry, the Rights of Man, or
perhaps the more practical innovations of the English industrial revolution or of Scottish political economy. After 1776, the rebellious
North American colonies offered a third alternative image of Western
modernity, and the list of possibilities could be extended further.

From this perspective, "modernity" in Latin America could draw
on strongly distinctive temporal and spatial resources, without pro-
posing any impossible restoration of a pre-Conquest imagined past.[10]
Creole elites could, for example, bolster their claims to independence
by reference to both the vulnerability of local culture and institutions
and to the magnificence and distinctiveness of their natural endowments. Since the Conquest they had helped to establish mining and
plantation enterprises, cathedrals, and universities. Creole elites might
challenge the privileges of Iberian colonists, but their ideas about
alternative futures were far from unconstrained.

Edmundo O'Gorman refers to this as an "inauthenticity or onto-
logical imbalance" at the heart of the Latin American patriotic project
(*la actualización del ser americano*). While it is true that the Creoles
tried to create "a new American Andean, they only managed to establish a peculiar type of Spaniard, who was still a Spaniard of sorts [. . .]
One must not confuse political independence nor economic nor technological independence, nor even all three together, with the onto-
logical independence presupposed by an original and autonomous
development [. . .] the new nations were constrained to continue
within the imitative framework that had prevailed in the history of
Latin America from its colonial beginnings [. . .] what happened with
the collapse of the colonial structure was a change in the model,

something very different from its disappearance. The generalised adoption of democratic republican systems and the hope that these would immediately fill the historical void left by a Spain which had missed the boat to modernity suffice to indicate that the new model [. . .] was not Latin, but Anglo-Saxon America."[11] This other America, also European in origin, would appropriate entirely to itself the name of "Americans," and came to achieve a historical success that would, in O'Gorman's view, permanently overshadow Latin America.

In different ways both the American and the French revolutions cast the stigma of backwardness over the Spanish and Portuguese empires and stimulated the belief that American Creole challengers might be better placed than Iberian incumbents to negotiate the region's adaptation to the modern world. After all, independence was not just a political rupture: it also involved a profound recasting of economics, society, and culture. In all realms the new republics had to work out new relationships with the leading Western powers, relationships no longer mediated through Lisbon and Madrid but negotiated directly. This involved the outward and inner projection of new identities. The distinctive physical endowments of each territorial unit inevitably became one privileged object of this identity formation. This involved geographical and scientific exploration and not just the inventorying of local national resources but also their presentation to the world as markers for the new nationalities. Modern methods of natural description and classification, accurate mapping, statistical compilation, and the assemblage of samples for systematic study all acquired the status of nation-building priorities. They involved a new, more active, approach to man's domination over nature and were partly associated with the search for a new international division of labor, in which the unexploited riches of each territory would attract foreign investment and secure new trade outlets. This was not just a case of neutrally applying the techniques of modern science to commerce, however. The new states were also adopting these innovations for more subjective and symbolic purposes. They were "imagining" if not communities, then territorial spaces bounded by newly defined lines of national jurisdiction, spaces stocked with natural marvels that validated their claims to separateness.[12] Nascent scientific communities often aspired not merely to add to established canons of knowledge but to reshape scientific understanding in the light of Latin American discoveries and reinterpretations. But in contrast to the United States such intellectual ambitions mostly ran far ahead of the capacity even to absorb, let alone to contribute to, modern science.

In summary, then, independent Latin America was created *either* in reaction to, *or* under the influence of, the Enlightenment, and its new rulers were structurally constrained to define themselves in relation to external idioms of progress and reform. These international origins meant that Latin American elites were discursively (if not necessarily substantively) biased toward the "modern." Indeed, Bolivarian discourse was explicitly drawn from European Republicanism, but what is more important for the purpose of this argument is that the other, apparently more "traditional" justifications for the independence movement (what Brading labels "Creole patriotism," or Guerra calls "sovereignty of the *pueblos*")[13] also reflected a universalistic outlook, which ensured receptivity to "modern" ideas and influences arriving from without. In this broader sense even the more conservative forces had a bias toward the modern: the Braganças preserved the hereditary principle in Brazil with help from Washington and London, Mexican conservatives turned to Second Empire France, and Guatemalan landowners promoted specialization in the export of coffee to Europe.

At this point, however, it is essential to enter a series of cautions, and to underline the modesty of what is being asserted. Otherwise this easy phrase—a "bias toward modernity"—can easily be misconstrued in a unilinear Whiggish or Anglo-Saxon liberal sense. To claim an elite bias or receptivity toward the "modern" is quite different from saying that the pursuit of modernity was the overarching preoccupation of all the *fuerzas vivas* of all these new republics.

Bearing in mind Charles Taylor's view of modernity, it would seem that for much of the nineteenth century this was more of an aspiration than a fact in large parts of the subcontinent. The "emergence of a market-industrial economy" was certainly fitful and uneven. This is hardly surprising given the primary product and enclave basis of initial economic growth, the instability of currency and credit markets, the minimal coverage of internal transportation networks, the persistence of servile labor relations, including slavery, and the general insecurity of property rights in large parts of the interior. Only toward the end of the nineteenth century were these productive deficiencies and economic obstacles to "modernity" systematically diminished and even then such progress was highly uneven. The creation of a "bureaucratically organized state" was also a patchy and delayed process,[14] although Brazil and Chile merit separate discussion in this regard. By contrast, at least on paper, Taylor's third, and more equivocal component of modernity—"modes of popular rule"—preceded the two ostensibly more necessary components.[15] So, if we accept Taylor's general contention that modernity progresses in a "wave like" fashion, we should certainly not expect Latin America, with its precocious republican politics and its delayed state formation and industrialization, to prove the unilinear exception. On the contrary, by the late nineteenth century the ruling elites of the various Latin American republics were unusually well placed to select and filter the various models and components of modernity that they wished to accelerate or deflect. The subcontinent may ultimately have faced the functional necessities that Taylor asserts made modernity almost irresistible but it was particularly sheltered from these disciplines and therefore possessed more latitude to experiment with its own choices than was the case elsewhere.

The question of direct rule from Europe no longer posed even a residual danger after Spain's defeat of 1898, and although U.S. expansionism constituted a serious problem (especially in the Caribbean, Mexico, and Central America) the danger was not of direct colonial rule. Thus, the rulers of Latin America were constrained to modernize rather than threatened by outright takeover. They retained at least some (often great) policy discretion within sovereign republics that could invoke liberal constitutional defences and that were sheltered from the brutalities of global power struggles by the—not entirely altruistic—shield of the Monroe Doctrine. At a time when local elites on the Indian subcontinent were primarily engaged in the struggle against British imperial rule, or when Africa and the Middle East were still in the throes of partition between rival European empires, the Latin American republics were already in a position to negotiate their own commercial, diplomatic, and cultural relations with the modern world. They were, for example, free to select their own immigration policies, to attract or exclude demographic influxes according to their own criteria of national interest and progress.

In such conditions of loose external constraints, "modernity" could assume many conflicting guises, and could be adapted to strikingly diverse local agendas. Although those with education and the possibility to travel (or better still study abroad) were best placed to present themselves as its intermediaries, it could be turned to advantage by a variety of nonelite groups as well.[16]

Eisenstadt's formulations are worth recalling here: "The orientations to the 'mother' country, and to the centres of Western culture, constituted continual models and reference points to an extent probably unprecedented in any other society, including the later Asian ones in their encounter with the West [. . .] the confrontation with 'modernity,' with 'the West,' did not entail, for the settlers in the Americas, a confrontation with an alien culture imposed from the outside, but rather with their own other origins. Such encounters often became combined with a search to find their own place within the broader framework of European, or Western, civilisation. Accordingly the relations between their own modernity, and those of other countries, constituted a continual concern about being at the margins of modernity."[17] Hence, a recurrent "bias toward modernity" can be identified as characteristic of Latin America since Independence, at least in contrast to the more stubborn forms of rejection and backlash found in the history of most other large world regions. While Eisenstadt's general line of thought is illuminating it contains some critical imprecisions that require mention here. It glosses the distinctions (of great historical significance within Latin America) between Iberian Catholic civilization, French republicanism, British commercialism, and the now ascendant U.S. liberalism, all of which could be considered key but competing components of the "Western civilization" to which Latin American elites might be drawn.

The "search for a place" within Western civilization needs to be disaggregated in various ways. One key theoretical distinction would be between a search based on "catching up," motivated by the desire to correct a perceived *deficiency*, and a search motivated by the desire to establish, and secure recognition for, *difference*. For much of the middle of the twentieth century (the period of the Depression, the Second World War, and the Cold War) inward-looking development in Latin America emphasized difference and the rest of the West was blamed for any perceived deficiencies. This was the *zeitgeist* of dependency theory. By contrast, both before 1930 and after the debt crisis of 1982 the emphasis has been on "catching up," given an acceptance that the leading countries of the West were achieving the kind of progress desired but not yet delivered in the subcontinent. Thus, searching for a place in these periods was about seeking to imitate, import, or in some other way latch on to, these extremely located sources of modernity. At another level of disaggregation one could distinguish between the domains where deficiencies needed to be corrected (finance, technology, property rights and human rights, for example), and other domains where difference could be celebrated (such as literature, music, ecology, and *indigenismo*).

Furthermore, any discussion of European projections of modernity into the twentieth century would need to include communism and fascism as additional but bitterly competitive rival images of the "modern," each eliciting a substantial response within a region troubled by its peripheral status. The multiplicities of modernity available to Latin America over the past two centuries can therefore hardly be overstated. Indeed, in the post-Cold War period it became critical to determine how far all the countries of the Americas shared an essentially common civilization or set of collective identities, or to what extent Latin America remained in need of further transfusions of western modernity transmitted from abroad.

So, finally, what if anything, does "a bias to modernity" exclude? It must be apparent from all that has been said so far that a vast array of diverse projects, interests, and viewpoints can be accommodated within the capacious terminology of "multiple modernities." But that does not mean that anything goes, or that nothing of significance can be asserted. Each *project* of modernity involves an evaluation of the present from the perspective of a hypothetical better future. Each *discourse* of modernity elaborates the implications of a given project invoking the normative categories of progress (necessary and desirable), and the obstacles, resistance, and parochialism (to be overcome). And also, in Latin America more than elsewhere, each *experience* of modernity exposes its ambiguities and hidden costs as it proceeds. As each experience unfolds, the starting project becomes more vulnerable to criticism and to the challenges posed by alternative projects—but these in their turn must also invoke modernity if they are to gain momentum.

This book aims to identify the key respects in which this part of the world has differed in its historical trajectory and in its *mentalités* from most other large world regions. The result is a recurrent and deep-rooted bias, or series of biases. Such biases do not guarantee any particular process or outcome, but they do structure the situation in a systematic manner and therefore make more probable certain kinds of developments, and render almost unthinkable or unsustainable certain others. No Islam, no mosques, no veils means an insensitivity to all the cultural and intellectual richness of that tradition (expelled from Spain and Portugal), but it also means no jihads, no rigid gender exclusions, no fundamentalist rejection of usury. The American and French revolutions mean congresses, courts, lawyers, journalists, and a discourse of universal fundamental rights. Belief in scientific progress means universities, specialization, openness to international exchange, and the benefits of fluency in other languages (once French and German, then English). These are all just biases but nonetheless powerful as guidelines and constraints shaping the course of a subcontinental history.

III. Successive Waves of "Modernity" in Latin America

Thus far this chapter has adopted a view of modernity that permits it to take multiple forms, arise in many different domains, and advance unevenly, or indeed remain incomplete as an aspiration more than as an achievement. These features all contrast to the unilinear and homogenizing implications of standard modernization theory, with its totalizing and univocal progression from "tradition" to "modernity."

Charles Taylor's metaphor of a wave-like pattern of historical change seems preferable and reference to "a bias" toward these many kinds of modernity means that structural and cultural constraints can play a part without predetermining either trajectories or outcomes. But all this could be accepted without clearly differentiating our twenty republics from other large regions of the world. Other parts of the "New World," including Australia and New Zealand, could equally be classed as essentially cut off from any pre-European past and characterized by a "bias toward modernity." Other regions subjected to centuries of European expansionism could be said to face multiple and cumulative pressures to "catch up" and reform in accordance with external projects or models of modernity. (Such models often have been transmitted from above by local elites seeking to stay in control but in general the dynamics of Westernization and of resistance to Western influence cannot be reduced to a Whiggish story of modernizing elites pitted against culturally resistant masses.)

In this section, the aim is to highlight an orientation toward modernity that may be more specific to Latin America, located between these two broader possibilities. As indicated in the introduction, the two features selected for emphasis here are, on the one hand, Latin America's bias toward modernity and, on the other hand, in light of the region's less-than-fully-modern present, the uneven and incomplete manner in which successive projects and models may typically have been assimilated there. Going beyond Taylor's general observation about wave-like patterns, a more specific possibility is considered: that of a sequence of "successive waves" that may be said to characterize the history of these republics. The essence of the "successive waves" hypothesis is that, more so than elsewhere, Latin America has tended to adopt innovations, reforms, and projects of transformation that are inspired "from above and without", and which elicit not so much root and branch rejection "from below and within", but rather distortion, delay, and qualified resistance. Thus, interests that feel unable to deflect or domesticate a particular manifestation of modernity (because it is too tightly controlled by its originators, or has been captured by rival interests) may attempt defensive absorption but will also be on the look out for alternative versions of modernity that are more congenial.

As most reforms and innovations are only loosely promoted from without and certainly not rigidly imposed (as might occur, say, under direct colonial rule), there is usually considerable autonomy to the process of bargaining by which any initial proposal is converted into a practical reality. So the typical modernizing initiative in Latin America may well be stabilized and eventually internalized but only after adjustments that may substantially modify initial expectations and intentions. Aspiring Latin American modernizers are, of course, soon likely to realize that, however highly they may value expertise in the best practices promoted by the most modern societies, their effectiveness will also depend upon the ability to win local allies and make the necessary adjustments to domestic realities. So it would be a mistake to reduce such intermediaries to mere instruments for the importation of foreign models, as dependency theory tended to do. Rather they should be viewed as brokers searching for projects and innovations that can be externally validated as "modern" but that can respond to the felt needs and potentialities of domestic societies as well. Another way to describe this would be to say that the region is receptive to the adoption of "modern" techniques but not necessarily to undertaking the social and cultural adjustments required if they are to operate as expected.[18]

If a particular modernizing initiative does not deliver on its promises this opens the way for challenges from alternative, similarly legitimized proposals, perhaps promoted by rival elite interests. Thus, we have a framework that implies a succession of reforms, each brought forward to remedy perceived deficiencies arising from a previous, incomplete, cycle of reform. With alternative sources of inspiration of best practices and multiple domains of modernity there should almost always be untapped possibilities for innovation, particularly since external models and modes of good practice change over time and since no modernizing reform has yet succeeded in overcoming Latin America's social heterogeneity and uneven development.

This extremely schematic framework can be elaborated on by directing closer attention to three main areas. First, there are the various competing external models of "modernity," each with its own structure and mode of transmission varying in intensity over time and space. Second, there are the specific elite groups, material interests, occupations, and professions within the region that are, at least partially, geared to promote the various "waves." Third, there are the social groups, communities, and cultural practices targeted for transformation with each wave, each with their respective capacities to absorb, resist, or deflect changes that are externally initiated and may not be welcome, or even understood.

Although each of these three very broad areas of enquiry must interact with the others, and although their specific weights will vary enormously from case to case, it is only possible here to consider them as separate from each other and at a very abstract level. In principle, however, this framework could generate the outcomes hypothesized in section one, namely: a series of modernizing initiatives each promoted from above and without, each carried forward far enough to create a durable impact and legacy, but each resisted and not fully internalized until its propelling force is exhausted, and an alternative push for modernity emerges.

Competing External Models of Modernity

The first area for discussion is also the most visible, and the best studied. British trade and French culture were obviously at the heart of any Latin American conception of "modernity" in the early post-Independence period. They were also rival sources of orientation, notwithstanding some commonalities. From the 1820s onward British shipping was a major presence in most South American ports, but the imperial court in Rio preferred to gossip in French. When it came to state building the Franco-Prussian war divided the region into countries that relied on French military missions to build up their armed forces, and those that turned to Germany. Again, there were rivalries and commonalities, and again these sources of external orientation each had their crescendo before fading over time. When modernity was conceived in terms of "whitening" by resorting to European immigration, it was mostly Italian and Spanish workers who were recruited, bringing with them the latest fashions in anarchism and labor organization. Here too, the influence built up to a peak and then waned. Similarly, if the British built most of the railways, the Americans took an early lead in the creation of enclaves for the export of minerals and tropical agriculture, and subsequently for the expansion of the automobile, while the Germans pioneered many of the early airlines. By the 1920s, the Soviet Union had become the mecca for an alternative vision of modernity, one that eventually took root in Cuba after 1959.

Obviously the list could be refined and extended. The point is, however, that each of these external models or influences was strong enough to produce a profoundly transformative and loosely "modernizing" impact on at least one domain, in at least one republic, over at least a substantial, if not unlimited, period of time. The impact could be primarily military or financial, or commercial or political or cultural or demographic, but it almost invariably spilled over from such initial confines and exerted a broader and more diffusely progressive effect. Most Latin American elites quickly became adept at tracking, anticipating, channeling and, if possible, monopolizing such external influences. Those that delayed or resisted were, as Taylor indicates, often induced to reconsider when they found themselves at a growing competitive disadvantage with the frontrunners.

We should consider briefly what motivated these various external actors and what were the biases and limitations of their rival offerings of modernity. For the purposes of this chapter the only question at issue is how and why the "West's" treatment of Latin America differed from that meted out to other large world regions over the same two centuries. Geopolitical location helped keep the subcontinent at the margin of great power confrontations, thus allowing more room for maneuver and more freedom to play off one source of modernity against another than was the case elsewhere. The precocious adoption of a liberal constitutional form of government may also have helped, signaling to all Western rivals that these were societies where influence and commercial advantage might be pursued without increasing the obligations of exclusivity or direct rule. The Monroe Doctrine was but the first of a long succession of sheltering signals of this kind.

Within this liberal international framework, the Latin American republics secured recognition in exchange for a tacit commitment to accept political, economic, and cultural impulses from without. Latin American elites in particular have displayed a record of openness and receptivity to almost all aspects of Western influence that is different in kind from experiences elsewhere.[19] From the standpoint of an external actor considering the advantages of a commitment to Latin America rather than elsewhere, this at least formal accessibility has often been reassuring, as has the impression that it was easy to locate like-minded partners and counterparts. They might often be brought together by some shared discourse of modernity. In practice, of course, there were always substantial costs and barriers to be overcome for any such partnership to work, but generally Latin America's perceived "bias toward modernity," its liberal republican makers, and its "New World" status have all served to mitigate such impediments to external linkages. There are notable contrasts here with Africa, Asia, and the Middle East. In post-Independence Latin America the early elimination of direct colonial rule softened the rigid, often racially defined, hierarchies and exclusions, while shared traditions of Christianity and European language and culture facilitated these cross-border alliances. The anti-Western pull of ancient civilizations and devalued rival traditions was also absent. As another part of the West—Alain Rouquié's "Far West"[20]— Latin America could connect on the basis of shared visions of a better future, although these connections were still prone to conflict and disappointment and to the ups and downs of "successive waves."

Reform Mongers[21]

The second area for discussion concerns the characteristics of the intermediaries who were best placed to promote and direct the various alternative innovations and reforms. Again there is great heterogeneity and a vast literature, though not so much geared to our purposes here. This could include harbormasters, ordinance officers, bank directors, engineers, lawyers, sanitary inspectors, printers, clerics, urbanists, and indeed a wide variety of rural elite interests as well. When one considers the specific occupational categories and professional groupings most likely to benefit from one or other modernizing initiative, it seems that almost all educated or propertied interests would be well represented, together with many significant nonelite groupings. This would seem to offer some sociological confirmation of the hypothesized "bias toward modernity" throughout the region. Whereas in the civilizations of Asia and the Islamic world strategic groups within the power elite would be likely to perceive Western penetration as inherently threatening to their status and prerogatives, it is hard to identify any substantial counterpart blocs with similar blocking powers in Latin America. Different elite groups would be likely to favor different projects of modernity, but that is all.

Beyond this general observation, it is possible to develop a more refined analysis, with a stronger cyclical component, by looking more closely at the history of certain key professions. In such key areas as military technology, sanitation, bulk transportation, and most recently macroeconomic management, there are periodic surges of scientific, technological, or analytical progress, which typically arise in the most modern and successful parts of the Western world. Latin American professionals working and studying in these areas have often gained a competitive advantage by picking up on innovations occurring outside the region and by taking the lead in introducing them to their own countries. In this way, at various times, experts in mechanized warfare, in port hygiene, in urban design, in civil aviation, and indeed in economic stabilization, have achieved remarkable concentrations of power conceded in deference to their possession of some vital form of expertise required to bring Latin America up to best practice standards in some area of "modern" performance. They have been allowed to concentrate power in order to change something that has been identified as a critical bottleneck or deficiency by the prevailing international standards of modernity. Typically, their monopoly of expertise is eroded over time as a broader professional community springs up around them and their claims to exceptional power are diminished, perhaps because they genuinely solve the specific problem in hand, or perhaps because, over time, that particular definition of deficiency is re-evaluated or superseded by another. Thus, through a study of the social history of key professions it may be possible to trace and define the nature of the cyclical rise of particular modernizing initiatives.[22]

At this point it is difficult to avoid raising the intractable problem of how to characterize—let alone generalize about—the Latin American state. It is easy to underscore the contrast between an ideal-typical Weberian idea of the state and its role in societal modernization, and the erratic and often over-extended and invertebrate forms of state organization so common in Latin America. Perhaps a better contrast for our purposes is between the capacity for sustained and cumulative social transformation displayed by the so-called developmental states of East Asia and the far more fitful and incoherent record of their Latin American counterparts, although all such dichotomies are suspect. The reality is that in some Latin American republics, on some key issues of social transformation, and for substantial periods of time, major efforts at modernization have been promoted from the state apparatus. Costa Rica's sustained emphasis on education and the implantation of an effective legal order may be cited as an unusually durable and benevolent example. The postrevolutionary order constructed by the Mexican state after the 1920s is another striking case. Other examples of ambitious and society-wide transformations promoted by the state could be studied, which were not necessarily directly driven from without in imitation of foreign models.

Our concern in this chapter, however, is with what has differentiated Latin America as a whole and in the long run from other regions. So, notwithstanding some important exceptions, the emphasis cannot be placed on those few instances where forceful and sustained state policies created a new social order in accordance with a domestic blueprint. Far more characteristic of these long-standing, loosely constrained, but poorly articulated state organizations is the launching of successive plans and programs, each neglecting the lessons of what went before and prone to denying inconvenient evidence about the realism and viability of the latest scheme. In order to overcome the public skepticism and resistance generated after successive public policies of this kind are experienced, Latin American governments discover the need to reinforce their credibility by associating with actors that have better reputations or track records. In some cases, domestic institutions (universities, influential newspapers, even individual prestigious thinkers) may supply the missing element of confidence; in others foreign advisers and international institutions or alliances may be sought out. Whichever the alternative adopted, the credibility of public policy is likely to be bolstered by reference to more successful models or experiences elsewhere.

Thus, even when "modernity" is pursued through government rather than through economic or societal channels, the state apparatus is likely to exercise scant autonomy and the imprimatur of external validation is often required. And so the Latin American state has frequently acted as an intermediary promoting "successive waves" of innovation and reform, each likely to end before fulfillment. Across a wide range of countries and time periods the record offers little support to those who claim the state *can* rather than just *should* offer an alternative to the patterns of modernity identified in this section.

This undoubtedly too sweeping appraisal of the Latin American state leaves open the related role of the region's intelligentsia and its associated educational establishment. Even if the state has a low capacity, is not the generalist Latin American intellectual unusually highly prestigious, and has he not the potential for formulating projects of far reaching social transformation? The existence of unbroken intellectual and institutional traditions stretching back over several centuries sharply distinguishes our region from most other parts of the "developing" or "third" world, where the impact of European colonialism was more recently and incompletely imposed and then withdrawn. Major republics such as Brazil, Mexico, and Colombia have extremely well-established systems of elite recruitment, socialization, and reproduction, which evolve only slowly and largely in accordance with internal rhythms and constraints. Even Bolivia—which may provide a yardstick of elite fragility—displays patterns of elite formation and political leadership recruitment that can be traced back to the *doctores chuquisaqueños* of the early postindependence period.

Innovation and Resistance

The third area for discussion is quite familiar to many social scientists at the level of theory but is particularly intractable at the level of evidence. How to explain not only the strength of successive modernizing initiatives generated from above and without, but also the fact that they remain incomplete, not fully internalized and incorporated into the mainstream of social life, so that when another initiative is launched it is not built on the foundations of what is already established but runs in parallel, perhaps leaving its predecessor stranded as a monument to a past and superseded future?[23] At a very abstract level we can borrow from Foucault and suggest that all the rival "modern" projects involve a high degree of abstract rationality divorced from the heterogeneous and conflictive lived realities of most popular sectors in Latin America. Such projects therefore collide with many local practices and understandings and are consequently prone to deflection, resistance, or even to being captured.

One of the most recurrent themes in Latin American public debate is the disconnection between the grandiose ambitions for a more progressive future typically developed within elite and governmental circles and the lacerating experiences of daily existence that shape the consciousness of the majority. Of course this divorce between the discourse of power and the "genealogy" of popular consciousness is not unique to Latin America but it may be more pronounced there because social segmentation is often so extreme, and also because the impulse toward "modernity" and transforming reforms is so heavily driven by elite and professional groups, which may be ultrasensitive to international fashions but well-insulated from the thoughts and feelings of their compatriots.

In the more stable, conservative, and densely institutionalized countries of Western Europe and North America there might be more resistance to such a succession of totalizing projects of transformation. Reformers would typically be more constrained by the need to acknowledge and incorporate the more successful achievements of their predecessors. In Latin America, whether for cultural reasons or, more concretely, because of the greater plasticity of institutional practice, a prevalent pattern is to launch an entirely new cycle of innovations and where possible to press them to the limit (or beyond). It is not energizing to admit that an incoming team is largely building on the foundations laid by its predecessors and will at best achieve incremental improvements on an established *status quo*. A more common assertion is that "only my project can save the nation," a stance that would justify root and branch activism and that may respond to opposition not by accommodation but by escalation. Although the record may contain successive episodes of this type, each with disappointing or unintended adverse results arising from societal resistance, this pattern still tends to repeat itself and to elicit new waves of enthusiasm (which take time to become exhausted).

Within the scope of a chapter of this kind it is obviously impossible to establish, or even to illustrate convincingly, such an ambitious and sweeping thesis. It was hard enough to find solid arguments for the preceding claims concerning external models and the role of intermediaries. Projects of "modernity" take so many diverse forms that any specific examples of resistance can scarcely be generalized. In any case, this third claim is not focused on outright resistance, which would at least be relatively easy to identify, but includes strategies of delay, deflection, and absorption. It even includes the acceptance of alternative modernities in order to frustrate the one seen as most threatening. Finally, it is a *relative* claim, which means one would somehow need not merely to establish its applicability in Latin America but also to establish that it was *truer*, or true in a different way for Latin America than elsewhere. Given these hurdles we can offer no more than an interrogation. If the rest of the argument is plausible, then this deserves consideration. But how might it be demonstrated?

In certain specific circumstances it can be shown to apply. The immunization campaign in Rio de Janeiro at the turn of the century has been written up in terms that fit the general account.[24] The Washington-backed proposal to "dollarize" the Ecuadorian economy generated indigenous and popular resistance that toppled President Mahuad in January 2000, and led to the brief occupation of the national congress. Three months later a *coordinadora* of similar complexion paralyzed the Bolivian city of Cochabamba and forced the withdrawal of an international business consortium that had contracted to modernize the local water supply. In December 2001, the President of Argentina fled into exile as a decade long experiment in "neo-liberal" restructuring reached its point of exhaustion. A similar pattern was repeated in Bolivia in October 2003. There is no shortage of historical and contemporary episodes of this kind that serve to demonstrate the heuristic value of an elite reform–popular resistance model of interaction. For every documented case of this type there are no doubt many more that remain undocumented, and still more cases where the reformers changed course before the crisis came to a head. Is this representative of the region as a whole? Does it differentiate Latin America from other large regions where modernizing projects clash with popular subjectivity? Of course the region is too large (and diverse) to fit neatly within any such framework. There are also some striking examples of incremental reform and the winning round of initially resistant popular opinion (as in Brazil since the early 1990s). And outside Latin America it may be possible to identify comparable cycles (although I suspect they are less recurrent and entrenched). The purpose of this discussion is to draw attention to some recurrent regional tendencies. It is not to construct a strictly regional account opposing this subcontinent to all others and still less is it to generate predictive knowledge. Rather than attempting to establish these non-falsifiable contentions, this chapter now changes tack. The next section explores the notion of a "littered landscape." If Latin America is characterized by successive waves of modernity, each superseded before it can reach completion, then we can search for evidence of what they left behind.

IV. The Littered Landscape

What could be more expressively "modern" than the Panama Canal? By creating a sea link for bulk carriers between the Atlantic and the Pacific and between North and South America, it transformed the

balance and reach of naval power in the twentieth century; it redistributed the commercial, financial, and political resources of great
cities, and indeed nations; and it symbolized the transformative
potential of modern technology when backed by the organizational
power of the U.S. government. Blasting the Cuebra Cut alone
required the use of 61 million pounds of dynamite—more explosive
energy than had been expended in all U.S. wars up to that time. It has
been billed as the largest, costliest single effort ever mounted
anywhere on earth in peacetime prior to the First World War.[25] Its
construction involved the displacement of France by the United
States, the marginalization of Nicaragua and Tehuantepec, and the
detachment of the province of Panama from Colombia to create a
semi-independent new republic. Its neutrality (and security) gave
Washington the flexibility of deployment needed to fight both Japan
and the European Axis powers simultaneously during the Second
World War, and helped to ensure that the western hemisphere
remained a secure rearguard during world conflicts. Here, then, we
find a great monument to "modernity."

It is a monument that has now become a relic. The canal machinery
"is a superb antique whose parts date back to 1914 [. . .] Large
tankers, which form the arteries of the international oil system—
cannot squeeze through the waterway [. . .] In early 1977 as many as
1,000 vessels were too large, either in width or tonnage, to travel the
passageway [. . .] One container vessel carries the cargo formerly
carried by three to five of the merchant ships using the Canal [. . .]
Containerisation, larger ships, air freight, truck trailer rigs with cargo
roll-on, roll-off techniques, and the increased processing of raw material near their sources—all are reducing the Canal's value [and] its
strategic value has also rapidly declined. Aircraft carriers cannot use it,
and nuclear submarines must surface while going through it."[26] All
that was written over twenty years ago. During the 1980s, the U.S.
rail network was adapted to carry the bulk of the container trade, and
pipelines were developed for bulk transport. In 1998, the water level
in Gatien Lake fell so low that the tonnage of ships passing through
the Canal had to be drastically restricted for months at a time. The
Canal that was finally handed over to the Panamanian government at
the end of 1999 was a nearly obsolete monument to a past era of
modernity based on naval power.

By 2005, 60 percent of outstanding orders for new ships were for
so-called post-Panamax vessels, which weigh more than 165,000 tons
and can carry 7,000 containers each. These ships are too large to pass
through the existing Canal locks (even though US$ 1 billion was
recently spent widening them to allow two Panamax size vessels to

pass alongside each other). The only way to further expand the Canal to cope with such developments in bulk transport would be to build a second set of locks, twice as large as the old ones, and to create enormous new reservoirs to supply the water needed for their operation. This is an extremely costly and environmentally disruptive option that would involve flooding large areas of central Panama. But in the absence of such expansion, which would require approval in a national referendum, world shipping will be rapidly diverted away from the Canal toward renewed reliance on the pre-1915, exclusively maritime, routes, notwithstanding the need to circumnavigate whole continents. Thus, Latin America's greatest engineering feat of the early twentieth century risks being left high and dry in the early twenty-first century.

Of course all innovations in the built environment are to some extent superseded by the passage of time. Europe is littered with castles, palaces, churches, and even waterways that were in the vanguard of change when they were constructed but that are downgraded and adapted for lesser uses as later functions and structures overlay them.[27] In the United States, following a more strictly market logic,[28] many no longer profitable assets are sold off for demolition and substitution. Western civilization in general conserves obsolete structures by converting them into objects of the heritage industry. But this requires the relics of past modernities to be adapted and absorbed by a rising tide of consensual consumerism. In some traditional settings (the Mosque at Ayodhya, the Temple Mount in Jerusalem, or the bridge at Mostar) violent conflict arises because this desacralization of historical monuments is socially intolerable. Latin America presents rather few examples of such "primordialism."[29] This perhaps provides some confirmation of Eisenstadt's suggestion about the relative weakness of primordial ties in the region and of my hypothesis about a "bias toward modernity."

Despite its nationalist symbolism, it may be impossible to apply these considerations to the Panama Canal because its size and function make it difficult to absorb as a heritage industry artifact.[30] In any case, the tide of consensual consumerism has yet to raise average income levels and available leisure time to the required degree, not least in Panama and its adjoining republics. Nor is this monument easily dismantled or parceled out for alternative commercial uses. Here we have such a grandiose, overbearing, and inflexible relic to a past modernity that a more plausible eventual fate would seem to be as an exhibit in a "mausoleum."

Perhaps, then, this example provides a practical illustration of the rather abstract argument presented in the introduction to this chapter. But we need more than one monument to constitute a mausoleum, of course. Those who have traveled in the interior of Latin America can usually assemble their own favorite somewhat folkloric selections. Spectacular examples of physical constructions might include the 367-kilometer Madeira-Mamoré railway closed in 1971; the Manaus Opera House; the re-tropicalized banana plantations along the Caribbean coastline of Central America; and the cannibalized sugar Centrales in eastern Cuba. These structures are all superseded expressions of modernity that are neither sacred nor absorbed into the heritage industry. They are remote and arguably marginal, although they could also be viewed as quintessentially Latin American because they are only possible in "new" lands characterized by an abundance of space ("nature") and a precariousness of human settlement ("culture").[31] For further evidence we need to consider more central locations such as the *Ascensor Polanco* that opened in Valparaiso in 1915 and was recently declared an historical monument. For this we need to visit such metropolises as Mexico City, Buenos Aires, Havana, and Brasilia.

Mauricio Tenorio Trillo has reconstructed a guided tour of central Mexico City as it was in September 1910, the centenary of independence, when the capital "had acquired the visible and lasting symbols of nation, progress and modernity, notions that the *Centenario* had actualised and intermingled."[32] This was the point at which the Porfirian regime erected its most celebrated monument—*El Ángel de la Independencia*—in the Paseo de la Reforma. It was the dictatorship's opportunity to map out its "ideal view of modernity, understood as harmonious and peaceful economic development, progress and science. The best embodiment of this ideal was the modern city— which contained the proofs of the nation's pedigree: economic progress and cultural greatness, but which was also sanitary, comfortable, and beautiful [. . .] a textbook of a civic religion; a city of monuments and well-defined public and private spaces. Finally, the modern ideal view, inseparable from the other two, of a cosmopolitan style. The quintessential incarnation of this ideal of cosmopolitanism was Paris itself."[33]

But in contrast to Paris, in Mexico City it was not necessary to destroy urban sectors or to relocate largely inhabited zones in order to build these new avenues and boulevards. "Instead, they displaced *campesinos* and Indian communities from the nearby *haciendas*." Indeed, "compared to Europe, where urban reform was considered a matter of social reform and internal security [. . .] in Mexico it was a matter of frontier expansion. The ideal city, therefore, was conceived as a conquest not only over tradition, chaos and backwardness but also over nature."[34] As Tenorio adds, the "Mexican elite shared with their European and North American counterparts a belief in the evil and degenerating characteristics of cities [. . .] But the Mexicans had an almost blind confidence that upon achieving a modern city— and not a bucolic return to nature—those evil by-products of urban development would be overcome."[35] Thus, the "ideal city was also demarcated by a sort of *cordon sanitaire*. A city free of miasma and ill-ness was a difficult achievement [. . .] Nonetheless [. . .] it hosted the first large popular hygienic exhibition, built a national penitentiary, opened a new modern mental hospital and forced Indians to shower and dress in trousers."[36]

Tenorio provides us with vivid insights into the ideal of modernity nurtured by the Porfirian elite and to some extent incorporated into the built environment on the very eve of the Mexican Revolution. The reality certainly fell far short of these ideals, but his account makes it clear why the ensuing projects of transformation would have come essentially "from above and without," and would have been met by various powerful forms of resistance, even without the Revolution. In fact, within three years Zapata's armed insurgents were feasting in Sanborns after which anarchist detachments from the urban working class helped tip the balance of the fighting against the Restorationists. The next attempt to "modernize" Mexico City invoked a very differ-ent imagery, both of a postwar Europe and of a *mestizo* Mexico as depicted by the murals of Diego de Rivera. This is obviously a very selective commentary on a much more elaborate historical process, but Tenorio's reconstruction of the Porfirian vision of a modern Mexico City deserves a prominent place in any mausoleum of Latin American modernities.

In a parallel endeavor Adrián Gorelik has examined the centenary of May 1810, and its urban manifestations in the city of Buenos Aires.[37] He reviews the succession of reformist projects through which such innovators as Sarmiento and Alvear envisaged the reconfigura-tion of the crowded colonial port into a modern urban metropolis worthy of Europe. The most critical steps in 1888 (incorporating an area of the pampas sufficient to roughly treble the size of the city's jurisdiction) had been completed by 1904. Jeffrey Needell regards this as one of the culminating achievements of Argentina's "Generation of 1880," proclaiming the "political consolidation and foreign economic dependency imposed by a new Europhile elite."[38] He notes that it permitted the rise of *Barrio del Norte* and the dis-placement of the area to the South of the main square, "the traditional seat of the proud old porteño elite," which became "more and more unfashionable and decrepit in style and appearance."[39] By contrast, the northward shift gave that part of the city a "Second Empire veneer so pleasing to a Francophile elite," with broad avenues, fine parks, and elegant modern mansions. This flourishing of a new economic and social elite was associated with the northern infrastructure of port and railheads, together with an associated financial and commercial district. At the same time mass immigration was creating a spreading metropolis of new workers who needed to be housed and assigned employment. During this period a leading role was played by the Anglo-Argentine Tram Company, which unified and monopolized public transport in the emerging metropolis and from 1905 onward imposed a uniform ten-cent tariff, thus stimulating suburbanization and the construction of popular housing in the more outlying districts. In 1909, this company reached its apogee when it obtained a municipal license to build three underground routes with the subway stations all linked to its tram routes.

This provides the background to the centenary celebrations in Buenos Aires, which revealed not one hegemonic elite project for the future of the city (as in positivist and dictatorial Mexico) but rather a clash of interests and objectives that reflected a greater freedom of expression and stronger capacity for contestation among the *porteño* popular classes. Official parades expressing the priorities of the better-off northern sector of the city were interrupted by protest marches from La Boca, which reflected what Gorelik terms an alternative "southern ideology."[40] Unlike Mexico there was no outright substitution of one project by another, but by 1919 the initiative in urban affairs had passed decisively from one view of modernity to another. In that year the Socialists and Radicals took control of the City Council and began a long campaign against the tram monopoly and the regulated vision of urban modernity that it articulated. The Generation of 1880 had lost its ascendancy by the time of the First World War and its vision of urban modernity had come under challenge from cultural nationalists and the municipal professions even before it was displaced from political control.

Then there is Havana, whose urban architecture is truly a mausoleum of successive and overlapping modernities. A great colonial city, of course, but for our purposes the twentieth-century structures merit particular attention. There are the glories of the *art deco* movement of the 1920s. The dictator Machado sought to curry favor with the United States and to symbolize Cuba's permanent alignment with Washington by having the Capitolio constructed as a copy of that city's Capitol building. In another gesture to an alternative modernity the Batista regime constructed public buildings inspired by Le Corbusier. After the 1958 revolution this built environment was mostly left to crumble, becoming a neglected mausoleum, although some Soviet style Brutalism was introduced, and the Plaza de la Revolución provides an eloquent monument to the superseded visions of the early revolutionary years.

No listing of this kind would be complete without some reference to Brasilia. Constructed in one frantic burst in the late 1950s this tribute to European modernism stands on a site unencumbered by previous urban design (on what was once virgin land). It was intended to assert the inward-directed orientation of the new Brazil but its inspiration was overwhelmingly external. The agent of transmission was Lúcio Costa, a Brazilian architect born in France, whose views were transformed by his attendance of a lecture given in 1929 by the Swiss Le Corbusier. Costa became director of the School of Beaux-Arts in Rio and designed an avant-garde mining settlement (Monlevade in Minas Gerais) in 1934. It was through Costa's influence that Le Corbusier's stress on the rationality of public spheres (the need for regularity to displace disorder) and on the primacy of functional and egalitarian structures became a part of the archisymmetrical design of Brazil's unlovable new capital.[41] Le Corbusier was literally "imported" to Brazil by the most modern means available in the 1930s—the Zeppelin (another Euro-Latin American exhibit in the mausoleum, perhaps?). Of course Brazil was already receptive to such influences. Indeed, Belo Horizonte preceded Brasilia by sixty years, a precedent that opened up the possibility of designing a capital *de raiz*.

James Holston has recounted the extraordinary *brincadeira* that Costa used to promote his Master Plan and beat the competition in 1957, and has uncovered the "hidden agenda" and sweeping Modernist social theory that lay behind its architectural schema. He has also provided an elaborate anthropological critique tracing the interplay between the dogmatic conception of the designers and the societal responses that ultimately absorbed and deflected their social project. The product of this interaction is the largest and most magnificent example of urban modernism in the Latin American mausoleum but also another superseded version of modernity, another dated and passé vision of the continent's future.[42]

The cities of Latin America evidently contain many monuments to past drives for urban transformation in accordance with what was then considered the culminating aspirations of modernity. But does this pattern of *modernitus interruptus* characterize this subcontinent more than elsewhere? In cities subject to direct colonial rule monumental structures were normally erected according to a different logic: to assert the superiority and intended permanence of European imperial systems. Perhaps the nearest equivalent to Brasilia is the handful of new administrative cities built after independence to affirm the national identity of the postcolonial state. James C. Scott has bracketed Chandigarh with Brasilia in his critique of the high modernist city.[43] Indeed, Le Corbusier was recruited in person by J. Nehru to design this city as the Indian substitute for Lahore, the historic Punjab capital alienated to Pakistan under the Partition. But the great Indian cities that are not dominated by Raj monuments are packed with sacred sites and immemorial traditions. It is not futuristic Chandigarh, but the supposed birthplace of Rama, home of Buddha, and the site of a Mughal Mosque, Ayodhya, that captures the collective imagination in India. Or we could turn to countries like China and Thailand, where formal independence was preserved, to undertake our comparisons. To at least a limited extent some Latin American patterns *can* be identified in these parts of the world. Michael Tsin recently reconstructed the way the walled city of Canton was "modernized" after the advent of the Chinese Republic in 1912.[44] Returning émigrés brought Western ideas and resources, and after the Kuomintang (KMT) made the city its headquarters the hitherto unknown discipline of "urban planning" was introduced. The result was a far-reaching physical transformation, in particular of the waterfront area abutting Pearl River. But Tsin's work indirectly reveals the limits of this experience. Canton was most unrepresentative of Chinese cities as the only port officially open to foreign trade since the eighteenth century. An entire section of the waterfront was granted to the British and French as a concession under the 1842 Treaty of Nanjing. Even in the 1920s the KMT modernizing project met powerful merchant and popular resistance and was only sustained through warlord support (the presence of "ghost armies") and under the influence of foreign, notably Soviet, advisers.[45] So the Canton example, at first sight a refutation of Latin American distinctiveness, on closer inspection seems to support the theses of this chapter.

At this point it becomes essential to turn away from the built environment, no matter how tangibly that kind of evidence illustrates the argument. The "bias toward modernity" envisaged here must extend beyond the realms of architecture and technological innovation to gain macro-sociological significance. It would also have to encompass such other aspects of the prevailing *zeitgeist* as literature and culture, political and social theory and practice and, as suggested in the previous section, an orientation toward economic modernity. It must touch on *all* these realms if it is to affect the distinctive patterns of Latin American identity and self-recognition. This brief section is obviously too slender to establish so sweeping a claim and so a single nonarchitectural illustration will have to suffice.

One long-standing and recurrent strategy for bringing the region closer to "modernity" has been the promotion of European immigration. (The contemporary counterpart to this is the promotion of direct foreign investment, which typically brings with it a certain influx of foreign managers together with opportunities for local professionals to upgrade their skills by working abroad.) In this case, the "bias toward modernity" took an unusually explicit and direct form. Large population groups, perceived as bearers of the advanced characteristics of Western civilization, would be literally incorporated into Latin American societies that were viewed as insufficiently modern and dynamic. Through the design and implementation of these programs it is possible to trace quite precisely where modernity was thought to reside (in different places at different times) and how much dislocation it was thought worth enduring in order to attract it. Thus Gilberto Freyre explicitly linked the modernizing thrust of the immigration policies adopted in Brazil after the fall of the Empire with a similarly dated esthetic concerning the built environment:

> "[. . .] the Negro was considered a 'blot on the national civilization', and was a source of great shame to Aryanists and racial purists of the time. It was felt in these quarters that only through great waves of white European immigrants could Brazil develop a modern economy and a modern civilisation and culture. In addition to invigorating the economic life of the country, these immigrants would hopefully also discharge a eugenic mission, that of 'Aryanising' the country through the absorption of the Negro, producing lighter-skinned children whose appearance and features would carry some distinguishable resemblance to their German, Italian, Spanish, or Portuguese parent. In this way the official propaganda would be sustained, propaganda that in Europe presented Brazil as a 'great Latin nation' or as a 'new European civilization', complete with photographs of white—or apparently white—citizens, European-style avenues, neoclassical theatres, and elegant Norman town houses."[46]

Obviously this is a complex and varied story with its own elaborate historiography and it produced a panoply of unforeseen and/or unintended consequences. Two general points are nevertheless worth stressing in this context. First, those arriving in the subcontinent as bearers of the desired characteristics (whatever they might be) could predictably anticipate a remarkably favorable reception. Often they could enter a very stratified social system at a considerably higher point in the hierarchy than they could expect to have accessed in their (mostly European and class ridden) countries of origin. The offspring of rather dubious military adventurers could become Presidents (Banzer and Stroessner, for example); businessmen with low reputations at home could become captains of industry in their new countries; agitators and outcasts could found powerful labor organizations; suitors rejected in Europe could make magnificent marriages in the Americas. Of course not everyone was equally successful or well received but even those who failed could occupy a relatively high position in Latin America's social hierarchies. To this day visiting Europeans and North Americans typically receive favors and advantages that would not be so easily available at home and these favors are more generous and unconditional than those that their equivalents receive in other, major world regions. This first point, if it could be sufficiently documented and generalized, would provide compelling evidence for the broader thesis of this chapter concerning the region's "bias toward the modern" and its inclination to push reform "from above and without." For a more complete picture we would also need the views of the popular classes—sometimes deferential and complicit with this *extranjerizante* outlook, but usually a complex mixture of reactions (think of the popularity of ex-President Fujimori, seen by many ordinary Peruvians as less remote and hostile than members of the old Lima oligarchy), and potentially available for a nationalist backlash.

The second point is the obverse of the first. If "whitening" was such a public policy priority then clearly large segments of the indigenous population were not beneficiaries and their interests did not count for much among the holders of power. The generosity and access extended to the "modern" foreigner were matched by attitudes of disregard and exclusion toward the "backward" and the local. In consequence we would have to expect periods of resistance and reversal. Certainly pro-immigrant policies were cyclical, and after 1930 the rise of nationalism and populism tended to redress the balance as far as new arrivals were concerned. But those who had already arrived were generally able to retain and benefit from their initial advantages. Popular resistance may have curtailed the form of modernization but it seldom entirely reversed it.

But how did these pro-European immigration policies contribute to the "littered landscape?" It is possible to assemble an inventory of scattered and unabsorbed legacies of this approach to "modernity" comparable to that for the built environment. Consider the Anglo-Chilean *Racing* of Viña del Mar; the Welsh speakers of Patagonia; the Swiss chalets of Gramados; the Mennonite farm settlements of lowland Bolivia; and the German coffee plantation elite of Alta Verapaz in Guatemala.[47] This is admittedly a highly impressionistic list, but it could serve as an introduction to an additional set of exhibits in our prospective mausoleum.

V. How Durable A Break with the Past?

Turning to the recent period, since the end of the Cold War there have no longer been such sharply antagonistic alternative models of "modernity" to choose between. The professions intermediating liberal internationalism are now much more broadly based and solidly implanted; and perhaps (if the claims of the democratization literature have any substance) the gap between official discourse and popular consciousness is in the process of being narrowed. On these arguments one might conclude that Latin America is at last entering fully into the western mainstream of modernity, and that the sequence of incomplete and uneven "waves" proposed in section two has been relegated to history.

It would be obtuse to underestimate the significance of the huge shift toward a more standard version of liberal economics and politics that took place across almost all of Latin America in the 1990s. In broad terms, the subcontinent embraced market-oriented democracy as never before, and the scope of the resulting change in model is such that there is now very little possibility of a wholesale reversion. This remains true despite the mounting evidence of various forms of resistance and disenchantment, including the Argentine default of 2001 and the "Bolivarian" movement in Venezuela.

While there are currently (2005) multiple manifestations of opposition and rejection directed against the most recent wave of reforms "from above and without" what they demonstrate is lack of consensus rather than the crystallization of an alternative project. The more interesting questions concern the coherence and legitimacy of the new liberal framework. How much scope remains for sharp variations and shifts within the basic parameters of the new market democracy model? This issue has become sharper since the end of the 1990s, at least in part because the strong and unified impulses that were reaching the region from the United States ("Washington Consensus" economic prescriptions and democracy promotion linked to free trade agreements) have since slackened. The current drivers of liberal innovation are now more heterogeneous and domestic. Some forms of internal resistance to conventional liberalization are now better supported from abroad. Viewed from this perspective, the late twentieth-century secular shift in favor of liberalization does not invalidate the underlying thesis of this chapter.

Liberalism, like other apparently universal abstract variables, assumes different guises in alternative contexts not only because it is a classic example of an "essentially contested concept"[48] expressing many and often contradictory political, economic, and social ideals but also because really existing conditions give body and substance to abstract concepts, such that liberalism in Argentina will look and feel different from liberalism in New Zealand. The latter, for example, experienced the same international paradigm shift as Latin America but it has a more homogenous and integrated society than most of those of Latin America: the change in model was assimilated in a different—more wholehearted and successful—way. To take a different example, the adoption of market democracy in Central Europe was more transformative because of the domestic, often Austro-Hungarian, traditions it reactivated and because of the unique geopolitical context that underpinned and defined it. Similarly, the frontier individualism celebrated in some parts of North America as the most authentic expression of liberal values cannot be a central variant in most of Latin America given very different perceptions of collective rights and state authority.

None of this is very surprising in light of the many alternative varieties of practises that "exist" within the cluster of ideas we call "liberalism,"[49] or given one distinctive characteristic of the fragmented societies of this region, namely the distance customarily separating proclaimed from actually delivered rights. The result is that in Latin American conditions competing elites and power contenders have great leeway when interpreting such key tenets of the liberal canon such as constitutional responsibilities, market disciplines, and even the rule of law. Almost throughout the twentieth century, and virtually across the entire subcontinent, this leeway has been greater than elsewhere in the world (where such a large gap between *hecho* and *derecho* has been impossible to sustain for so long). At the end of the twentieth century even Latin America has come under increasing pressure to reduce this gap and to convert ostensible rights and duties into really observed practices. But even if this does indeed come about, regional understandings of the commitments required by a liberal order are likely for historical reasons to remain at some variance with the international mainstream. Thus, it is possible to envisage broad agreement on the need to reform society in accordance with modern liberal principles, but that leaves great scope for rivalry and disagreement between advocates of different components of the liberal "package" (economic, political, civil), and between alternative practical manifestations of each component. Similarly, the external models and sources of modern practice invoked by liberal activists can be very diverse, including the United States but also Spain, Germany, and ranging from Hayek to the Greens.

If the prevailing *zeitgeist* of the 1960s was state-led development and "dependency" in the 1970s, by the 1990s an opposite outlook had become hegemonic. The catchphrases became the "Washington Consensus" on economic policy, the "third wave" of democratization, and even the "end of history" as global liberalism appeared to displace all alternative worldviews. Of course, since there are twenty republics in Latin America there have always been differences of timing and emphasis and that remains true in the 1990s. However, before evaluating the significance of the remaining countercurrents it is essential to take on board the scale and coherence of the latest modernizing consensus.

The resurgent liberalism of the 1990s was both economic and political. It rested on strong intellectual foundations and derived practical inspiration from the apparently successful liberalizing reforms associated with the names of Reagan and Thatcher in the 1980s. The worldwide collapse not only of the Soviet Bloc but also of the socialist doctrinal alternative to liberalism gave it an immense boost in credibility. The sustained economic expansion of the post-Cold War decade, reinforced in the last few years by growing confidence in a long innovation and technology-led cycle boost to productivity in the United States and other leading economies, dispelled many of the early warnings that unconstrained global liberalism was inherently unstable. Thus, if the 1990s constituted a break with Latin America's past experience of incomplete cycles of modernization this must be evaluated in the context of an apparent international break with the past regarding the viability and dynamism of global liberalism. Within this framework we need to consider in what ways contemporary Latin American experiments with liberalism and with liberalization may differ from those of the past, such as the apparently successful half-century of externally driven liberalizing initiatives that followed from about 1870.

It is possible to identify four key sources of strength in contemporary global liberalism, each of which contrasts with the pre-1929 equivalent version of the same tradition. These are the intellectual foundations of the doctrine; its wide practical application; the sources of support it can mobilize; and the sweeping disarray of its opponents. Each of these sources of strength can be summarized briefly, and contrasted with earlier cycles of Latin American liberalism. Under each heading, the global inspiration may have become stronger than before, but that by no means resolves competing interpretations of how it should be applied in the regional context.

Foundations of Liberalism

By starting with an, albeit very synthetic, account of the strong intellectual foundations of current doctrines it is also possible to clarify the terminology employed here. All references to "liberalism" are intended to be broad, including liberal doctrines, ideologies, and practices, and including both economic and political liberalism. From this perspective, the intellectual foundations of contemporary global liberalism are both narrower and more tightly constructed than was true of earlier variants present in post-Independence Latin America. These earlier variants were often richly textured, with multiple sources of inspiration, but they contained inconsistencies of doctrine and practice and did not constitute an all-encompassing system. Thus, nineteenth-century liberalism might have coexisted with slavery, or aristocracy, or with imperialism or suffrage restrictions. The contest between religious faith and secular liberalism was still hard fought and, on the other side of the spectrum, socialism and Marxism were also serious challengers to liberalism.[50]

In contrast, the global liberalism of the 1990s could take secular assumptions for granted, treat socialism as a defeated alternative, and project both democracy and markets as values of universal applicability. Liberal doctrines were no longer constrained by the need to defer to any inherited source of tradition or institutional authority. Even such key institutions of global liberalization as the World Bank (WB) or the International Monetary Fund (IMF) might find themselves subjected to the same critique from liberal first principles as can be directed at all other collective agencies and authorities. The first principles in question were more rigorously and parsimoniously articulated. The intellectual foundations of contemporary liberalism are uncompromisingly radical. Individualism provides the building block for all understanding of both values and behavior. Thus, the old divide between political and economic liberalism is superseded and collectivist concepts such as solidarity or altruism are deconstructed. Working from such postulates the underlying "rationality of the market" can be put beyond question at least at the level of theory and ideal, with the "imperfections" of "really existing" markets being subject to correction. Political and social critiques of this radical variant of liberalism can be delegitimized as manifestations of "rent seeking" and constituency building by self-seeking brokers and intermediaries. This system of thought is doctrinally solid and all encompassing. It has greater transformative power than the earlier, more tentative and contextually restricted, variants of liberalism. In contemporary Latin America (as elsewhere) its intellectual elegance continues to win new converts (especially among the younger generations).

Not only is contemporary liberalism intellectually well grounded but it also has very wide practical applications. The central proposition is that all forms of monopoly—economic, political, and even social concentrations of power—can be presumed collusions against the interests of outsiders unless proved otherwise. From this one can derive "liberalizing" prescriptions that apply as much to the professions or the arts as to trade and finance and political representation. The implications for "the state" are particularly wide-ranging in Latin America, where so much hope has been invested in an institution that has fallen so far short of its pretensions. The subtlety and sophistication of some of these practical applications merit considerable elaboration, but here we are only concerned with the basics. In practice, however well structured and comprehensive they may be, not all the prescriptions that can be logically derived from first principles are taken up with equal enthusiasm. That is as true of global liberalism as it is of all other social doctrines.

If the liberal case for liberalization of trade and financial exchanges across international boundaries is so powerful that it has become an almost unquestionable mantra on grounds of doctrine one could conclude that the liberal case for dismantling immigration controls or for legalizing the sale of narcotics is almost as compelling. In practice, the analysis becomes inarticulate when challenged to explain why the doctrine applies so well to capital but not labor flows; or why alcohol and tobacco markets should be legal and competitive, but marijuana should be criminalized and cartelized.[51] It is not necessary however to adopt the view that contemporary liberal prescriptions are meant to apply equally to *all* social relations. What is claimed here is that the doctrine has very wide practical applications, and that it is a major source of strength that these essentially quite simple principles can be elaborated and refined to address such a large array of both large and small policy issues.

In the Latin America of the 1990s these principles were widely disseminated and a considerable variety of important policy problems were tackled from within that perspective. But many areas of social life have yet to be liberalized. The full potential of this doctrine as an instrument for transforming social relations in the subcontinent is far from being fully revealed as can be illustrated from the example of Lula's Brazil, where the government of the Workers Party (PT) government shifted to a remarkable degree compared with earlier expectations of it. This shift was driven and directed from the top of the party and its supporters have not yet fully assimilated it (it may not have to, in light of the current corruption scandals threatening the survival of the government) so the final outcome is by no means settled, although the old guard remains continually on the retreat. This is a powerful reason for concluding that the current cycle of reforms, inspired as always "from above and without," may still have a considerable distance to run.

Global liberalism has by no means yet exhausted its impact on contemporary Latin America. But equally, the well-entrenched pattern of eventual resistance and backlash has not been eliminated either (as in Argentina or Venezuela).

Social Support, Weak Resistance

Liberalism's two other sources of strength concern the nature of the social support it can mobilize and the weakness of the resistance it encounters. On both these fronts contemporary liberalism also occupies a stronger position than its predecessors. Starting with sources of support, the key point is that contemporary liberalism can present itself as inclusionary. Critics may be right to assert that the material benefits of liberalization are often very unequally distributed. From this standpoint it may seem as though only a narrow stratum—financial operators, managers, and large shareholders of international corporations, and associated consultants and media types—have strong reasons to back contemporary liberalism. But such a reductionist perspective overlooks two other sources of attraction that generate support from much wider constituencies.

The first is that in its present more robust and parsimonious form liberal doctrine is seen as occupying the intellectual high ground. If it appeals to the bright and the ambitious in many societies, whether or not they stand to gain any immediate material advantage, it is because it seems to provide convincing and practical answers to a great range of questions that are so inadequately addressed by alternative doctrines. It has high academic prestige, a strong pedigree, a succession of unexpectedly convincing successes to its credit, and its analysis is bold and unmistakable. Small wonder, then, that recent cohorts of the "best and the brightest" in Latin America and around the world have rallied around liberal positions rather than the nationalist or socialist doctrines that exerted so much pull over earlier generations.

The second feature making contemporary liberalism appear so inclusionary is that it has demonstrable appeal not only to business elites and to yuppies, but also much broader sections of the populace at large. This is often dismissed as "middle class" support, but that is quite misleading. Democratization has facilitated the emergence of a wide array of new "civil society" organizations extending far beyond the old (and often shrinking) middle class. More individualist, consumer rather than producer-oriented, forms of social expression underpin social demands for liberal "rights," and these are reinforced by a new ethos in the mass media. Developments in information technology and mass travel make it possible for broad social strata to "see" themselves from a more detached perspective and therefore to think in terms of liberal rather than corporatist identifications. The huge expansion of international remittances, now reaching large proportions of the popular sectors in many Latin American countries, exemplifies the scale of these innovations and their social reach far beyond the "middle classes." Of course these are all two-edged developments—they can mobilize mass support for a successful liberal project but they can also generate mass discontent when it fails.

Another key point is that liberalization, conceived as challenging "insider" privileges and the extension of access through broadened competition, strikes a chord with all sorts of real or imagined outsiders. Public ownership provides one good example of the kind of issue that can mobilize consumers, competitors, and indeed all non-participants against a cozy-looking monopoly. Even well-run and socially responsible public enterprises find it difficult to defend themselves against this broadly based reflex. Trade unions offer a similar target, especially in the parts of Latin America where corporatist privileges really have been enjoyed at the expense not only of society as a whole but of much union membership as well. Menem's Argentina provided a vivid illustration of the broad social appeal of contemporary liberal arguments in a society that had invested so much hope in antiliberal doctrines to so little avail. More generally, it is often the votes of the lower income deciles that have sustained recent liberalizing initiatives in Latin America in the face of opposition from organized challengers. Indeed, if anything, the "middle classes," however vaguely that term is defined, may be more susceptible to critiques of liberalism than other social strata.

Here it may be worth briefly noting a contrast between the broad inclusionary potential and intellectual self-confidence of contemporary liberalism in Latin America as compared to its late nineteenth- and early twentieth-century forerunners. At that time, as already noted, the doctrine was more complex, more compromised, and less focused, and its Latin American sources of social support were considerably more constrained. In still heavily agrarian societies its appeal was mainly urban. In cities where conservatives and socialists might both seek lower class support, the educated middle class was most likely to put up liberal ideas. But the main sources of liberal doctrine were foreign—French, American, and British—at a time when nationalism was stirring. Merchants and those in export enclaves might claim allegiance to liberal ideas but their ways of pursuing self-interest would not necessarily win them converts in other sectors of society.

This brings us to the relatively weak resistance to contemporary liberalism. First, the Catholic Church no longer opposes either democracy or the market with anything like the militancy of the past. In any case, its capacity for influencing social thought has plummeted. To a large extent it—and other sources of religious influence that carry increasing weight in various parts of Latin America—have come to terms with a secular, liberal, and worldly order, except on a narrow range of "moral" topics. Within the Church, Opus Dei probably has more influence in promoting liberal doctrines than liberation theologians have in resisting them. Second, the collapse of the Soviet Bloc not only discredited Bolshevism: it also destabilized Western social democracy, leaving the main ideological initiative to resurgent liberalism. Admittedly, large parts of the Latin American Left still manifest considerable nostalgia for these fading nostrums. Castro, Chávez, and "Tirofijo" all remain defiant in their different ways, but these examples can be taken as confirmation of the weakness of resistance to contemporary liberalism rather than as evidence to the contrary. The evolution of the Chilean Socialist Party reveals more about the power of liberal doctrine and the difficulty of resisting it (rather than seeking to "tame it" from within). Third, we should note that contemporary liberalism is a *global* doctrine and derives much strength from the apparently inexorable advance of what is loosely known as globalization. The key point here is that whatever else it involves, this process signifies the shrinkage and wholesale restructuring of the "Latin American State." State expansion and the associated doctrines of political and economic nationalism constituted the most formidable source of resistance to liberalism in Latin America from the 1929 Depression to the 1982 debt crisis. If statism and nationalism are no longer seen as viable options, then the most serious obstacle to the advance of contemporary global liberalism has been removed.

In view of the robust intellectual foundations, varied practical applications, broad basis of support, and weakened sources of resistance to global liberalism it is hard to avoid the conclusion that the 1990s represented at least a fairly substantial break with the past. Contemporary liberalism offers a series of ambitious and wide-ranging projects of transformation, catch-up, and "modernity," which even if originating "from above and without" may be carried through to fulfillment and anchored in the collective institutions and memories of the subcontinent to a far greater extent than earlier initiatives. It may define the contents of "modernity" in a more precise, specific, and operational form than ever before, and it converts its vision of the future into a realizable present. That, at least, is what the liberal *zeitgeist* presumes. Barring some major discontinuity on the scale of earlier setbacks to the liberal view of progress (1914, 1929, and 1939, among others), the current process in Latin America seems likely to continue more or less on course for a considerable period to come. It is therefore too soon to judge the full effects of the reforms undertaken in the 1990s. Perhaps the defining characteristic of a prevailing *zeitgeist* is that it structures social perceptions in such a way as to obscure or screen out discordant tendencies. However, some historical perspective on the question might be obtained from a brief reflection about the general relationship between social doctrines, ideologies, transformative policies, and their eventual outcomes.

The general pattern might be presented as follows. The starting point is a period of crisis or paralysis in which prevailing ideas, doctrines, and ideologies are no longer convincing as sources of guidance for the future. Alternative social doctrines therefore find a more receptive audience. These may be entirely new, or they may be restatements of old ideas that had passed out of fashion. But most probably, though claiming a respected pedigree, they will be somewhat renovated. In this case, they should have some initial credibility but can also be adapted to the specific requirements of the crisis of the moment. A good social doctrine needs to be pitched at a high level of generality. It should not be too obviously tailored to an immediate *conjuntura* that may be superseded quickly but must highlight underlying regularities that serve to explain what alternative doctrines cannot, and thereby point to relevant remedies. It is perfectly possible to argue that the rooted-ness of existing errors makes it extremely difficult to introduce appropriate remedies let alone enjoy their benefits any time soon. A robust social doctrine can envisage a better world that is very distant and costly to attain, but the more visionary the doctrine the more penetrating must be its critique of the existing situation.

Let us assume, then, that these initial ideas are articulated into a coherent and far-reaching doctrine that wins the necessary assent and are then translated into action. As the old assumptions crumble and failed practices are swept aside, the doctrine will become identified with more specific innovations and with conflicts in which its protagonist and antagonists acquire well-defined identities. This is the point at which doctrine can be said to generate ideology. The success or failure of specific innovations carries implications not just for the coherence of the theoretical ideas that may inspire them but also for the power and success of the authors of these policies. Even so, if the initial doctrine is sufficiently coherent and prone to generalization it is not so easily damaged by the failure of any particular innovation it generates. Usually, such failures can be accounted for from within the originating belief system. If the crisis that started the whole process was sufficiently severe, as was the crisis of the inward-looking development model in the Latin America of the 1980s, then successive reform failures may merely pave the way for further, more ambitious, root-and-branch proposals from within the same doctrinal school. Thus the process of feedback from policy outcome to questioning of the doctrine may be long delayed and deflected.[52]

Eventually, however, any social doctrine faces increasing pressure to answer for its results and is no longer able to rely solely on its promises. With the passage of time the triggering crisis will gradually fade from memory and the next generation of policy-makers, however steeped in the assumptions of the newly hegemonic doctrine, will be expected to explain when their initiatives generate undesired consequences. Particularly in the case of liberalism, ideology cannot indefinitely cover up an inability to achieve promised goals because the foundational doctrine provides both principles of freedom and criticism and practices of accountability through democratic processes that eventually expose failure and incoherence to criticism. On this basis, we may hypothesize that in due course the current liberalizing wave in Latin America will become more subject to effective critical feedback to the extent that it proves incapable of fulfilling the expectations it has raised. But "in due course" could be some considerable time in the future bearing in mind the severity of the 1980s crisis and the continuing disarray of liberalism's Latin American (and global) critics. Indeed, on these grounds one could also hypothesize that the most effective sources of criticism may well be generated from *within* the liberal framework of analysis, rather than from outside and against it.

So there *has* been a real break with the past and the subcontinent's linkage with western "modernity" *has* become more secure and broad-based, but the characteristic pattern of reforms impelled "from above and without" has not yet been broken conclusively. In consequence, it remains an open question how far the modernization drives of the 1990s will lead to a cumulative and internally guided dynamic of transformation or to what extent they will once again generate partial, incomplete, and eventually superseded outcomes that can be added to the existing stock of relics in the regional "mausoleum of modernity."

Thus far this section has emphasized arguments about the status of liberal theory and the distinctiveness of the current liberalization drive. But from the standpoint of this chapter as a whole contemporary liberalism should be situated in the context of two centuries of a regional history biased toward "modernity." If so, the 1990s can also be evaluated in accordance with the three areas discussed in the second section of this chapter. With regard to external "models" or reference points, in the 1990s the range of available alternatives was much narrower, but within that constricted field there was more scope for detailed negotiation and for country-specific adaptation. The Soviet alternative has of course been eliminated but so has the model of the social democratic welfare state and also that of Franco-style corporatism and authoritarian modernization. Although that may seem to reduce the possibilities to just one single nonnegotiable model—"neo-liberalism" or the "Washington Consensus"—the reality is somewhat more pluralist. There is a North American Free Trade Agreement (NAFTA) model promoted by the United States but there is also a Common Southern Market (MERCOSUR) variant closer to the European approach. There was the Argentine fixed exchange rate and various proposals for "full dollarization" but there are also experiments with "floating" currencies. And Brazilian constitutionalism and federalism contrasts with Venezuelan personalism and centralism. An important consequence is that when external models are invoked as guidelines for reform they are now more detailed, more closely evaluated, and more likely to include other Latin American experiences and not just an idealized account of a distant North America or Europe. Thus, Bolivian reformers recently borrowed some specific proposals from Chile and then passed on their experience and advice to Honduras and Haiti. Some Central Americans are even promoting their model of conflict resolution in Chiapas and Colombia. Some of the models being debated seem more problem-oriented than in the past and the region may be displaying more pragmatism and greater reciprocity. But this cuts both ways of course. If dogmatic neoliberalism fails in Argentina pragmatic imitators can take up the lesson elsewhere; and if illiberal measures produce desired results in one country its neighbors may take them up. After September 11, 2001 the international climate has also shifted back from an emphasis on liberalization to a renewed emphasis on security. And given the severity of Latin America's inherited social and political problems an increase in pragmatism (results-orientation) and local learning gives no guarantee of a permanent thrust toward liberal institutionalization.

This connects, of course, with the second area of reflection: the emergence of a denser and more internationally integrated network of policy advisers, specialists, and intermediaries. Again, the range of possibilities is narrower than before. Mexico used to dispatch officials from *Petróleos Mexicanos* (PEMEX) and land reform experts to Bolivia to advise on the creation of state oil companies and the enactment of sweeping land redistributions. By contrast, within the broadly liberal democratic and market-oriented framework of current policy-making the region is developing a much larger community of well-trained, competent, and versatile professional experts and advisers. There is less scope than before for the isolated Renaissance man empowered to implement his transformative vision. Today's reformers are more dependent upon teamwork, mutual monitoring, and comparative evaluation. That said they still operate in deeply unequal societies where the trust and consensus needed for the shared implementation for reforms may well be lacking. They often derive their expertise from education outside the region and their career advancement may be far more linked to the approval of foreign investors or a credentialist bureaucracy than to the satisfaction of popular needs. They are still, therefore, often biased toward reform "from above and without."

To some extent the democratization of Latin America is creating countervailing pressures but this is only a relative and uneven process, and so with regard to the third area of reflection the patterns of popular resistance and incomprehension that used to block successive waves of modernizing reform are probably weakening, although they have by no means disappeared. On the one hand, greater political freedom, press criticism, and institutional accountability may lead to more consensual strategies of reform, with greater diffusion of responsibility and more of a sense of "local ownership" (the internalization of modernity). On the other hand, where transformative initiatives threaten to harm sectional interests, greater democracy and a more autonomous civil society can produce intensified resistance. Overall, then, it would be prudent to retain an open verdict on the extent of the post-1990 break with the past.

VI. Conclusion: Reflections on Multiple Modernities

This chapter has attempted a very broad survey of the issues raised by the notion of "multiple modernities" as they relate to post-Independence Latin America. It has presented the region's republics as long-standing and geopolitically relatively secure regimes constructed from an early date on basically liberal foundations. These societies were fundamentally disconnected from their pre-Conquest histories but were well placed to fashion or reshape their national identities in accordance with the ideologies—and more broadly the mentalities[53]—prevailing among the dominant strata. And, for a multiplicity of reasons—part historical, part geopolitical, and part socio-structural—these mentalities were heavily influenced by European and North American ideas of progress and visions of "modernity." The resulting republican and loosely liberal elites were relatively unconstrained either by demands for physical security in a conflict-ridden world or by the weight of social traditions. So they found themselves comparatively free to *hacer patria* (nation build) and to pursue modernity in accordance with their own aspirations and views of the proper place for them and their nations through a "bias toward modernity." Clearly, however, for most of the past two centuries this must be understood essentially in terms of intentions more than in terms of outcomes. These intentions were only partially fulfilled before being superseded by alternative modernizing projects the result of which is what I have called the existence of a "littered landscape."

Certain categories and hypotheses have been highlighted that might be used to organize one's understanding of the region's distinctive historical experience and trajectory, and which could shed light on how this region can be contrasted in very broad aggregate terms with other major world regions, and on where it fits in some very loose and overarching theories in historical sociology. It conforms to Collingwood's view "that the historian himself, together with the here-and-now which forms a part of the process he is studying, has his own place in that process, and can see it only from the point of view which at this present moment he occupies within it." This being so, "every new generation must rewrite history in its own way, every new historian, not content with giving new answers to old questions, must revise the questions themselves; and [. . .] even a single historian, working in a single subject for a length of time, finds when he tries to reopen an old question that the question has changed."[54]

From that perspective, the questions I raised here about Latin America's "bias toward modernity," its tendency to reform "from above and without," and its propensity for leaving such projects uncompleted and not fully absorbed, are questions made more vivid by the region's current engagement with neoliberalism. Whether this is a repetition of earlier patterns or a break with the past is critical to the standpoint of this chapter. Is the mausoleum complete or is undergoing yet another extension? There is an empirical side to this question but it also depends on how one views "modernity" at the conceptual level.

"Multiple modernities" is an elusive category that might easily come to embrace everything. For example, the chapter has presented the region's late nineteenth-century "whitening" policies in favor of European integration as a good example of a transformative modernizing initiative. However, the nationalism of the 1930s and 1940s, which was partly inspired by European fascism, could also be viewed in the same vein even though it involved exactly the opposite measures: deportation of foreigners and the reservation of jobs for nationals, among other measures. Globalization, possibly including the regional and international convergence of labor markets, represents the latest international modernizing fashion. It is even possible to view the transformation of some parts of Central America through dependence on emigrants' remittances as another externally approved path to "modernity."

But if all these contrasting demographic strategies can be slotted into the same conceptual framework then surely nothing is excluded and so nothing can be explained. Fortunately, in this example, it is possible to illustrate how a bias toward modernity can structure some options and exclude others. All these rival demographic policies reflect and express a distinctively "modern" view of the state and its purposes.[55] Consider the machinery associated with all these policies: passports, entry visas, censuses, vaccination certificates, identity cards, birth certificates, evidence of military service. All these are impregnated with the assumptions of modernity. Moreover, it is not just the machinery but also the intellectual inspiration for successive demographic policies that is located in the "West" and lends authority to these strategies of transformation when they are adopted in the region. Currently, international institutions like the WB and the United National Development Programme (UNDP) standardize and propagate these visions of modernity. Latin America is not alone in receiving these impulses but they came early, met an easy reception, and worked to powerful effect in the subcontinent.

Although the debate over modernity is partly conceptual, there must also be an empirical part to it so we must face the question of how to evaluate the evidence bearing on this argument. As mentioned in the second section, we are dealing with tendencies only, and with relative differences between regions, not unambiguous dichotomies. Thus, against the Panama Canal we could pit the Suez Canal; against Brasilia there is Canberra; against the Porfirian ideal capital of 1910 one could quote Victorian Delhi; and so on. The "littered landscape" of section four is hopefully evocative but does it also establish a convincing case for Latin America's distinctiveness? What is involved here is not a matter of formal proof but of informal judgment. How significant and representative are these examples as an expression of an underlying *zeitgeist* in Latin America? There is plenty of scope for debate and elaboration, but at least, as my examples indicate, the region's historians are sensitive to the issue and have begun probing from this angle. Even if it were concluded that they are indeed relatively representative of Latin America how far does that distinguish the subcontinent from other major world regions? Here the comparative expertise is much thinner. It should in principle be possible to assemble parallel evidence from, say, Asia, so that the questions raised here in a preliminary manner in relation to Latin America can be evaluated on a comparative basis.

Michael Tsin's study of Canton in the 1920s has been used here as an illustration of that possibility. In a similar vein, Xiaoqun Xu has traced how the native Chinese physicians of Shanghai staged a counterattack against the assault of "modern" (Western) medical knowledge in the 1930s. In Latin America western medicine has often encountered low-level popular resistance but the "bias toward modernity" has precluded any counterattack on this scale or at this level of sophistication.[56] A further example would be Sudipta Kaviraj's analysis of the "invention" of India, a product of the nationalist imagination of the nineteenth century. To my mind his interpretation of Indian nationalism permits comparison with what has been said here about Latin America but also confirms an essential point of difference.[57] Similarly, his analysis of the changing attitudes toward public space in Calcutta, "the first modern city" of India, evokes a sense of recognition for those who try to understand street life in such Andean cities as Lima and La Paz, but his conclusion about the "public sphere" in Indian cities ("neither the central concepts nor their direction of transformation is the same as in the West") posits an end-state that in Latin America remains contested.[58]

Obviously much more work would need to be done before such impressionistic contrasts could be confirmed. Indeed, even with much more evidence the debate would remain open since these are difficult questions of judgment. But it is perhaps worth setting out the strong case for Latin American distinctiveness if only to force the comparative enterprise and stimulate a debate on these commonalities and differences. As Eisenstadt has written, "the systematic comparative analysis" of such matters "is yet very much before us."[59] In our informal discussions about these ideas, Wolfgang Schluchter drew attention to the contrast between difference conceived as *pattern* and as *deficiency*. The standpoint of this chapter is that if Latin America has a "bias toward modernity" this should initially be presented as a distinctive pattern rather than to judge it as either a merit or a deficiency. It has both a positive dimension—its transforming and rationalizing power—and an accompanying cost—the results of importation for an unwilling or unconvinced section of the population. The pattern should be established before it is judged. However, it is important to add that from the standpoint of the elites who have repeatedly launched and sustained so many self-serving projects of modernity the region is always conceived as suffering a deficiency in comparison to their view of the most advanced and "modern" models available. This negative assessment is required if they are to generate the unity and drive to push through a project of transformation against the predictable (and confirmatory) resistance of their putatively more backward compatriots.

Finally, this chapter has made two potentially conflicting suggestions that need to be reconciled. On the one hand, it has argued for an overall "bias toward modernity" in the entire post-Independence history of the region; on the other hand, it has focused in particular on the notion of a succession of transformative initiatives driven from "above and without" (inspired by external models rather than rooted in local practices). The first claim implies that the desire for modernity is society-wide, whereas the second suggests that the driving force is external and subject to popular resistance. But Latin American societies are highly stratified so it is possible for well-organized elites to drive through specific foreign-inspired projects of transformation that do not adequately reflect the interests or aspirations of the population at large. At the same time, the society as a whole can display receptivity to "modern" models and practices in general even while resisting specific elite projects that are perceived as one-sided or threatening. Indeed, although this chapter has emphasized certain types of initiatives that are relatively easy to isolate and reconstruct because they had elite sanction (such as projects to reconfigure the urban landscape, to "whiten" the population, or to promote elite-favored medical reforms and hygiene), those are not the only areas where evidence of a "bias to modernity" might be sought. Popular aspirations can also be traced, for example, through the demand for literacy, or through the examination of *telenovelas*, or in the area of sport.[60] While the most visible and directed forms of change may have come "from above and without," this chapter has also indicated that the appetite for modernity has been widely diffused. Not infrequently, however, what popular opinion has demanded is a variant of reform and transformation different from that being offered from on high.

Chapter 2

Latin American State Organization*

I. Introduction

This chapter surveys more than half a century in the development of state organization in twenty formally sovereign republics of Latin America.[1] As a historical survey rather than an exercise in abstract theory it pays close attention to the particularities of individual cases and analyzes them in a comparative context. Specific aspects of state organization—territorial control, public employment, fiscal capacity, scope of economic regulation, and accountability to citizens—are singled out. The aim is to isolate the main long-run trends in state organization in Latin America since 1930, and to formulate some generalizations about their determinants.

These Latin American states can be differentiated from most others on a number of dimensions. At Independence they were *creole* states, which as Benedict Anderson says, were "formed and led by people who shared a common language and common descent with those against whom they fought."[2] This they had in common with the United States, and although the latter has been celebrated as the "first new nation" the former are more likely to be singled out for what François-Xavier Guerra refers to as their "precocity."[3] In fact, as political units displaying almost unbroken administrative continuity they often date back further than their North American counterpart, in some cases as far as the sixteenth century. By world standards this is an exceptionally long record of continuous territorial jurisdiction, certainly as compared to nearly all the contemporary states of Africa, Asia, and the Middle East, but also by the standards of much of Europe. The consequence of this long history—reinforced by the strong geographical separations arising from greater distances and poor communications—has been the nurturing of local political elites often infused with a powerful sense of their autonomy, and their connected-ness to a distinctive institutional past. At the same time, as argued in the previous chapter, dominant attitudes toward institutional design are highly attentive to international practice and metropolitan fashion, and the sense of connected-ness with the past does not extend beyond the European Conquest (at least not in the sphere of political organization). In comparative terms, therefore, Latin America's main political elites display what in this book is called a "bias toward modernity," combined with a considerable degree of local autonomy, which results in intra-elite competition over alternative models of political innovation. This competition can broaden the range of political actors with a chance to participate and press their demands but usually within an institutional framework still heavily tilted to the elites. Hence the prevalence of successive "modernizing" political projects, each of which tends to run into the ground before achieving fulfillment.

Such projects require and tend to presuppose the existence of a comprehensive, authoritative, and effective national state apparatus, but precocity and autonomy are not sufficient to deliver this. So the history of the region is replete with efforts at "state building," "state reform," and even "state shrinking," all arising from the hope of reorganizing inherited political institutions so that they live up to collective, broadly modernizing, aspirations. However, the state organizations that developed following Independence did not reflect these aspirations: at best they served to develop and coordinate a range of mostly long established elite interests, and perhaps also to provide opportunities for transformative action led by narrow cohorts of state recruited "experts." Even that was by no means assured, let alone a capacity to generate stable consensus across the whole of society, or to overcome conflicts arising from persistent inequality and exclusion. It was not until the mid-twentieth century that the question of how to extend the reach of the state became more pressing. Between about 1930 and 1980, the role of the state was transformed throughout the subcontinent, and although there were many variations in detail, the general pattern was for ambitious expansions of responsibilities and pretensions, which the 1982 debt crisis eventually proved to be unsustainable. This chapter deals with these efforts at modern state organization and their regionally distinctive trajectories and outcomes.

It is not "the Latin American state" that is considered here but rather a range of different kinds of state organizations that respond to quite varied conditions with respect to economic development, geopolitical location, and sociopolitical context. However, there are some important limits within which these variations occur, and rather than thinking of twenty totally distinctive national experiences it is possible to identify several clusters of states with sufficient similarities to permit commonality of treatment. The rest of this introductory section briefly outlines major shared characteristics of Latin American state organizations and indicates the classificatory criteria used here to identify subgroups of states within the region.

But first some caveats: this is not another account of the development of state capitalism, although all the countries considered developed forms of state organization intended to mediate the crucial relationship with the capitalist world market. Second, given space limitations, there is little consideration of the varying ideological climates which have shaped state organization since 1930. Changing doctrines of, and attitudes toward, nationalism in particular merit closer attention than they receive here. Third, changes in social structure discussed in other chapters—urbanization, mass education, the rise of organized labor, for example—which interact with changes in the organizational structure of the state, are not fully elaborated on. While not entirely overlooked, the number and variety of distinctive national experiences under consideration preclude rigorous treatment of changes in social structure. And fourth, there is no attempt to trace key developments in state organization throughout the entire region over the whole period, but rather a focus on selected aspects, countries, and periods. In particular, the early 1930s are highlighted and compared with certain later periods, notably the early postwar years, the 1960s, and the early 1980s.

So what did our twenty Latin American states have in common in the early 1930s, and what characteristics distinguished them from the other forty or so formally sovereign states in existence at that time? They were long established, having more than a century of independent existence in most cases; they were not empires like most of the European states were, or aspired to be; they were republics, not monarchies; they were not socialist republics, although Chile and Cuba witnessed brief attempts to follow the Soviet example during the trough of the 1929 Depression. They suffered no casualties or direct war damage in the First World War. Indeed, they were far less exposed to international warfare than other states in the world in the twentieth century: there were no veterans of foreign wars and not even many serious rivalries over territory (certainly not over inhabited territory). The 1932–1935 Chaco War between Bolivia and Paraguay constitutes a major but isolated exception to this rule. Although the Catholic Church had a not infrequently powerful, and for the most part reactionary, influence on society, all the states had at least formally liberal, and often progressive, constitutional structures. There were no theocracies and no hereditary dictatorship—at the time, the Trujillo and Somoza regimes were just beginning. On the contrary, secular education was acceptable in principle and rising in practice, often led by higher education sectors in which remarkably radical ideas about university autonomy had acquired widespread momentum. The normative political structure of the region included regular—albeit suffrage-restricted—elections, the separation of powers, and at least some degree of autonomy for the legal system and the press, as well as some appearance of federalism. The principle that modern society should have a "public sphere" separate from the private was widely acknowledged, even though access to the former was extremely selective and relatively unstable and patrimonial and clientelist reflexes pervaded nearly all the public administrations.

In fact, the social underpinnings of these republican forms were often weak, and class, ethnic, and regional fragmentation was the norm, as were local or personalist loyalties. Elite groups were typically unaccustomed to the notion that general public rules might also be applied to themselves. As Loveman notes, "from independence political life was informed by republic, rule of law values, and the aspiration of elites to liberty, prosperity and even democracy: "[. . .] this was the dream, the promise, the passion, and the rhetoric of Spanish American political elites in the nineteenth century. They shared this dream with North American and European liberals, even when they meant it to apply, like their European and North American counterparts, only to the affluent, the educated, the male and the non-coloured."[4] The paradox is, however, that the practical reality of the political life of the region was as, if not more, authoritarian and dictatorial than democratic or liberal: "Spanish Americans wrote constitutions proclaiming popular sovereignty while military officers, brigands, would-be national saviours and aristocrats sought to impose order on peoples tormented by despotism, instability, and misery. This reality was reflected in the juridical regimes and historical constitutions of the region, which both expressed "the dream of liberty and contain[ed] its negation", in the form of emergency or extraordinary powers."[5] In short, these were not fully consolidated liberal republics with fully internalized constitutionalist principles that had become "second nature" in society as a whole, and indeed, the Depression of the 1930s marked a turning point in the trajectory of Latin American liberalism after which even the most highly advanced expositors of liberal principles (in Argentina, Chile, and in particular Uruguay) were driven into frank retreat. Nevertheless, compared with most of the world in the early 1930s Latin America seemed an unusual haven for republican virtues.

Most of the distinguishing characteristics listed above fail to separate the states of Latin America from such Anglophone liberal states as the United States, Australia, Canada, and New Zealand. Some care is needed when making crucial distinctions. Overall, the Anglophone countries enjoyed a higher living standard than the Latin American republics—although Argentina and Uruguay were not so different in this respect from Australia and New Zealand. More decisively, a clear majority of citizens in the English-speaking nations enjoyed relatively full and secure participation in the social and political life of the time. This statement needs to be placed in context (we are referring to the 1930s), but compared with even the most favorable Latin American experiences liberal rights and guarantees were more of a reality in the ordinary lives of average citizens in North America and Australasia. A convenient way to sum up this contrast is to say that even during the Depression there was an important difference for those experiencing it firsthand, between the *achieved* liberalism of these developed capitalist-market economies, and the *rhetorical* and *aspirational* liberalism of Latin American societies.

Latin American societies were, of course, characterized by markedly uneven development—so-called "enclave" development in the dependency literature—and an often incomplete and insecure form of insertion into the world market economy.[6] In this regard the "peripheral" or "semi-developed" countries of the region had more in common with the newly established republics of the Balkans and Eastern Europe. But their geopolitical location was more fortunate, and their experiences of uninterrupted self-government were for the most part much longer.

The great majority of these republics had already celebrated their first centenaries of independent existence in the 1930s. Such longevity raises complex questions about the origins and morphology of the state organizations under consideration. To what extent can their state structures and workings be traced back to the three centuries of Iberian colonial administration? Intellectual influences derived from European and North American liberalism are clearly present in many constitutional documents and speeches by the founders of the independent states although doubt remains as to how far these ideas were transmuted in the course of adoption, especially since the institutions that came to embody them were at least initially very fragile and in many respects ineffective. Perhaps it would be more accurate to trace the effective organization of these states not from independence but some later stage in the nineteenth century, when stable administrations finally proved capable of successfully upholding "the claim to the monopoly of the legitimate use of force" throughout the territory, to use the Weberian formulation.[7] Important as they are in their own right, these issues open a larger question: did Latin American state organization precede and perhaps give rise to "civil society," or did these two social abstractions emerge together? Or was it the preexisting social structure that largely shaped and penetrated belatedly organized state structures?

There is no simple answer to such complex questions, least of all when discussing the history of twenty diverse republics. However, a few general observations can be made. Concerning the legacy of Iberian administration, for example, nearly all the states in existence in 1930 were governed from cities that already performed some administrative functions prior to independence. However, while some capital cities had glorious colonial pedigrees (such as Havana, Lima, Mexico City, and Santo Domingo), others were more transient (Rio de Janeiro, the Brazilian capital from 1763 to 1960), others arose from relative obscurity (Asunción and Montevideo, for example) and a few were parvenus (like La Paz, Managua, and San José). Similarly, the boundaries of these republics bore a recognizable relationship to colonial jurisdictions, although the fit was far from perfect. There were other continuities—in the language of administration, some forms of property law and rights, some aspects of the professions like university faculties—all of which could be cited by those claiming to identify a continuous and dominant Iberian tradition ("centralist" to some, "Catholic corporatist" to others). Yet, such arguments overlook the fact that for much of the colonial period distant centralizers learned to coexist with a remarkable array of local diversities, and disregard the rupture brought by independence (or by the overthrow of the Empire in 1889 in the case of Brazil).[8] Of course there were well-known continuities between colonial and postcolonial elites and social structures but at least at the level of state organization the discontinuities were sometimes drastic. Even Claudio Véliz, who has made the strongest claims for the historical persistence of an underlying bureaucratic and centralist political tradition of colonial origin, concedes that Independence was initially followed by a wave of anti-Absolutist, decentralizing, and federal experiments and that in the second half of the nineteenth century the region underwent what he calls a "liberal pause," which lasted until the Great Depression. Moreover, to the extent that he is able to identify a concealed centralist tradition beneath this appearance of fragmentation he is forced to recognize the appearance of a variety of *competing* centralist authorities no longer subject to political restraint or control from Europe.

An alternative perspective emphasizes the powerful impact of liberal and republican political ideas emanating from Europe and North America, but also recognizes the local realities distorting their transmission to Latin America. To dispense with hereditary rule and openly aristocratic governance was a bold innovation in the early nineteenth century; so too was the abolition of slavery, the adoption of the principle of the division of powers, and experiments with federalism and secession. The underlying rationale was some notion of popular sovereignty clearly traceable to European liberal currents of opposition to Absolutism. Whether the dominant current was French, British, North American, or Iberian need not detain us here, although all these influences contributed in varying proportions, and the Spanish strand in particular has frequently been underestimated. From the standpoint of state organization what matters is the huge gulf that opened up between abstract endorsement of these principles, and their effective embodiment in authoritative institutions. The "precocity" of Latin American constitutionalism has therefore been suggested as a key explanation for its debility. One very concrete aspect of this precocity, which can be studied systematically by historians, arises directly from the extreme difficulties of overland physical communication throughout almost all the subcontinent, which rendered largely theoretical the claims to territorial authority of the new state administrations. Another aspect of particular salience in the Andean republics and Meso-America was the widespread prevalence of indigenous peasant communities who traced their ethnic identities to pre-Conquest civilizations rather than to any political models derived from Europe.[9]

Oszlak's summary of the sources of "disorder" confronting these twenty states reflects a situation that in many cases extended well into the twentieth century: "On the one hand there were many instances of armed confrontations, which in different countries occurred as uprisings of local caudillos, *campesino* rebellions, Indian raids, secessionist attempts, and other forms of opposition to the claims of concentrating and centralising power. On the other hand, tradition conspired against the centralisation by the state of certain instruments of social control: civil registers, the educational system, uniform commercial practices [. . .] Sub-national divisions (states, provinces, departments) continued to have their own armed forces, coin their own money, establish internal customs, and administer justice based on varying constitutional and legal norms."[10] Indeed, it was not uncommon for the best-organized and most dynamic administrative structures to arise on the periphery of these established states and for these subnational bureaucratic units to present a significant challenge to central authority. Consider the two largest republics during the 1920s: Mexico and Brazil. In the former, it was the so-called Sonora dynasty political networks that drew some of their strength from the surviving administrative structures of the northwestern and north-eastern states, which occupied many dominant positions in national politics following the collapse of central authority occasioned by the revolution;[11] and in the latter, the southern state of Rio Grande do Sul played a crucial role in backing the Vargas revolution, which led to the re-centralization of the invertebrate old republic.[12] There are other examples. In Bolivia, the city and Department of La Paz rose to such supremacy that in 1898 it displaced the nominal capital, Sucre, as the effective seat of government. In Ecuador, Guayaquil posed an increasing threat to the central authorities in Quito although it never captured or superseded them. Given the multiplicity of instances in which such conditions still applied a full century after most republics had obtained their independence, it is hardly possible to defend the hypothesis of an underlying "centralist" tradition except by classifying every assertive periphery as a new center.

This may be why Oszlak goes so far as to state that, "In Brazil, many still maintain that we can speak of a truly national state only since the 1930s while in Peru the very existence of a nation and a national state is still a topic for discussion."[13] This goes much too far. The problem with such arguments is always to determine an appropriate standard of measurement by which to gauge the progress, or absence thereof, of any particular state organization. Matched comparisons between Latin American republics are more instructive than contrasts with an ideal-typical state modeled on, say, Prussia. Steve Topik provides one such comparison between early republican Brazil and Porfirian Mexico that redresses the balance. According to his—overstated—alternative view, at the turn of the century "the state in Brazil was internally strong and internationally respected, while the Mexican state was fragmented internally and internationally dependent. The republicans who took power in 1889 inherited a fairly well-institutionalized national state that had elite support. Brazil's path to independence had been smooth. A weak church, relative ethnic homogeneity, and the social cement of slavery tended to convince the country's ruling class of the necessity to maintain a united front. Arguably, a nation was built and a state formed earlier in Brazil than anywhere else in Latin America."[14] In reality there are multiple dimensions to state organization, and Porfirian Mexico outranked republican Brazil in some major respects (more extensive regulation of land-ownership, and mineral and water rights, for instance) while falling well behind in terms of tax effort ("extractive capacity"), spending on public works, or the size of the state bureaucracy.

As for the relationship between "state" and "civil society," in very general terms we may classify almost all these pre-1930 regimes as "oligarchic republics," in which such public authority as existed was broadly at the service of a restricted sector of the population that derived its coherence from various non-state sources of social power, such as land-ownership, family lineage, or a position of advantage in international trade and finance. Yet, any such "oligarchic" predominance was typically fragile—perhaps vulnerable to internal feuding or liable to contestation from below. Moreover, as state organization proceeded and as the formal structure of republican and constitutional government acquired substantive policies and capabilities, the emerging bureaucracies tended to pursue ambitions and sources of justification that were liable to diverge from the outlook of the so-called oligarchic sectors. This became especially manifest as a consequence of the Depression since it weakened both the material position and the ideological legitimization of the liberal oligarchies, and simultaneously thrust new tasks of national integration and economic management into the hands of governmental structures that were abruptly cut loose from their preexisting international alignments. The rise of economic nationalism involved these states in a multitude of new commitments, and impelled them to generate new sources of social support to substitute for, or counterbalance, traditional "oligarchic" alignments.[15] To say that these newly assertive state organizations began to "create" new, more participatory, and truly national societies might be to overstate the case, but certainly the balance of initiative passed from oligarchies to bureaucracies as the process of import substituting industrialization got underway.

Since state structure in Latin America has multiple dimensions and since state–society relations varied considerably over time and between countries and there was a socially and geographically very uneven development of institutional structures in most republics, the question inevitably arises whether the states of the region could—in the 1930s or the 1990s for that matter—properly be analyzed as a collectivity and, if not, what kind of subdivisions would be appropriate. Given the focus on the characteristics of state organization, this chapter must distinguish between the extreme cases of, say, Chile and Uruguay, on the one hand, and Haiti, Honduras, and Bolivia, on the other. What is more problematic is to identify criteria of classification that remain stable over time, and to discriminate not just between these two extremes but between both and the more typical intermediary levels of state articulation (apparent in Brazil, Colombia, and Mexico, for example). This suggests a rough-and-ready threefold classification. At the top of the range, the most sophisticated and in some sense "modern" forms of state apparatus are found in the countries of the Southern Cone. This can be sustained even for the early 1980s, although the normative implications are far different from those implied by "modernization" theory. At the bottom of the range, the simplest and most improvised forms of state organization are broadly "Central American" in type (although this shorthand does an injustice to Costa Rica). Except when I refer to either Southern Cone or "Central American" subcategories, the more typical forms of state organization, those that receive the most attention here, fall into an intermediate range. Brazil and Mexico will often be cited as representative in this sense.

This threefold classification has the virtue of simplicity but the defect of crudity. One significant implication should be underlined at the outset. Taking Brazil and Mexico as representative of the middle of the range biases the interpretation toward the overstatement of the advances made since 1930, as both these countries had rather poorly organized, and in many ways defective, forms of state organization at the beginning of the period. On the eve of the 1982 debt crisis, however, they possessed perhaps the most sophisticated and effective, and certainly the most ambitious and self-confident state bureaucracies of the region. By contrast, at either of the two extremes, we witness far less in the way of positive change and also much less growth in self-confidence. After 1982, the impression of a relentless advance is reversed throughout the region by the debt crisis and the ensuing near bankruptcy of most states, a topic discussed briefly at the end of the chapter.

In general the state has at least three essential and interrelated characteristics: territoriality, administration, and command over resources. Where all three elements have been effectively developed and brought together we have a "modern state," and otherwise not. Relatively few "modern states" in this sense existed around the world in 1930. Latin America was of course much further advanced than Africa or Asia along this route and it is at least arguable that some of the Latin republics (those of the Southern Cone) were more like "modern states" than many countries in Europe, notably in the Balkans. However, as we shall see, for most countries of the subcontinent the three essential requirements were only incipient or partially developed in 1930. A half-century later the situation was very different, especially in Mexico and Brazil. Enormous strides had been taken toward the consolidation of "modern states" throughout Latin America, although this is certainly not to claim that all was rational, well organized, and impartially dedicated to the public good in any of these countries.

The three characteristics proposed here should be regarded as minimum sufficient conditions for modern statehood rather than as some

Hegelian historical end product. Even by this minimalist yardstick there were still many loose ends, many partial and incomplete processes at work in the countries under review. Indeed, in certain cases, there was a degree of regression as some earlier extensions of state organization were eroded or undermined. Moreover, as the "state shrinking" tendencies of the 1980s made clear, even the most impressive and sustained efforts at state building proved to be deeply flawed, resulting in over-extended, inflexible, unresponsive, voracious and often very politicized bureaucracies that proved highly vulnerable to predatory attacks (in the lexicon of Mexican neoliberals, the state had become *el ogro filantrópico*). Nevertheless, the broad picture is clear: between 1930 and the early 1980s nearly all of Latin America underwent a remarkable process of state organization. The ambitions, resources, and capabilities of virtually all the region's public authorities became incommensurably greater than they had been a half-century earlier even though a yawning gap between aspiration and reality often persisted; state accountability to society usually remained highly deficient, and a systemic crisis loomed.

It is no easy task to determine either when or why this happened in each instance, let alone why some countries lagged behind in relative terms while others took such impressive strides. Since we are dealing with a continent-wide—indeed worldwide—process we must take into account the major international forces at work, although there is no consensus about the level of generalization appropriate for the purpose. At one extreme, for example, it can be argued that given Latin America's physical characteristics, effective and uniform territorial control could only be established by means of air transport. In almost all countries simple airplanes and primitive runways first made their appearance in the 1920s, and by the 1950s and 1960s air transport had become a vital and strategic aspect of internal communication and state affirmation.

From the other extreme point of view, however, this type of analysis would be regarded as of minor significance. The spread of modern state organization can, from this standpoint, only be understood if the global spread of capitalist forms of social organization is first delimited. Progress or retrogression in particular Latin American countries would always have to be interpreted in the context of an unfolding world system driven essentially by forces that are external to Latin America. What we have characterized as the "modern states" of the hemisphere would, in this perspective, have to be re-labeled "dependent states." An intermediate line of explanation would argue that the expansion of state organization increases its political and economic weight and therefore its capacity to pursue its own self-interest—albeit in the guise of serving the interests of all. Thus, the state bureaucracy may have a built-in tendency to grow exponentially regardless of whether or not this expansion reflects genuine public policy requirements. Such differences of viewpoint are of fundamental importance, and it is another limitation of this chapter that no direct attempt is made to resolve them. However, after tracing the process of state organization in a number of countries it may be a little easier to identify some of the proximate causes at work.

Among other considerations, it can be suggested that the 1930s Depression often tightened command over resources exercised by central authorities. The Second World War gave rise to a much intensified effort to assert effective and centralized territorial control, a concern renewed in the 1960s under the impact of guerrilla challenges; and postwar international institutions such as the United Nations (UN), the General Agreement on Trade and Tariffs (GATT), and the United States Agency for International Development (USAID), among others, played an important role in spurring the growth and upgrading of modern administrative and bureaucratic structures. However, such external stimuli must not be over-emphasized. Even in Bolivia, for example, where attempts to organize an effective modern state have faced exceptionally severe difficulties and external forces have played an unusually active role, it is clear that a powerful internal logic was at work throughout the period. Throughout this half-century, Bolivian statesmen and administrators of a variety of political persuasions were intensely concerned about the need to "catch up" with their neighbors in the area of state organization. Social Darwinist explanations should not be too lightly dismissed where the growth of state organization is concerned. "Organise or perish" is the stark alternative that has recurrently motivated state initiatives throughout Latin America in the contemporary period.

There is also another type of internal logic at work. Between 1930 and 1990 the inhabitants of Latin America were socially transformed by, for example, urbanization, literacy, mobility, capacity for organized self-expression and "citizenship." In the extreme case, in the 1930s, incipient and in some ways "oligarchic" Latin American states confronted a largely rural and uneducated population most of whose civic skills and material possibilities confined them to the status of subjects for most purposes. The early twenty-first century state is forced to recognize that for good or ill the people to whom it must respond are rapidly acquiring all the characteristics of active citizenship. Of course the growth of the state has itself done much to promote this transformation, as in the history of public education considered below, but whatever the causes the consequences are clear: Latin

American politicians and administrators are obliged to elaborate more complex and sophisticated forms of public policy because they are in the last analysis answerable to a far more complex and sophisticated public. This secular transformation (the "modernization" and "massification" of all these societies) provides the single most powerful impulse toward the construction of "modern states" throughout Latin America.

Perhaps a fourth characteristic—democratic, constitutional, and popularly accountable government—should be added to the three essential and interrelated elements of modern statehood already mentioned.[16] Certainly that is the implication of much contemporary discussion about the wave of democratization that swept Latin America in the 1980s, but on the long view it is too early to judge the profundity of this change.[17] The criteria of state organization adopted here are therefore minimalist, a choice that can be justified both on theoretical grounds and in the light of Latin American experience. There is very strong evidence of the growth of state organization in the realms of territoriality, administration, and command over resources, and there are good reasons why this should, almost necessarily, have occurred. By contrast, in the realm of constitutionalism, or in terms of democratic and accountable government, there is no such clear-cut progression, nor are the reasons for expecting it nearly so compelling. Indeed, a plausible case can be made for the claim that in the 1920s quite a few Latin American countries witnessed a high point of constitutional government. Much broader strata of society may have participated in aspects of political life in the 1980s but the state structures organizing such participation were in many cases even less adequate to process increased demands from below than in the past. This is especially true of sectors and regions where the state's presence, always uncertain, increasingly faced eclipse. However, although history and theory both suggest that constitutional accountability may be an "optional" rather than an integral component of the concept of a modern state, the recent wave of democratizations do at least confirm that it is one very important possible form of state organization. Accordingly, the patchy and reversible expansion of "citizenship" is discussed in a postscript at the end of this chapter.

The relationship between the development of state organization and "capitalist expansion" also requires a brief comment.[18] A wide range of public policies implemented between, say, 1870 and 1930 can certainly be viewed as state-initiated efforts to reshape internal socioeconomic arrangements (with the creation of property laws, the establishment of credit systems and transport infrastructure, among others) and to integrate the region more fully into the prevailing capitalist international market system. Similarly, in our period this has been a dominant theme of public policy in various countries and in certain specific periods (the Alliance for Progress can be interpreted in this way, as can the late 1980s). Another wide range of public policies, loosely labeled "import substituting industrialization," can reasonably be viewed as forceful state-initiated efforts to promote a "national" form of capitalism partially sheltered from the instability and inequality then attributed to the international capitalist system. The policies associated with this phase sometimes resulted in extremes of state interventionism and state ownership that were, at least with hindsight, often judged to have hampered or stifled private enterprise rather than to have reinforced it. Where such judgments were made, the policies in question were generally reversed, which might be taken as confirmation that the underlying logic of state action was directed to the "promotion of capitalism." However, another large array of public policies have been directed toward the mitigation and even control of class conflict (such as social security provisions, corporatist labor legislation and various forms of co-optation and repression). Again, it seems reasonable to suggest that such measures can be broadly interpreted as being motivated by an intention to "legitimize" and stabilize capitalist development.

For a variety of reasons, however, this chapter does not stress such an interpretation. First, such an approach makes the central object of study the development of capitalism in Latin America rather than the development of state organization. Second, it involves lumping together highly diverse systems of economic organization that share the "capitalist" denomination only in the sense that they preserve space for private ownership of some of the means of production and do not involve comprehensive central planning. Third, it tends to downplay, or even preclude from consideration, all factors contributing to the expansion and reorganization of the state other than those that are "functional" for the promotion of capitalism. The Second World War is presented here as a powerful stimulus to certain forms of state organization that were only very indirectly connected to the promotion of capitalism, for example. More proximate causes like national security, the wish to secure access to scarce and critical indigenous natural resources, provided adequate motivation for pro-capitalists and anti-capitalists alike. Similarly, although innovations designed to regulate social conflict may well prove functional for the subsequent development of a private-ownership based market-system this was not always and necessarily their intention or consequence (think of Velasco's Peru). For all these reasons, this chapter treats the development of state organization as a subject for study in its own right. Once that has been accomplished, the interrelationships with various forms of capitalist development may be traced more accurately.

In the light of these very general considerations, let us now consider with more historical and geographical precision the development of each of the three elements that can be characterized as *essential* to statehood.

II. Territorial Control

By 1930, nearly all the states of Latin America had a century of experience in asserting governmental control over their respective territories. As direct successors of the Iberian Empire they exercised a territorial control that reflected an even longer history. And yet, as late as the second quarter of the twentieth century, effective and uniform administrative control was in most cases more an aspiration than a reality. By the 1960s this, the most primitive aspect of modern statehood, was far more securely implanted but even in the last quarter of the century it was still possible to highlight certain respects in which territoriality was still incompletely established (a few *republiquetas* in Colombia; some Amazonian provinces in which the national currency circulated only infrequently; even a small number of unresolved boundary problems such as those that gave rise to armed conflicts between Peru and Ecuador, and Britain and Argentina, in the early 1980s). Clearly, the process of asserting centralized control throughout a given territory can be very protracted. It is also a complex and multifaceted affair. The crucial point is that the generation of leaders that emerged in 1930 presided over a very rapid advance in this process, a qualitative transformation in the degree of territorial control exercised from the national capital.

One way to illustrate this transformation is to ask what was required in the 1920s for a new appointee to take up responsibilities in a far-flung province. In Bolivia, for example, before the advent of air travel, an official appointed to the rubber-producing provinces controlled by Suárez Hermanos would take a train to the Chilean coast, a boat through the Panama Canal to England, and then a return boat to Manaus in Brazil, and proceed upriver from there. He would find that the pound sterling rather than the Bolivian peso was the currency in local circulation. Although this is an extreme case, it illustrates a fairly general Latin American phenomenon of the 1920s. Consider the Colombian official sent to Chocó, the Brazilian official responsible for Acre, or the Nicaraguan responsible for the Miskito coast. Even the compact and reputedly "modern" state of Costa Rica fits this pattern. The journey from San José to the northwestern provincial capital of Liberia in the 1930s proceeded as follows: it was possible to take a train to the Pacific Coast at Puntarenas (although some families still made the journey by ox-drawn *carreta*, which took eight days—typically with stops to cut wood or pick coffee, for example), but from there to Liberia the overland route was passable only six months in the year so the alternative was a circuitous boat ride to the Guanacaste coast, followed by eight hours on horseback into the interior.

Reviewing any list of relatively uncontrolled outlying provinces it soon becomes apparent that a variety of very different factors may account for the lack of central control. One possibility is simply that the region in question might be so inaccessible, so lacking in "governable" population or in realizable economic advantage, that its theoretical administrative needs could be relegated to some distant hypothetical future. Trans-Andean sections encompassing Bolivia, Peru, Ecuador, Colombia, and Venezuela mostly fell into this category in the 1930s. However, even in these cases the presence of neighboring states with a potential capacity for seizing and controlling whatever a sovereign government might fail to protect provided a spur to colonization and settlement. Every Latin American statesman of the 1930s was conscious of what might otherwise occur. The loss of Texas and California by Mexico, the loss of Panama by Colombia, the loss of Patagonia by Chile, and the loss of Acre by Bolivia all stood as salutary reminders. The Chaco War and the Peruvian–Ecuadorian conflict of 1941 would ensure that such considerations were not forgotten. Indeed, the more obviously valuable the province, the greater the temptation for a neighbor to covet it. In such circumstances the central authority might well judge that the only effective defense was to delegate virtually all its authority to locally organized interests and not to interfere in their affairs except by invitation. Much has been written about the economic dimension of "enclave" development, but the political—and geopolitical—logic behind this type of arrangement seldom receives sufficient attention.

It would be misleading to suggest that the only important examples of uncontrolled territory within the formal state boundaries of the 1930s concerned provinces suitable for annexation by predatory neighbors. The reality was that large swathes of the interior, far removed from international frontiers, fell into the same category. This was surely the significance of the 1920s odyssey of the *tenentes* through the backlands of Brazil right up the São Francisco River, not to mention comparable exploits of exploration and discovery in various other countries at the time, like Bingham's discovery of Macchu Picchu and archaeological finds in southern Mexico, to mention only the most publicized. These physical precursors of the "inward-looking" development of the 1930s helped to awaken a sense of nationality in a new generation of officers and administrators. Overcoming physical obstacles to communication certainly played a vital part in this stage of apprehending the national territory, but the process should not be reduced to that. A crucial aspect of the "external orientation" of the Latin American economies in the 1920s was the emphasis on coastal settlement and development. Lands that were not directly accessible to international shipping routes depended on rail or road links to the coast to give them their place in national life. Vast extensions of sometimes highly productive and heavily populated land often remained at the margin of official consciousness because, in the absence of interior communications, its contribution to the flourishing international division of labor could only be marginal. Where such an outlook prevailed the national government might have little interest in asserting central control over "abandoned" internal territories. The problems of Goias were of little interest to Rio de Janeiro, and the *puno* was a world apart from Lima, as was Guerrero from Mexico City. Here too, even though there were no "enclaves" the central authorities were typically complacent about extreme delegation of power to local elites, perhaps an incipient bourgeoisie based on internal colonialism, or an archaic and isolated landlord stratum or perhaps simply *caciques*, whose control originated neither from capital or land but from more "primitive" forms of accumulation based on the unimpeded monopolization of local force.

Finally, to this necessarily brief and schematic list we must add the characteristics of the national governments with nominal responsibility for asserting such control. In some important cases—most notably Brazil—a high degree of federalism limited even the nominal powers of the central authorities. Regionally semiautonomous governments were often reluctant to enforce any more control than they would tolerate emanating from above. More generally, the administrative capabilities and material resources of most Latin American states were very modest in the 1920s, certainly by comparison with later developments. In short, there was a widespread lack of means to assert uniform central control, to some extent reinforced by a relatively general lack of will. The need was also far less than it would become later as communications improved and a surging population filled out the empty spaces of the interior. The main exception to this generalization concerned certain geopolitically vulnerable territories and some economic enclaves. A new generation of military officers, as well as intellectuals and journalists stimulated public awareness about such "nationalist" issues but only slowly and unevenly did the objective and subjective conditions fall into place that would give real momentum to their campaigns.

Enough has been said to demonstrate that extreme unevenness of territorial integration and control affected nearly all Latin American republics in 1930. By contrast, of course, in the 1980s not only national governments but also the international media and even the global tourist could expect to obtain easy access to the remotest corners of all these lands (only communist Cuba and highland Peru excepted). Roads, airstrips, telecommunications networks and even satellite photography covered the entire territory bringing it into almost instant contact with the central authorities. Without laboring the point, it may suffice to note the ubiquity of the fax machine as an aid to the coverage of the 1989 Chilean plebiscite; the increasingly national scope of most Latin American broadcasting networks, above all in television; and the high quality and detailed coverage provided by Bolivian maps of even the most inaccessible corners of the Andes. Admittedly, not all these changes operated in the direction of enhancing state control over national territory. In parts of the Andes it is the narcotics cartel rather than the official administration that possesses the best aviation and telecommunications equipment. But our attention here must focus on the main trends, and in particular on the stages and processes though which Latin American territorial integration was transformed between the 1920s and the 1980s.

The principal modern means of transport and communications in the 1920s were boats, trains, trams, and the telegraph.[19] Modern communication was therefore confined to a small number of well-defined channels—coasts, navigable rivers, and a very restricted range of overland routes linking major cities or regions capable of generating high value surpluses for export. Transport was expensive and "outward-oriented" toward European and North American markets, as was the whole structure of economic development. There was a marked contrast between the minority who could easily travel (and were citizens) and the majority who could not, and were not. The arrival of the internal combustion engine changed all that. The first commercial airlines got underway in the late 1920s just as surfaced roads began to break the monopoly power of the railways. It has become a cliché that the 1929 Depression produced an "inward-looking" economic reorientation, but perhaps it only accelerated and dramatized a shift that would have occurred in any case because of this transport revolution. Be it as it may, the spread of road and air travel made possible policies of national integration, not only in the economic sphere but also in politics, with the forging of new national identities and loyalties that within a generation had done much to displace previous regional and local affiliations. There is no more dramatic and visible demonstration of the significance of this process for state organization than the transfer of Brazil's federal capital from Rio to the entirely new city of Brasilia in 1960, a shift that would have been physically impossible to achieve before the advent of the internal combustion engine.

Rather than dwelling on the spectacular episodes, the historian needs to consider the multitude of incremental advances that took place almost unnoticed throughout the continent. In Bolivia, in the middle of the Second World War, for example, the post and telegraph service underwent a series of major changes, which considerably enhanced the efficiency and control of the central administration. In 1942, the Bolivian state dispatched three quarters of a million telegraphic messages and instructions to its agents throughout the republic; all provincial public servants began receiving their salaries in accordance with reliable new procedures for the transmission of postal orders; and air delivery of both national and international post began to displace rapidly the slow and unreliable system of overland distribution.[20]

The Second World War was in fact a crucial turning point in the process of state formation and consolidation throughout Latin America. The impact of the war was particularly direct and forceful with regard to questions of territorial control, now conceived more in terms of defense against extra-continental aggression than of national integration. Three aspects—surveillance and control of "fifth columnists" and Axis nationals, naval defense, and airspace control—merit a mention. It must be acknowledged that much of the initiative for all these measures came from the United States so that in most cases (except for the Southern Cone countries) the war signified a considerable external loss of state autonomy. Between 1941 and 1946 the U.S. State Department followed London's example by issuing a series of "blacklists" and "Blue Books" naming individuals and enterprises regarded by Washington as security risks to be controlled. However, when the war ended the steps that had been taken to increase national policing powers and the capacity for political control were preserved and extended, and in most cases the national authorities ended up with increased powers and relatively little external supervision.[21]

Comparing the 1950s with the 1920s it seems clear that a profound transformation had taken place in the capacity of even the least well organized of Latin American states to assert control over even the most intractable portions of territory. One of the last major countries to acquire this capacity was Colombia where the *Violencia* of the late 1940s only slowly gave way to a fairly uniform national system of government in the early 1960s, a system that again seemed under siege by the late 1980s. Of course the process was far from complete in the mid-1950s. Indeed, in some respects it was incomplete even today, as the problems of narcotics control make clear. But whereas the first quarter century after 1930 witnessed unprecedented advances, what followed thereafter was the further elaboration and filling-in of a structure of control that was already firmly in place virtually throughout the hemisphere. Such a nationwide structure had been little more than an aspiration in most countries (the Southern Cone always excepted) as recently as 1930.

In the 1960s, the issue of territorial control acquired a new significance, as a consequence of the Cuban Revolution and its repercussions in almost all countries of the subcontinent. Batista's military proved extraordinarily inept in the face of Castro's insurgency. Although police state methods were effective in the major cities and although Castro was extremely fortunate to survive until he reached the Sierra Maestra, in 1956–1958 Latin Americans of all persuasions looked on with amazement as a miniscule band of *guerrilleros* managed to entrench themselves in a mountain fortress, broadcasting daily to the entire population of the island, and eventually precipitating the disintegration of the entire Batistiano state apparatus. It is hardly surprising, then, that through most of the 1960s a succession of Castro-inspired movements sought out weaknesses in the interstices of official territorial control in a whole succession of countries, notably Venezuela, Guatemala, Argentina, Peru, and Bolivia. The capture and execution of "Che" Guevara in the last of these adventures in October 1967 brought that particular cycle of illusions to an end.[22] What these quixotic undertakings had clearly demonstrated was that, with the help of some emergency counter-insurgency measures under the Alliance for Progress, all the Latin American states of the 1960s were capable of exerting a sufficient degree of territorial control to make the rural *foquista* route to social revolution unviable. Indeed, the preventive land reform programs and the military civic action projects that accompanied counter-insurgency drives both served as the conduit for greatly increased central control over the most insecurely held provinces and regions.

During the 1960s and 1970s state territorial control was even extended outward and upward as Latin American governments took the lead in promoting a law of the sea that extended their jurisdiction two hundred miles out into the oceans,[23] and in increasing regulation of national rights to airspace and radio frequencies—although the trend was to scale back legal restrictions and welcome foreign investors and licensees by the 1980s.

The 1980s also witnessed a new cycle of insurgencies, this time concentrated in Central America. It is too early to formulate a historical judgment of these experiences but it is already apparent that under the pressures of protracted civil conflict and international involvement the central authorities of these countries proved relatively effective at securing territorial control—the price paid for this in terms of deaths and expulsions is a subject for separate discussion. The Salvadoran military ensured that their *volcanes* did not become local equivalents of the Sierra Maestra; their Guatemalan counterparts imposed a "peace of the cemetery" on vast areas of the Indian interior; and even the Sandinista security apparatus in Nicaragua proved capable of retaining territorial control in the face of counter-revolutionary encirclement. Indeed, by that decade almost all Latin American states possessed a capacity for centralized territorial control quite beyond anything that existed when Vargas marched on Rio in 1930.

In concluding this section, advances in national integration achieved in the great majority of countries must be emphasized. As roads opened, surplus population moved into underpopulated areas of the interior in much of Latin America. State-provided primary and even some secondary education was extended more or less throughout the populated territory. These schools propagated standardized ideas about national history, geography, language, and culture, all of which tended to cement bonds of loyalty to the nation and thus, implicitly, to the state. Many students hoped to qualify for public employment. Not only were such schools soon accompanied by local bureaucrats and agencies of administration but they also produced a national market for radio programs and even printed news, and, later, television. Thus, knowledge about the central state's activities become much more extensively available, and with it the potential for a more uniform pattern of administration. In certain parts of Central America, however, and in a few "Central American" type regions elsewhere, it was not until the 1980s that the full force of these integrating processes reached substantial swathes of the national territory, and when this finally did occur—as in the Miskito coast of Nicaragua—it often proved highly conflictive.[24]

In sum, then, an essential precipitating condition for the massive expansion of state territorial control over the past half century was the spread of roads, airstrips, radio and television stations, telephones, aerial photography, and radar throughout the hemisphere. At the outset this was accompanied by the tendency to "turn inwards" and develop domestic resources as substitutes for foreign exchange in the wake of the collapse of world trade in the 1930s. The Second World War and the Cold War introduced additional "national security" motivations. In any event, the old semiautonomous enclaves tended to lose their immunity from central control, as "national integration" became a central political priority. Although it has been recently fashionable to make sweeping condemnations of the inward-oriented development strategy, it should not be forgotten that for rather a long period the economic benefits appeared to be quite considerable. Moreover, in almost all republics, policies of "national integration" appear to have crystallized sufficiently strong sentiments of territorial identity to shield the region from balkanization or interstate conflict. During the "inward-looking" phase of development, communications became available to a mass populace, while international travel and communications remained the prerogative of a privileged elite for reasons of cost, language barriers, among others. By contrast, from the 1960s onward contact with and information about the rest of the world became more readily available to a mass public in most Latin American countries. Television displaced radio as the main source of public information, bringing with it a more international outlook, at the same time that cheap mass air travel brought in visitors and tourists from the rich north, a movement soon followed both by middle-class tourism from Latin America and by large-scale international migration of poor and unskilled workers seeking better incomes abroad. As Latin Americans developed a more sophisticated view of the outside world and as the economies of whole regions and sectors became dependent on the provision of international services or the delivery of foreign-earned remittances, the mid-century surge of Latin American nationalism and statism gave way to a much more relativist outlook.

Thus from the 1960s onward, as processes of internationalization overtook the earlier phase of national integration,[25] and as the extended territorial reach of the state came to be more generally taken for granted, state activities could no longer be justified in terms of the need to create a national identity (now more secure) but instead required a more pragmatic indication. Indeed, the apparent fading of ultra-nationalism in the region in the 1980s may be regarded as the final proof that earlier policies had been successful. The nationalist period had required the rapid establishment of a large and ambitious system of public administration, often with little regard for cost or rationality of organization, but as the justification for state activism shifted toward pragmatism it became impossible to ignore the deeprooted deficiencies of many of these administrative structures, especially when fiscal crisis became the norm. This brings us to developments in the sphere of administration and the question of resources.

III. Administration

Any modern state must organize not only to control its territory and marshal its economic resources but also, and most crucially, to administer the subject population. Effective administration of the population is, of course, intimately related to the questions of asserting territorial control and of securing a reliable tax base required for building a viable "nation." Nevertheless, these aspects can be disaggregated and indeed they must be if we are to trace the historical evolution of state organization in a large number of countries. The basic question of how central authorities established their writ over far-flung or highly autonomous provinces has been addressed schematically. This section calls for a similarly schematic perspective on the growth of administration, beginning with a charting of the growth of public sector employment in Latin America and then examining the activities of these expanding state agencies, paying particular attention to the "cognitive" dimension of public administration.

Consider first the evidence on aggregate public employment as a ratio of total population. It seems that "government" provided direct employment to less than 1 percent of the total population before 1930. In the 1930 Mexican census, for example, public employees constituted 0.93 percent of the population.[26] The Economic Commission for Latin America (ECLAC) estimates that in 1935 government employment involved 0.8 percent of the total population of Latin America (about 400,000 state employees in the whole sub-continent), rising to 1.1 percent in 1950 (about 1.7 million), and to 1.2 percent in 1960 (about 2.5 million).[27] A different source, using different methods and including public enterprises and state banks, produces a figure of 4.8 percent of the total population (around 17 million employees),[28] employed by the public sector in 1980.

These very aggregate numbers may distort the trend and they also conceal the different rhythms of public employment in different countries. In 1930, there were many republics with systems of public administration as "backward" and "clientelist" as the most retrograde Brazilian regions. In some, such as Guatemala and Venezuela, the attitudes and practices of nineteenth-century Latin American public administration still survived almost unscathed. It has been said for example that President Juan Vicente Gómez (1908–1935) "invented nothing new in the way of government, [and] showed no imagination in his organisation and administration of Venezuela Instead [he] applied the same principles of sound patriarchal management to the task of running Venezuela that he had applied to the job of raising cattle in his rural properties."[29] Others, such as the Dominican

Republic and Nicaragua, were just emerging from lengthy periods of government under the supervision of the U.S. Marines. In these cases, administrative reforms had been externally introduced, enormously increasing the effectiveness of post-occupation governments and making possible an unprecedented level of social control.[30] When Ubico took over the administration of Guatemala in 1930, the balance on hand in the National Treasury was exactly US$27. The archives of the Foreign Ministry were filled with missives from representatives abroad reporting their desperate straits and complaining that both salaries and maintenance allowances for the legations were months in arrears. In the interior many provinces had left teachers and minor officials to fend for themselves. Ubico responded by cutting all government salaries by 30 percent, dismissing "surplus" employees from the Central Customs Office and the Finance Ministry, severely cutting the health service, and closing provincial schools. Total government expenditure was reduced to only US$8.5 million in 1933 (US$5 dollars per head of population).[31]

There is no space to trace the history of administrative growth and transformation in all the Latin American countries since 1930, so what follows is a brief account of the expansion of administrative ambitions and capabilities in Brazil, the largest and one of the two most "representative" countries of the region. Brazil, like the other major republic Mexico, had relatively weak and incipient administrative structures at the beginning of the period under review, whereas half a century later on the eve of the debt crisis both appeared to be among the more highly and effectively organized states. On the face of it, then, they were "success stories" rather than representative cases. They are also, of course, the two largest countries, with relatively diversified economies and impressive records of aggregate economic growth. In fact, state-led national integration and "inward-looking" industrialization were exceptionally successful in these two countries because the underlying endowments were particularly favorable. It is the greater dynamism and sustainability of these processes in the two largest countries that goes far to explain the high and sustained rates of progress in terms of administrative organization and coverage. At the beginning of the period, of the two Brazil's administration was even less well articulated than that of Mexico—where the Revolution had accomplished significant institution-building in the 1920s—and seems to have progressed more rapidly and consistently, probably overtaking Mexico in the 1950s or 1960s, although in the 1970s the Mexican state may have caught up again. In the 1980s, the Mexicans moved more rapidly than the Brazilians to "roll back" state involvement in the economy and to slim down the public sector.[32]

The immediate aftermath of the 1930 Revolution in Brazil saw the creation of the Ministry of Labour, Industry, and Commerce, popularly known as the "Ministry of the Revolution," and a new Ministry of Education and Public Health, together with the establishment of various retirement funds for certain categories of public employee and for transport workers. The 1934 Constitution established a unified judicial system with strong authority, an emphasis on professionalism, and substantial autonomy from vested interests. Minimum wage commissions were created in 1936 and when the *Estado Novo* was established, a new administrative department, the *Departamento Administrativo do Serviço Público* (DASP) came into being to introduce reforms and prepare the annual budget. There was general agreement that the much-enlarged responsibilities of the federal government, as expressed through the new ministries and the recently created planning bodies, would require a highly trained professional civil service "based on merit and tested in examination."[33] Although it is generally agreed that the DASP and the other new agencies fell far short of any Weberian ideal it is also accepted that they represented a very large increase in federal administrative capabilities, particularly as the much enlarged federal bureaucracy was able to attract many able new recruits by offering attractive salaries and an impressive array of privileges.[34] Moreover, DASP central administration controlled so-called *daspinhos* in all the state administrations who were even empowered to override decisions of the *interventores*.[35] Thus, whereas the *Interventor* might act as a political coordinator following instructions issued directly by Vargas, the administrative department, which was run by bureaucrats and staffed with engineers, agronomists, statisticians, and other professionals who considered themselves immune to clientelism, functioned as a kind of proxy legislature.

The dismissal of an *Interventor* was not necessarily accompanied by any reshuffle of the heads of interior, justice, education, and labor administrative departments who had served as administrative advisors. The President of the São Paulo DASP boasted that he, along with six colleagues, was able to perform all the duties previously assigned to the former State Assembly and Senate and to 271 municipal councils.[36] The São Paulo model was not applied uniformly, however, and in Minas, for example, the same *Interventor* served continuously from 1933 to 1945 and therefore exerted more authority over the administrators. At the end of the *Estado Novo* an attempt was made to abolish the DASP,[37] but by 1948 it had managed to survive in a reorganized form and so provided an important source of continuity and focus for administrative centralization. In Brazil as elsewhere, technical rationality and administrative centralization were accompanied by more modern forms of repression. In contrast to countries more directly in the U.S. sphere of influence, most of the main measures taken against domestic communists, fascists, and Axis nationals were introduced well before the Second World War began, and in association with the DASP structure.

With the tasks of government becoming ever more massive after the Second World War, it was a constant effort for the federal administration to keep pace with the rate of change. Following his return to office as a democratically elected President in 1951, Getúlio Vargas evidently judged the 1945–1950 period to have been a failure in this regard: "The Federal Administration is notorious for duplications, parallelisms and conflicts of responsibility, all of which demand a general overhaul. The current state of administrative disorganisation is an obstacle that must be tackled resolutely. This is required not only by the universal tendency of the state to assume additional responsibilities, but also because of the abnormal international situation, and furthermore because of Brazil's status as a new nation," he declared in his 1951 presidential message.[38] Much of the most important administrative innovation to take place during the 1950s was, of course, the transfer of the seat of national administration from Rio to Brasilia, a physical assertion both of the "inward orientation" of the state and its vocation for national integration, and of the official determination to free the state apparatus from identification with any one regional or sectional interest.

However, the shift to Brasilia in 1960 and the imposition in 1964 of a twenty-year long military dictatorship should not deceive us into confusing an explosive expansion of the state apparatus with the emergence of a unified and purposeful state actor disconnected from sectional interests. Luciano Martins proposes a more persuasive interpretation: ". . . the recent expansion of the state came about through a process composed both of centripetal forces (the concentration of financial resources and decision-making authority at the Federal level) and of centrifugal forces (through relatively independent agencies and/or relatively autonomous centres of resource allocation and decision-making). No doubt the Brazilian experience is far from unique in displaying such contradictory tendencies. They are easier to detect, together with the intense bureaucratic rivalries which accompany them, when the state is viewed not as a unitary actor confronting society, but rather through the prism of its internal structure. What is, perhaps, distinctive about the Brazilian case is that the very mode of state expansionism appears to imply an ever-growing tendency of the agencies towards independence and of the actors towards relative autonomy."[39] Martins explains this tendency as follows: "One of the most persistent features of our history since 1930 has been the comparatively high stability of administrative career structures (in contrast, for example, to the precarious "life expectancy" of officials in the business world), regardless of the political upheavals through which Brazil has passed since then. However, this stability never became an obstacle to the promotion of successive waves of "new" *técnicos*, who emerged from the successive phases of the development process, largely because the bureaucracy grew by a process of sedimentation. No sooner had the old officials begun to adapt to a new political situation than the state would create space for the emergence of new strata."[40]

While this seems an accurate and helpful characterization of some underlying trends within the general process of state expansion in 1930–1980, it is clearly incomplete, as the scale and gravity of the crises of the 1980s revealed. After 1982 the Brazilian state seemed spectacularly to lose its capacity either to co-opt new social sectors, or to promote any coherent pattern of economic development, a capacity not regained until the mid-1990s. One stark indicator of this was the acceleration of inflation to such a level that public finances become almost totally disorganized and the private economy severely disoriented. Successive attempts to restore order to public administration only redistributed the problems. Thus, for example, in the face of the legal privileges protecting many Brazilian public employees from dismissal, the state responded to prolonged fiscal crisis by allowing their real, after inflation, incomes to fall precipitously, apparently by as much as two-thirds between 1980 and 1990. O'Donnell notes that before the crisis "in many areas of the public sector to be a functionary was to be inserted in a career. This meant to work in a bureaucratic setting that provided a reasonably predictable path towards promotions, and to receive a monthly income and various fringe benefits, which allowed a solid middle-class life-style (which usually included good housing and affording the university education of the children). Except for some privileged pockets (typically the Central Banks) [that was] no longer true [. . .] A bleak picture result[ed] from the decapitation of the top and more specialised bureaucracies due to the exodus of the more qualified individuals, the politicisation of those positions [. . .] and the spectacular decay of the physical plant."[41] The result, in his view, was an upsurge of demoralization, leading to numerous public sector strikes that far from rectifying the situation fuelled an ever stronger reaction of public opinion against state employees in general. But whereas such tendencies have persisted or even intensified in other South American nations, from the early 1990s it has been possible to observe a patchy and incremental process of state reform and even "state-crafting" in Brazil that could revitalize this historic project.

In fact, for nearly all of the period under study some kind of equilibrium was maintained within the public administration. On the one hand, Brazil has probably never—even during the most puritanical and authoritarian of moments—experienced uniformly effective and honest administration of public affairs. There have always been major geographical zones and administrative enclaves within which clientelist, patrimonial, and in all probability even sultanistic practices, have been the norm. Only thus could social stability be maintained across such a vast, unequal, and in some places backward territory, especially given the limited apparatus of coercion available to the central authorities. Moreover, we cannot assume that the moments of greatest centralization were the moments of least corruption. On the contrary, there are indicators that one motive for centralization is sometimes to curb the incidence of local parasitism so as to concentrate the resources available for misappropriation at the highest levels. On the other hand, however, there have almost always been even larger zones and sectors in which legal and administrative formalisms were properly observed and any occasional misconduct was liable to result in routine sanctions.

Indeed, it would have been impossible for Brazil to achieve the industrial and social modernization of the last seventy-five years except through the observance of a reasonable degree of efficiency, responsibility, and honesty by a substantial proportion of the productive population. The line of demarcation separating productivism from parasitism seems often to have been shifting and uncertain and the mechanisms maintaining the two realms in equilibrium were clearly weak and improvised. But Brazil is no Zaire.[42] It would be too simple to assert that the state administration in Alagoas was always corrupt or that the city government in Curitiba was always pure, but local authorities with very different traditions did manage to coexist within a single framework. Certain federal agencies are known to be the instruments of unfettered patronage, whereas others pride themselves on their technical competence and professionalism.

IV. "Cognitive" Capacity

One way of investigating the existence of a competent and professional sector in a state organization able to operate on its own terms despite the need to coexist with a clientelistic or "rent-seeking" sector, is to examine an aspect of public administration that is seldom studied historically: the development of a "cognitive" capacity. By this is meant sustained organization to collect, process, analyze and deliver the types of information about a society that is necessary for a modern state to monitor and interpret the impact of its measures, and to adjust or reformulate them when they prove ineffective or counterproductive. In Latin America, the record of this is extremely uneven and variable over time. There is a wide range of experiences, from cases where even the most basic information is lacking about the internal workings of the state (what it owns and who it employs) to extremes of both personalized and bureaucratized control (the Trujillo dictatorship or the Uruguayan military regime for example). Both extremes can be cited as confirmation of a "parasitic" or "predatory" image of the state in diametrical contrast to the Weberian ideal type of a "rationalizing" modern bureaucracy. But the developmental and "nation-building" dimension of state activism also represents an at least partial and intermittent element of the historical experience recorded here. In other words, there is a serious tradition of providing "public goods" through the state, tangled up with other, more self-regarding or predatory, traditions. The empirical study of advances and retreats in the "cognitive" capacity of the state should help to clarify the nature and purposes of public administration at different times and in different places, and thereby enable us to qualify overgeneralized claims about the "predatory" or "over-extended" or indeed the "developmentalist" state.

The "cognitive" capacity of a public administration can be studied historically by examining two issues: first, the kind of information available to the central authorities (how accurate, comprehensive, timely, and easily processed it is), and second, when the authorities formulate a public policy, how difficult is it for those affected to discover what the policy consists of and what impact it might have on them, and what scope might exist for corrective measures if the process of implementation diverges too radically from the intentions of the policymakers. These are large questions. All that can be done here is to touch on some relevant considerations and examples. The Southern Cone countries receive special attention because they were "advanced" in this respect at the beginning of our period. However, they may not be representative, particularly since in some respects they may actually have regressed, so evidence from Bolivia, Brazil, and elsewhere is also considered.

By 1930, virtually all Latin American state administrations had assembled various types of economic and statistical information, such as foreign trade statistics and information about money and credit transactions. In the more advanced countries of the Southern Cone this information was of a very high quality by international standards.

Accurate, comprehensive, timely, and effectively administered information was an integral part of the Uruguayan welfare state, a world leader at this time. Argentine and Chilean administrative processes were also of high quality although not quite up to Uruguayan standards since geographical conditions were less favorable and the provision of welfare benefits less extensive.

As a result of the Great Depression and associated political struggles, the quality of administrative processes probably declined well into the 1940s. Census data, for example, became less reliable and comprehensive and long delays built up between the collection and release of many types of official information. Tax rolls were often not revised as efficiently and punctually as before. Civil servants were increasingly overworked, underpaid, and badly supervised during the 1930s. During the war a number of additional emergency administrative responsibilities were taken up such as price controls, credit allocations, import controls, even some rationing, and these were often not well run. Although information on these questions is hard to assemble, it seems fairly safe to conclude that on balance the administrative systems of the three Southern Cone countries were probably less efficient in 1950 than in 1930. However, it must be stressed that these are relative judgments. By world standards, and certainly by the standards of the rest of Latin America, the Southern Cone administrations were far ahead in 1930 and still had much to their credit at the end of the Second World War. The same applies if we consider administrative processes from the viewpoint of a subject population. With generally high standards of literacy, good internal communications, a language of administration that was accessible to almost all inhabitants, and a relatively stable and open system of political communications, it was generally not so difficult for members of the public to discover which government decisions might affect their own affairs, and reasonable possibilities existed for the better-informed and better-organized sectors to influence the implementation of such policies.

How then can we characterize the development of state administration in the Southern Cone between, say, 1950 and 1980? This was a period, as we have seen, in which many other Latin American countries took enormous strides forward in the area of administrative capabilities. By contrast, as is well known, during the 1970s these countries all experienced prolonged periods of severe repression, political closure, censorship, and administrative contraction. To quote a single, but highly telling example of closure, Chile's electoral registers were deliberately and systematically destroyed after 1973. And severe inflation rendered the process of tax collection extremely arbitrary and indeed chaotic, at least for a while, in all of these countries.[43] Undoubtedly there were very severe setbacks in the quality of some administrative processes in all these countries. In some respects they may even have been worse off than in, say, 1950, although this would not be true overall. At any rate, the great gap that separated them from the more typical countries of Latin America had been almost completely bridged during the 30-year period. This was largely because countries such as Brazil and Mexico took such large strides forward, but also because the Southern Cone countries slipped back in key respects.

It would be radically misleading, therefore, to think in terms of a simple unilinear progression from administrative backwardness to "modernity." The example of Uruguay illustrates the variety of different situations that can be encompassed by the general label "effective administration of the subject population." In 1930—and indeed even as late as about 1960—the Uruguayan state was exceptionally well organized to deliver social services and welfare benefits to the great majority of the population. Around 1970, the state apparatus was at its most chaotic, corrupt, and ineffective, and its capacity to perform traditional functions seemed on the verge of collapse. Yet, by 1980, a highly organized "national security state" had replaced the bankrupt welfare state, now geared to social control with very heavy reliance on repression. The characteristics of Uruguayan society, which had formerly favored the near universal distribution of state benefits, now proved equally favorable to the distribution of state sanctions. The entire population of the country (those who had not been driven into exile) was apparently classified in the central records of the administration either as A (reliable), B (doubtful), or C (in opposition) and public policies were geared accordingly.[44]

Consider Bolivia, one of the more "backward" republics in this respect. To take the most basic of indicators, there was no population census between 1900 and 1950. In fact, both social arithmetic of the type required for modern administration and the more general knowledge of the social sciences were virtually nonexistent before the midtwentieth century. The changes that came about after that were altogether too drastic and too rapid to be properly absorbed. Thus, for example, the 1950 census generated more misconceptions than understanding about inequalities of land tenure. Within two years the new revolutionary government had launched upon a most ambitious program of state expansion and regulation, including national economic plans, and a sweeping Agrarian Reform Law, both of which were in practice founded on almost complete official ignorance of the relevant facts.[45]

Indeed, it seems probable that until substantial foreign technical assistance arrived in the mid-1950s the Bolivian state was unable to establish even a rough picture of the true state of its own finances. Even a generation after the revolution, most of the administrative information available to the authorities was being produced or processed by missions and advisers from the United States.[46] It was not until the 1970s that a reasonably competent and informed technical bureaucracy began to take root, although by the end of our period Bolivian public administration had reached levels of sophistication and accuracy that were much more comparable to the regional norm.[47] There was, for example, no real difficulty over the registration of voters and counting of results in the complex series of national elections held from the mid-1980s onward, and the national accounts had become relatively trustworthy.

The materials presented here are too scattered and impressionistic to permit any very firm assessment of the overall development of the "cognitive" aspects of state organization in Latin America after 1929: the starting points varied immensely from country to country; there were bursts of advance followed by countercurrents of regression; the timing and rhythm of these developments lacked any apparent international uniformity; and more fundamentally, the objects of cognition are also quite disparate (quite different for a state geared to internal regression as under Trujillo than for one focused on "developmental" tasks like postwar Mexico, or for one concerned with consolidating a participatory democratic system like Venezuela after 1958). In addition, the effective cognitive capacity of a state depends not only on the object it pursues but also on the coherence and thoroughness with which it organizes itself.

At one extreme, therefore, we find highly centralized and effective regimes with clearly delineated objectives. (What could be more clearcut than the spectacle of President Gómez personally reading all the telegraphic messages summarizing the existing state of knowledge about Venezuelan affairs in the 1930s?) At the other extreme, we have administrations in Lima in the 1980s buffeted by endless fiscal crises, lacking effective control, wracked by administrative incoherence, and a perverse structure of incentives that destroys all sense of public service. In addition to all this, the contemporary Peruvian state is saddled with a multiplicity of competing official objectives nearly all of which exceed its grasp. The information available to it may be far richer and more varied than that received by Gómez but its cognitive capacity or ability to sift and apply relevant information is much inferior. Indeed, it suffers from "information overload." The contrast between these two extremes indicates the wide range of factors bearing on the cognitive capacity of a modern state, and suggests that although technical advances in data collection may create the potential for the performance of a more complex and extensive range of administrative functions, they provide no assurance that these potentialities will be exploited effectively.

To conclude this section, let us take a closer look at a rather specialized but basic state activity that is eminently "cognitive" in nature and also highly relevant to the section on command over resources: mapping. The modern state requires maps of all sorts; maps to delimit the boundaries between administrative subunits; to demarcate the property rights of taxpayers; to guide the provision of public works; to conduct elections; to collect census data; or to create "Indian reserves," national parks, or ecological reservations. In the last analysis, states need maps to create and protect their national security. The activity of mapping is therefore an essential if unspectacular feature of public administration and, indeed, it is one of the first things every new state does. So an examination of how it is done in Latin America may tell us something more general about the condition of state organization there.[48]

Looking at the case of Brazil, the history of mapping indicates the fluctuating ambitions and achievements of the state in this eminently practical realm. The point dramatized by the saga of the Prestes column in the 1920s was that a vast interior remained virtually abandoned—indeed almost literally "unknown"—as far as the ostensible authorities of the Old Republic were concerned. Geographical and cartographical knowledge was hardly institutionalized with the exception of a scattering of "topographical engineers" who were dispatched to survey pioneer zones. These were "more akin to eighteenth century naturalists than to contemporary European geographers"; they lacked specialization, and their conception of national identity was based only on territoriality without concern for the society occupying a given geographical space.[49] Following the 1930 revolution and especially under the *Estado Novo, tenentista* and nationalist conceptions of state building stimulated a major effort to improve territorial cognition and to strengthen centralized social control. The state therefore created the *Conselho Nacional de Geografia* (CNG) in 1937, and the *Instituto Brasileiro de Geografia e Estatística* (IBGE) in 1939. Fitfully (particularly in the early 1940s and the late 1960s when military influence was at its highest and geopolitical theories were most in vogue) such institutions modernized and professionalized Brazilian territorial self-consciousness. Yet as in not a few other areas of Brazilian state building, sixty years later the practical results seem comparatively modest and uneven whether judged by international standards or by the yardstick of official ambitions. Of course, until recently, the mapping of Brazil was a gargantuan task. Only in the past few years has aerial and satellite photography achieved the necessary precision—a development that Brazilian nationalists view with apprehension since it frees foreign interests from dependence on official authorization.

It was not until 1984 that regular and comprehensive satellite images of the entire Brazilian landmass became available from Landsat 5. These images were received at a station in western Brazil, where they could be processed to generate photographs containing information on forest cover, geology, settlement patterns, and economic activity (including illegal airstrips) on a scale of 1:250,000. In the early 1990s, 334 maps on this scale, covering the entire 5.2 million square kilometres of the Amazon Basin became available, although over one-third of the country still lacked maps on the scale of 1:100,000, the level of detail required for most economic and social development projects. Only 4.3 percent of Brazil has been mapped at 1:25,000, which is the appropriate level of detail for most local government purposes. In order for the Ministry of Agrarian Reform to delimit land grants it required maps on a 1:10,000 scale, and in urban areas maps at 1:2,000 were required for the proper provision of services and the collection of land taxes. The general absence of such maps meant that these public policies could not be accurately implemented. Brazil is huge, of course, but the obstacles to better cartography were bureaucratic as much as physical. In the North East, for example, 31 different agencies used 121 separate though similar institutions, some producing maps for irrigation projects, others for transmission lines. At the federal level, responsibility was disseminated across 13 ministries, which frequently disregarded the authority of the central *Comissão de Cartografia*.[50] Small wonder, then, that conflicts over rural land-ownership often escape the official framework of legal regulation and are still liable to be settled by bribery and local acts of force.

There is probably only one country in Latin America with an entrenched tradition of reliably adjudicating private land disputes through the courts rather than by direct action, where land taxes are more or less rationally assessed and collected, and where since about 1960 house construction only proceeds when there is an official permit, including professional advice on standards of earthquake resistance, and guaranteed connection to a potable water supply. That country is Costa Rica, where the whole territory has been accurately mapped to a scale of 1:50,000, and in even greater detail in urban areas.[51] The result is that nearly all boundaries are clearly demarcated and can therefore be legally protected, especially since in contrast to the rest of the subcontinent the courts are well funded and readily accessible to the public at large. The contrast between Brazilian and

Costa Rican styles of administration could hardly be starker. As illustrated by the specific example of cartography, the two states are at opposite ends of the organizational spectrum. Most Latin American countries are still closer to the first model than the second, but both advances in technology and continuing pressures for socioeconomic modernization and democratization favor the production of more accurate maps that may in principle permit a more secure pattern of property ownership, a more rational provision of public services, and a more efficient structure of taxation.

To summarize, some agencies of some Latin American states have performed well and have progressed steadily in the provision of the information required for sound public policy-making. Many others have a much more fitful record, and there are plentiful examples of the "capture" of public agencies by private interests or even of their "cannibalization" by their own employees. In most countries politicians and bureaucrats can provide a fairly accurate account of which agencies fall into which categories but there is very little academic, let alone historical, analysis of these patterns. The implications of this variability require further attention. If the state is to provide any kind of "public goods," public administrations have to acquire appropriate cognitive capacities. This is as true for a privatizing or "state shrinking" administration as for an expanding "developmentalist" state. Even an opulent "rentier" state requires considerable cognitive capacity if it is to distribute its abundance rationally. In the absence of such capacities there will be no orderly means by which the state can capture and allocate the resources required for its activities—and that can only lead to the adoption of "predatory" strategies of state financing.

V. Command Over Resources

This section surveys the transformation of Latin American states in the half century following 1930 in the areas of taxation, state ownership, and economic regulation: in short, in terms of their command over resources. It includes some tentative discussion of "state shrinking" in the 1980s, and concludes with an illustrative account of the history of social security, which bridges the themes of resources and citizenship.

In general, in the 1920s, principles of economic laissez-faire still prevailed in most of Latin America even if practice often diverged substantially from principle. State involvement in economic management was largely confined to the provision of a basic law-and-order framework, including attempts to guarantee respect for legally constituted property rights together with some minimal infrastructure provisions (roads, which were often partly financed by users, railways, which were state guarantees for foreign bondholders, and ports, which were recognized and supported to the extent that they housed valuable customs facilities). Notwithstanding the provisions of liberal constitutions and the aspirations of lawmakers, many aspects of property ownership were not yet fully regulated by the constituted authorities. For example, an accurate Land Registry was hard to find, cadastral surveys were in their infancy, and hopelessly conflicting claims to land titles and mining rights were still the norm. Taxes were levied on sales but seldom on income or profits. Local financial institutions were incipient, and often the only or major sources of credit lay in the metropolitan countries and thus beyond the reach of any national regulation. National currencies circulated and found acceptance either if they had some intrinsic value (silver coin, for example) or were reliably backed by some international currency.

In sharp contrast, by the early 1980s state interventionism had become a long-established, and apparently ineradicable, reality throughout the subcontinent. Cuba was the only fully socialized state, and it is essential to resist any temptation to conflate the Soviet model of a command economy with the more typical Latin American experience of a mixed economy in which public and private enterprise coexist in a possibly precarious, but still essentially market coordinated, equilibrium. In most of Latin America, state ownership expanded dramatically in the 1970s but even at the highpoint the public enterprise contribution to GDP was below the average for all developing countries and not radically out of line with the pattern prevailing in developed capitalist economies. The most important difference was that public enterprise undertook a higher proportion of gross capital formation in Latin America than in the advanced industrial countries.

In tracing the growth of the interventionist state a good starting point is the response to the economic crisis of 1929–1930. Nearly all countries adopted exchange controls, import rationing, and other strategies of economic *dirigisme*, often chosen for reasons of desperation rather than conviction or theory. Most state resources prior to 1929 had come from taxes on foreign trade and the brokering of foreign loans, the two sources most severely affected by the crisis. In many cases, therefore, it was almost a question of survival for the state to tap new sources of finance. A conventional route was to introduce new or enhanced taxes on income, profits or sales. This was the path taken in some cases. Raúl Prebisch, for example, can be credited with much responsibility for the introduction of Argentine income tax during the trough of the recession, an aspect of his long career not much remembered by his latter day denigrators. But it was hard to bring about such reforms in the midst of a crisis. Less conventional expedients also proliferated, such as forced loans; forced savings; regulations and the creation of monopolies from which the public sector could profit; and the issue of unbacked paper currency (which might result in inflation although in Mexico, for example, when the government began settling its bills and paying its employees with promissory notes the initial result was to overcome an acute liquidity crisis caused by the hoarding of metallic currency).

At first, these tentative and provisional expedients may only have served to keep the state apparatus afloat, but as the 1930s wore on and the efficacy of the new techniques became apparent the inclination grew to undertake new forms of public expenditure—road and school-building, for example—as part of a strategy of "inward-looking" development. Later on, this was followed by more ambitious schemes of economic interventionism often encouraged, if not necessitated, by the exigencies of the Second World War, including the establishment of public enterprises in such "strategic" sectors as steel and power. In the immediate postwar period there was something of a reaction against these statist trends, no doubt partly reflecting the gradual restoration of liberal institutions in the international arena. (The IMF experimented with its first conditional financing programs in Latin America in the late 1940s.) However, there was no outright restoration of the status quo ante, and by the Korean War "inward-looking" development was becoming more of a conscious strategy rather than just an improvised response to external shocks. By then the ECLAC, under Prebisch, provided some intellectual counterweight to the IMF and World Bank. And particularly after the Cuban revolution various Latin American governments took on more social welfare commitments and attempted to demonstrate that they were not in thrall to private enterprise. Indeed, starting in 1960, the Inter-American Development Bank (IDB) was authorized to channel external finance into Latin America's public sector.

The scale and range of public enterprise increased rapidly from the 1960s onwards, and the "sovereign lending" bubble of the second half of the 1970s accentuated the trend toward state sector economic expansion, only loosely restrained by market discipline. Then, abruptly, after August 1982, nearly all Latin American states ran into a fiscal and external financing crisis that proved at least as durable and far reaching as the shock of 1929. Once again the search for alternative sources of revenue led first to a variety of emergency expedients, including some major bank nationalizations and some external interest moratoria, followed by a major shift in economic strategy.

Thereafter, the unconventional—some would say "heterodox"—
tactics that eased state resource constraints in the 1930s and 1940s,
and perhaps again during some of the nationalizations of the late
1960s and early 1970s, were no longer effective. Indeed they proved
counterproductive and their long-term legacy is now widely viewed as
harmful.

As is well known, after 1982 the inflations that had characterized
much of Latin America during most of the inward-looking development phase became so virulent that it was no longer possible to
achieve other public policy goals without curbing inflation first. If the
much enlarged and diversified state organizations of the 1980s were
to continue receiving the resources they needed to perform at least
their most central functions after external credit had dried up, they
evidently needed to "restore market confidence." In place of the
increased state discretionality that characterized the post-1930 period,
the typical strategy to capture resources was to demonstrate increased
state responsiveness to the dictates of the market. Privatization, the
focus of chapter five of this volume, is one element in this general
process of "state shrinking"—the state can capture resources by sell-
ing off public enterprises, as easily as by nationalizing private ones.
But a new equilibrium between the public and private sectors in what
continue to be "mixed" economies can only be stabilized when the
state has been not just scaled back but restructured, so that it functions more effectively within its prescribed sphere. This is not just a
question of curbing inflation through budget discipline, necessary
though that will be. It is also a question of restoring coherence and
structure to organizations that have become acutely demoralized and
disorganized. Not only market disciplines, but also legal and political
controls needed to be tightened. One way of illustrating this is with
reference to the question of the state's "cognitive capacity." Whether
the objective is to promote an interventionist state or a market-
supporting state such a capacity is required. Even the most limited
objectives of fiscal discipline require the assemblage of accurate and
timely information about the state's assets, liabilities, obligations, and
resources.[52] As already pointed out, such cognitive capacity cannot be
taken for granted in much of Latin America. Indeed the state shrinking
of the 1980s may quite frequently have diminished such capacity as previously existed. Resource mobilization is not just a question of physical
availability: it requires effective organizational structures as well.

Synthesizing a range of national histories makes it possible to identify a small number of major innovations since the 1930s that account
for much of the expansion of state resources over this period. Starting
with the external sector, the bond issues, the railway loans, and the

bank credits that had played such an important part in the public finances of most Latin American republics before 1930 came to an abrupt end with the Depression, which also terminated the era of "dollar imperialism" in which not a few domestic revenue resources were earmarked for priority use to service external obligations. During the 1930s, various alternative strategies were adopted by different states. Some, like Venezuela and the Dominican Republic, paid off their external debts in order to achieve freedom from foreign interference in their domestic economic affairs; others, like Brazil, negotiated large debt reductions that created similar domestic room for maneuver; yet others resorted to forced loans from foreign investors, backed up by the exchange controls that became possible once the region was allowed to go off the Gold Standard. Where this proved insufficient, nationalization, and even expropriation, came into play, most notably in Mexico.

It is hard to judge where such expedients might have ended but for the outbreak of the Second World War. Thereafter, in any case, the panorama changed, with wartime security interests displacing commercial advantage. Lend-lease became a new potential source of external finance available to Washington's allies and a large array of "New Deal"-type public investment plans and initiatives received encouragement from without. In the postwar period, however, the reconstruction of Europe and the rise of the Cold War soon curtailed much of this external assistance. Venezuela introduced the 50–50 profits tax in 1948, and a variety of other strategies were attempted to increase the "return value" of foreign investments in the region. Perón used sterling balances to buy out the railroads. Bolivia nationalized the tin barons. The Guatemalans attempted to tax United Fruit. And in 1960 the Cubans finally closed this cycle by expropriating the largest single concentration of U.S. investment in the region. On the whole, however, between the late 1940s and the late 1960s the external financing environment was fairly stable and enforced greater "orthodoxy" on the region's public finances than in the previous two decades.[53]

The external financing panorama changed again from the late 1960s, with the rise of "sovereign lending" by commercial banks, and with renewed tolerance for various nationalizations, particularly in the oil sector. This relatively permissive international environment goes far to explain the rapid expansion of state activism in the 1970s. The diversity of national experience is noteworthy, as the pattern of public enterprise financing in a range of Latin American countries and the extent of budgetary burden, and the degree to which public enterprise deficits were financed from abroad vary considerably, although enterprise deficits were generally unacceptably high. Equally, the violent reversal of conditions that followed the 1982 debt crisis goes a long way to explain the subsequent (lagged) shift toward "state shrinking." Important though this external dimension has undoubtedly been, it would be a mistake to overstress its salience or to neglect the domestic counterparts. For example, the establishment of Central Banks in most of the region in the 1920s and 1930s, and their disengagement from international sources of support prior to the creation of the IMF, provided many states with a powerful means of supplementing the inadequate revenues generated through the tax system. Paper currency and domestic bank credit became the principle means of payment in most economies. Under conditions of inconvertibility this made it easy for many Latin American states either to collect *seignorage* or to levy an implicit "inflation tax," and to capture and allocate domestic resources through an array of nonconventional policy instruments, such as directed credit, selective price controls, and implicit subsidies (or tax exemptions). In addition, conventional policy instruments such as income tax became widespread in the 1930s, sometimes with unconventional extras such as compulsory payroll taxes levied on large employers, ostensibly to finance social security systems.

Traditional revenue sources, such as taxes on foreign trade, dwindled in significance in comparison with these powerful new methods of resource appropriation. Moreover, from the middle of our period onward, the proliferation of state enterprises and decentralized agencies provided additional potential sources of revenue generation. Over time, however, many of these striking innovations displayed declining efficacy. Thus, in an increasingly internationalized economy the inflation tax tended to lose its bite, as savers held out for the more sophisticated, indexed, or high interest returns, or resorted to capital flight. The captive savings generated by an immature social security system were gradually depleted, as ever increasing cohorts of beneficiaries demanded the services they had subscribed to. Similarly, state enterprises, which may have initially "captured surplus" for the public sector, often degenerated into fiscal burdens, especially when, as with the *Corporación Minera de Bolívia* (COMIBOL) or *Petroleos Mexicanos* (PEMEX), they were used as "milch cows" until they accumulated a heavy backlog of postponed investment. Thus, in the 1980s, instead of viewing nationalization as a potential source of fiscal relief, a majority of Latin American states embarked on ambitious program of privatization motivated, to a considerable degree, by the expectation that foreign bidders would contribute the additional resources the state could not provide.

State ownership of mining and oil production has constituted one of the most contentious public policy issues, repeatedly pitting "nationalists" against apparently overbearing foreign lobbies. Set-piece confrontations over this issue extend across the whole of the subcontinent and occur almost throughout the sixty years under analysis. The most famous episodes concern the Mexican oil nationalization of 1938, the creation of the *Companhia Vale do Rio Doce* (CVRD) in Brazil in 1942, the nationalization of Bolivian tin in 1952, the struggle to create *Petróleos Brasileiros* (PETROBRÁS) in 1953, the Cuban oil refinery seizures of 1960, the Peruvian oil and mineral nationalizations of 1969–1975, the Chilean copper nationalization of 1971, and the Venezuelan oil nationalization of 1976. At the beginning of the 1990s, five of the resulting enterprises—PEMEX, CVRD, PETROBRÁS, the Chilean Copper Corporation (CODELCO), and Venezuelan Petroleum (PDVSA)—were still among the economic giants of the region, while the Bolivian and Peruvian enterprises were prostrate.

Experiences in this sector are sufficiently diverse to cast doubt on all categorical judgments. Not all these state takeovers were inevitable; not all the resulting enterprises lost focus or fell prey to predatory interest groups; not all are beyond rational reorganization and reform; and not all should be judged as historical failures. What does seem true is that in all cases one result of state ownership was to convert these key generators of foreign exchange and tax revenue into at least semi-captive sources of "rent" for the state, with far-reaching consequences for the balance of the whole fiscal system. In such conditions it is not easy to maintain a managerial structure that is sufficiently autonomous and efficiency-oriented to do justice to the long-term economic potential of the sector. However, not even the Chileans have proposed the outright privatization of CODELCO, which provided critical resources to sustain the Pinochet dictatorship, and which, like key Argentine, Bolivian, Brazilian, and Peruvian public enterprises, offered a "second career" to elements in the armed forces. The various joint ventures and contractual agreements between these enterprises and major transnational corporations, which became fashionable at the end of our period, could serve gradually to displace this model of public enterprise, or could potentially give the model a new lease of life.

A full history of the growth of public enterprises in Latin America would have to consider the wide variety of state development banks and public development corporations set up from the 1930s onwards (the *Corporación de Fomento*—CORFO) in Chile in 1938; the *Corporación Boliviana de Fomento* (CBF) in 1942; the *Corporación*

Venezolana de Fomento (CVF) in 1946; and other state holding companies charged with such tasks as opening up the interior and electrifying the countryside). It would be necessary to trace the various phases of expansion into steel, capital goods, light manufacturing, and tourism. Equally, the history of state banks and the dramas of bank nationalization and reversal would need attention. That is not a task that can be attempted here. It must suffice to say that the early history of many of these enterprises was a world away from what they would become in the 1980s. None of the modern conditions that are taken for granted by most current critics of state enterprise were yet in place in most of the region. Forceful state action was required to go where the private sector would never venture on its own if the framework of an integral market economy was to be established.

By the 1980s, around one-tenth of national income was typically being devoted to social security expenditures in the three Southern cone countries, and Cuba. In Brazil, Costa Rica, and Panama the comparable figure was typically in excess of 5 percent of GDP. As a result, for example, the *Sistema Nacional de Previdencia y Asistencia Social* (SINPAS) managed by the Mexican Ministry of Social Security had become one of the largest enterprises in Latin America: "only the Brazilian federal government as a whole, PETROBRÁS, the state petroleum company and elsewhere in Latin America, the federal government of Argentina, are larger."[54] The impact of these systems on social inequality, citizenship rights, on overall economic performance and on the quality of state-society relations can hardly be overestimated. The growth of the state and its success in displacing the theoretical alternative sources of welfare provision (the family, the community, and the church, for example) had been made socially acceptable over most of our period by its promise to provide an ever-rising proportion of the population with a range of health and pension benefits. By 1980 coverage was almost universal in some countries, and for Latin America as a whole it covered an estimated 61 percent of both population and workforce. (The fact that benefits were frequently highly unequal, often regressively financed and tilted toward powerful minorities, in no way weakened their legitimizing function given the severely stratified characteristics of most Latin American societies.)

The demonstrable inability of most Latin American states to honor any such promise set the stage for the almost universal shift toward "state shrinking" that characterized the end 1980s. The privileged minorities that did best from state welfare provision in its expansionary phase included many who were among the first to believe that their interests would be better served by a market-related provision of benefits. Their defection undermined the cohesion of the interventionist alliance, the core of which shrunk to those in public employment whose jobs were at risk. Thus perceptions shifted from the state as a means to better society, to one in which state agencies were seen to be only out to better themselves. (It is worth noting that in the mid-1980s over 15 percent of social security expenditure in Mexico and Venezuela was spent on administering the system, compared to 3 percent in Argentina and a half percentage point in the Unites States).

The vantage point of 2005 is bound to affect interpretation of the earlier history of the Latin American welfare systems. The term "social security" does not precisely translate the original notion of *previsión social* or *previdência social*. This was for most of our period essentially "a system of state-enforced obligatory insurance."[55] The point is that neither private employers nor individual clients of the system ever really had a choice as to whether or not to affiliate, nor did they exercise control over the uses to which their funds were put. Social security contributions were therefore in essence a form of disguised employment tax, and often quite onerous. Governments used these funds to finance programs that would generate support, buy off dissent, and enable them to co-opt what might otherwise prove to be troublingly autonomous social groupings. Since these were disguised as earmarked taxes, they were not directly misappropriated even by the most cynical administrations, which knew they could not administer the funds as if they were directly incorporated into government revenue. Rather they were regarded as semiautonomous "soft" funds, which could be raided from time to time when fiscal or political conditions were pressing. It is symptomatic that from the 1950s onward reports became widespread of nonpayment or late and inadequate payment of the contributions that governments themselves owed to these funds on behalf of their employees. Not surprisingly, then, contributors also tried to evade their obligations (over one-third of all Argentine payroll taxes were unpaid in 1983). Pension funds were also commonly required to invest in government paper, often paying artificially low interest rates. The counterpart of this covert depletion of contributors' real resources was that the central authorities typically delegated control over these systems to politically favored groups and interests, which they knew would not be subjected to rigorous supervision or fiscal control. In the extreme case of Peru no accounting records were kept from 1968 to 1978.

In the long run this meant that these schemes were so underfunded and mismanaged that the central budgetary authorities were bound to face demands for large subsidies (especially if, as in Argentina, Brazil, pre-1973 Chile, and Uruguay, the insurance was on a pay-as-you-go basis rather than being properly capitalized). After generating quite significant volumes of "forced savings" in the 1960s and 1970s, the region's social security institutes barely broke even in the 1980s, and can be expected to generate large deficits, as the demographic profile of contributors matures. Central government subsidies are already necessary in Argentina, Brazil, Costa Rica, and Uruguay. In the 1980s, the Chilean system was only made solvent through a drastic privatization program with major re-distributive implications. (Whereas the beneficiaries of the privatized Chilean system now have greater security and better pension prospects than before, and public subsidies have been eliminated, a large sector of the population has no coverage.) With hindsight, then, many of the deficiencies that reached crisis point in the 1980s can be traced back to the genesis of these program generations earlier.

This brief review appears to confirm the relevance of the threefold classification of state organizations proposed at the outset. The Southern Cone states were already highly advanced in this area before 1930, and their systems stagnated in the postwar period and entered into crisis and decline during the 1970s and 1980s. Brazil and Mexico, the two largest countries were far behind in 1930 but achieved impressive organizational advances over the ensuing half century. They were affected by the fiscal crises of the 1980s as well but they arguably retained some scope to rationalize and strengthen the existing systems without necessarily experiencing such drastic dislocations as in the Southern Cone. A third group of smaller and less indus-trialized countries started organizing their social security provision much later, and still have some way to go before they achieve the coverage—or face the challenges—of the others. In all three group-ings, despite these big differences of timing and impact, the realloca-tion of resources through social security program required a major and well-elaborated intervention of the state in the economy. It was part of a broader shift toward economic interventionism and was at least partially motivated by the need to "legitimize" economic activism by the state. However, during the 1980s this tide turned, and rising dissatisfaction with the results of the social security system contributed to a new climate favoring restraint on, or even reduction in, the state's claims on the nation's economic resources.

The full significance of these post-debt crisis trends is only now emerging. Perhaps in the long run they will prove to have been more cyclical than structural.[56] On the other hand, Malloy's 1979 portrait of the Brazilian system written before the "lost decade" seems to have a remarkably general application: the "concept of a meritocratic elite civil service was consistently undermined by the expanding reality of a politically controlled patronage-based civil service. This fact contributed to the paradox evident especially after 1945 that, while the state apparatus grew in size and formal power, its capacity to act effectively in a number of important policy areas actually declined. The power of the state receded in part because its administrative apparatus was colonised and parcelled among a complex array of political and labour leaders."[57]

With such an administrative background, and caught between the rival long-term imperatives of fiscal solvency, on the one hand, and the need to address a vast accumulated backlog of unmet social demands, on the other, Latin American states reached a point where they were no longer able to tap the new sources of finance and popularity that were available to them in the early days of welfare provision. This left them with two main alternatives; either to recognize the inevitability of some "state shrinkage" and plan an orderly retreat that might eventually produce a somewhat small and more targeted system of welfare provision or, if that proved too hard, to resign themselves to the consequences of a disorderly rout.[58] Vacillation between these alternatives has generated instability and insecurity, which continue to obstruct the consolidation in most of Latin America of what liberal theorists regard as the essential underpinnings of a constitutional state: a defined sense of mass citizenship in which individual rights and obligations are minimally balanced. Unless social security provision can be overhauled in broad accordance with this general principle much of the positive potential of existing systems may be destroyed. Clearly the outcome will have far-reaching implications for the quality of "citizenship" in contemporary Latin America and for the nature and durability of the region's experiments with democracy.

VI. Postscript on Citizenship

There are two possible relationships between the state and the people. Viewing them as subjects, the state's main concern is with securing their compliance and providing for their security; if they are treated as citizens, they acquire rights that the state is supposed to uphold. At the beginning of our period most of the population of Latin America were little more than subjects and at the end of it they were rather less than full citizens.

A few summary points must suffice to link this discussion to the bulk of the chapter. First, normative conceptions of a participatory constitutional republicanism retained strong appeal throughout the region during the period under review. Initially only an oligarchy enjoyed the benefits of this system and even at the end of our period efforts to extend the coverage of citizenship rights were still uneven and imperfect. Nevertheless, the aspiration remained powerfully intact and strongly constrained those administrations and elites that attempted to disregard it. Second, there seems to be a rather close affinity between "inward oriented" development, national integration, and the populist mode of collective mobilization and incorporation. Arguably then, the current switch back from nationalism to re-integration in international markets seems rather directly associated with the affirmation of a more individualistic and privatized image of citizenship. Third, whereas the normal assumption about liberal regimes is that they either uphold a fairly standard and universal model of citizenship rights throughout the society, or they collapse and citizenship collapses with them, in Latin America the more typical pattern has been for declaratory rights to bear rather little relationship to social realities, both under liberal and illiberal regimes. In either case, most subjects experience insecurity and unpredictability in their rights; citizenship is a promise that must be repeatedly re-negotiated; there are no reliable guarantors, or stable rules of inclusion/exclusion. And finally, the institutions and modalities of state organization that expanded most during the inward-looking phase of development were subsequently most exposed to curtailment. In contrast, other state institutions—the courts, congress, the municipalities—which seemed to flourish under the oligarchic constitutionalism that lasted until the 1920s, and tended to atrophy thereafter—may experience a renaissance under new conditions of liberal internationalism.

VII. Conclusion

Between the late 1920s and the late 1950s "oligarchic" states disappeared almost entirely from the subcontinent. They were replaced by what might be labeled "modernizing" states in the sense that many of the processes stressed in the "modernization" literature not only occurred but also took place in a fairly uniform manner during this period. There was the virtual revolution in territorial control, made possible at least partly because of the massive diffusion of the internal combustion engine, the telephone, and other new technologies. Further, not infrequently there was a quantum leap in administrative responsibilities and in some cases, albeit with less certainty, in capabilities, with much more extensive provision of education, health (mortality rates fell dramatically in the 1930s and 1940s), and urban services. The material basis for all this was a considerable expansion of the tax base, of official powers of economic regulation, and even of the entrepreneurial responsibilities directly assumed by the state, although in the first half of the period these were often more qualitative than quantitative shifts in the macro-economy. A changed international setting—the economic contraction of 1929 followed by the statism of the 1940s—gave this process its external impulse and supplied ideological models and sources to substitute the previously dominant doctrines of laissez-faire. The Cold War, of course, served to "de-radicalize" this shift toward *dirigisme*, but nationalism, Keynesian economics, and modernization theory all justified a continuing expansion in the range and depth of state activism. Civil society became much more urban, literate, industrial, and "homogeneous" in the sense that old enclaves and parochialisms eroded. At the same time, in critical aspects this "massification" of society made it far more complex and even at times unmanageable. Notwithstanding the considerable advances in "cognitive capacity" that have been made possible by recent developments in information technology, the strong tendency to reduce direct state involvement in many policy domains, and to extend the role of the market (known as "neo-liberalism" in short-hand), was often less a choice than a necessity forced by previous overreach.

Although a little forcing of the evidence makes reconciliation with modernization theory possible, the teleology and the predictions of that theory have not been borne out. Advances have not been unilinear and cumulative, but rather fitful, uneven, and reversible. Latin America did not simply develop uniform democratic market-regulated participatory societies. No stable and harmonious relationship emerged between the growth of state organization and the social incorporation of the lower classes. On the contrary, the "modernizing" states of the 1950s progressed with considerable uniformity into the "national security" states of the following generation.

The basic characteristics of these authoritarian systems are well known. In the simplest terms, all the features of centralization, control, intrusive administration, and sequestering of resources that had appeared in a relatively positive light during the early stages of the "modernization" and "state-building" processes now proceeded at an accelerated pace, at least temporarily overriding any countervailing pressures. Liberal mechanisms of public accountability and restraint had never been very strongly developed. In some cases, they were identified with the protection of pre-1930 oligarchies, and it was therefore considered "progressive" to sweep them away to extend opportunities to a wider array of social forces. Moreover, they were often simply seen as obstacles to the necessary processes of state building. In other, probably more common, cases the dominant classes (increasingly complex successors to the old oligarchies), preserved too many of their privileges and veto powers in exchange for acquiescence in the process of state expansion. Public accountability was all very well in principle, but was not to be used against them.

The "democratizing waves" of the mid-1940s and late-1950s might have given rise to more stable and effective institutions able to counterbalance the emerging bureaucratic Leviathan, but the Cold War and the aftermath of the Cuban Revolution swept away these experiments before they could become entrenched (although Venezuelan and Colombian exceptionalisms are both in their different ways highly significant). For a combination of developmentalist and counterinsurgency reasons, then, during the 1960s the ostensibly "modernizing" states of the 1950s were mostly closed off systematically from the pressures and constraints of an autonomous civil society. Needless to add, not all sectors of society were equally excluded from influencing and restraining the state apparatus: on the contrary, it is very well known that some very small sectors of the dominant classes gained enormously from the constitution of a national security state. These military, financial, and entrepreneurial groups often had very strong links with foreign interests, mainly in the United States. Hence, there was some objective basis for the "dependent capitalism" characterization of the underlying social basis of the "national security state" although this was a gross oversimplification as academic research and recent history both show.

One conclusion to emphasize is that processes internal to the pattern of state expansionism were very important in contributing to the emergence of the "national security" form of state organization and its subsequent disintegration. The tutelary state was too extensive and intrusive to serve as the lasting instrument for domination by any specific sector of society, no matter how conspiratorial or well organized. Indeed it could be argued that, not infrequently, the tendency of the state to usurp leadership responsibilities formerly exercised by private interests, sapped the will and/or destroyed the organizational capacity of what may be called "dominant interests" to formulate global strategies or to pursue autonomous hegemonic projects. In any case, Latin American society as a whole has now become far too complex, elaborate, and "modern" to be governed as the old oligarchies sometimes wished to do. The very tasks of contemporary government—including debt management, environmental protection, technology transfers—often require wider consultations and participation in decision-making.

Thus, the previous phase of centralization and authoritarian control not only yielded diminishing returns in the 1980s, but also proved incapable of providing either economic development or even "rational" administration. The "national security" state was therefore rejected by civil society more or less as a whole (note the part often played by business organizations in undermining them), and for the third time since the Second World War the possibility of establishing a reasonable degree of public accountability and democratic control over the apparatus of the state is being considered. The international setting for this new phase may seem relatively favorable when compared to the late 1940s or the early 1960s, but as became evident in September 2001 that can change very rapidly, and for reasons that have little to do with features internal to Latin American societies. But the political task of democratizing the state is made more difficult by the fact that it is widely believed that the scope of state activitism must not only be halted, but vigorously "rolled back" if any lasting equilibrium is to be restored to the mixed economy.

The establishment of an institutionalized equilibrium is a task for the future not only in the economic realm, but also in a wide variety of political and social fields. If they are to occur at all, such processes of institutionalization must be achieved through collective consultation and negotiation. By definition they cannot emerge as the product of administrative edicts or centrally imposed plans. Yet, the long established pattern of pushing reforms from above (with outside legitimization) and against the resistance of heterogeneous domestic actors and interests, has recurred during the recent era of democracy and neoliberalism, as will be seen in later chapters.

Chapter 3

The Politics of Expertise*

I. Introduction

All public activities are, in some broad measure, political, and all require certain specialized skills that may be termed "expertise." Over time and space, however, the realm of the specifically "political" may either expand (as during wars or revolutions) or contract (as after the discredit of a utopian schema). Equally, what counts as expertise, and how much autonomy it is granted, also varies over time and space. Horsemanship, literacy, oratory, textual exegesis, and an understanding of global financial derivatives have each been regarded as the hallmark of the modern expert in one setting or another. The relationship between the "generalist" politician and the expert "specialist" is one of the most ancient and recurring themes in political science, as is the conflict between the authority and competence of the specialist, and democratic accountability.[1] Effective and durable rule requires the enlistment of a range of competences, yet government is not reducible to technique. How, then, are the rulers to be guided by their advisers without being usurped by them? This problem presents itself in many different guises depending, for example, on whether it arises in a hereditary monarchy or a constitutional republic; under conditions of technological leadership or of educational backwardness; or on whether the dominant preoccupation is with state-building or with state-shrinking. But whatever the prevailing form of rule, and whatever the dominant source of expertise, the fate of the polity will be heavily determined by the manner in which these two are coordinated, and the ways in which the tensions between them are resolved.

Such recurring tensions between politics and expertise are readily visible in Latin America, as elsewhere. But what distinctive characteristics do they display in the particular regional context? This chapter outlines a very broad historical sketch of the issues, and then concentrates on contemporary developments, after the waning of the Cold War undermined the claims to authority of previously dominant military and security expects. At the broadest level, different varieties of expertise come to the fore in accordance with shifts in the main challenges facing a society. Thus, legal expertise might be crucial at the point when a new republic engages in constitutional design. Or engineers could claim an over-riding authority when basic infrastructure such as bridges and railways is to be installed.[2] During epidemics and medical emergencies doctors may come to the fore.[3] Since the 1982 debt crisis it has been the economics profession that has been most in the ascendant. But the states of Latin America have experienced unusually long periods of unbroken self-government, during which time they have had to contend with many diverse challenges, and they have therefore accumulated multiple and overlapping clusters of expertise, each with its own *esprit de corps*, its track record of addressing national issues, and its history of rivalry with other expert claimants to social prestige and state resources.

During the twentieth century, as state organization progressed in the ways outlined in the previous chapter, many more elaborate and specialized variants of expertise developed and received official sanction. In fact, as argued in the previous chapter, modern state organization necessarily involves the creation of various "cognitive" capacities—cartographical and statistical, and all the other specialized abilities required to design, monitor, and implement ever more complex and refined public policies—all of which presuppose the existence of appropriately skilled professionals. During its long phase of "inward-looking" expansion the typical Latin American state took on an ever-increasing range of responsibilities and so became involved in promoting and employing many more varieties of expertise. In the course of this period of turning away from the outside world it was not uncommon for the state to embrace certain "heterodox" versions of expertise that were out of step with dominant practices elsewhere, but even in these cases a high international reputation was still viewed as a precious endorsement of local claims to expertise. Prior to the 1982 debt crisis there were quite a few domains where the state was virtually the sole sponsor and user of key skills. State bureaucracies built from the "top down" to promote various aspects of "inward-looking" development (as outlined in the previous chapter) were typically authoritarian in style and outlook. In each policy domain, the expending state would designate a particular cluster of specialized operatives as the bearers of the latest idea of modernity and rationality—which could range from the builders of steel mills to anticlerical educationalists, to "money-doctors," or labor lawyers, or even the most up-to-date practitioners of repressive policing, and, indeed, torture. Such "experts" would typically be granted something approaching monopoly rights in their respective domains, and were seldom encouraged to cooperate with more traditional practitioners in the same field, so that there was often more inter-bureaucratic conflict than cooperation between rival clusters of expertise. They would derive their authority from a claimed possession to specialized knowledge essential for the latest cycle of state-building, and would usually try to bolster such claims by authentication from some prestigious external source, often either in Europe or North America. But such claims to expertise were not necessarily subjected to any particularly rigorous internal, or indeed external, scrutiny: state sponsorship was often enough to shield them from professional challenge. Even if their claims to expertise were less than fully authentic, that would not necessarily deter these Latin American "philosopher kings" of sorts from using their access to public power to override opposition. So, instead of accepting them at their own evaluation as the bearers of an incontrovertible modern rationality, they should perhaps more plausibly be viewed as inheritors of a characteristically Latin American oligarchic-patrimonial policy style—one that, as we shall see, predated modern state-building, and has to some extent persisted under state-shrinking. This style is to disdain all criticism as ignorant, irrational, or self-interested, and to persist regardless of opposition, and using private or public power to prevail rather than relying on persuasion and reasoned argument. Where such a policy style has become entrenched, rival elites and preexisting professional interests do not respond to such claims to expertise through dialogue, but rather by sponsoring their own clusters of experts, grouped around their own alternative claims to rationality.[4] The key test becomes not who has the more convincing claim to expertise as a result of open debate, but who can grab and hold onto state sponsorship.

If this was the dominant policy style under "inward-looking" development, it has changed only gradually with the subsequent shift to more market-based allocations of responsibilities and functions. One feature of the region's distinctiveness is therefore the compartmentalized existence of a variety of competing clusters of expertise (sometimes of high caliber, sometimes more a competence), nearly all historically dependant on state patronage, and none of them securely in the ascendant (contrast, for example, the *enarques* of France, or the traditional Oxbridge establishment in Britain). These clusters of experts tend to be organized in a very hierarchical manner. The few at the top of each pyramid may enjoy great leeway to express their views and to disregard the reactions of the lower ranks. They are likely to compete intensely for state recognition, and those who obtain it may then be subject to few restraints from their colleagues when they push their agendas to the limit. But this intense elite competition and top-down transformism tends to be unstable, as rival claimants to expertise with competing projects of reform often clash with each other, without any of the contenders securing a permanent hegemony. Since rivals are never permanently eliminated, nor definitively co-opted, they remain in play, and simply await the next opportunity to counter attack with an alternative formula. So although each expert-sanctioned initiative may seem to enjoy irresistible momentum at the point of its introduction, repeated experience has taught the society to anticipate the emergence in due course of various forms of resistance and backlash that can be used to promote a policy reversal.

In Latin America, a region characterized here as being "biased to modernity," successive and rival groups of elites and their associated experts each need the validation derived from international recognition and good standing in the relevant epistemic communities. To be credible as a modern expert in Latin America normally requires some form of external certification or legitimization in a specified profession or policy domain. But, as has been stressed already, in this region there is still no one exclusive external template of modernity (even the United States projects several rival alternatives). Instead Latin America still operates in most respects in a context of "multiple modernities" and this means that competing claimants to influence on the basis of expertise can invoke rival professional or doctrinal sources of international validation, from alternative metropolitan centers of endorsement. In practice, it is necessary to add, there can often emerge a strong disconnection between how prominent Latin American authorities are evaluated internationally, and what they actually stand for within a domestic setting (a particularly spectacular illustration of this phenomenon was provided in the 1990s by Domingo Cavallo, the miracle maker of Argentine stabilization).[5]

In post-Cold War Latin America the prevailing form of rule has been liberal constitutionalism, and the dominant *zeitgeist* that of state-shrinking and market liberalization. These are conditions in which the strictly "political" realm tends to contract, and market-related forms of expertise claim increasing autonomy. They have inspired some excellent studies of the recent rise of economic "technocrats," and some sweeping denunciations of the evils of politicized rent-seeking and populism.[6] But allegedly technocratic rule is no novelty in Latin America—consider the *científicos* of Porfirian Mexico—nor is it confined to narrowly economic forms of expertise—as in the case of the *positivistas* in Republican Brazil. In Latin America, however, as contrasted with some other large regions or the "developmental states" of East Asia, this massification and segmentation of professional expertise did not involve the displacement of an earlier cohort of generalist intellectuals. On the contrary, mid-ranking professionals who only possess certain defined technical skills are typically no match for the traditional *pensadores*, when it comes to social prestige or the capacity to form public opinion. In that area not only historians and social scientists but also philosophers, poets, and latterly even television presenters, exercise much more influence than specialists and technicians. The latter's claims to expert understanding are readily overridden by these socially authoritative generalists, who have even gained ground as the more functionally inclined military rulers have been replaced in power by argumentative civilians. In these heterogeneous and loosely integrated societies there is often little understanding for the intricacies of technical analysis, and little trust in the disinterestedness of those who claim to possess special expertise.

This chapter aims to situate contemporary trends in their broader historical and socio-geographic settings. The hope is that by sketching out the distinctively Latin American antecedents to the rising power of this latest cohort of experts it may be possible to de-mythologize some fashionable judgments about the present.

II. Antecedents

During the colonial period access to positions of political and bureaucratic power in Latin America was drastically restricted by stringent birth, race, gender, education, and property requirements. The dominant principles of recruitment were aristocratic and/or patrimonial. European birth and family or courtly connections were formidable assets, and active Catholic observance was virtually indispensable. Good command of the language of administration, in both its written and spoken forms, was essential, together with a working familiarity with colonial laws and institutions. A reasonable degree of numeracy was also normally required. In the social circumstances of the period these were highly restrictive prerequisites, but not such as to preclude intense competition to fill the positions available, since these were very few in number. Even so, effective colonial government required the performance of some complex and specialized tasks. Advancement on merit, or as recognition not just of experience but also of the expertise that could be derived from diligent public service was already an established career path. Not only were military promotion structures based partly on training and experience, but also credentialism was strongly developed in the main civilian professions of public life—the church and the law.[7] Military colleges, seminaries, law schools, and even universities were busy cultivating the "expertise" required for colonial rule well before Latin America's wars of independence. Not infrequently, such training institutions had the potential to develop into seats of learning, producing not just technically competent servants of the status quo but critical thinkers and potential leaders of a distinctively American orientation.[8]

Following the American and French revolutions new models of political organization and new sources of influence and power displaced colonial rule from Europe. European birth or aristocratic connections shed their political advantages, sometimes drastically as in Paraguay, sometimes more gradually as in Brazil. Depending upon the course and intensity of the battles for independence, new channels of political recruitment opened up, with opportunities for advancement extending to some who lacked property or education, or had been excluded on "caste" grounds in colonial times, although those classified as *mestizos* were far more likely to benefit than those who were considered Indian, let alone of African origin. Non-Catholics secured access to the higher levels of political power only very gradually, mostly not until well into the twentieth century, and women, of course, were virtually excluded from public life until after the Second World War.

For the first century or so after Independence most Latin American political elites continued to be recruited overwhelmingly from a narrow social stratum that, although differing in form, typically retained significant sociological continuities with its colonial precursor. Clearly, an important distinction must be made between regional and provincial levels of political leadership, which was often semi-autonomous and based on extra-legal control over local resources, and the formal positions to be filled at the national level in the state apparatus. Our concern here is the latter, since that is where technical competence and political professionalism was necessarily concentrated. In many countries and over substantial periods this level of government did not concentrate any very large proportion of social power but, however that may be, political recruitment at this level continued to privilege various skills and educational attainments that were scarce in the society as a whole. Indeed the shift from a colonial to a republican principle of legitimacy greatly increased the value of a higher educational qualification for those seeking either a bureaucratic or a political career. This was as true for imperial Brazil as for republican Spanish America.[9] Although university education for long remained heavily oligarchic and weighted toward the more traditional vocations (especially law and medicine) republican institutions of higher learning were no longer subject to colonial censorship or to such strict ecclesiastical discipline as in the past. On the contrary, and as suggested in the first chapter, they became major centers of illumination, within which successive new generations of aspiring political leaders could aim to debate all the ills of society, to imbibe the latest philosophies of social reform, and to formulate their respective programs of political action. Many major Latin American political parties can be traced back to specific student cohorts, like the Colombian "Generation of 1880" or the Venezuelan parties founded by the Central University of Venezuela (UCV) leaders of 1928. Typically this pattern of elite formation encouraged generalists rather than specialists (the student leader-cum-journalist who subsequently became a legislator-cum-lawyer).

To make a top leadership career in this setting required high intellectual prestige, and attainment on a broad front. Like the *philosophes* of republican France, the aspiring political leader of pre-Castro Latin America was likely to respect no intellectual or disciplinary boundaries. Historian, poet, philosopher, and legislator were all attributes that could be embodied in a single individual. Figures such as Benjamin Constant Botelho de Magalhães, José Vasconcelos, and even the more contemporary Rafael Caldera indicate the real political power that could accrue to such individuals. Of course many students who attempted to imitate this style ended up with no political power, and no real field of professional competence either. They could be dismissed as mere "cafe intellectuals."

Various factors have been suggested as explanations for the distinctive political role of the general intellectual in Latin America between the 1850s and the 1950s. First, there is an analogy with intellectuals in postrevolutionary France. Having decapitated a hereditary aristocracy and overthrown an *ancien régime* legitimated by powerful traditions, the isolated *philosophe* wielding only his pen seemed capable of remarkable feats of social transformation. His prestige and ambition soared, and to some extent the Paris intellectual came to substitute the overthrown nobility at the apex of the French pyramid of social prestige. Latin American intellectuals were deeply influenced by this model, particularly during the century in which Paris seemed the center of world civilization and culture. Second, most of the newly independent states were genuinely in need of a new republican legitimacy, or alternative overall principles of economic and social design, to replace the colonial model that had collapsed on them. General intellectuals with a capacity to synthesize ideas from a variety of sources and disciplines were therefore needed to address quite pressing and fundamental questions of public policy that could not be resolved through inertia or *ad hoc* improvisation. Those who seemed the most effective bearers of the most "modern" ideas drawn from the experiences of the most successful liberal regimes were likely to secure a receptive following. Third, there was generally plenty of obscurantism and anti-intellectualism for these thinkers to struggle against. In particular, the Catholic Church offered a coherent worldview, and a compelling source of traditional authority, which long resisted secular republicanism and the rule of reason to its foundations. Latin American intellectuals were required to address unresolved foundational issues, whether opposing traditional clericalism or seeking to modernize it. They could not limit themselves to "specialized" or narrowly "technical" areas of competence. This helps to explain why, from the early twentieth century until the 1970s, the secular religion of Marxism rose to prominence as the most complete and coherent alternative to submission to the priesthood. Finally, as the modern state became consolidated, it sought to "co-opt" this republican intelligentsia, granting it public favors and creating educational and cultural institutions that glorified its most ambitious intellectual endeavors, which were placed beyond the reach of criticism (so long as the beneficiaries returned the favor by abstaining from directly criticizing the *gobiernos de turno*).

III. Actualities

These long-run antecedents are highly germane to any discussion of the politics of expertise in contemporary Latin America. The existence of unbroken intellectual and institutional traditions stretching back over one or even several centuries sharply distinguishes the region from most other parts of the "developing" or "Third World", where the impact of European colonialism was more recently and incompletely imposed and then withdrawn. Such major republics as Brazil, Mexico, and Colombia have extremely well-established systems of elite recruitment, socialization, and reproduction, which evolve only slowly and largely in accordance with internal rhythms and constraints.[10] The sinuous career of Casimiro Olañeta—who switched loyalties at the very last stage of the struggle against Spain, thus outliving many patriots and surviving to exercise great influence in the new republic—provides a significant precursor to various late twentieth-century Bolivian political biographies. Alain Touraine's mostly rather negative account of the politicized Latin American intellectual will probably strike a chord with many readers of this collection:

> Intellectuals shifted from one ideological theme to another with the greatest of ease, from modernization to dependency, from authoritarianism to

democracy, not allowing ideas to take on a practical form as action [. . .] Successive fashions paved the way for the emergence of numerous but fragile groups of semi-professional intellectuals who intervened both at a very general level and in the domains calling for more specialised professionals. These doctrinaire intellectuals produced few original political analyses or solid professional work [. . .] intellectuals usually emerged in the empty spaces left between a declining oligarchy and an increasingly powerful State and [. . .] they followed two main paths: that of professionals, particularly in the area of education and the social sciences, and that of extreme right or extreme left wing radicals, whose ideas had a weak capacity to mobilise [. . .] The weakness of the doctrinaire intellectual is all the more visible more recently, and in particular under the military dictatorships, in the face of persecution there emerged a category of intellectuals that was completely different from those preceding it, in which professional quality improved rapidly, often attaining top international standards. These intellectuals put forward general analyses that went well beyond doctrinaire interpretations.[11]

For our purposes the most important point here is the shift that Touraine detects from what he characterizes as impractical "doctrinaire" theorizing to more effective and well-grounded political analyses that are still general in scope and broad in their implications, and not just technical.

Albert Hirschman made a parallel observation in his study of economic policy-making in Latin America in the 1960s, when comparing U.S. and Latin American political styles: while the former consisted of pragmatic "logrolling," the latter was governed by "*toderos*," or "people who count have a finger in every pie, and [. . .] like to acquire and express an opinion of every issue"—in other words, in Latin America there was a tendency for upper class decision-making groups to situate any specific decision within some overriding political framework and to feel honor-bound to develop strong opinions and "right" answers to every question. Although he acknowledged that this generalist attitude might be "beginning to be eroded by a more "modern" specialist-lobbyist type of attitude" he added that "it [was] still strongly entrenched," and proposed the following inference arising from his comparison: "the more principled the individual decision-makers, the more unprincipled will be governmental political behaviour, with yesterday's allies being jettisoned today, and yesterday's enemies suddenly being honoured in surprising turnabouts."[12] These observations can be interpreted as partial support for my claims about the prevalence of conflicts for control of power between rival elites, each with its own top-down project of modernity, none of which permanently eliminates its competitors.

Such observations tend to be pitched at a very sweeping level of generalization, and realities on the ground remain extremely heterogeneous, if not also hybrid. Nevertheless, the case can be made that in a post-Cold War, democratic, and internationally liberalizing Latin America, the politics of expertise is being rapidly and perhaps irreversibly transformed. The rest of this chapter consists of a statement of that case, a review of some of the most pertinent objections to it, and a brief discussion of a few major contemporary instances that can be used as "reality checks" in the debate.

The contrast between Cold War Latin America and the post-Cold War period provides the best starting point for the claim of irreversible transformation. As a consequence of the Cuban Revolution, foundational issues of political philosophy and identity took the center stage for a considerable period, roughly in the 1960s and 1970s. Fidel Castro never acquired any specific field of expertise, and he never allowed experts to flourish around him who might constrain his leadership style. General Arnaldo Ochoa seems to have shown signs of developing that kind of potential in 1989, before he was given a show trial, and then shot. The Sandinistas were almost as casual about managerial competence. Priests and poets were highly valued, but not accountants or administrators. Neither Allende nor Velasco paid much attention to the politics of expertise. They were all engaged in voluntarist efforts at social transformation, and therefore valued commitment to this normative ideal above training and know-how.

It was not just on the radical left that this syndrome manifested itself, however. A brief study of the *Falangistas* of Bolivia in the 1970s led to the rather surprising discovery that they were less flexible or reality-oriented than the Marxist utopians they opposed. More generally, the national security states of the 1970s relied heavily on ideological commitment and often coexisted uneasily with technical competence. That is a major reason why they did not endure: as the Marxist threat faded, their business and elite allies turned elsewhere for effective government. In Argentina, for example, the Dirty War produced a systematic process of negative selection within the armed forces culminating in the leadership of General Galtieri, perhaps the most incompetently nonexpert military leader one could hope to recruit.

Even where such polarization was avoided, it was often an uphill struggle to consolidate "pockets of competence" in limited parts of the state apparatus. The Itamaratí in Brazil is an example of a successful pocket of competence. It was the child of the Barão de Rio Branco, the longest serving foreign minister of the country, whose obituary stated that with his death "Brazil [had] lost one of its favourite sons and one of its most dedicated servants."[13] It is considered in and outside Brazil as an exceptionally professional and technically competent foreign services, with a strong *esprit the corps* and a powerful sense of tradition and continuity. For example, Brazilian diplomats at the World Trade Organisation have the reputation of being among the most effective negotiators from the "developing world." Central banks and foreign ministries, perhaps because of their specialized functions as interfaces with the outside world, were more likely than most political institutions to promote professional expertise, but they were often enclaves with little spillover effect on the political systems as a whole. Admittedly, professional economics was on the rise, but at first this manifested itself in specialized academic centers and think tanks (and in international financial institutions) rather than in national politics. Many governments continued to operate with a relatively low level of economic expertise until the debt crisis, and even where higher levels of technical competence became more embedded in parts of the state apparatus that did not necessarily signify—as the next two chapters show—unilinear progress toward abstract rationality. To the contrary, unaccountable and intolerant experts, out of touch with the social realities surrounding them, might still use their privileged access to state power to impose supposedly modern projects that were in fact based on mis-specified theoretical assumptions. If such initiatives did not turn out as expected, it could well be because their authors had oversold their expertise, or because their abstract predictive models were not calibrated for Latin America's distinctive regional characteristics.

The end of the Cold War, following on the heels of the 1982 debt crisis, created a new set of opportunities that were seized upon by a new generation of technocrats and managers—usually foreign trained—who believed that the latest version of modernity must consist of a top-down liberalization and a regional shift to outward orientation. During the 1980s, it became progressively clearer that the Soviet bloc offered no alternative model to liberal capitalism in Latin America and indeed that socialism no longer constituted much of a threat to the established order. As the aftermath of the debt crisis lingered on it also became more apparent that Latin America would be forced to adjust to the requirements of the outside world, rather than vice versa. This obviously increased the scarcity premium and political leverage of those judged competent to design and manage the necessary adjustments. At the same time, the establishment or restoration of (usually fragile) democratic regimes shifted the axis of political debate from the kind of foundational issues on which intellectuals traditionally vested their authority to the resolution of more specific policy questions of direct concern to a mass electorate, questions typically neglected by "doctrine-oriented" theorists, although not necessarily beyond the range of a younger generation of western-influenced and often U.S.-educated reformers. In the international climate of accelerated economic liberalization that followed the end of the Cold War, expertise in foreign commerce, finance, technology, and the workings of modern market economies acquired an enhanced value. Equally well, in a climate of fiscal austerity, "state shrinking," and retreat from universal formulae of welfare provision, expertise in socioeconomic regulation, trade union issues, and state-organized health and education, among others, no longer commanded any scarcity premium. Military expertise was also downgraded, whereas journalism gained ground. Some new channels of professional training and recruitment therefore surged to the forefront while some old established channels struggled to adapt (one example is the contrast between the National Autonomous University of Mexico (UNAM) and the Autonomous Technological Institute of Mexico (ITAM) as rival sources of economic expertise).

In summary, then, the case for an irreversible shift in political elite training and recruitment rests on the assumptions that: first, the foundational debates of the Cold War era have been durably resolved; second, the fragile democracies of the region are, if not *en route* to consolidation, at least reasonably secure from breakdown; and third, the internationally oriented new economic model is here to stay. If these assumptions are valid, the remaining vestiges of the old generalist and doctrinal politics may well fade away with the passing of time, and a more educated, articulate, and cohesive civil society may perhaps demand progressively more competence and effective service delivery from their political and bureaucratic leaders.[14]

Having summarily stated the case, three main objectives to it deserve consideration. First, insofar as there has been an "eclipse" of foundational politics in contemporary Latin America, this astronomical occurrence has been decidedly partial, rather than total. There is still at least one unattained utopia to struggle for—the vision of a fully consolidated democratic market economy founded on the rule of law and compatible with elementary social justice. Were this to be attained in Latin America to, say, the same extent as it has been in western Europe, then politics could be reduced to just the "technical" or expert business of keeping the established order in trim. This is so far from being attained in all the countries of the region at present, however, that much more than mere administrative or technical competence is required to bring it about. Admittedly, at least for the time being, alternative foundational projects are conspicuous by their absence. As a result even "doctrinal" intellectuals mostly concentrate on propounding competing interpretations of the same basic vision.

Second, the conflict between those competing interpretations can still be highly unsettling, though, and the failings of "really existing" liberal capitalism, while perhaps less acute than those of "really existing" socialism a decade ago, are sufficiently serious to raise doubts about whether "the end of history" really has dawned even in the advanced market societies. Insofar as this is the case, the rebirth of alternative Latin American utopias cannot be entirely discounted for the indefinite future. "Foundational" politics may be dormant but they are not yet dead. The continued prominence in public life of many who made their careers through their identification with alternative utopias—from Fidel Castro to Augusto Pinochet, and from Cuauhtémoc Cárdenas to Hugo Chávez—reinforces the hunch that such disputes could still be reawakened. As all these examples indicate, it is still possible to achieve transformative effects in the Latin American region through the pursuit of "grand" general visions. Thus, at least in this region, rationality (meaning the deployment of means appropriate for a chosen end) can still be foundational, and not merely technical.

Third, so far the strongest argument for "irreversibility" has been the inability of critics of the emerging political-economic model to formulate a coherent and workable alternative, or to demonstrate any success outside the liberal market framework. That seems likely to remain the most formidable obstacle to the resurrection of foundational disputes in Latin American politics, but it is not completely decisive. Continued social exclusion, gross inequality, and personal insecurity may provide a large social base for alternative visions, even if political leaders are incapable of articulating programs for that constituency. The rise of evangelical Protestantism seems partly to reflect such unsatisfied aspirations, as do the emergence of "historically displaced" nationalist populist projects and some currents of indigenous political organization. Sometime, somewhere a half-plausible alternative model may always present itself. In any case we should guard against too stark a dichotomy between the "doctrinal" politics of the past and the "professional" politics of the present and future. The reality was, is, and seems likely to remain, substantially hybrid. That is not to say that nothing is changing, but only that we should concern ourselves more with questions of balance and proportion than binary oppositions.

This point can be illustrated by reference to one of the outstanding political and economic figures of twentieth-century Bolivia. Here, I draw on my work on the evolution of the career of Víctor Paz Estenssoro. Quoting articles he wrote in 1930, emphasizing the preeminence of economic phenomena, "which in reality and beyond apparent causes, regulate the life of nations," I labeled him "Boliva's first technocrat."[15] Subsequently tracing his career as Finance Minister in 1945; as leader of the party that made the social revolution of 1952, the MNR; as intellectual author of the 1956 stabilization plan (although he allowed credit and blame to accrue to a specially recruited and supposedly "technical," but in fact highly ideological foreign adviser, George Jackson Eder); and eventually as the one leader capable of bringing about a neoliberal counterrevolution in the management of his country's economic affairs (the 1985 "shock treatment" that did so much to build the reputation of Jeffrey Sachs), it is possible to find strong technical competence in the field of economics indissolubly welded with intense political leadership skills of a foundational, revolutionary-populist variety. These apparently incompatible ingredients coexisted in his persona throughout his sixty-year long career at the center of Bolivian politics. To call Víctor Paz Estenssoro a mere "technocrat" is to profoundly misjudge his historical significance, but to underestimate his expertise would be equally mistaken.

Is this case unique? Probably not: the career of Raúl Prebisch spans approximately the same period and displays similar characteristics. His authority as a technical expert was fused with his charisma as a prophet of social transformation. Moreover, from the earliest years, and like Paz Estenssoro, Prebisch combined vision with technical know-how. Important parts of his career have been analyzed elsewhere,[16] and the contribution here is just an anecdote he told me about his experiences in the military government of General Justo in the early 1930s. He came to the conclusion that, as a result of the Depression, it would be necessary for Argentina to introduce a most unpopular new measure: an income tax. His dilemma, however, was how to explain to the ignorant conservative President that he must adopt an innovation so contrary to the preferences of all his friends at the Jockey Club. No technical presentation, no rehearsal of the figures, no review of international experiences would do the trick. What Prebisch had to do was present himself to the General as the most impeccable servant of the established order, and to persuade him that it was a patriotic duty to demand sacrifice from the public just as an officer expects discipline and abnegation from his soldiers in times of armed conflict. It may be wondered whether discussions on economic policy between Cavallo and Menem were any more technically demanding than that between Prebisch and Justo in 1933.

The broader point illustrated by these career sketches is that complex policy reforms require both a good measure of technical competence and authoritative political endorsement. Sometimes the two may be combined within a single personality, as in the case of Paz

Estenssoro in 1985. Sometimes they may be harmonized within a strong bureaucratic administration like the *Gabinete Económico* in Mexico in the 1980s.[17] Or, perhaps, they may be reconciled through an informed process of parliamentary debate and interparty elite negotiation (as in Chile under the *Concertación*). But it is not unusual for those with the necessary political authority to lack the appropriate technical competence—there was no meeting of minds between President Reagan and his budget director, David Stockman, for example.

All sorts of hybrid combinations have been found in the past, and even the experience of the most advanced liberal capitalist democracies provides us with little reason to doubt that these multiple forms will continue to operate in the future. Sometimes they work well for a while, as under President Fujimori and his relationship with his Economy Minister, Carlos Boloña; sometimes they break down, as was the case with President Caldera and the Venezuelan technocrats; and sometimes the appearance of collaboration proves deceptive, as the Cruzado Plan under the Sarney presidency shows. Undoubtedly, the secular processes emphasized in modernization theory are genuine and powerful. Overall levels of education are rising fast, and more or less "middle class" lifestyles and values are on the increase. Dense and overlapping networks of specialized competence and expertise continue to develop, informing public policy and constraining some forms of misgovernment. But these are merely loose tendency statements, leaving plenty of scope for the perpetuation of inherited authoritarian policy styles. Despite the many structural changes associated with the end of the Cold War, the transition to democracy, the liberalization of the economy, and the increased leverage of the business community, there is really no conclusive evidence that hybrid, potentially unstable, and erratic patterns of policy-making have been eliminated from contemporary Latin America. How can there be any "irreversible" triumph of the technocrats, or even of expertise more broadly understood, as long as many traditional patterns of policy-making continue to persist? The evidence that has accumulated since the collapse of Domingo Cavallo's reckless "convertibility" project in Argentina in 2001 points to the huge backlash that can build up against such pretensions.

IV. Conclusion

"Technocrats" derive their authority from their claimed mastery of certain specialized areas of knowledge that are deemed essential for effective government. If a central problem facing a society is the threat of yellow fever, then those who know best how the disease propagates and how it can be combated may have an irresistible claim to the public resources required for its defeat. If the central problem becomes the threat of hyper-inflation a similar logic may empower those economic experts who alone know how to restore monetary stability. But there are two very striking limitations to the power that can be obtained by such means, even in the most extreme of circumstances. The first is that once the "emergency" has passed other sources of concern will return to the center of public debate, and there is no reason to suppose that the expert in disease control will also possess the specialized skills required to tackle nonmedical dilemmas. Similarly, there is no good reason to suppose that the expert in monetary stabilization will possess the skills required to combat, say, the reappearance of cholera. Particular types of expert may therefore enjoy brief periods of concentrated power, but if they live up to their promises they will thereby undermine the conditions for their preeminence. Either they may prove false experts and lose power altogether, or true experts who, having overcome one policy emergency, retreat from center stage to occupy a no doubt honorable and durable, but also secondary, role in public life. True expertise becomes professionalized, institutionalized, and even depoliticized, as a society moves from national emergency to routine administration. As Kathryn Sikkink has persuasively argued in relation to the ideology of "developmentalism," unless such ideas acquire institutional embodiment they will lack the staging power and detailed follow-through required to shape public policy over the longer run.[18] Yet if they *do* become institutionalized they also become subject to broader processes of political bargaining and analytical dilution.

This relates to the second limitation. When technical expertise is scarce, valuable, and a source of empowerment these rewards will attract an influx of new entrants. Scarce knowledge is therefore likely to become diffused throughout the society, the early technocrats will find themselves held increasingly accountable to a more informed community of peers, and the opportunity to make further breakthroughs on the basis of privileged expertise can be expected to decline. Broader and more "generalist" forms of policy discussion will therefore reassert themselves. Twenty first century Latin America manifests a range of characteristics that might be expected to reinforce the authority of political generalists and to curb the arrogance of unaccountable experts. Contemporary features favorable to the influence of generalists might include: the reassertion of constitutional rule; international détente and regional cooperation; the failure and discredit of various forms of authoritarian social engineering; advances in education and science diffused through an increasingly assertive and rising stratum of young professionals. All of this is reinforced by a high degree of media freedom as compared to the past. These are surely conditions that ought to favor the emergence of a stratum of political brokers and entrepreneurs capable of assimilating expertise without surrendering to its dictates. Their communication skills and capacity to persuade will be needed to synthesize and popularize the valid insights of the experts. To some extent, the new cohort of technocrats and neoliberal experts have also learnt some of the skills of mass communication, and there is often a competition between them and the more traditional intelligentsia over who can dominate the airwaves, but neither have a monopoly and the battle could prove salutary for both. The overall quality of public policy-making may rise as hitherto esoteric forms of expertise become incorporated into the collective understanding of the whole community.

For the sake of simplicity this discussion has taken such expert claims to authority at face value. In any real political process we can expect to find dispute over the validity and extent of such claims. Inexpert politicians will have to make judgments about who to believe and therefore how much authority to delegate. Often such judgments may remain contested even with the benefit of hindsight. Here is a further reason why an apparent "triumph of the technocrats" may so often prove ephemeral. Even with all the reinforcement they can now muster from Latin America's reinvigorated business class, today's neoliberals still seem engaged in an endless campaign against an array of critics who may shift their ground but never seem to disappear. These critics can never be eliminated, in part because insulated technocrats characteristically overreach themselves, but more fundamentally because the viewpoints and interests that the critics represent extend far beyond the reach of any form of bureaucratic rationality. Further, and above all, because they have failed to produce the results everyone desires—wealth and greater distribution and sustainability of the economic model.

Chapter 4

Economics in Mexico: The Power of Ideas and Ideas of Power*

"Once the military phase of the Revolution had ended [. . .] the intellectuals became the secret or public advisers of the illiterate generals, the labour or peasant leaders the political bosses. It was an immense task and everything had to be improvised. The poets studied economics; the jurists, sociology; the novelists, international law or pedagogy or agronomy [. . .] Within a short time the country possessed a considerable group of technicians and experts, thanks to the new professional schools and the opportunity to study abroad [. . .] However, their situation is extremely difficult [. . .] The Mexican intelligentsia as a whole has not been able to use the weapons of the intellectual—criticism, examination, judgment—or has not learned how to wield them effectively. As a result, the spirit of accommodation [. . .] has invaded almost every area of public activity. In addition, government service has become a sort of cult or sect, with the usual bureaucratic rituals and 'state secrets.' Public affairs are not discussed, they are whispered."[1]

I. Introduction

This chapter surveys the changing role and outlook of economists and the economics profession in Mexico since the 1930s, identifying some distinctively Mexican features of the story that can be compared and contrasted with roles assumed by economists in various contemporaneous South American policy transformations. The chapter concludes with some speculations about the consequences of the Salinas legacy for the profession and the economy. Indirectly, it suggests some implications of the Mexican case material for more general theorizing about the power of economic technocrats in a broadly "neoliberal" era, and about the problems of "democratizing" economists and economic policy-management in Latin America. As noted by Sarah

Babb in a volume published after the first version of this chapter had appeared, "Mexico has an economic and institutional history similar to that of many developing countries, particularly those of Latin America. Relative backwardness, import substitution in the post-War period, credit-financed populism in the 1970s, and the debt crisis of the 1980s—these are all historical factors that Mexico shares in common with other Latin American nations."[2]

As indicated in previous chapters, it was the Mexican state that initially created this cluster of expertise, and to date the latter remains far more heavily dependent on state sponsorship and direction than is the case of economists in the metropolitan centers. From the outset, the history of expertise was heavily shaped by dependence on foreign models—note the plural, since both liberalism and Marxism vied with statist Keynesianism for acceptance as the most authoritative modern doctrine. Consequently, the profession has always tracked international trends in its field, while nevertheless operating according to a distinctive institutional logic within the national context. As tasks of economic modernization, and more recently, of international economic integration, have come to the fore, so have these experts enhanced their power within the state apparatus. But they have acquired and deployed their power in a more top-down and transformative manner than would be typical of economists in developed countries. Since the democratization of the late 1990s, they have had to contend with the hitherto concealed reality that their outlook and agenda rests on scant support from, and understanding, by Mexican society at large, even though these experts are now repositioned as allies rather than as enemies of the business community.

II. Origins of the Profession

In the 1950 quote at the begnning of this chapter, Octavio Paz was expounding both a creation myth, and an early critique of the role that would be played by social scientists in serving—and protecting—the postrevolutionary political bureaucracy in Mexico. This chapter challenges the creating myth, and reinforces the critique, particularly as it applies to the second and third generations of economic specialists, whose *déformations professionelles* reinforced by their corporate and personal self-interest, and spiced by their intolerance of critical debate, generated a considerable backlash after the "Tequila crisis" of 1995.[3] Octavio Paz's original creation myth, that the Mexican revolution engendered a social science community tailored to the requirements of state service, was succeeded in the late 1980s by a new one, according to which the exhaustion of the revolution's state-centric development model opened political access to a cohort of foreign-trained economists and technocrats whose expertise will at last transmit international standards of rationality and market competence into Mexican public life.

Perhaps every generation of professionals needs its distinctive creation myth. In reality, of course, Limantour and Matías Romero were thoroughly schooled in European financial and commercial practices before 1910, and Alberto Paní, Eduardo Suárez, Narciso Bassols, and Manuel Gómez Morín were far from amateurs or hastily retrained poets when they constructed the postrevolutionary economic institutions of the 1920s and 1930s. Even former President Calles, when he became director of the Bank of Mexico at the height of the Great Depression in 1931, was more a seasoned military Keynesian *avant la lettre* than an illiterate general, and his re-flationary policies were at least a match for those that FDR would improvise in the United States two or three years later. As Sarah Babb has summarized: "following the Revolution of 1910–1917, Mexican state-builders explicitly looked to foreign models in their construction of a central bank, development bank, the finance ministry, and a host of other institutions. Indeed, the founding of Mexico's first economics programme in 1929 was conceived as a project for training students in the latest economics knowledge and techniques developed abroad, to the end of developing a corps of competent administrators to work within the government bureaucracy."[4]

Concerning economics as a professional career in Mexico, in 1929 the *Escuela Nacional de Economía* (ENE) was founded as a dependency of the Law Faculty of the *Universidad Nacional Autónoma de México* (UNAM). The founders of the school, who designed the curriculum, had degrees in law, philosophy, and engineering. Two of the main founders—Narciso Bassols and Manuel Gómez Morín—each served as finance minister before going on to help found opposition political parties, the first on the Left and the second on the Right. Daniel Cosío Villegas was named director of the school in 1929, but encountered many difficulties in getting good professors for the program. When only three students registered for the second year he proposed to eliminate it and to send good students on scholarships to foreign universities, but Jesús Silva Herzog and other early professors and students rejected the idea.

It was not until after 1935 that the school gained independence from the law faculty. Between 1929 and 1954 only 174 persons obtained their degrees under this program. But even if the numbers were few, the school soon trained an elite of public officials. Most students already held middle-level positions in government, and had degrees in law or accounting before they entered the school. Camp found that 17 out of the 159 graduates whose subsequent careers he could trace went on to hold high-level positions in public life. From the earliest days, professors would often recruit graduates of the school into employment in the various new state agencies that began to proliferate. Camp found that the two largest centers of recruitment were the Ministry of Industry and Commerce and the Finance Ministry, although it is not clear whether or not he included the Bank of Mexico in his analysis.[5] By the 1940s, as a high level official of the Finance Ministry, Silva Herzog was able to obtain funds to send many of his best students to study in graduate institutions in the United States. Economists almost exclusively staffed the Federal Income Tax Department within the Ministry. Similarly, Gilberto Loyo, who became Dean of the School of Economics in 1944, gave a great impetus to the career of economists by employing many of them in the Industry and Commerce Ministry that he headed in 1952.[6]

III. The Rise of the Economic Technocrats

By the 1960s, U.S. analysts were identifying the emergence of a new category within the ruling elite. Raymond Vernon of Harvard, where Cosío Villegas had also studied, introduced the notion of the *técnico* as follows: "In the development of nations the economic technician is rapidly coming to be thought of as the indispensable man. By general agreement, such subjects as exchange rate policy, fiscal and monetary policy, investment and saving policy, and similar esoteric matters can no longer be left entirely to the rough-and-ready ministrations of the politician. For one thing, the economic techniques have grown so complex that they are beyond the easy understanding of the amateurs; for another the increasing flow of communications between nations and with international agencies on these subjects has demanded that every country develop a class of responsible officials which is capable of holding up its end in the interchange. In Mexico the economic technician has become an integral element in the decision-making process on issues affecting Mexico's development."[7]

Thus was the stage set for a takeover of decision-making in Mexico by such "indispensable" economic experts as Carlos Salinas de Gortari (educated at Harvard) and Ernesto Zedillo de Leon (trained at Yale). They would be trained to communicate on "esoteric" matters beyond the comprehension of the ordinary Mexican politician, with others of a like background. The literature on *técnicos*, "technocrats," and "techno-bureaucrats" in Mexico is quite extensive and exhaustive— not to say exhausting.[8] But despite Raymond Vernon it does not specially single out *economic* expertise: all these categories are also held to cover engineers, doctors, and law specialists as well, even though in the past generation it is clearly this specific variant of specialized knowledge that has come to dominate the recruitment process. Moreover, this literature proposes clear-cut definitions in principle, but acknowledges that in practice it is often difficult to attach precise labels to individual power-holders. Thus, Peter Smith, one of the scholars most sensitive to the peculiarities of the Mexican political system in its totality, repeatedly notes that his informants seldom seem to correspond neatly to the divisions implied by the typology. Furthermore, the typology conveys the impression that Mexican ruling elite composition and behavior is comparable to that of the other Latin American countries in which economic experts have acquired positions of prominence, when in reality other regimes were the products of military power seizures, and the terms upon which economists were invited to serve was determined by that stark fact— a situation that was far from the case in PRI-ruled Mexico.[9]

Since this chapter is about economics in Mexico, rather than about technocrats, it will take much of the general literature as given. The focus is on the rise of a specific subset within the system of technocratic governance—the *economic* technocrats, and the influence their success has exerted upon the economics profession, and on the character of debate on economic policy questions within Mexico. Unfortunately, it is not possible here to compare the development of the economics profession in Mexico with its development in the Anglo-Saxon and West European democracies over the same period. It must be acknowledged, however, that some of the key issues discussed in this chapter such as the increasingly closed and technical character of the discipline, its propensity to generate one-sided diagnoses and prescriptions that are insensitive to social context or to noneconomic variables, and the consequent tensions that can arise between the need to win democratic understanding and consent, and the need to satisfy professional economic standards of discourse and proof, tend to arise elsewhere too, and not just in Mexico.[10] Moreover it was not just in Mexico that what Peter Hall has called "the Keynesian policy paradigm" collapsed in the early 1980s, thereby opening the way for so-called third order change in economic policy-making, involving the wholesale substitution of a broadly neoliberal framework of interpretations and prescriptions.[11] However, for several reasons these issues arise in a more acute form in Mexico than in developed market economies. The Mexican dominant party regime of the time was more authoritarian, the general level of citizen education and understanding was lower, and the divorce between the Mexican social context and the tacit assumptions built into most models of market behavior was more extreme. Also, as the economics profession has developed in Mexico under strong external tutelage it has advanced much more rapidly in the production of economic policy managers and analysts who focus on the *conjuntura* rather than on the realms of economic theory or doctrine.

One of the features of both apolitical *técnicos* and the more politically empowered "technocrats" or "techno-bureaucrats" is that they tend to apply, with great authority and self-confidence, ideas they have derived at second-hand and without drawing on a strong local tradition of theoretical elaboration or debate. For many years, until the mid-1980s the history of economic thought in Mexico was dominated by a dogmatic type of Marxist economics in no way linked to the policy concerns of the economic managers in power. With the collapse of the Soviet bloc, and the decline of state autonomy in the 1980s, Mexico's economic *técnicos* were freed from even these elements of professional critique and competition. Without state patronage, the statist wing of the profession atrophied very quickly.

Miguel Centeno constructed an analysis of the development of the economic technocrats in Mexico, which enables us to identify the break in continuity that occurred during the 1970s. Up until the death in 1970 of Rodrigo Gómez, the long-term head of the Bank of Mexico, government economic expertise was concentrated under his supervision. President Echeverría disrupted this line of continuity, and after the foundation of the *Secretaría de Programación y Presupuesto* (SPP) by his successor at the end of 1976, an alternative institutional base emerged. By 1983, 66 percent of the SPP personnel traced by Centeno had economics degrees, as compared with 36 percent in the Finance Ministry, and 21 percent in *Gobernación*.[12] Centeno adds a highly significant (and controversial) qualification to this finding. Accordingly to him "it would be incorrect to assume a functional relationship between such expertise and empowerment. The government did not necessarily need economists to make policy. Rather, a cohesive group inside the state first established their dominance and *then* utilized supposedly meritocratic criteria to benefit those with whom they shared key attributes."[13]

On this view, then, the rise of the economic technocrats was not mainly attributable to their condition as possessors of economic expertise, but rather to their other—class, education, family network—characteristics. Centeno overstates his argument here because, although nontechnical considerations were certainly important, over the past twenty years successive Mexican governments have confronted extremely complex economic dilemmas that many potential candidates for power were incapable of evaluating at an adequate level of precision. This is why the *Gabinete Económico* rose to preeminence in the decision-making apparatus of the federal government in the 1980s, and why a substantial level of economic competence became a prerequisite for participating in its deliberations.

Nevertheless, if we review the family and educational background of the key economic decision-makers in Mexico in the 1980s and 1990s, it is not just academic training that seems to matter, but also ancestry and network connections. For example, the leader of the radical statist faction within the regime prior to the 1982 debt crisis was Carlos Tello Macías, son of Manuel Tello, who was Foreign Minister in 1958–1965. Carlos Tello's father-in-law was the grandson of the dictator Porfírio Díaz, and his brother followed in his father's footsteps by becoming Foreign Minister under Salinas. His radicalism derived from his connections with the well-heeled student revolutionaries of the 1960s (particularly Rolando Cordera). Although Miguel de la Madrid studied public administration rather than economics when at Harvard, his thesis for the law school at UNAM was on the economic ideas behind the 1857 constitution, and from 1953 onward his career was mainly in the public banking sector.

The key economic policy-maker from 1982 to 1986 was Jesús Silva Herzog Flores. He was the UNAM-trained son of the distinguished nationalist cofounder of the ENE and under-secretary of Finance. Between 1956 and 1964 he worked as an economist in the research department of the Bank of Mexico and subsequently served as a sometime economics professor at the *Colegio de México*. He was also—of particular importance after 1982—a personal friend of US Federal Reserve Board Chairman Paul Volcker. The presidential ambitions of Silva Herzog Jr. were thwarted in mid-1986 when he was outmaneuvered by his rival for the succession, Budget Secretary Carlos Salinas de Gortari, himself the son of Raúl Salinas Lozano, the former Minister for Trade and Industry (1958–1964), who had studied economics at UNAM in the 1940s. Although Carlos Salinas is now seen as an economic technocrat there is little economic content in his U.S. doctoral thesis about peasant producer organizations. At first his rivals in the bureaucracy dismissed him as another lawyer lacking economic expertise, but in 1980 he took on Armando Labra and won an argument in the *Colegio de Economistas*.

Prior to the debt crisis, from April 1982 right up to the Tequila Crisis, the director of the Bank of Mexico was Miguel Mancera Aguayo, a Yale graduate and son of Rafael Mancera Ortíz, an accountant by training who had served several terms as a deputy minister of finance. The only interruption to Mancera's tenure was a brief three-month interlude in 1982, after the bank nationalization, when Carlos Tello Macías struggled with the thankless legacy of resource rationing decisions that followed the debt moratorium. In academic terms the main effect of this incident was to eclipse the previously influential Keynesian scholars associated with the Department of Applied Economics at Cambridge in Britain, and therefore to leave the U.S. Ivy League schools in virtually sole possession of the entire field of Mexican economics.[14] The 1980s Director-General of the state oil monopoly, *Petroleos Mexicanos* (PEMEX), was Mario Ramón Beteta, nephew of Ramón Beteta, an early Professor of the National School of Economics, who became Treasury Secretary in the late 1940s. He was also the son of General Ignacio Beteta, the head of presidential security in the 1930s, which indicates the extent to which technical training and family ties were entangled with other types of political responsibility. During the 1990s, the head of PEMEX was Adrián Lajous who studied economics in the 1970s under Joan Robinson at Cambridge, and who was initially identified with the statist wing of Mexican economics, but who successfully advanced inside the oil industry in the 1980s and 1990s.

These biographical sketches are extremely superficial, and fall far short of either explaining the policy choices of the individuals described or illuminating the extent to which their political influence was bolstered by their educational or technical skills in the field of economics. They are included here merely as illustration of the points being made by those who write of the rise of the "economic technocrats" in contemporary Mexico. It will be seen that a large number of key political appointments have more recently fallen under this rubric. This is in contrast with earlier periods in Mexican political history when military experience was the touchstone for high office until 1946; or between the Second World War and the 1976 devaluation, when general legal and political management skills were at a premium. It may also turn out to be in contrast to career profiles of those now rising to prominence following Mexico's recent transition to genuinely competitive electoral politics.

Before turning to the relationship between the economics profession and the rise of the economic technocrats in Mexico, it will be useful to take a quick glance at the South, to assess the degree to which these Mexican developments reflect a more general Latin America-wide pattern.

IV. Comparisons

It was not only in Mexico that analysts referred to the "rise of the technocrat" during the 1960s. The military regimes established in most of South America between the mid-1960s and the early 1970s needed economic expertise to legitimate their power seizures, and to strengthen their ties with the international investment community. The best example is probably the Brazilian military regime (1964–1985). The comparisons and contrasts between Brazil and Mexico with regard to the status and orientation of the economics profession would be worth pursuing further,[15] not least because in Brazil (though not yet in Mexico) the transition to a liberal democratic system of political representation has significantly affected the career paths and self-images of these engaged in the dismal science. It would also be worth considering broader comparisons, for example with Argentina and Chile, where the influence of Prebisch and the UN Economic Commission for Latin America (ECLAC) was strongest and where the Chicago school produced its greatest impact, or with Colombia where a competitive oligarchic democracy spawned a rather more pluralist yet high quality community of local economists and economic policy-makers.

Comparisons between Mexico and other developing countries are always fraught with difficulty, and in this chapter it is hard enough to discuss Mexico convincingly without taking on further problems. The purpose of this section is not to attempt an impossible assignment,[16] but merely to warn against the assumption that superficial resemblances or journalistic labels express deep underlying identities. For example, there persists a French and Positivist tradition within Brazilian intellectual history that includes Brazilian economics, a current that disappeared from Mexico with the eclipse of Limantour. U.S. academic discourse is not so hegemonic in South America as it is in Mexico, and heterodoxy was not routed as early, or as thoroughly, in the aftermath of the 1982 debt crisis. The structural characteristics of the South American economies include some features that are absent in Mexico—a more extensive history of wage and price indexation, for example, and greater scope for regional integration between Latin American neighbors (as opposed to Mexico's asymmetrical integration in the North American Free Trade Agreement (NAFTA)).

This may reflect a political science bias, but it seems that what is most important is the contrast between the durability and capacity for co-optation of the regime of the *Partido Revolucionario Institucional* (PRI) in Mexico, and the instability of politics—and academic and professional career structures—in most South American countries. It would appear that Mexican social science operates with a shared set of tacit assumptions about what it is in one's career interest to investigate, and what topics and/or approaches are likely to attract official hostility. These assumptions are quite widely understood, stable over time, and periodically confirmed by dramatic examples of promotion or demotion. State vigilance is therefore quite effective in setting the agenda for not just policy, but also academic debate, and stimulating new fields of enquiry in both and rendering others marginal. By contrast, in most South American countries it is much more of a lottery as to which approaches will be rewarded or penalized, and both universities and research centers have often learnt to live with a condition approximating Trotsky's vision of a "permanent revolution." In these latter circumstances professional careers are more frequently interrupted by political or institutional upheavals (and even bouts of exile), but state authorities are typically much less effective in molding the agenda of debate. Different cohorts of scholars establish different support networks that encourage more diversity of methods and perspectives—although, unfortunately, the result is sometimes just outright academic warfare over a diminutive and unstable system of spoils. Whereas in Mexico it is nearly always sound career advice to avoid head-on confrontation with those in authority, and to cultivate a degree of ambiguity, in Chile or in Argentina it has sometimes been far more rewarding to mount a high profile challenge, or to establish a reputation as the standard bearer of a controversial position.

To give some examples, Domingo Cavallo was as entitled to the designation "economic technocrat" as any member of the Salinas *Gabinete Económico*, but it is difficult to imagine his style of operating being transferred from Argentina to Mexico. There is no Mexican counterpart to Delfim Netto: when Ortíz Mena served successive Mexican presidents it was as the custodian of stability and not the active author of transformative "miracles." The "Chicago Boys" of pre-1982 Chile were doctrinaire neoliberals at the service of an implacable dictatorship, and were constantly resisted by an equally competent and cohesive team of "CIEPLAN monks"[17] quite unlike the opportunistic and politically manipulative network of PRI insiders who captured the designation as "the neoliberal technocrats" of Mexico. These marked contrasts between those labeled the economic technocrats in differences systems both produced and reflected substantial differences in the character of the respective economic professions. With this sketchy digression concluded, we will now go on to consider the economics profession in Mexico.

V. The Profession

All over Latin America—Mexico included—the rise to power of economic technocrats produced strong repercussions throughout the new profession. On the one hand, it stimulated an influx of very able new recruits, attracted by the extremely favorable career prospects associated with the possession of this powerful new type of expertise. The career came to offer not just a high income and social prestige, but the prospect of international travel and indeed even for some a shortcut to political power. Moreover, a feature of particular importance, given the nature of PRI politics, in Mexico economic expertise seemed to offer a "clean" way to tackle the perplexing and often distressing problems of underdevelopment that disfigured Mexican society. On the other hand, and above all in Mexico, the career leapt to prominence so quickly that the incipient local resources and traditions were overwhelmed. Moreover, the accretions of power attached to the claim of economic expertise have been so great that arguably the development of the profession was distorted and politicized. In the absence of a strong preexisting community of scholars or a dense community of economically literate consumers it has been tempting for newly minted economists to vault from ignorance to the status of *iluminados*, who feel unconstrained by the critical judgments of the ignorant people around them.[18]

Since the 1970s, the best shortcut to this desirable status was a postgraduate qualification from a favored U.S. university. With this credential one would be insulated from most of the cross-pressures afflicting others in the Mexican bureaucracy or in the academic world. One could hope to enter a charmed circle—a self-protection society of *cognoscenti*—with privileged access not just to bureaucratic positions, but also to well-paid employment in the increasingly autonomous private sector, particularly the flourishing banking community. As a consequence, some have suggested that in the 1980s, Mexican economics became essentially an arena for competition between alternative U.S.-based academic networks, none of which were particularly closely tailored to the problems confronting the Mexican economy. Local traditions of expertise and indigenous perspectives were sidelined or forgotten.[19] Prior to the student rebellion of 1968, the primary establishment promoting the development of economics in Mexico was UNAM, which began this work in 1929, and enjoyed much official sponsorship and encouragement in the 1940s and 1950s. In 1934, Daniel Cosío Villegas founded *El Trimestre Económico*, which from 1937 onward was published by the state-backed *Fondo de Cultura Económica* (FCE), particularly after the arrival of a cohort of Spanish intellectual *emigrés* who sparked Mexican interest in European academic debates. *El Trimestre* became a major vehicle for generating awareness of economic ideas throughout Latin America. Until the 1970s it was much concerned with publishing Spanish translations of leading articles from the international economic community.[20] During this period a few Mexican economists began making contributions to the international debate on development, which were taken up elsewhere in Latin America.[21]

The 1960s saw the culmination of this effort at inward-directed and state sponsored professional development. But after 1968 the situation was radically changed. A much more politically assertive and intellectually radical generation came to the fore in UNAM, just as the university lost its intellectual hegemony and its capacity to sustain professional standards of training, recruitment, and publication. Under Echeverría's patrimony minister, Horacio Flores de la Peña, this more radical generation enjoyed their brief tenure in the sun, but their rapid ascent and their policy mistakes provoked the emergence of rival centers of training and research that would soon overshadow them. Until 1982 UNAM economics preserved a foothold in the internal debate by embracing the "post-Keynesian" doctrines being propagated from Cambridge in England. But after 1982 the possession of a UNAM (or even, for a while, a British Cambridge) qualification became a handicap rather than an asset within the Mexican economics profession. The UNAM faculty responded by publishing ever more arcane and *recherché* work in the area of Marxist economic theory, a line of thought that more or less petered out with the collapse of the Soviet Union. Their journal, *Investigaciones Económicas*, combined exquisite exegesis of the theory of surplus value with lamentably ill-argued condemnations of Mexican capitalism and its crisis.

The *Colegio de México* remained an elite institution with a broad social science base that might perhaps have compensated for the eclipse of UNAM. It certainly sponsored some very high quality work, in particular on areas of Mexican political economy, notably demography and urbanization. On the whole, however, it steered away from the more controversial and politicized debates over the central issues of Mexico's economic strategy, and its economists concentrated on maintaining technical standards, perhaps to the detriment of policy relevance.[22]

By the 1980s the initiative had passed from these long-established and domestically rooted institutions to newer elite centers of training and research, such as the *Instituto Tecnológico Autónomo de México* (ITAM) and the *Tecnológico de Monterrey*, which drew their inspiration directly from the U.S. academic community and regarded Mexico's indigenous economic traditions as outmoded. It was symptomatic that the highly selected students entering these establishments were more likely to come from business elite backgrounds, and expected to read their English language economics in the original. Thus, the *Trimestre* and the *Fondo* lost a key sector of their old readership as the new establishments plugged their students directly into mainstream U.S. economics.

Of course there were also countercurrents. In particular, the *Banco de Comercio Exterior* managed to sustain a relatively large readership for good quality policy-relevant economic analysis in the pages of its monthly *Comercio Exterior*. The pluralism and seriousness of this publication is notable, particularly because although sponsored by a public institution it never succumbed to political censorship or *oficialista* orthodoxy. This was in marked contrast to the mixture of technical pretentiousness and *oficialista* servility that marked the pages of the privatized *Informe Mensual*. But if *Comercio Exterior* was an honorable exception, it could not conceal the generalized absence of economic literacy displayed by even the upper reaches of the Mexico City print media.

The influential weekly *Proceso* has never made much effort to present economic issues to its readership, nor has this been a priority for the prestigious monthlies *Nexos* and *Vuelta*, at least until recently. Anyone who tries to follow an argument in the economic pages of *Excelsior* or *El Universal* will often find it hopelessly garbled. Even the specialist and sometimes very instructive daily *El Financiero* contains a disconcertingly high quota of howlers that suggest that neither its writers nor its readership are exercising sufficient critical vigilance. Only recently has the situation begun to improve, notably in the business pages of *Reforma*. Sarah Babb detected some changes, as follows: "Today [2001] Mexico seems to be a country that is saturated in foreign-trained economic experts, some of whom are interested in bringing their views from the halls of academe to a more public forum. Elite discourse in Mexico has a long tradition of 'public intellectuals,' whose literary fame and political involvements qualify them to speak authoritatively on a range of issues, from democracy to development to cultural affairs. More recently, however, a new sort of expert has appeared on the editorial pages of Mexican newspapers, the individual with a profound knowledge of a circumscribed topic (such as monetary policy), often with a degree from a prestigious U.S. university. The increased visibility of these experts has been promoted by the growth in a number of business-oriented publications, such as *El Economista*, *El Financiero*, and *Reforma*."[23] For the most part, however, the Mexican economics profession tends to operate in a vacuum, cut off from its historical roots, screened from critical feedback from the society, distorted by the power plays of the technocratic elite, and filtered through a "U.S. literature" that is poorly adjusted to Mexican realities.

VI. The "NeoLiberal" Ascendancy

No one in Mexico studies Hayek or von Mises, and few are interested in the ideas of Milton Friedman. So in one sense there is in Mexico no intellectual grounding for neoliberalism, as the doctrine is understood in Chile or more generally. A central feature of neoliberal theory that is strikingly absent from Mexican practice is the rejection of state "discretionality" in economic affairs. Despite Salinas, the state bureaucracy retains great allocative discretion (as with financial rescue packages). Yet, scholarly works on the economic reforms promoted by Carlos Salinas de Gortari and his erstwhile acolytes commonly use this catchphrase (Salinas himself preferred the characteristically ambiguous term "social liberalism"). Privatization, deregulation, state shrinking, financial and commercial liberalization, fiscal orthodoxy, central bank independence, monetary restraint, however one sums up this policy package, the Salinas team promoted it with energy and determination for a full decade after the oil price collapse and near default of 1985–1986. The inheritance of these reforms dominated the economic policy agenda of the Zedillo administration, and their critics and opponents remained ineffective and dispersed. This is what justifies the title phrase of this section. To explain this ascendancy I would highlight the following points.[24]

First, economic liberalism was nothing new in Mexico. It had a powerful institutional base in the financial sector, and had made a fairly successful accommodation with the PRI during the 1950s and 1960s. What changed in the 1980s was that Mexican neoliberals began to repudiate Mexican statism and even, to some extent, Mexican nationalism, and became more intellectually self-confident, and more outwardly oriented. These changes took time, they built up cumulatively on a variety of fronts, and they were consecrated by successive crises. However, by the end of the 1980s the landscape of Mexican economics had undergone a profound transformation as compared to a decade earlier.

Second, the rise of "neoliberalism" was promoted initially by the collapse (through internal dissension and demoralization) of its traditional counterweight: statist and nationalist approaches lost what Tello had called *la disputa por la nación*. This may have been due more to their own failings and contradictions than any overwhelming offensive by their rivals. By the time Tello himself relinquished his post as director of the Bank of Mexico, it was becoming clear, even to his own side, that further interventionism was politically and economically unviable, and that some kind of at least temporary and partial retreat was unavoidable. At the time, it was still just possible to believe that this could be a case of *reculer pour mieux sauter*, but when oil prices collapsed again in 1985–1986 this was no longer credible. This explains why the *Gabinete Económico* remained cohesive and proved capable of pushing ahead with a deepening of the reform process in the wake of the economic crisis of 1985–1986. If the economic statists had retained some degree of cohesion and self-confidence they might have been in a position to argue that the liberal reformers had had their chance, and had undertaken their program of reforms between 1982 and 1985 with disastrous results. On that basis they could have pressed for a mid-term course correction, a zigzag back from the market-liberalizing policies of the early 1980s. But in practice they were mute, and this cleared the way for a much more ambitious and far-reaching loosely "neoliberal" strategy of reform. It is not as though the political and social balance of forces in Mexico ensured this outcome: on the contrary, nationalist and leftist forces retained sufficient political strength to sustain the first really deep split in the ruling party, followed by a serious electoral challenge in 1988. After 1994 the submerged opposition of broad sectors of Mexican society toward the neoliberal project resurfaced in various disconcerting ways. But neither the political nor the social opposition had coherent economic leadership. So what has emerged in recent years, especially under the new conditions created by genuine electoral competition, is not so much a direct frontal challenge to neoliberal economics in the domain of ideas and professional expertise, but rather a diminution of its policy ascendancy, and the marginalization of some of its key personnel, given the often lukewarm public reaction to their ideas, and indeed, because of the political advantages that can be obtained from launching rhetorical attacks against them. In key parts of the state apparatus, such as the *Banco de México*, however, they remain well entrenched and sheltered from much public accountability.

Third, there is good reason to argue that this disintegration of the intellectual opposition to neoliberal reform reflected more than just the irresolution or analytical failings of the statist economists. It expressed the "crisis of the inward-looking model of development" that Mexico had pursued since the 1930s. That crisis was not peculiar to Mexico, and it could not be wished away by the economic analyst, however talented. In order for those who lost this political battle to preserve some intellectual capital to return to the policy-making arena later on, they would have needed to undertake a considerable amount of rethinking, self-criticism, and retooling. But this is not what they were encouraged to do by the Mexican system of co-optation and control. If they were not willing to switch camps the Mexican system tended to sideline or purge them. This is, for example, what happened at the *Centro de Investigación y Docencia Económica* (CIDE) in the early 1980s, where a talented team of anti-neoliberals was dispersed. It is instructive to contrast the fate of CIEPLAN, under the Chilean dictatorship—which was kept alive by the Ford Foundation and the

Christian Democratic Party (PDC), and nurtured until the final restoration of democracy—with the fate of CIDE, which was dependent only on Mexican state patronage, and identified as a focus of potentially dangerous dissent.

Fourth, the "conditionalities" associated with the restoration of international investor confidence in Mexico exerted some broad pressures in a generally liberalizing direction from the 1982 debt moratorium onward. However, it took some time for the requirements of the international financial markets to assume a clearly neoliberal form. This depended upon responses from within the Mexican ruling elite, as economic managers explored alternative avenues for re-engagement with the main sources of external capital. Later on the Salinas reforms created a powerful group of domestic vested interests pressing for their continuation, and capable of bearing down with great force on any within Mexico who threatened to reverse them. After the Brady debt deal and the opening salvoes in the NAFTA process, U.S. government and business influences came to play an active role in cementing this coalition and ensuring that it would persist even after the *salinato* came to an end. But this alliance acquired its solidity *after* the reform process had begun to produce its effects, and was a *result* rather than a *cause* of the neoliberal ascendancy in the state apparatus. It was held together more by self-interest than by commitment to any very precise economic ideology. It may therefore prove of uncertain value as a source of orientation in the future, given that the basic reforms are already in place, but their results are not seen as very satisfactory (a general theme returned to in subsequent chapters). Certainly, the first few years of the Fox administration proved to be highly disappointing from this standpoint, with a series of missed opportunities to enact further reforms (as in the energy sector and the tax system), which are widely perceived as contributing to the erosion of the competitive advantage of Mexico *vis-à-vis* rising powers such as China. In this respect, as in many others, Mexico still seems to be following a path that brackets it more with the rest of Latin America than with the more successful new economies of East Asia. The U.S.-educated, NAFTA oriented neoliberal generation of economists are therefore still vulnerable to challenge from counter-elites invoking alternative models of modernizing reform derived from elsewhere. In this case, it could be that China's success as a regime created from a revolution and seeking insertion in world markets on the basis of a home grown and hybrid political-economic model, will cast a shadow over the recent claims of the Mexican economics fraternity to be the exclusive proprietors of the one sound path to development.

VII. External Derivations

As noted above, certain economics departments in leading U.S. universities like Harvard, Yale, and of course, Chicago and the Massachusetts Institute of Technology (MIT), with their special links to ITAM were influential, and external Anglo-Saxon influences tended to overwhelm, or even at times to obliterate Mexican traditions of economic training and analysis that may have been more sensitive to local realities and peculiarities. Since this can easily be interpreted as a reductionist "intellectual dependency" argument some important qualifications are in order.

For one thing, there has long been a two-way flow between the Mexican economic establishment and the English-speaking academic world. Exiles (the old CIDE was not encouraged to continue practicing economics in Mexico City, for example) have had the opportunity to take up teaching posts in well-regarded U.S. institutions. Academic collaborations such as those between Brothers and Solís or Reynolds and Luisselli have clearly been intellectual partnerships as each stood to learn much from the other. It is patently clear, then, that the economics community in the United States offers not only high quality and depth of resources to its Mexican counterpart, but also breadth of outlook and openness to heterodoxy and innovation. The question at issue is how well equipped the Mexican academic establishment has been to take advantage of this range of potential benefits, and to what extent the policy preferences of the Mexican state, or even of the sectional interests of the *tecnócratas de turno*, have limited or distorted Mexican use of these resources. A more democratic and pluralist Mexico would probably have appropriated a wider range of international influences, and would have incorporated them differently.

This connects with another, perhaps more subjective, argument against reductionist dependency interpretations. Looking at a range of Mexican students in British and U.S. universities indicates that the socialization experience abroad is on the whole secondary to the constraints on beliefs and behavior encountered upon returning to Mexico. While studying at a foreign university and trying to succeed in a foreign language it is natural to try to adapt to the prevailing ethos and assumptions of the host institution. In the long run, however, most Mexican professionals know that their career advancement will depend upon how well they fit in to the situation they will encounter back home, and that opportunity structure remains heavily conditioned by Mexican presidentialism and by the hierarchical disciplines of the *camarilla* system and of bureaucratic politics.

For the most part, Mexican economists returning from the United States carry out rather little professional research beyond the work they undertook for their thesis, since career incentives seldom point strongly in an academic direction. As returning professionals reinsert themselves into Mexican career patterns they may well have to reconsider, and perhaps distance themselves from, some of the ideas they encountered abroad. That said, it remains significant that the economics profession in Mexico is so weak by comparison with the U.S. profession that trains its best students; and that both the scholarship program and the career structure established in Mexico to receive the returning economists is under such heavy and one-sided pressure to serve the requirements of the reigning technocratic elite. The hypothesis proposed here—it is no more than that, in the absence of independent evidence—is that these two features of the sending community significantly distort the pattern of exchange, and result in Mexico deriving less benefit from its investment in U.S. education than would be available to a more self-reliant and pluralist regime. Admittedly, this is pretty speculative, but perhaps more comparisons with Brazil would help test out the hypothesis.

If there was a serious and wide-ranging debate *within* Mexico about where the "neoliberal" economic strategy had gone astray, and what policy alternatives were now viable, then the U.S. academic community would likely be drawn into that discussion, and enrich it all round. But so long as the Mexican economics profession remains passive on this issue the only American voices likely to make themselves heard are those engaged with the promotion of the existing strategy. Just as there is widespread complicity within Mexico between the neoliberal technocrats and the economics profession that was swept along by official co-optation and control, so too in the United States, despite its greater pluralism, powerful interests are engaged on one side of the policy debate, and American economists are also not immune to predominant incentive structures. Of course, there are examples of criticisms directed at some aspects of Mexican economic policy by well-known U.S. economists. Rudiger Dornbusch attracted particular attention for his polemic with Pedro Aspe concerning the appropriate exchange rate policy in 1994. But these tend to be debates over tactics rather than strategy, and it is notable that very few U.S. economists would regard themselves as specialists in the problems of the Mexican economy.

Sarah Babb discusses the role of financial market disciplines in enforcing neoliberal policy convergence on Mexico in particular, and on Latin America in general, and notes the potential for countervailing pressure from the domestic electorate. Writing in 2001, her

verdict was that while "there is little doubt that Latin American countries are more subject to these sorts of financial pressures than their
European counterparts, the notion that Latin American governments
are less subject to the pressures of domestic electorates is more
controversial [. . .] The idea that Latin American technocracies are
compatible with democratic participation is supported by recent
scholarship on Chile [. . .] However, there are also some less optimistic signs. As we have seen, in Mexico, democratic transition promises to transform neither neoliberal policies nor the technocratic
profile of economic policy makers. One interpretation of these policy
continuities is that the electorate at large has endorsed the continuing
presence of foreign trained technocrats and the policies they prefer
[. . .] However, given the tremendous problems of social inequality
and social injustice that continue to plague the continent, it seems
more likely that economic policy is being placed beyond the reach of
democratic institutions."[25] The durability of such arrangements to
"insulate the technocrats" remains to be tested in Mexico, but this
formula has not proved very robust elsewhere in the region. To the
extent that the neoliberal imposition from above remains at risk from
popular backlash from below, this would seem to fit with the analytical
framework proposed in this volume as a key to regional distinctiveness.

VIII. The Authoritarian Style

Miguel Centeno has propounded a strong version of the argument
considered in this section: "The key to the technocratic revolution is
not necessarily the victory of a specific social or economic dogma," he
writes, "but rather the triumph of a world view that is linear, formal,
orthodox, and intransigent. We must understand this perspective not
as an ideology of answers or issues but as an ideology of method [. . .]
That is, what the elite shares is an epistemological rather than an economic ideology, an agreement about the source and nature of policy
knowledge not its actual content. *How* the technocrats thought was
more decisive than *what* they thought. The elite shares a cognitive
framework, a unique way of analysing social problems, formulating
solutions and implementing policy that limits the potential for public
participation and that inherently denies the inevitability of conflicting
social interests."[26] Centeno attributes the following "perfectly closed
logic" to those who have ruled Mexico since 1982: "we are the best
at what we do, therefore our policies are the best possible solutions
given present circumstances, therefore anyone who opposes them is
unrealistic and simply not worth listening to."[27] This logic also
absolved the technocrats from any moral responsibility for their

policies, he asserts: "Mexico was undergoing a process of modernization that was imposed by the reality of the international economy, and
there was no other choice but to continue."[28] His final flourish
perhaps reflects his background as a Cuban-American, the son of a top
official of the Castro regime in the 1960s: "the *tecnócratas* sounded
strikingly similar to another set of revolutionaries who also had
absolute confidence in their monopoly of the truth. Their economics
was capitalist, but their politics were Leninist."[29]

This is a bold thesis by a serious scholar, and so deserves consideration here. It dramatizes points made more circumspectly in the other
sections of this chapter. Anyone who is inclined to reject the argument
out of hand should first read the *Sexto Informe* of President Salinas,
delivered to the people of Mexico in October 1994. Nor was the
authoritarianism of the Salinas presidency confined to its public
discourse. One characteristic indicator of the persistence of executive
discretionality is the fact that whereas the *Gabinete Económico* met
57 times in 1993, the president only chose to convene it seven times
in 1994.[30] Salinas still had the means to open up or close down the
degree of debate over economic management issues according to his
convenience. His decision to close it down in 1994 must have helped
the Bank of Mexico to disguise the true state of the foreign exchange
reserves, until his departure from office precipitated a sudden awak-
ening to disagreeable realities.

Nevertheless, Mexican public policy styles have always been more
ambiguous than this one-sided account would suggest. The contrasts
with today's Leninist-capitalist Cuba are far stronger than the similarities. Presidential authoritarianism predates the rise of the *tecnócratas*
(the *Sexto Informe* of Díaz Ordáz in 1970 was quite as spine chilling
as that of 1994). And the scope for pluralism and serious technically
competent debate between rival schools of Mexican economists is far
greater then Centeno suggests. Moreover, the post-1982 technocrats
made a vital point when they asserted that the international economy
greatly constrained the range of viable options open to any responsible Mexican policy-maker. Although with hindsight it must be the
case that there were preferable alternatives to at least *some* of the
Mexican regime's recent economic policy choices, the country's margin
for maneuver was never very large, and in the absence of hindsight the
choices made were at least worthy of consideration. To enter a serious
economic debate it is not enough to oppose, or to invoke the cause of
one social group whose interests are opposed to those of another.
Rhetoric and voluntarism are no substitute for tough and well-
grounded economic analysis of the objective possibilities. Critics of
the *tecnócratas* have an obligation to face that challenge if there is to

be genuine economic debate in Mexico. If they *do* rise to the occasion it shall not be too hard for them to demonstrate from the record that past policies were not always the best possible solutions. Indeed, such critics could argue that those who committed mistakes have a moral responsibility to assume the consequences of their errors, to rectify the flaws in their analysis, and to participate in further economic debates in a correspondingly tolerant and modest manner.

But why claim that the potential exists for a responsible debate between rival schools of Mexican economists?[31] Admittedly much of the analysis has highlighted the impediments to such an outcome. Nevertheless, assuming Mexican democracy continues to advance, it may be possible to achieve a better level of responsible pluralism in economic analysis.

The attempt here has been to show that there is a longer and more respectable tradition of indigenous economic analysis than this new cohort of technocrats wished to recognize. Some intellectual pluralism can be constructed by revisiting this history. In particular, Manichean judgments about the failures of the 1970s require reconsideration in the light of the failures of the 1990s. This could readmit some lost or neglected talent in the arena of Mexican economic debate. (By this I do not mean that unrepentant statists shall be invited back to repeat their errors; rather *all* the competing contenders of the 1970s should be encouraged to reconsider their positions, and thereby contribute to the contemporary debate, as is to some extent recurring in democratic Chile.) It is not as though all pluralism of economic thought was stamped out, even under the *Salinato*. David Ibarra, for example, carried on doing serious work in the broadly *cepalista* tradition.[32]

Private consultancies such as *Economía Aplicada* have supplied rigorous critical commentary. The breadth of coverage of economic opinions in *Comercio Exterior* was noted above. Even the *Banamex* monthly review has become less dogmatic, and more cross-disciplinary.

The *Trimestre Económico* established an editorial review committee in 1986, and has subsequently achieved more consistently high standards, partly perhaps due to increased competition, for example from *Estudios Económicos*, published by the *Colegio de México*. Even the sorry experience of CIDE in the 1980s was not the whole story. In the 1990s, under the direction of Carlos Bazdresch, a serious effort was made to rehabilitate that center of economic and political research as an international standard scholarly institution and as an arena for serious investigation of controversial contemporary issues, and a journal, *Economía Mexicana*, was inaugurated. There may still be a strong undercurrent of official authoritarianism constraining the dynamism of Mexico's social sciences, but the power of the state has never been sufficient to crush independence of thought in the country, and future generations of Mexican scholars will not be entrapped easily within the anti-democratic cognitive framework Centeno claims to have identified. One way or another they are bound to question the results of "the best possible solutions" as they survey the country that not only the *salinistas*, but also the *zedillistas* and the *foxistas*, have bequeathed to them.

IX. Performance

One of the crucial arguments legitimizing the rising power of economic specialists, not only in Mexico but also in Latin America and indeed more generally, is that they can improve a country's economic performance. This proposition seems so obvious that it is seldom submitted to critical scrutiny. There is one version of it that does indeed seem highly probable, and for which Latin America provides considerable evidence. This is the idea that, in modern conditions, if those governing a country willfully disregard basic economic realities they can substantially reduce national economic performance not only in the short run but also more durably. On one reading of recent Mexican history, that is precisely what happened under the presidency of Luis Echeverría, and more arguably, under the presidency of José López Portillo. However, it should be remembered that both these leaders received conflicting advice from apparently well-qualified professionals. Echeverría's deficit spending binge in the early 1970s was certainly damaging, but it reflected some sophisticated economic analysis then in vogue in Mexico and elsewhere. Similarly, surprisingly orthodox experts initially endorsed the oil boom financed under López Portillo (including from the World Bank, some of whom went on to be highly regarded neoliberal technocrats and hastily buried the memories of such past misjudgments).

When López Portillo took the fateful decision in 1981 to reverse his earlier steps toward liberalization it was under the influence of an apparently authoritative group of post-Keynesian advisers. This is different from the case of, say, Alán García in Peru, who simply ignored expert opinion. Mexico's economic performance in the 1970s and early 1980s was certainly erratic and disappointing overall, but it remains open to debate how much this was due to ignorance of economic principles, and how much to deeper difficulties in the structure of Mexico's development model, difficulties that would have perplexed the most lucid of economic technocrats.

For about a decade after the debt moratorium of August 1982 these arguments in partial exculpation of the economic competence of the Echeverría and López Portillo teams would have been dismissed out of hand as special pleading by those wedded to a discredited version of economic analysis. With the hindsight of 1996, however, the time has perhaps come for a more evenhanded assessment. If the economic setbacks of 1976 and 1982 were mainly attributable to presidential ignorance and irresponsibility, what are we to make of the equally bad experience of 1995? Indeed, on many indicators Mexico's economic performance under the liberalizing *salinato* (1986–1996) was actually inferior to that under the interventionists.

It is, of course, still possible to argue not only that bad economic policies harm performance, but also that wise and expert ones enhance it. But this line of justification for Mexico's pro-market economic model now has to contend with the fact that between 1995 and 2005 per capita growth averaged just over 2 percent (no higher than the United States over the same period, despite all the hoopla about NAFTA), and there has been little progress on the equality front either. In the light of Salinas's economic achievements, it is now possible to reexamine the experiments of the 1970s in a somewhat more charitable light.

Worldwide, there is no obvious direct and single correlation between the distribution of economic expertise, or even the empowerment of economic technocrats, and superior economic performance. For many years Britain, and the United States more recently, had a disproportionate concentration of top-level academic talent in this field. But in the light of the relative international decline of these countries compared to say the Asian "Tigers," it may be that the distribution of such talent is a lagging indicator rather than a leading cause of economic dynamism. The quality of the economics profession in post-Maoist China is inevitably quite modest, although there have been rapid improvements in the last few years. The Chinese Communist Party is reluctant to allow such technical experts to escape from its overall political control, but the Chinese economy has performed far better than other economies that have been placed more directly under the control of the reputedly best-qualified economic experts in the world (the post-communist regimes of Eastern Europe, for example). So international comparisons tend to reinforce the case for skepticism about the ability of economic experts to transform a country's growth performance. If Mexico's economic technocrats cannot legitimate their accumulation of power in terms of the desired results that they alone can deliver, then it might be expected that they would come under pressure to scale back their pretensions and re-build their alliances with other interests and national sectors of opinion.

X. Conclusion: The Prospects

Immediately after President Zedillo took office in December 1994 the Mexican economy plunged into yet another of its post-sexennial downswings, and the Salinas-orchestrated euphoria about the brilliance of Mexico's neoliberal technocratic elite gave way to a further bout of demoralization. However, although many aspects of Mexico's social and institutional inheritance were subjected to searching reexamination, there was not much serious debate concerning the conduct of the nation's economic policies.[33] There are several possible explanations for this taboo: the incoming president and his economic team were too closely identified with this aspect of the predecessor's record to risk opening that debate; U.S. support for the new team depended upon a restoration of the "investor confidence" that had been created by Salinas's economic reforms, and to question those reforms would therefore—allegedly—have jeopardized U.S. support; in a climate of social tension, with debtors threatening to repudiate their obligations, and multiple other sources of insecurity, the Mexican private sector and the middle classes could defect from the regime altogether if it began questioning the interests created by the previous decade of market-liberalizing initiatives; neither the opposition parties, nor critics in the press, nor dissidents in the ruling party, were able to produce much of a practical and intellectually coherent alternative to the prevailing economic strategy. For the reasons discussed above, there were few outside the administration that were able to analyze the central issues clearly, let alone formulate alternatives. Those within the administration, or close enough to have hope of office, have seldom judged it expedient to be too directly critical of the ruling orthodoxies; and finally, perhaps, as the ruling technocratic elite apparently continued to believe, "there is no alternative," given the degree and character of the international integration to which Mexico is now committed.

In 1998, the seventeenth Assembly of the PRI rewrote the statutes of Mexico's then still dominant ruling party. In a vote against the official leadership the delegates resolved that in future only those with a decade of PRI membership, or a record of elected office, on a party slate, would be allowed to run as candidates for the presidency, state governorships, or the Senate. Under these rules none of the presidents elected since 1970 would have been eligible to stand, nor would any of their economics ministers. The result of the rule change was that such key economists in the Zedillo administration as Guillermo Ortíz and Herminio Blanco would only be eligible to stand as PRI candidates for the presidency in 2000 if they resigned from the cabinet and secured nomination and election in the 1997 mid-term congressional elections, a step that deprived the Zedillo administration of its main economic managers. The press described this resolution as a party "revolt against the technocrats," and undoubtedly marked a sharp break with the past. Whether it will produce a more democratic cohort of top economics managers remains to be seen. However, as this is not a policy paper, it does not espouse any particular diagnosis or course of action concerning Mexico's economic policy options. The focus has been rather on tracing how some Mexican economists rose to the positions of political supremacy, and how they have used that power. A major concern has been with the narrowness of the debates that guided their decisions, their lack of self-criticism in the face of unanticipated results, and their inability to connect with an informed public that might both generate social consent for, and also moderate, the policy excesses of the ruling caste. Those negative features were, of course, thrown into particularly sharp relief by the peso crisis of 1995, but they were equally troubling at the height of the *salinato*.

For all the increased pluralism and lively debate that has developed since the mid-1990s, the basics of economic policy remain largely beyond dispute. To the extent that democratization gradually expands public deliberation in this area, it may well be that the professional consensus established by the educators of Mexico's economic policy community will remain essentially U.S.-oriented. But, as Sarah Babb has insightfully observed, "although American visitors may still be impressed by the apparent familiarity of Mexico's most elite economics departments," the "institutional logic [. . .] under-girding Mexican economics remains radically different from that of its disciplinary counterpart in the United States [. . .] Mexican economics is still fundamentally guided by the logic and resources of the Mexican state—a very different base from that of American economics, which is fundamentally an academic profession."[34] Because of this underlying structural difference between the United States and Mexico we should not think in terms of simple convergence, and we cannot assume that the latecomers will always behave in the manner felt appropriate by their metropolitan mentors. Here is another example of why context matters, and why Latin America's distinctiveness requires systematic analysis.

Chapter 5

Privatization and the Public Interest: Partial Theories, Lopsided Outcomes*

I. Introduction

Throughout the twentieth century, if not before, Latin American governments have been searching for the right overall development strategy—one might even say philosophy of development—that would achieve accelerated economic growth, structural modernization, social integration, and a respected status among the advanced countries in the international community. As described in the first chapter of this volume, this search has given rise to a number of at least partially successful experiences of modernization "from above and without," but it has also encountered a succession of disappointments, with the result that successive initially popular development strategies enter into discredit and are then vigorously repudiated.

The recent, strong, region-wide drive in favor of "privatization" can be viewed as just the latest example of this underlying historical pattern. Privatization is an umbrella term used to refer to many discrete reforms, and it has often been driven—or even captured—by quite specific, highly organized, interests. Nevertheless, it also has a broader ideational logic: it fits within a particular framework of Western "liberal" thought that is mainly, although not exclusively, economic in character. It derives a good part of its momentum and its appeal from the claim that it expresses the latest in "best practice," the most "modern" version of what has to be done to promote "good government" in the leading Western market democracies. As shown in chapter three, it has generated its own distinctive cohort of "experts"—real and supposed— whose influence derives from the strong external endorsements they are able to muster, and who, as a result, become characteristically overconfident and intolerant of dissent.

Although privatization in Latin America has been associated with state shrinking, it has actually required more forceful state-led initiatives imposed from above in order to override impediments to the latest model of transformative modernity once again. And as shown in chapter two, to achieve completion and social legitimization, systems of market regulation and stabilization and legal security are necessary to an extent that far transcends what Latin American state organizations have been able to accomplish. Although some of these reforms have evolved considerably in some of the more advanced economies of the region, overall the record is decidedly mixed and the prospects for their consolidation remains uncertain.

As privatization evolved from a visionary theory into visibly divisive and imperfect practice it conformed to the pattern indicated in chapter one, eliciting multiple forms of criticism and resistance. So it would not be uncharacteristic of Latin America if this most recent experiment ended up like others recorded here, superseded before it has become hegemonic, leaving in its wake another "littered landscape" of discarded but not wholly forgotten monuments—state enterprises, regulatory agencies, and floundering private monopolies—of the more distant as well as recent past.

From this standpoint, the current wave of privatization initiatives deserves to be situated within the broader context of Latin America's long independent history of externally driven attempts at economic liberalization, offset by internal disputes over the scope and content of market reforms. It should be recalled that the international liberalism of the 1870–1914 period was increasingly rejected in the interwar years, and displaced by inward-looking strategies that became prevalent by mid-twentieth century. In the 1960s and 1970s there was division over whether these by then languishing strategies should be "deepened" in an increasingly state-dominated and potentially socialist direction (although anti-Communist regimes such as the Brazilian military might also favor "deepening" on nationalist grounds), or reversed. Following the 1982 debt crisis and the global discrediting of central planning, the 1990s witnessed the emergence of a strong and broad-based consensus around a liberal and outward-oriented development strategy, sometimes referred to in short-hand as "neoliberalism" or the "Washington Consensus."

Privatization or divestiture of state assets has been central to this model. It can perform a variety of strategic functions such as creating new management incentives, enhancing competition, relieving fiscal burdens, eliminating subsidies and price distortions, attracting flight capital back, or drawing in new multinational investors, strengthening local capital markets, providing reliable assets for privatized pensions schemes, funding huge, otherwise unaffordable, capital investment programs, and more generally, signaling an irreversible commitment to the prevailing philosophy of development. It is best to understand privatization as an integral component of a broader liberalization process, rather than narrowly and in isolation. However, the different components of such a broad process do not invariably fit harmoniously together. In a context where reforms from "above and without" are often left half finished, privatization unaccompanied by other requisites of economic liberalization (including legal redress against insider abuse) can be hijacked by rent-seeking elites.[1] Where the "public interest" is inadequately protected, privatization can therefore replicate the vices that orthodox economists attribute solely to state enterprises. So it is important to keep in mind the longer term historical context. If Latin America has now finally ended its search and settled on the right development strategy for the indefinite future, then privatization is a foundational element in the new order; but if the features that gave rise to disillusion with earlier development models have not been fully overcome, then the Latin American tradition of first promoting and then rescinding alternative patterns of property rights may continue to reassert itself.

At present, there does not appear to be much of a prospect for an early and major reversal in the privatization trend. The protests and even reversals in Argentina, Bolivia, Costa Rica, and Uruguay do not yet constitute a clear counter trend, and may not be sustained. Privatization might be slowed or redirected, but except in extreme situations it is unlikely to be frontally challenged, at least for some time yet. The most clear-cut and recurrent factor triggering the wave of privatization across the subcontinent has been the overstretched state of public finances and that impetus remains powerful throughout the region. In the absence of adequate tax revenues, government after government has been forced to recognize its incapacity to supply all the resources needed to finance public enterprise investment or to supply the goods and services demanded by citizens and consumers. Thus, privatization has swept the subcontinent, not just as a source of short-term revenue enhancement but also as the only way to tap private capital markets and so pay for economic modernization. Whether it will ultimately clear the backlog of unmet demands remains to be seen, although the process has been underway long enough for some provisional judgments to be made. This chapter attempts such a preliminary review.

The first section defines the phenomenon under study (the boundaries of which are less clear-cut than one might suppose) and draws attention to the various issues of public interest that are not resolved merely by expressing a preference for privatization. The second section considers questions of timing and sequencing related to the alternative styles of privatization that have been undertaken, and the third offers a "snapshot" of the current scene, indicating where the momentum is still building up, and from where the main points of difficulty and resistance are emerging. The fourth section reviews a series of alternative theories of privatization, comparing each with the Latin American experience so far.[2] The conclusion returns an as yet open verdict on the relationship between privatization and the public interest, and on the prospects for an enduring pro-market policy consensus. Privatization theories seem to provide only partial and incomplete accounts of the story so far. They cannot tell us whether the current consensus necessarily represents an irreversible break with the past, particularly because prospective outcomes are often lopsided and imbalanced. On the other hand, the forces promoting privatization remain largely unabated and the alternatives are sketchy and unconvincing, so the present tide of pro-market reform almost certainly has further to run.

II. "Privatization" and "The Public Interest"

Privatization is a flexible term: it can be narrowly understood or it can be used to describe a wide-ranging series of phenomena. To illustrate the point, it is worth comparing the following definitions used by U.S. academics to describe the Latin American experience: one defines privatization as including "all types and increments of transfer of ownership, partial or complete, from the government to the private sector. Privatization also occurs when previously excluded persons or groups, such as foreigners or limited liability corporate entities, are re-categorized as 'eligible' private owners."[3] Another defines privatization as including "divestiture, the liquidation of uneconomic public enterprises, the conversion of government-owned ventures into mixed enterprises or joint ventures with private investors on the basis of market performance, the contracting out of management or subsidiary operations, and the requirement that parastatal managers meet ordinary standards of profitability in discharging their functions."[4] Add to this a third formulation by a leading analyst of privatization in Britain: "The privatisation programme [. . .] was a much broader policy than asset sales, involving a host of measures including the withdrawal of industrial aid, deregulation, and franchising. The policy followed a number of phases, as did the emphasis on its intellectual justification. At first, the State withdrew aid and subsidies, radically pruning industrial policy as traditionally conceived [. . .] The next step was to increase competition in the State sector [. . .] The next phase concentrated more directly on ownership and the transfer of public assets to the private sector [. . .] In addition, there were a number of other variants of the new competition policy. These included the contracting-out of services traditionally performed by State organizations (such as dustbin collection and health service laundry) as well as more ambitious franchising arrangements. Thus, what started out as a relatively well-defined policy came to be directed towards the achievement of other objectives which sometimes conflicted with competition."[5]

Each of these three definitions has its advantages, but their boundaries and focus differ substantially. It is therefore important to be alert to these variations when using the term. The first definition is the narrowest. It is concerned only with ownership transfer, and explicitly disavows the "privatization of management" in the absence of ownership change. Although it acknowledges complexity, and posits a continuum rather than a dichotomy, it takes as given a set of legal categories such as "state" ownership and "private" ownership, which other analysts have viewed as contested and problematic. For example, if the Honduran military pension fund owns strategic productive assets, is that adequately characterized as state ownership? If shares in Bolivian state enterprises are transferred to collective pension funds administered by private foreign financial managers is that a shift into "private" ownership in the same sense as quoting share of *Yacimientos Petrolíferos Fiscales Bolivianos* (YPFB) on the New York Stock Exchange after the Bolivian government changed the pension contract?[6] If so, what are the rights of the ultimate owners? In 1998, Bolivian pensioners proved bereft of legal protection when their government unilaterally changed the pension contract. Thus, the first definition has the advantage of being empirically observable, but there is room for doubt as to the true meaning of what is thereby observed.

The second definition, offered by Glade, apparently includes everything covered by the first, given by Armijo, but adds two further elements that considerably redefine the issues. If an enterprise can be privatized through *liquidation*, then we need to pay much more attention to bankruptcy procedures and to the residual claims of the various creditors and stakeholders. If privatization can include some continuation of state ownership, moderated by the requirement that enterprise managers are subject to market disciplines, then at least some of the public enterprises operating in Latin America before 1982 would have to be classified as privatized (the *Petroleos de Venezuela* (PDVSA) after the Venezuelan oil nationalization of 1976, or the

Puerto Rican Telephone Company between 1973 and 1998, when it was finally "privatized" in the sense posited by Armijo).

Acknowledging the "strikingly entrepreneurial behavior" of the Venezuelan state petroleum company, Glade describes this as "a form of simulated privatization when managers of state-owned enterprises must conform to the behavioral constraints applied by the market to private firms."[7] Glade's definition invites further consideration of various aspects of the "public interest" (like those concerning bankruptcy, or the social behavior of market-oriented management), assessed in the fourth section below. He also stresses the points that privatization must be seen as part of a broader package of market-oriented policies, and that its effects must be evaluated in terms of the general signals it transmits as well as the specific economic results it delivers. But his analysis is structured around the dichotomy conveyed in his title and he therefore tends to assume that the broad thrust of current policy is both positive and irreversible.

The third definition or evaluation, by Dieter Helm, follows Glade on some key points, but includes various qualifications downplayed by the latter. In this instance privatization is viewed as a broad policy orientation with an initial pro-market theoretical foundation that fails to account for successive policy applications and variations. Privatization is not necessarily pro-competitive. It may be distorted to serve political necessity (as Armijo notes, albeit in a reductionist manner), or it can involve the redistribution of social power against welfare dependants and organized labor, points discussed below as they redirect our attention to key aspects of the "public interest."

This chapter adopts the more wide-ranging view of privatization. It is an umbrella term, encompassing a number of subcategories and national variations. As it has grown in popularity over the past twenty years, the term has also been extended in scope so that it can now be used to include social security and welfare provision,[8] and even a range of government services in addition to directly productive activities. Considering Latin America's superabundance of relatively untouched or only locally appropriated natural resources, it is also essential to include here hotly resisted attempts to privatize what Anthony Hall, referring to Amazonia, depicts as the "commons."[9] Even prisons and police forces may be contracted out to private suppliers, though not— at least as yet—the legislative or judicial functions of the state. At the same time, as the term has been inflated, broader changes in economic ideology and organization have also taken place so that the policy significance of any particular measure of privatization must be assessed in a specific policy context. In one setting the main objective might be to reduce fiscal subsidies or strengthen management incentives; in another the rationale could be the elimination of vestiges of state socialism, or attracting modern technology and direct foreign investment. Privatization may be a central pillar of economic strategy in one context, and in another simply one alternative option within a market-oriented reform program. What gives this disparate range of possibilities some underlying unity is not so much a precise or technical meaning, as a prevailing pro-market, internationally oriented mood in favor of liberalization—the *zeitgeist* is as powerful as calculated choice. What matters from a public interest perspective is precisely how this general orientation works out in particular contexts. This means further distinctions are necessary.

First, privatization has different implications when applied to a natural monopoly than to a competitive industry. Its significance varies when the product is in relatively fixed supply (such as water) or when the product is in headlong expansion (like telecommunications). Two examples illustrate this point. The Chilean Water Code of 1981 is widely regarded as a pioneering initiative in privatizing water rights. It set up a legal framework for the free trading of water rights, transferring oversight from administrative agencies to the judicial system and leaving the rest to private initiative. It has been generally interpreted as a faithful application of the theories of the "Chicago" school to one particular conflictive area of public policy, and regarded as a vindication of those theories. However, this understanding has not been based on careful examination of the experience on the ground. A recent study of the rural water system by Carl Bauer, which seeks to rectify that deficiency, found that in practice the Code was something of a compromise aimed at accommodating traditional conservative and military interests rather than a wholehearted application of neoliberal theory. Although trading in water rights was introduced, little of it actually occurred. The really difficult issues involved sociopolitical conflict (between power companies that sought to store water in the summer in order to meet peak electricity demand in the winter, and irrigators who aimed to store water in the winter to meet agricultural demand in the summer). Neither the markets nor the Chilean judiciary were particularly well placed to resolve these disputes, as the 1998–1999 drought and power cuts in much of rural Chile showed.

More generally, Bauer argues that to "define property rights to natural resources simply as commodities tramples on difficult issues. Such property rights cannot be private, exclusive, and transferable, because different resource uses are physically inter-connected and people's activities directly and indirectly affect one another. New definitions of property rights affect not only their owners but also other resource owners and users. Thus property rights to nature affect collective interests, and consist partly of overlapping rights to use shared resources, rather than private freedom to alienate and exchange." Resolving water conflicts "requires qualitative measures and comparisons of value, and a qualitative logic to weight and choose among a web of rights, rules, purposes and interests. This again is an inherently judicial and political task for which private bargaining and exchange cannot substitute."[10] Bauer concludes that as competition for scarce water increases in Chile, the sclerotic and tradition-bound judicial system will need to be reformed. Public interest considerations will demand greater weight, and the market-determined allocation of private rights over water will have to be reformulated. Bauer's study refers only to the rural sector. And it should also be noted that in Santiago the municipally owned water utility has succeeded in balancing market constraints with social objectives to a greater extent than elsewhere in Latin America.[11]

A second example concerns telecom companies, which occupy pride of place in Latin America's new corporate rankings. According to the London *Financial Times*, 29 out of the region's top 100 companies, ranked by market capitalization as of September 30, 1998 were in this sector.[12] Topping the list was *Teléfonos de México* (TELMEX); fifth and sixth were the two São Paulo components of *Telecomunicações de São Paulo* (TELESP); seventh and tenth were the rival private telecom monopoly in Argentina, and fourteenth came *Telefónica de Chile* (CTC). However, the fact that private investors can buy and sell such shares on the stock exchange by no means tells the whole story about the scope and limits of private ownership in this most strategic and dynamic of industries. Even the old state-owned monopolies frequently released a proportion of their equity to the investor public. More important have been legislative changes to introduce competition and perhaps subject management to the possibility of challenge and even takeover. In Mexico the transformation was partly driven by the need to satisfy business demands on the US–Mexico border, and to cater for the explosive growth of international traffic,[13] while in the Dominican Republic the demands of the tourist industry were paramount. In any case, according to Noam, "once governments make the decision to liberalize markets and to permit multiple providers, they can organize domestic telecom markets to allow various amounts and types of competition. The licensing of operators can be used to limit the number of competitors and services and to impose obligations on providers. Licenses for spectrum access can be allocated according to specific use or assigned according to specific users. Once multiple providers are permitted in domestic markets, governments can restrict the extent of collaboration among competitors with limits on vertical and horizontal integration and separation of territories of operation. Foreign PTOs [Public Telephone Operators] [. . .] can be regulated as common carriers and required to meet minimum quality of service and investment criteria specified by the regulatory entity. Particularly important in developing countries with low teledensities is the mandate to strive for universal connectivity."[14] In sum, the world of privatized telecoms is about as far removed from laissez-faire as one could imagine. If we accept the stereotype that state interventionism encourages rent seeking and collusion, then privatization of this sector by itself can offer no guarantees that the public interest will be more honorably served. If possible at all, this can only be achieved through vigorous supervision provided by a well-structured and resourced system of regulation.

The issue of regulation arises in many guises, depending on the specific characteristics of each industry. The telecoms example is focused on here because of its quantitative importance, and its exemplary complexity and relevance to the public interest. But it is illustrative of broader patterns. When the Mexican government sold TELMEX between 1990 and 1994, the privatized enterprise was granted a domestic concession until 2026, and a monopoly on long-distance services until 1997. The largest shareholder, the Carso Group, was accused of acting as a front for the most powerful politicians responsible for the privatization, and the *Partido Revolucionario Institucional* (PRI) was almost universally perceived as having manipulated privatization to secure party and patronage benefits. In Venezuela, in 1991, "the government and the state telecom company, the *Compañía Anónima Nacional de Teléfonos de Venezuela* (CANTV), renegotiated the company's contract prior to the privatisation to ensure CANTV's monopoly for the first 9 years after its sale and its continued contribution to the National Treasury; this policy was supported by the major political parties in Venezuela."[15] The electorate later comprehensively repudiated Venezuela's traditional parties, as it judged them to have become irredeemably corrupted. In Argentina "the government increased tariffs prior to the sale of the *Empresa Nacional de Telecomunicaciones* (ENTEL) to increase the basic rates from which future increases would be calculated. Also, in Argentina, entrenched suppliers were able to secure continuance of existing contracts in order not to lose market share." Alejandra Herrera's study of the Argentine experience concluded that, "the post-privatization period in Argentina [was] inherently unstable because of the institutional weaknesses of the national telecom regulatory agency; the two regional monopolies [were] virtually unregulated. The agency [was] excluded from all major disputes among companies and between the companies and the government [after] privatization. The companies [used] the regulatory vacuum to their advantage to consolidate their position in the major service areas."[16]

Overall, Noam notes that "as a result of privatization, private monopolies, sometimes foreign-owned, have, in many countries, replaced the old state monopolies." Arguably this policy was necessary to provide sufficient incentive in the form of monopoly rents to promote high levels of investment and greatly expanded network coverage. Also, the policy contributed to the high price realized by the state for the privatizations. But a problem amply documented in the Noam volume is that adequate, consistent regulatory controls of private monopolies have yet to be instituted. Moreover, as part of the initial sale agreements, purchasers of telephone companies demanded policy changes that undercut many of the supposed benefits for the public of sector reorganization. Noam thus concludes that "governments [. . .] pledged to regulate private companies in a way that [would] expand and modernise the public network and eventually extend service to all who want it, but to date, [there is] little evidence that government officials have made the necessary political and financial commitments to create and to sustain credible regulatory agencies. In some cases, regulatory agencies were supposed to have been established prior to the sale of the state companies but either became entangled in domestic political disputes or, according to the cynical view, were purposefully not created and/or not funded in order to give the new owners a free hand."[17]

As in the case of water, Chilean telecoms privatization is seen as exemplary. It began earlier than elsewhere in Latin America and went further. It was based on laws barring monopoly and periods of exclusivity, authorizing international involvement, and promoting competition among equipment suppliers. Noam describes Chile as coming the closest in Latin America to developing an institutionally advanced federation of subnetworks, or what he calls a "pluralistic stage network."[18] However, while privatization resulted in a tremendous increase in the quality, variety, and quantity of services, it also exposed the problem of the institutional weakness of the regulatory regime: "Power is being transferred from executive and administrative action to the judiciary. This transfer has consequences for the government's ability to promote social objectives in the sector, particularly in the extension of services to rural areas and cross subsidies [. . .] there are many unresolved questions about the proper role of government and the means to achieve universal service and to structure competitive markets."[19] Once again, the Chilean judiciary appear as guardians of the rights of property, charged with screening the market from the interference of elected politicians. As in the case of water, it is questionable whether Chilean judges have the necessary skills and incentives to serve the overall long-run public interest in this dynamic area of the economy.

A third and final "public interest" point concerns the question of foreign ownership. Even with a complete transfer of operations to the private sector, governments often reserve the right to nationalize vital infrastructure to safeguard national sovereignty. Historic examples are found in Britain, Spain, and Sweden, or the United States, where "governments may place restrictions on the permissible level of foreign ownership of the telecommunications infrastructure [. . .]."[20] This quotation refers to telecoms but the point is more general. For example, laws concerning the U.S. merchant marine, ports, and harbors, and air traffic control systems all include national security protections. Yet many forces in favor of privatization in Latin America have been inclined to dismiss any such provision as an archaic residue of interventionism. Foreign advisers, in particular, should be pressed to explain why deregulation should go further in Latin America than in their own countries of origin.

Another area of U.S. law and practice that merits the attention of Latin American "privatizers" concerns the question of bankruptcy. As mentioned above, one key practical consequence of allowing free market forces greater scope is that some privatized enterprises may face liquidation. One of the most recurrent reasons why public ownership increased in Latin America in 1930–1980 was that governments were unwilling to allow large enterprises to be dismantled through bankruptcy and the forced disposal of assets. Whenever this prospect loomed the state tended to step in and take over the management and eventually even the ownership of the ailing enterprise. If privatization is truly to generate a fluid and efficient market economy in Latin America it will have to be accompanied by more frequent and much smoother processes of asset reallocation among qualified creditors.

It is as well to notice that U.S. practices in this regard are considerably more fluid than those found in Western Europe, as well as in Latin America. Whereas in Europe bankruptcy is a status meant to carry great stigma (Italian bankrupts lose their passports or even their right to leave their city of residence), bankruptcy in the United States is only considered a rather minor violation of the social contract. In Europe it is likely to be involuntary, and the result of a decision taken by one or more creditors, whereas in the United States it is almost always a voluntary choice, a decision taken by the insolvent debtor. European bankruptcy procedures have a bias toward immediate liquidation and prompt distribution to the creditors, whereas U.S. practice favors reorganization, with a multi-year stay on creditor demands. The consequence is said to be that Europeans are less willing to take on debt, whereas Americans are more entrepreneurial.

Latin American legal systems are generally so sluggish and overloaded that they would be unable to operate either of these systems reliably and on a large scale. But if privatization is to work in accordance with liberal expectations of an efficient market system, this is a further area of public policy that requires definition and reform. The choice between the alternative models of bankruptcy procedure is not a simple technical matter, but raises broad issues of public interest concerning the model of capitalism underlying privatization processes. As yet there is not much evidence about how Latin Americans intend to develop this aspect of the new economic model.[21]

III. Alternative Styles of Privatization: Timing and Sequencing

When, as in this chapter, privatization is viewed as a broad-gauge process embedded in a larger strategy (or even ideology) of market-oriented restructuring, then it becomes possible to identify a variety of alternative possible stages and trajectories. This section distinguishes between three alternative styles of privatization, each with its own specific rhythm and temporal sequence: *root-and-branch; incremental,* and *opportunistic.* The respective rhythms are *intense and sustained; gradual and measured;* and *erratic.* Actual examples are always somewhat hybrid, of course, but in Latin America the contrasts are sharp enough to illustrate these distinctions. Chile provides the prime example of a root-and-branch process; Brazil can be taken as an illustration of incrementalism; while the Venezuelan path has been highly erratic.

Root and Branch Privatization in Chile

The Pinochet dictatorship exercised unrestricted power for over sixteen years. It originated as a reaction to the socialism and statism of the preceding Allende administration. Its pro-market orientation was "root and branch" in the sense that it systematically aimed to strengthen and guarantee the private property system that had come close to suppression. In this context, "privatization" was only one element in a broader ideological program. The regime could work within a long time frame across a wide array of policy areas, deploying its concentrated power to produce a holistic transformation. Nevertheless, it was driven by a sense of urgency and its activities were intense as well as sustained. The military probably had a bias in favor of emergency measures, and the propertied classes had been unified by the Allende threat. In addition, Chile initiated privatization at a time when the regional and to some extent even the international climate was still against it, and the aim was not just to restore the *status quo ante* but also to consolidate an exemplary and irreversible new model of post-socialist enterprise and economic dynamism. In short, and in contrast to most other Latin American countries, the Chilean administrative apparatus was more capable of implementing a coherent and integrated program of national transformation.[22]

Even with this root-and-branch objective and a capacity to carry out policy in a sustained and intense manner, the privatization process was neither simple nor straightforward. Eduardo Silva distinguishes between three strongly contrasting phases, which he labels "gradual-ist," "radical," and "pragmatic." We have already mentioned the gap separating ideology from reality in the case of privatized water rights, and the problems of judicial oversight in the telecoms sector. As is well known, the state-owned copper company, the *Corporación del Cobre* (CODELCO), was never privatized but rather run in competition with new private mining investors by state managers who knew that 10 percent of their foreign exchange earnings had become earmarked revenue allocated directly to the armed forces. In the same national security spirit, when the state electricity monopoly, the *Empresa Nacional de Electricidad* (ENDESA), was privatized in the late 1980s, the military government insisted on spinning off the Colbún-Machicura dams as a separate state company that might provide some counterweight to private monopoly power. There were also fluctua-tions in policy over time. In particular, the most dogmatic phase of the Chilean program took place before the deep financial crisis of 1982. The new privatized banks plunged into insolvency at that time, and the Chilean taxpayer had to rescue them. Thereafter, the program was recalibrated and conducted in a more pragmatic and successful manner.

Incremental Privatization in Brazil

In conception, Brazilian incrementalism offers a clear contrast to Chilean maximalism. However, as the process has gathered momen-tum there have been certain signs of convergence. In Brazil, the pre-ceding state interventionist economic model was identified not with Marxism and a politicized labor movement but with statist nationalism and military rule. The model did not end in spectacular defeat but was eroded by a protracted crisis that still left many elements of its legacy looking viable and enjoying influential support. The post-military democratic regime was not initially much in favor of market-oriented reform. The 1988 Constitution contains many provisions that restrict domestic competition and an international economic orientation. Over the subsequent decade, however, attitudes toward economic liberalization became progressively more favorable, although the process of change was stepwise and incremental. Privatization began slowly, experienced a setback between 1992 and 1994, and gathered momentum thereafter as large inflows of foreign private capital became available. Following the *real* crisis of January 1999, pressures to accelerate the program of market-oriented reforms intensified, but resistance also increased given that the foreign appetite for Brazilian assets weakened and the terms available became less attractive. However, the long feared arrival in office of a PT-led administration under President Lula in 2003 did not precipitate the wholesale reversal of pro-market reforms that had been so widely anticipated by financial markets. On the contrary, while there were certainly some shifts in the regulatory framework that could trouble particular sectors, in broad terms the established policy thrust was maintained. Market strengthening policies are still advancing incrementally, accompanied by measures of "state-crafting" designed to counter the risks of an Argentine-style collapse.[23]

In contrast to the Chilean process, privatization in Brazil may be classified as "measured" in the sense that each step was taken as a distinct operation rather than arising from an overreaching commitment. There was time for lobbyists to bring their preferences to bear both for and against privatization, and the key decisions were subject to legislative and party political debate and oversight. In fact Brazilian democracy provides for multiple (possibly excessive) institutional veto points—legislative, judicial, electoral, administrative, and state and/or federal.[24] Nevertheless, it needs to be emphasized that over time and through a succession of discrete decisions the Brazilian government has ended up authorizing an interlocking set of market-oriented reforms, public enterprise divestitures, foreign investment incentives, and product and capital market liberalization, which may be cumulatively almost as transformative as the Chilean experience. The differences of conception, timing, and process may be greater than the variations in eventual outcome.

Erratic Opportunism in Venezuela

The erratic course of privatization in Venezuela illustrates a third possible style, with a different rhythm and probably also a very different outcome. In this case the preexisting system was a highly interventionist

and politicized electoral democracy structured around the distribution of rent derived from the state ownership of massive oil revenues.
As illustrated by the case of telecoms, there were some large-scale
privatizations in Venezuela in the 1990s. Indeed, the administration
of Carlos Andrés Pérez (1989–1992) might even be described as
starting out with ambitions for root-and-branch transformation along
the lines of the Chilean model. However, if this was the aim, it soon
encountered sufficient resistance not only to block such ambitions but
also to bring the entire political order into question. After President
Pérez was impeached, President Caldera was elected on an antiliberal
economic platform. Even so, in the wake of a massive crisis in the
financial system the pressures for a return to market-oriented reform
prompted a change of course.

But with the election to the presidency in December 1998 of
former coup leader, Colonel Hugo Chávez, Venezuela once against
departed from the prevailing regional norms of economic liberalization and market strengthening. Rather than working toward the
establishment of a functioning market economy, the controversial
"nationalism" of the regime and opposition to it has given rise to
political mobilization, with the emergence of two rival and polarized
blocs of opinion, and of a battle over control of the country's abundant oil revenues. These events and struggles are partly a reflection of
Venezuela's exceptional resource endowments and of a political economy tradition adjusted to its long experience as a rentier state. At present, it seems unlikely that the Bolivarian Republic will return to
a "Washington Consensus" anytime soon, but it is also difficult to
see how the Chávez experiment could be replicated elsewhere
in absence of huge oil resources. At a minimum, however, the
Venezuelan experience indicates that in Latin American conditions it
is possible for the logic of privatization to be blunted or even frus-
trated by domestic opposition; it is possible that the interests built up
around an alternative model of rentier politics are able to block cumulative advances in a market-oriented direction, even though the
consensus is purely negative and no coherent public interest alternative is available. If the main benefits of privatization arise from its
signaling a long-term commitment to market-related patterns of
allocative efficiency, then erratic, and potentially reversible, divestitures of state assets may fail to deliver such reassurance and may even
transmit the opposite message.

The three styles of privatization above in no way exhaust the range
of observable alternatives. Menem's Argentina, for example, presents
many features of the "root and branch" approach associated with
Chile, but it was the product of a constitutional government, subjected

to electoral constraints, and followed from a previous administration
that displayed a more unstable Venezuelan kind of evolution. The last
privatization of the Menem administration was of the *Correo
Argentino*, for which the local concessionary never paid the annual
royalty (due since 1999). In September 2001, the private holding
company filed for bankruptcy and eventually in November 2004 its
concession was revoked, meaning that in practice the Post Office was
re-nationalized. The Kirchner government has insisted (April 2005)
that this represents no precedent and that the Post Office will be
privatized by mid-year in any case. However, it has also set up *Energía
Argentina SA* (ENARSA), a new state oil company in the area previously occupied by YPF, and the privatized water and utility companies
are hemorrhaging cash because the rates they can charge have not
risen to reflect the new costs they have incurred. The present situation
in Argentina therefore remains undefined. In due course it will become
necessary to run these enterprises either for profit or for public service,
or perhaps some regulated mixture of the two. In the meantime, they
are de-capitalized and vulnerable to erratic policy lurches.

The Mexican process also contains several stages with different
prevailing styles, and the country's energy companies are only a little
better placed than their Argentine counterparts. They are not subject
to the same emergency conditions but they also need a financially
clear-cut framework within which to operate if they are to undertake
the long-term investments that their customers will in due course
require. At present they are in policy limbo. In Uruguay, incrementalism of the Brazilian type has proceeded even slower because of the provision that privatization can be overturned through popular plebiscites.
In Bolivia and Peru, extreme hyper-inflationary crises paved the way
for urgent root and branch transformations, whereas in Puerto Rico
the benefits of the U.S. dollar, the American legal system, and a generous flow of federal subsidies has meant that decisions to privatize are
adopted within a framework of normality rather than under the spur
of emergency conditions.

There appears to be at least as much variation in styles of privatization in Latin America as are found in post-Communist Eastern
Europe, if not more. The Treuhand in East Germany, charged with
dismantling state companies in the former German Democratic
Republic (DDR), certainly obeyed a very different logic from that of
the Hungarian Privatization Agency, or the Czech Voucher Scheme,
and Romanian policies seem almost as erratic as those of Venezuela.
The Ukraine offers yet another model of privatization wrought in the
midst of intense regional rivalries and in the absence of secure property rights. In this region, as in Latin America, lopsided policy

experiments are followed by sharp course corrections. Thus, the Czech voucher scheme failed to provide much legal protection for minority shareholders who were then mistreated, so that Prague later tried to introduce US-style securities regulation.

One additional observation is pertinent here. At least in Latin America, there are considerable analogies between the various styles and rhythms of privatization identified above, and the styles and rhythms of state interventionism that preceded them. An equivalent to Chilean "root and branch" privatization under dictatorship is Cuba after 1959 or Peru after 1968. A counterpart to the incrementalism of Brazilian privatization might be found in the progressive expansion of the Mexican public sector in the 1960s and 1970s. The erratic policy course recently exemplified by Venezuela resembles many earlier experiments in which state ownership was blocked or contested. Viewed from this perspective, perhaps the current upsurge of privatization initiatives in Latin America should be seen in a less unilinear manner: the range of privatization styles, rhythms, and eventual outcomes may prove as diverse as the preceding range of statist experiments. Indeed, differences are a product of the nature of state organization in each instance, and are therefore subject to the "configurative" context in which they occur. We lack the historical perspective needed to reach firm conclusions about the range of eventual privatization outcomes but these processes have now been underway long enough to permit some provisional or "snapshot" evaluations of the current scene.

IV. The Contemporary Scene: Momentum and Resistance

If one adopts a narrow definition of privatization as divestiture of state assets, there comes a point when not much is left to transfer to the private sector. Argentine under Menem disposed of most what could be sold and, tellingly, the last items on the list were the Post Office and the air traffic control system. There are some obvious hard cases, such as *Petroleos Mexicanos* (PEMEX), CODELCO, and PDVSA— but these are finite in number and may eventually be reduced to residual status. The pendulum would only swing into reverse if the remaining state enterprises started growing much more rapidly than their private competitors (if PDVSA or CODELCO, for example, developed large low cost reserves), or if another private sector crisis delivered a new cohort of insolvent enterprises whose losses the state was willing to socialize. Only PDVSA had much potential to follow the first route, and under the current Chávez administration

Venezuelan policy is headed in very much the opposite direction, with the disposal of the state enterprise's assets in the United States, and the reinforcement of Energy Ministry control over a much weakened and increasingly politicized management. As for the second alternative, the hypothesis is harder to assess, but the evidence from East Asia is that in the event of a massive private sector crisis, emerging market governments are placed under intense pressure to sell off assets cheap to multinational investors or, failing that, to liquidate failures. Certainly the 1995 peso bailout and the Mexican congressional debates over the *Fondo Bancario de Protección al Ahorro* (FOBAPROA) resulted in the wholesale transfer of the Mexican banking system from domestic to foreign private ownership (making it far harder to reverse bank privatization than if these had remained domestically owned enterprises). In the energy sector, for constitutional reasons it is proving almost impossible for a more divided Mexican political system either to privatize PEMEX and the electricity companies, or to re-capitalize them so that they can grow as viable public enterprises.

A broader definition of privatization, however, leaves a lot more to be done, and the relevant time horizon becomes far longer. To establish and routinize effective and predictable insolvency procedures is mainly a task for the next generation, for example. To generalize competitive markets so that all managements—private as well as public—can be ejected for failure to perform will take even longer, particularly in countries where family firms continue to operate in much the same as during the "old days" of state capitalism. To create authoritative, professional, accountable, and speedy systems of market regulation will also require much further work, as judicial legislative and media oversight remains weak or incipient in most countries. So if privatization is understood in these terms, the process is likely to take much longer and the momentum behind it is considerably more open to question.

This brings us to the actual or potential sources of resistance. With regard to divestiture, in most instances the nationalists and statists within the political elite have been marginalized or bought off.[25] Trade union opposition can still be found and may cause delays (the 41-day strike against the sell-off of Puerto Rico Telephone Company (PRTC) in 1999, and mass demonstrations in 2000 in defense of the *Instituto Costarricense de Electricidad* (ICE), which is responsible for telephony as well as power, is an example), but most state enterprises remain vulnerable to renewed privatization campaigns over the long run. In current conditions of high fiscal pressure, governments almost always have a strong financial incentive to override or compensate the most influential losers.[26] As international capital flows to emerging markets contracted in the wake of the Asian, Russian, and Brazilian crises, the Washington-based international financial institutions stepped up their pressure in favor of accelerated economic reforms as a condition for financial support, although on one issue—the abolition of all restrictions on short-term capital movements—they softened their stance.

Nevertheless, on a broader view of what constitutes a privatization process, and in light of trends at work in the international economy since the late 1990s, the signs of resistance seem to have grown. For example, on taking office the Chávez administration in Venezuela revoked a 38 percent rise in electricity charges authorized by the outgoing Caldera administration at the end of 1998, causing a one-third fall in the share price of *Electricidad de Caracas* (EDC). The telephone company CANTV feared that the government might also violate the terms of the contract drawn up during the 1991 privatization, which, as noted above, were politically controversial. Similarly the Brazilian Minister of Justice imposed a maximum fine of 2.9 million *reais* on each of the two major telephone companies for São Paulo and Rio, which had been privatized in July 1998, for providing inadequate services. In February 1999, during the hottest period of the summer vacation, half a million inhabitants of Buenos Aires were subjected to electricity blackouts that deprived them of light and of water for about a week, for which the privatized Chilean operator, the *Empresa Distribuidora Sur Sociedad Anónima* (EDESUR), faced a fine of no less than US $75 million.

Perhaps the only general conclusion to be drawn is that such problems are sufficiently widespread, visible, and recurrent to elicit a substantial risk premium in world capital markets, and that a great deal of further confidence-building and institutional reform will be required before these doubts can be fully dispelled. Given the scale and complexity of the privatization and post-privatization tasks that remain, it seems almost inevitable that further resistance will be generated and it is uncertain whether the reform momentum can reliably be maintained. According to the ILO, between 1990 and 1998, privatization and deregulation reduced the amount of good quality employment available in the major economies of Latin America. It estimated that for the region as a whole the proportion of the labor force consigned to the "informal" sector rose from 52 percent to 55 percent over that period. This was attributable to a decline in public sector employment from 15.5 percent to 12.9 percent of the workforce, and a decline from 32.7 percent to 28.4 percent in the formal private sector. In such circumstances, and in conditions of electoral democracy, the potential and actual losers from privatization could be expected to generate some degree of resistance and even obstruction. Of course, this discussion provides no more than a very partial indication of the balance of forces at work.

There is still legitimate scope for debate between alternative perspectives, with those enamored of privatization and market reform entitled to argue that further advances in the same direction will eventually produce the promised benefits—though some honest self-criticism and more open-mindedness would add to the credibility of such assertions of faith—and their critics need to develop a more positive alternative. From the standpoint of this volume what matters is how this dialectic is likely to play out in the specific regional context we have identified. While it is too early for a final verdict, it is already apparent that privatization in Latin America is likely to conform to earlier regional experiences of reform "from above and without." The results are likely to be mixed and subject to being superseded. The initial theoretical impulse was lopsided, and the outcomes are predictably uneven and partial.

V. Lopsided Theories

This section summarizes five alternative ways to account for the region-wide upsurge in privatization initiatives, in each case checking the argument against pertinent examples. The assumption is that each approach, although one-sided, contains at least some degree of insight, but that more than one approach is needed to account for the range of experiences. In the recent period only one of these theories—liberal universalism—has dominated the public debate and the thinking of most policy-makers. By setting this "hegemonic" viewpoint alongside other, equally useful, alternatives, the aim is not to refute liberal universalism but rather to underscore its incompleteness. These possible approaches are liberal universalism; cyclical interpretations; wave theories; catch-up theories; and structural explanations.

Liberal Universalism

Privatization in Argentina bears sufficient resemblance to privatization in Poland to permit a systematic comparison of the two. A doctoral dissertation on the Hungarian Privatization agency highlighted analogous writings about the Mexican state bureaucracy without too great a sense of incongruity.[27] Although this is more speculative, it is at least possible that those knowledgeable about Romania would find points of reference in the experiences of Nicaragua. More generally, then, this provides a *prima facie* case that the processes under study are, if not completely universal, then at least very widely disseminated. Wherever liberal values, private property rights, and processes of peaceful exchange between unconstrained juridical equals are understood and appreciated a similar logic of pro-market reform can be anticipated. This broad predisposition toward this version liberal universalism can be reinforced from various directions. An influential school of economic analysis regards the reduction of transaction costs as a virtually universal imperative, from which far-reaching and recurrent institutional consequences can be derived. Desire for individual autonomy and security can be posited in a similar way, as can the foundations for an almost universal endorsement of standardized property rights (and fundamental human rights of a broader kind). More contingently, but equally powerfully, the logic of the contemporary international economy may be so relentless and universally present that economic agents and enterprises with the most dissimilar histories may be subject to its homogenizing impact.

These are weighty considerations, and they help us understand what might otherwise seem inexplicable—the sustained pursuit of remarkably parallel programs and policies in so many diverse and structurally distinct societies. However, the analysis would be incomplete if it failed to deal with another aspect of these disparate realities, namely that before 1989 in Eastern Europe, or before 1982 in Latin America the desire and need for, or feasibility of, wholesale privatization was perceived only by a handful of visionaries. Neither a liberal cultural heritage, nor the wish to reduce transaction costs, nor aspirations for individual self-realization, nor indeed the need to earn a living in the international marketplace, gave rise to any serious drive for the divestiture of state assets or the enhancement of economic competition. If anything, the dominant tendency was toward greater state ownership and regulation. In this period, liberal universalism seemed to be under siege. So this theory needs to take into account prior constrictions before it can explain current success, let alone predict an unconstrained future ascendancy. This may seem unproblematic to East Europeans, for whom subjugation by the Red Army could be thought to account for everything. But Latin Americans, securely lodged in the U.S. sphere of influence, cannot dismiss the difficulty so lightly. Even in Chile, Peru, and Nicaragua, where functional equivalents of the Red Army can be conjured up, everyone knows that there was widespread popular support for increased statism before the switch to privatization. And elsewhere—the Brazilian Constitution of 1988, the Uruguayan plebiscites, and the electoral preferences of Venezuelan voters—testify to the limits of liberal universalism. International market pressures may have intensified, but that is not enough on its own, certainly not for the indefinite future. So this theoretical position is insufficient to explain why privatization was not sought before the 1990s and cannot reliably promise that privatization will be favored in coming decades. It may help to underpin current policy choices, but seems thin on its own. Other explanations are necessary to supplement it.

Cyclical Interpretations

One such alternative is a more cyclical interpretation, which posits a relatively stable "public interest" that is best served by privatization at one point and by nationalization at another. On February 2, 1999, President Ernesto Zedillo announced his intention to reform articles 27 and 28 of the Mexican Constitution so that, with effect from December 2000 (the date of his departure from office), private domestic and foreign investors would have the right to acquire or construct new electric power stations. The justification offered for this measure was surprisingly similar to the terms that his predecessor from the same party, President Adolfo López Mateos, had used to justify the nationalization of the electricity industry on September 27, 1960, (its purchase from its foreign owners through a stock market takeover). The then Secretary of Finance, Antonio Ortíz Mena, explained that the rapid growth of demand exceeded the likely increase of supply that the private foreign companies were willing to create through their investments, and that the country required an integrated national network, in particular capable of delivering electricity to the regions and to the countryside. Zedillo justified the opening of the electricity sector to private investment on the grounds that large new investments in modern capacity were necessary and he preferred to use state resources to meet social needs.

On the basis of this example one could construct a cyclical theory where the underlying public interest is rather stable and may be best served by one or the other option at different times. It is important to note that in this instance the Mexican authorities were not claiming that nationalization was an error or that the resulting state enterprises were inefficient. On the contrary, President Zedillo stated that the objectives pursued in 1960 had been "very satisfactorily" fulfilled by the *Comisión Federal de Electricidad* (CFE).

Latin American economic history provides various other examples that would seem to confirm a cyclical interpretation. Most striking is the history of oil production in Bolivia. In the 1920s, Standard Oil was brought in to provide the capital and technology needed to tap the country's geological potential. In 1937, it was expropriated, and the state-owned YPFB acquired a monopoly over these promising assets. In 1955, the monopoly was revoked and foreign companies were again invited in to do what the Bolivian state was unable to do on its own. In 1969, the Gulf Oil concession was nationalized and YPFB regained its monopoly status at a time when hydrocarbons were becoming the country's leading economic activity. In 1997, YPFB was "capitalized," meaning that the new multinational partners effectively acquired control over the sector in return for a commitment to bring in large amounts of new capital and technology. In early 2005, the Bolivian Congress was once again deeply divided and subject to intense popular pressures over a new law on hydrocarbons that might deter private investors and perhaps recreate a state-led energy sector. What this example seems to demonstrate is that throughout the last century the Bolivian state sought to reconcile conflicting aspects of the public interest. Privatization was found to serve one of these public policy objectives (modern and capital intensive prospection) but at the cost of another (national control and the formation of national expertise in the exploitation of a key natural resource). The solution was to alternate between policy stances. On this cyclical interpretation it remains to be seen whether the capitalization formula will prevail for the indefinite future or whether it too will prove exhaustible and reversible after another generation.

More debatable examples of a cyclical pattern involve the privatization of state-owned banks in Argentina, Chile, Mexico, and elsewhere. When these banks proceeded to engage in unsound borrowing, and thereby entered into a state of generalized insolvency, they were "rescued" by the public authorities, which effectively nationalized the risks that the private sector had assumed. This provided an attractive one-way bet for the beneficiaries of privatization. They were effectively licensed by the state to gamble with the funds of their depositors. If they won, they kept all the proceeds, and if they lost, the taxpayer would have to assume the liabilities. So long as prevailing doctrine insists on the evils of state ownership in the financial sector, investors may be tempted to repeat this cycle indefinitely. (And this is not a phenomenon confined to poorly regulated "emerging markets" as the US Savings and Loan *débâcle* of the 1980s amply demonstrates.)

Another area where this kind of long-term cycle is particularly likely concerns the pensions industry. The failings of universal state provision in Latin America require little elaboration. They have given rise to a very widespread shift toward privatized pension provision. However, in at least some countries it is foreseeable that with the coming to maturity of the privatized schemes, a large section of the elderly population will have been left in indigence. If democratic processes exist, some reaction against the fashion for personal pensions may occur in favor of a restoration of universal coverage and defined benefits.

Each of these examples is rather distinct, and could provide the basis for a specific variant of cyclical theory. However, what they all have in common and what distinguishes them all from the unilinear assumptions of liberal universalism is that the conditions leading to a decision to privatize are viewed as time-limited. Once privatization has occurred a new constellation of forces and incentives emerges, which is itself subject to shifts over time. Thus, in a first post-privatization phase the restoration of state ownership may seem unthinkable, not least because it would render worthless all the adjustment costs incurred to bring about the new state of affairs. But over time those adjustments may come to be seen as "sunk costs" and the relative merits of private as opposed to public ownership can again be assessed in terms of a pragmatic evaluation of the locus of the public interest. And in due course that evaluation may shift again against private ownership. The coalitions that support it may come to be seen as self-serving and as acting against the collective good, leading to more state intervention.

Although there are some good arguments in favor of the cyclical hypothesis the counterarguments also deserve consideration. If we regard privatization as essentially no more than a component within a broader process of economic liberalization, we have to consider whether liberalization as a whole is likely to go into reverse. Provided trade liberalization and the opening of capital markets remain intact, a bias toward privatization will be "locked in" to economic policy. For the present it is difficult to envisage what would be needed to produce a wholesale reversal of the overall trend toward liberalization. Nonetheless, in particular markets and specific political conjunctures individual privatizations could fail or be repudiated. This could take the form of re-regulation rather than re-nationalization. In federal systems, for example, the center may privatize, but the states may try to reassert control.

At the most abstract level, one might hypothesize that any particular system of ownership or management of productive enterprises may become complacent and collusive with the passage of time. A drastic change in public policy can have the effect of galvanizing management into making greater efforts, and subjecting long-standing systems of economic organization to critical scrutiny. The extension of state ownership in Latin American may initially have served some efficiency enhancing purpose of this kind, just like the current wave of privatization. But what happens thereafter is more of an open question.

Wave Theories

Cyclical theories concern long-run patterns of change within a single continuous process. Present and future outcomes are understood as developments from, or reactions to, earlier stages in the same cycle. What causes the shifts over time may be structurally determined, or may be subjective reactions to unfolding experiences, or even the need for successive adjustments that aim to secure a single functional result (higher efficiency, for example, might be achieved through state intervention against private sector laxity, or later as a private sector corrective to public sector indiscipline). In contrast, wave theories concern interaction effects linking parallel processes going on at more or less the same time. Such interactions may take the form of "contagion," or may involve the more intentional exercise of influence or power, transmitted from one process to the next. (This could include joint consultations, training missions, or the transfer from one country to another of "experts" with relevant experience.)

For example, the Peruvian oil nationalization of 1968 was clearly a factor in precipitating Bolivia's action against Gulf Oil the following year, and both helped to create the climate of opinion for the Chilean copper nationalization of 1971. The privatization of British Telecom (BT) in 1984 opened the door to successive measures of the same kind in other European countries and, more recently, in Eastern Europe. These two examples indicate wave theories and cyclical theories are not necessarily mutually exclusive. Both can be in operation simultaneously and mutually reinforcing.

There are alternative variants of wave theory just as there are variants of cyclical theory. All need a precipitant cause in the first episode; a transmission mechanism from early to late instances of the process; and some way to account for the limits of the wave. The key task is to adequately identify the initial precipitant factors. Transmission may then be at least partly explained by the operation of similar causes in analogous cases, encouraged by a first "demonstration" that the process is feasible. The limits of the wave may then be understood either in terms of the absence of analogous conditions, disillusion with the results of previous experiences, or some deliberate reaction or blocking mechanism. (The same reasoning applies to sequences of military takeovers, or waves of democratization, including the collapse of the Communist regimes of Eastern Europe.)

With regard to privatization there are three main areas that can be explored in a search of initial precipitant factors. The first, as emphasized in the introduction, is fiscal crisis or, more generally, economic overreach by the public sector. In Latin America this is generally associated with the 1982 debt crisis, although it arrived earlier in some countries like Chile and Peru, and was postponed until later in others like Venezuela. Typically, privatization followed, but not until after a considerable time lag. Initial steps were mostly quite timid. In general, the wave did not build up into a crescendo until around the mid-1990s. This means looking at a second supplementary area related with academic and intellectual debate and even fashion. During the 1980s socialist ideas lost ground in the face of challenges from reinvigorated liberal theories and the emergence of new orthodoxies in economic analysis. The "Chicago Boys" in Chile were very conscious of this aspect of causation and they aimed to prove the superiority of their ideas by applying them more quickly and wholeheartedly than elsewhere. In other countries the intellectual debate moved more slowly and it was not uncommon for new policies to be introduced before the rationale for them had been fully internalized. Brazil is a good example of a reluctant and somewhat "heretical" convert. In Cuba the debate is still rejected although some liberalizing policy measures have nevertheless been adopted.

To account for this disjuncture between theory and practice it is helpful to turn to a third possible area of explanation: pressures and incentives generated by the international economy. The collapse of the Soviet bloc eliminated an alternative source of resources, and increased the confidence of international investors and multinational corporations in the safety of expanded operations in the "Third World." The Washington-based international financial institutions, greatly empowered in the wake of the debt crisis, became much more active in promoting market-oriented structural reform in Latin America. Again, different countries were affected differentially. To give just one example, Mexico, with the prospect of entry into the North American Free Trade Agreement (NAFTA), was subject to particularly compelling international inducements to privatize, whereas, in the absence of such external inducements, Ecuador was not.

This sketch of precipitant factors should serve to illustrate the potential explanatory power of wave theories. But it is not by any means fully specified, and only scratches the surface of the issues.[28] When all three types of inducement are weak, it is more likely that privatization will fail to take hold. In Venezuela, for example, the hope still exists that an expansion of the oil industry will overcome the fiscal crisis. Venezuelan elites have not been won over by neoliberal theory.

And the international economy may not exert the same pressures in Venezuela as on nonoil countries.

Catch-Up Theories

The most celebrated "catch-up" theory is that of Alexander Gerschenkron, whose *Economic Backwardness in Historical Perspective* published in 1962 argued that whereas the United Kingdom, as the first industrializing nation, required very limited state involvement in the economy, subsequent industrializations required a great collective effort of discipline to mobilize resources if they were to catch up with the leader. Hence German industrialization was more statist than Britain's. Extending the argument to its limit, Gerschenkron suggested that it was the great backwardness of the Russian economy that explained the extreme statism of the Soviet system. The limitations of this theory as an account of these cases is nowadays all too apparent, but a version of this hypothesis can be adapted for use in the comparative analysis of privatization. In this context, the independent variable would not be the absolute level of economic development but rather the scale of the economic failure associated with the pre-privatization regime. The further below potential, the greater the justification for a policy effort that induces a national economy to "catch-up" with its neighbors and match the standards of competitive efficiency achieved in the outside world. On this reasoning, Chile and Argentina have made greater and more sustained efforts to promote pro-market reforms (including privatization), because of the depth of their preceding systemic crises. Brazil never underwent such a severe setback, and was therefore never forced to muster the unity and resolve to pursue comparably drastic "catching-up" strategies.

This is obviously simplistic, but it may have some explanatory power, at least when undertaking selected and controlled comparisons. The question of case selection is of particular importance here—only after screening out irrelevant or inappropriate cases is the analysis likely to generate much leverage. Clearly, the Cuban economy is performing further below its potential than most in Latin America, but it does not follow that an exceptionally far-reaching program of privatization is to be expected there. The Uruguayan economy has long performed poorly, and underwent a period of extreme crisis at roughly the same time as Chile but with different results. Unlike Chile, re-democratized Uruguay did not inherit an economy transformed from its state-led history by military fiat. The progress of liberal reforms there has long been slow and fitful, in part perhaps because that was the preference of an ageing and relatively egalitarian population, reinforced by the constitutional provision allowing voters to block legislative reforms by means of a popular plebiscite. The election of Tabaré Vásquez and his left wing third force coalition in late 2004 may mean that long-standing assertions about Uruguay's policy inertia will require revision. President Vásquez took office under the constraint of a last minute constitutional amendment entrenching the state monopoly over water and sanitation services. Despite his leftist credentials—or perhaps because of them—he insisted on a retroactive implementation clause that would allow the fourteen private companies that had been taken over by the state utility to maintain the rights they enjoyed prior to the amendment, and he has also pledged to privatize the telecommunications and energy sectors. His view seems to be that this is the best way to generate the resources needed to meet the expectations of his electorate. Uruguay may be better placed than most South American countries to sustain the levels of regulation and accountability to the public interest that would vindicate this option. At a time when Argentina, Brazil, Paraguay, and Uruguay are all undertaking extensive adjustments in order to make their economies compatible within Southern Common Market (MERCOSUR), it is reasonable to expect that the pressures for reform in any one country will intensify if voters and consumers find that this is the only way they can "catch-up" with the higher standards or faster improvements being enjoyed by their now more directly comparable neighbors. Similar considerations probably apply within other experiments in "open regionalism" like NAFTA and the Caribbean Common Market (CARICOM).

As a tentative suggestion, one might hypothesize that "catch-up" effects may be more powerful levers of change in certain industries and sectors than in whole economies. For example, if an outdated national telephone monopoly fails to meet business demand in one country when a privatized and digitalized service is boosting the efficiency of competitors in another, then the logic of "catch-up" may induce a telecom privatization without necessarily stimulating broader reforms. Similar considerations could apply in particular to other types of international business service, such as airlines, banking, and insurance. This hypothesis leads to a fifth and final, more structural, kind of theorizing.

Structural Explanations

A final set of explanations for privatization processes directs attention to the requirements of industrial structures. These differ, both between industries and over time. At the height of the railway age, for example, the logic of a unified and coordinated transport system seemed to exclude the disciplines of competition and to maximize the potential for monopolistic exploitation. This industrial structure favored state ownership and in due course that was the system that came to prevail in almost all major railway systems, including Latin America and Europe where, to be sure, the logic of war always played a part. For a variety of reasons that deserve further examination, it is currently believed that many railway systems can better serve the public interest through privatization.[29] Here we have an example of an explanation based on industrial structure, including the changing requirements of an industry in its stages of growth, maturity, and decline. Something approaching the reverse pattern might make more sense for the information technology industry. In its early days it required huge investments of capital and specialist know-how, and offered only very uncertain and long-term prospects of commercial reward. The industry therefore required the nurture of lavish public investment and the shelter of government-imposed controls to protect dissemination of the most promising lines of discovery. Large missile defense and space research budgets and classified communications systems in the public sector financed the development stage of the industry. But as it reached maturity, the range of commercial applications multiplied in an explosive and unforeseeable manner. Secrecy and monopoly became the enemies of industrial development. Whereas the Soviet system clung to these statist arrangements, and so lost its position in the development of the industry, the Americans in particular promoted forms of private appropriation and dissemination of the technology, thus giving the United States its current ascendancy in this hugely transformative industrial sector.[30]

Most industries are located somewhere between these two extremes, obviously, and in any case it would be reductionist to conclude that industrial structure *alone* determines the pattern of state or private ownership and/or management. Nevertheless, there are some quite promising lines of enquiry here. Large domestic markets may provide better benchmarks for competition between privatized firms than small ones that either shelter a monopoly supplier or retain no domestic supplier at all (airlines are a case in point). In very general terms we might distinguish between standardized mass production, involving the reliable but repetitive performance of precisely defined tasks and interactive customized variable lines of production. The first, Fordist, kind of process could be delivered through large-scale, vertically disciplined, production that might be a candidate for public ownership (like the great nationalized industries of western Europe of the mid-twentieth century). The second "flexible specialization" process can only occur through knowledge-intensive, horizontally coordinated networks that can monitor and respond rapidly to shifts in customer demand or in technological possibilities. Insofar as any economy's productive structure shifts from Fordist to flexibly specialized systems it could reasonably be argued that this will virtually necessitate some accompanying shift from state ownership to privatization.

VI. Conclusion: Partial Outcomes

In the last decade of the twentieth century, an unusually wide and deep consensus has emerged that the best from of government is democracy, and that the most appropriate developmental strategy is outward-oriented and pro-market. Privatization gathered momentum as an integral component of this new consensus and as a powerful means to cement the linkage between political and economic liberalization. Privatization was also promoted with a number of both macroeconomic and sectoral objectives in mind. The idea was that it would help to "depoliticize" economic life and to stimulate a more entrepreneurial society. In view of this multiplicity of objectives, and the still incomplete nature of the associated reform processes, we can hardly expect to arrive at a definitive and uniform evaluation of its success.

This chapter has emphasized complexity, diversity, and the potential for chain-effects of results spread over time, some of which may correspond to initial intentions, and others not. That assessment must not disguise the fact that in many cases some form of privatization—and a more general shift toward economic liberalization—was unavoidable given that the previous economic model had reached an impasse. Moreover, there are at least as many examples of spectacular success as of unanticipated difficulties. Privatization gathered momentum in the 1990s because, in many cases, it was found to work surprisingly well.

This may eventually turn out to be the final verdict. We may conclude that at the end of the twentieth century Latin America finally managed to settle on both a form of government and a strategy of development that could be continued, deepened, and made irreversible for the indefinite future. However, the broad-gauged, long-run, comparative perspective adopted in this chapter has drawn attention to at least three potentially substantial qualifications to this optimistic scenario.

First, by comparing the current wave of privatization with an earlier wave of nationalizations, and by highlighting cyclical, catch-up, and structural considerations it has brought into question the dichotomous reasoning that underlies the current consensus. Instead of viewing all aspects of previous interventionist experience as misconceived and all aspects of a current market orientation as inherently superior, it has provided a perspective through which to relativize such judgments. In particular, it leaves open the possibility that the current wave of reforms will turn out to be one more episode in the long succession of Latin American experiments in search of the right development strategy. In that event it will deliver some benefits, encounter some resistances, deteriorate over time, and in due course, lead to another round of experiments that, rightly or wrongly, aim to overcome the perceived failings of the latest model.

Second, this raises the question of the potential "reversibility" of measures that are currently sold as irreversible (they must be, otherwise private investors would not respond appropriately). Both the sketch of the current scene, and the various explanations of privatization above raise doubts about the irreversibility of the current property regime. Historically, external shocks—violent fluctuations in the availability of international capital inflows, and in the openness of the markets to which Latin American trade has been oriented—have destabilized earlier sequences of market-oriented internationalism. Perhaps the international political economy has now been rendered secure against further upheavals of this kind, but that is to take a lot on trust. Were the international environment again to become less favorable, the irreversibility of the new model would depend upon the solidity of its domestic foundations. Thus, for example, the preservation of private property rights would depend substantially upon the strength of the rule of law, and the quality of the legal and justice systems in place in Latin American countries. If impunity for violating property rights persists, then arbitrary infringements of the property system will tend to recur. Similarly, if social inequalities are left untouched.

Perhaps the most specific way to underscore the continuing reversibility of the privatized economy is to focus on bankruptcy procedures. There are really only three basic possibilities, although actual outcomes may be hybrids: either market failure leads to liquidation of the enterprise and the reassignment to other agents of the assets thus released; or it leads back to public ownership; or, if the absence of bankruptcy proceedings is accompanied by a rejection of public ownership, there will be repeated cycles of privatization of profits and socialization of losses, creating a "moral hazard" each time the balance sheet is cleaned up and assets are returned to private ownership. Until the first option is securely established in contemporary Latin America, the privatized economy will not be fully irreversible.

Third, there is the issue of the "public interest" under conditions of political democracy. Neither democracy nor the market are entirely secure as yet in Latin America, but let us work on the assumption that both are likely to persist and become more deeply entrenched. In that context, defining where the public interest lies involves a complex process of debate, bargaining, and political interaction. If democracy becomes consolidated, then voters, citizens, and parties will expect to play their part in shaping that public debate. In broad terms they may be constrained by the wish or need to respect market rationality. But, as this chapter has indicated through its discussion of definitional issues, and of the range of timing and sequencing possibilities, the market does not generate a unique static equilibrium solution to every problem of allocation and distribution. These are the realities of privatization as uncovered by recent experience, not only in Latin America but also in developed democracies elsewhere. The market economy has to be constructed, reshaped, maintained, and monitored by a whole array of state initiatives and public policies that always involve a succession of complex balancing acts. The current political preoccupation with fighting terrorism and curbing market abuses that facilitate the covert financing of terrorist networks demonstrate how quickly the climate of opinion—and regulation—can change even in the most mature market democracies.

If both democracy and the market are to coexist and interact in accordance with the public interest, a considerable degree of mutual adjustment will have to take place. This would mean not merely that a durable liberal democracy must be market-friendly, but also that a broadly privatized economy may be subject to extensive political re-regulation. These are the challenges facing all market democracies, but in this chapter we have also seen that they assume a distinctive and acute form in the Latin American regional context. Here, the advocates of Privatization are likely to rely heavily on external accreditation and protection to validate their purported expertise. Here, a poorly coordinated and easily captured state apparatus may lack the specialized capacities and staying power required to design, implement, and monitor successful transformations of this kind. Here, the lessons of history and the division of interest may both generate a reasonable expectation that the public interest rhetoric of the "privatizers" may prove a poor guide to what they are really trying to achieve, or how it will turn out in practice. Consequently, in Latin America, more than elsewhere, it may prove difficult to sustain a minimum social consensus around this latest project of modernity. As we shall see in the next chapter, the extremes of social inequality and exclusion that still characterize almost the whole region despite its embrace of markets and democracy, exposes all such projects to potentially destabilizing resistance and even backlash.

Chapter 6

Democracy, Inequality, and Insecurity: A Paradoxical Configuration*

I. Introduction

Earlier chapters in this volume have highlighted a Latin American proclivity for projects of modernizing reform that are imposed in a "top down" manner and thus encounter societal resistance and fail to "take." This very schematic interpretation might seem to fit the broad pattern to be expected from a long history of authoritarianism, but over the past twenty years the region has become a haven of democracy where, in principle, former undemocratic practices should be less prevalent, and give way to greater participation of a broader array of actors and communities, more open dialogue, collective deliberation, more institutionalized procedures of decision-making—leading perhaps to more consensual and legitimate reform outcomes. At the same time, projects imposed from "above and without" are replaced by projects negotiated and internalized "from within." It is possible to detect some patchy shifts in this general direction (reforms à la Tabaré Vásquez, rather than à la Pinochet), but the old reflexes have proved to be remarkably resilient. After two decades of democratic rule, experts often remain arrogant and disconnected from their societies; state organization remains geared to the imposition of inflexible programs; liberalization obeys an externally directed logic that deprives citizens of a sense of ownership over collective choices. The ostensible rules of the new political game continue to be bent and twisted.[1] The sovereignty of the electorate continues to be impaired by the persistence of *de facto* powers, and by the frequent need to resort to direct action in order to affect policies that are not simply the product of legislative decisions. The flip side of this is a fragmented civil society that is unable to mobilize for greater accountability in a sustained and effective manner: elite disconnection, arrogance, and imposition is, after all, only sustainable if the people subjected to such *caprichos* are unable or unwilling to demand greater proximity to and control over power-holders.

This is not to say that democratization has made no difference in these respects, but it would be equally misguided to underestimate the extent to which the long-standing regional characteristics highlighted in this volume have persisted, and served to filter and reshape democracy in accordance with contextual traditions. A common comparative politics response to the persistence of such nondemocratic phenomena is to propose some alternative variant of institutional design to realign the incentives of political actors and lead them to behave in the expected or desired democratic fashion. One application of this approach in the Latin American context is to advocate a switch from presidentialism to parliamentarism. This kind of approach, when presented as *the* key policy prescription, disregards regional contexts and traditions, and assumes that some universal incentive structure will simply override local configurations of power and practice. It is not very credible in a region where formal rules are so frequently changed and flouted. An alternative standpoint is to focus on the channels through which Latin America's distinctive sociohistorical characteristics may be expected to shape the way democratic government operates in this particular region. Indeed, rather than looking at Latin America "from above and without," this perspective involves looking at the region imaginatively, and, with the benefit of accumulated "tacit knowledge," from "within" in two ways—from within the region and from within its societies.

Previous chapters have drawn attention to some of the main characteristics involved—bias to modernity; top down projects; competitive state-promoted elites; external orientation; institutional instability and indiscipline, among others. But this characterization would be incomplete if it only concerned leadership groups. Throughout the analysis we have referred to a constellation of societal forces and characteristics that react to, or feed back on, the outlook of the dominant sectors. In a highly condensed summary, these distinctive regional features limit the scope for stable and broad-based consensus around any particular elite-led project or vision. They include such attitudes as parochialism and distrust of authority, and may be partly founded on the parallel existence of many poorly integrated communities and subgroups—including ethnic, class, gender, religious, and other identity-based divisions. The historical force of oligarchic and statist authoritarianism can live on in the form of "illiberal" democracy.

In addition, under current conditions of economic liberalization in a context of generalized underemployment many workers and citizens must face endemic insecurities concerning any supposed rights and entitlements. This is a reality even for those with jobs in the "formal sector," and all the more true for the often large sections of the workforce who have to scrape a living in the precarious conditions of the "informal" sector. The heterogeneity and internal complexity of so many Latin American societies make it impractical to fill out these synthetic observations within the space of a single chapter. Instead, the focus will be on two topics that contribute powerfully to the distinctive societal characteristics of most interest here: acute and persistent social inequalities, and severe problems of public insecurity. The argument is that while in the early 1980s it may have been necessary to separate political rights from social justice issues in order to achieve democratic transitions, in the long term this separation has come at a high cost in terms of social cohesion and the "quality of democracy" itself; that twenty years later, many of these new democracies have yet to make clear cut progress in overcoming this sin of origin; that such social policies as have been attempted have often displayed the characteristically debilitating technocratic rigidities described in previous chapters; that in the absence of progress in that direction it would hardly be surprising if electorates were once again tempted by "populist" appeals; that citizen security has also proved elusive, feeding anxieties that can reinforce the attraction of *mano dura* and authoritarian responses; and that both the analysis and search for solutions to the problems posed by entrenched inequality and insecurity require an approach that looks at the region not from above and without but from within the complex maze of reality on the ground.

II. Inequality and Social Injustice

Over the past twenty years Latin America has carried through a more comprehensive and successful sequence of democratic regime transitions than any other major region of the world in any historical period. But when we turn to social justice, the region is an outlier of a different kind. According to one estimate, the per capita product received by the richest fifth of the region's population is more than eighteen times the product received by the poorest fifth. This compares with a worldwide average of about seven to one, and an average for all developing countries of about eight to one.[2] Of course these figures are very approximate, and one might argue that they reflect the inheritance of previous exclusionary politics. But other comparative indicators of social justice confirm the same stark message, and the time series that are now becoming available offer little support for the contention that Latin American democracies can bring the region back into a more normal range of income or asset distribution within a measurable time frame. So we are left with the paradox of a successful region-wide shift to democratization that makes little or no difference to the subcontinent's notorious inequality.

In fact, on some key indicators, the poor in Latin America have fared worse since democratization than the poor in other regions where democracy has been less salient, or nonexistent. The 2004 International Labour Organisation (ILO) report on worldwide employment, for example, indicates that in 2003 half of workers worldwide (1.400 million out of 2.800 million) earned less than US$2 a day, and 20 percent (550 million) earned less than US$1 a day. In absolute numbers, these figures are the highest in recorded history. However, as the proportion of the global labor force, the poorest workers (living on less than US$2 a day) fell from 57 percent in 1990 to 50 percent in 2003, with a predicted further decline to 40 percent by 2015. But whereas at a global level it is possible to observe a positive tendency in terms of proportion, in Latin America and the Caribbean productive employment did not increase proportionally with the economically active population. Thus, despite its "democratic status," Latin America in the 1990s "exported" an important part of its labor force—mainly to Europe and the United States—and left many young people unemployed or surviving in the informal sector. In contrast to the global trend, the ILO figures for our region indicate that per capita income did not increase, absolute poverty did not decline, and the GINI coefficient on income inequality also failed to improve. There were positive developments in some countries (Chile is a case in point) to compensate for deterioration in others (like Argentina), but in general the middle class has been subjected to intense pressure, and unqualified workers have had to compete fiercely for low quality jobs, while many of the old and the very young live in desperate conditions.

Democratization has occurred in several other large regions of the world since the 1970s, but with different implications in terms of social justice and integration. In Southern Europe democratization was accompanied by integration into the European Union (EU), and with it, the delivery of new welfare provisions and benefits deriving from European integration. In East Central Europe, the dismantling of Communist structures removed some protections and generated new social inequalities, but this was generally accepted as a necessary price to pay for rectifying other kinds of injustices and to ensure societal transformations backed by an underlying consensus. In Asia, where democratization has occurred its impact has been less on social justice *per se*—which was arguably equally served by authoritarian-led national developmentalist policies—and more citizen demands for a say in how to distribute the benefits of a development model generally perceived as successful. In the few instances of democratization in Africa the focus—if not the practice—has been on the need to build up states that are accountable and able to deliver social benefits to the population at large. In sum, democratization has generally included a focus on distribution even if the area of social policy emphasized in each case varies and is conditioned by different local realities and varying popular demands. By contrast, in Latin America the decision to embrace political democracy was accompanied by a shift away from redistributive and welfare priorities.

This is partly a product of the negative experiences of the recent past: left wing contestation and popular mobilization in the face of inequality and authoritarian repressive responses to it. Given the traumatic effects of that experience, the reformists of the 1980s made a strong case, both analytical and political, for highlighting the distinction between the establishment of a democratic political regime and the satisfaction of popular aspirations, including a desire for social justice. It was considered essential to challenge the widespread tendency to conflate "democracy" with "the good society," understandable in light of the polarizing experience of past mobilization and authoritarian reaction. Thus, most analysts focused on a rather precise and perhaps somewhat narrow view of political democracy concerned above all with procedural issues. This focus necessarily excluded—or at the very least pushed to the margins—many concerns that are central to most discussions of the "quality of democracy," such as the existence of widespread illiteracy, vast pockets of rural and urban poverty, and situations of structural "exclusion." The issue of literacy illustrates this point. Historically, the issue of the compatibility between modern democratic regimes and widespread illiteracy has been a serious question, with some well-respected democracies confining votes to literates, others granting universal suffrage, and yet others using literacy tests as a covert form of discrimination against social groups they wished to disenfranchise for different reasons. The 1980s signaled a practical and an analytical consensus in Latin America, and more generally, that a democratic electoral regime involves universal suffrage. This ignored the old argument that those without the capacities to exercise political autonomy should not be enfranchised, since they would vote at the behest of their masters. In theory, it would have been possible to advocate universal suffrage, but only in conjunction with a mass literacy drive and other reforms, like land redistribution, to free all voters from the status of dependency. Instead, the consensual definition of democracy of the 1980s advocated a "minimal" or "procedural" definition. Implicitly or explicitly this was justified on the grounds that if illiterates were enfranchised they would be able to press their representatives to provide them with education, and that waiting until illiteracy was eradicated before establishing full democracy would be playing into the hands of the authoritarian elites. It was also argued that the experience of South Asia and elsewhere showed that a partly illiterate electorate could sustain a worthwhile system of democratic institutions, and further, that in Latin America at least, since it had been radical demands for confiscatory land reform and socialist literacy campaigns that had paved the way for authoritarian repression in the first place, it seemed advisable to adopt another, more restricted, but "safer" interpretation of what democratization should be about. The underlying theme was that "the best was the enemy of the good." These mostly pragmatic considerations were bolstered by more theoretical arguments about democracy as an institutional system based on structured bargaining within an agreed framework of rules, and about the centrality of elite compromise, especially if a new regime was to be established by consent and maintained without extra-constitutional conflict. In any case it would be quite misleading to regard traditional forms of welfare provision as necessarily the central plank of any modern social justice agenda. Whatever their ostensible reform justifications when introduced in Latin America, such programs have often been captured or perverted by narrow sectional interests that are far from reflecting the claims of social justice more broadly understood. If international integration weakens the monopoly power of such interests and forces a restructuring of welfare provision to make it more accountable, it may support rather than undermine the cause of social justice. In fact, a broad social justice agenda will include a wide variety of elements, some of which (such as indigenous rights, the rights of women, and the nonexploitation of children) may be promoted by international pressures, while others (trade union rights or public health care provision) are more likely to be downgraded.

A generation later, we can observe the results of this distinctive route to political democratization, one disconnected from direct association with much of the region's traditional substantive social agenda.[3] While there may be no causal connection between the two phenomena, it remains of great political significance that since the transitions to democracy in the region, per capita incomes have mostly stagnated while traditional inequalities have not diminished and the economic welfare of much of the electorate has failed to improve.

Traditionally, of course, "social justice" is about the establishment of equitable arrangements *within* a bounded national community, only weakly supplemented by provisions to encourage "international social justice," which essentially involved the emergency transfer of resources to assist those living in extreme destitution as a result of man-made or natural disasters. However, since the liberalization and adaptation of national economies to the demands posed by globalization over the past generation this traditional compartmentalization between the national and the international has become increasingly difficult to sustain, and the pretence that the governments of poor countries can deliver on promises of universal welfare provision becomes ever less credible. In Cuba the illusion is foundering, despite sustained and politically very costly efforts, and even the "model" democracies of Canada and Sweden have been incapable of resisting these international pressures and preserving their welfare systems. So it is to be expected that insecure neodemocracies sometimes recently emerged from bankruptcy and hyperinflation will not easily achieve such ambitious equity goals.

If there have been relative social equity improvements on a global level, this is because of the accelerated growth rate of some Asian countries, particularly China—countries that are not necessarily democratic. In Latin America, however, what has predominated and will likely continue is a level of inequality that is only second to that of the predominantly nondemocratic Arab world,[4] and for the most part stagnation in the generation of high quality employment. So, compared with Africa, Asia, and the former Communist countries, or with the Middle East, Latin America's democratic performance has been stellar over the last twenty years, but in the field of combating poverty and acute inequality the region is in a state of stagnation and even moving backward. We are thus faced with the paradox that Latin America and the Caribbean is perhaps the region in the world that has achieved the most in terms of democratization—understood in the classic and formal sense—but which has simultaneously failed dismally where the so-called social requirements for democracy are concerned. In short, Latin America is a whole subcontinent, where poverty and social injustice appear to be as, if not more, entrenched as democracy and political freedom.

When attempting to understand the origins of this paradox, various issues need to be taken into account. Perhaps the most vital question concerns the *sources of social injustice*. In other words, which aspects of a broad "social justice" agenda are most likely to be addressed by strengthening of democratic institutions, and which are less responsive to that process? There are directly *political* aspects of social justice, such as freedom from police persecution, torture, and being disappeared if one is an opposition activist, that are constitutive of a democratic regime, and strikingly absent under authoritarian regimes. Other aspects of social justice are not so directly deducible from regime type, however. A democratic constitution *may* contain ambitious social justice provisions, like the Brazilian and Mexican charters, but other equally democratic regimes may stress property rather than social rights. In addition, many of the social injustices that characterize the subcontinent can be attributed more to *economic* possibilities and choices that are only very indirectly affected by the political system. It is also the case, however, that many of the most extreme forms of social injustice and exclusion are not attributable *either* to recent political structures *or* economic policy. Parts of Latin America display deep, centuries-old forms of social inequality, like those resulting from a history of conquest or a legacy of slavery. These entrenched forms of social injustice can be expected to change only very slowly, independently of the regime type. Indeed, a transition to democracy may raise the visibility of discrimination without actually alleviating its impact, and thus apparently worsen victims' sense of injustice and exclusion.

Redefining the Democracy–Justice Nexus

The theorists of democratic transition of the 1980s and the analysts of democratization of the 1990s are more or less in agreement in minimizing the connection between the establishment of a democracy and the reduction of extreme poverty. Other variables are invoked to explain variations in the poverty head count, and it is argued that, at best, democracy may be indirectly positive in this respect. Nevertheless, these different components of social injustice all interact, and democratization can affect the overall climate of opinion and the structure of incentives within which equity issues are tackled. Even people living in severe poverty stand to benefit from the modest improvements in civic rights that usually accompany a process of democratization. The right to have your vote counted honestly, to petition, to associate and communicate freely are also aspects of social justice that are of value in themselves, and can be directly associated with political regime change. Admittedly, this is a rather abstract claim, and ethnographic evidence points to a more complex reality, but the principle is clear: some aspects of the social justice agenda can be directly connected to the contemporary discourse of democratization.

Beyond this very general assertion, it is essential to remember that within the limits set by the new political rules of the game, the claims of social justice will be open-ended and vary in structure and salience according to the preferences of the electorate. Thus, in Brazil the claims of landless and indigenous groups have recently reoccupied the political agenda to an unexpected degree; in others, physical insecurity and the absence of a reliable justice system have emerged as the central themes of public policy; and in yet others issues of gender inequality have come to the fore. These and other issues besides are plausible components of a broad "social justice" agenda. All of them can be taken up and processed through the democratic political system, not only in ways that contribute to the eventual overall strengthening of social justice, but, to the contrary, also in ways that institutionalize injustice, as when an unreliable penal regime is made even harsher, or when the rights of one group are strengthened to the detriment of the entitlements of other, equally valid, claimants. In short, there can be no neat one-to-one equivalence between establishing democratic institutions, however "substantive," and achieving social justice.

It is remarkable that in most of Latin America the persistence of a multiplicity of acute forms of social injustice has coincided for over a decade with more or less stable and routine democratic governance. Unless we make the drastic assumption that the region's new democratic leaders are somehow entirely insulated from the social aspirations of their constituents (an assumption that would need detailed justification), we have to accept that the justice most people seek is in some way—slowly, partially, distortedly—being processed by existing institutions. Insulation, distortion, and delay can all be plausibly invoked to *weaken* the postulated link between democratization and social justice, but of course they all imply that some linkage does exist. Following this line of analysis, then, it may be necessary to reflect on what characteristics of the region's new democracies mesh with what facets of the contemporary understanding of justice to produce at least a fragile *modus vivendi* between the two.

Looking at the relationship from an institutional angle, and generalizing very broadly, it can be said that the public policy priorities emphasized to date have involved a rewriting of the rules of the political game, which is now about stabilizing the economy in a climate of state-shrinking, and about preserving social peace without unnecessary resort to overt coercion. This is a fairly demanding agenda for any society, and in those characterized by severe inherited inequalities and injustices, especially those with a previous tradition of "populist" political mobilization and incorporation, it has been especially difficult to pursue. So instead of raising expectations by promising to right past wrongs, the emphasis has generally been to minimize "unrealistic" expectations, conciliate formerly antagonistic interests, and to reduce the stakes involved each time an elected government gives way to another. This is not to say that all grievances concerning past mistreatments have gone unattended, as the range of "truth and justice" policies for past human rights violations show. But on the whole, and compared to the earlier history of democracy in the region, the new democracies have been low key, downbeat, and demobilizing. The emotional intensity of previous crusades for social justice has been conspicuous by its absence.

This generalization can be connected to a second, even more broad-based and approximate one, concerning societal perceptions about the nature and possibilities of justice. In many countries it seems clear that the failings of populism and the traumas of authoritarian rule had a very sobering impact on social expectations, and for large sectors of opinion that effect has not been merely transitory. Anyone who witnessed the intensity of feeling that accompanied demands for redistribution and equitable participation in Chile before 1973 or in Argentina before 1976, or in Bolivia just before 1985, will be impressed by the contrasts evident in those countries throughout the 1990s. But if under the current hegemony of international liberalism the claims of social justice no longer legitimize demands for expropriation or quasi-insurrectionary strike action (to take the most extreme manifestations of the old syndrome) that does not mean all aspirations for equity have been abandoned. For example, as a result of liberalization it has evidently become more acceptable to demand justice in the form of equitable treatment for individuals as citizens and consumers. Such demands express a much more privatized and nonconflictive understanding of entitlements, but they are nevertheless quite ambitious and still only erratically and imperfectly met. And they are still strong enough to generate waves of protest that can prove intermittently capable of destabilizing top-down reform initiatives, although they are almost invariably too volatile and incoherent to sustain structured alternatives to the prevailing orthodoxies.[5]

In the 1990s much official policy-making was shaped by an alternative, and equally ambitious, theory linking the promotion of social justice, not to regime type but to the sustained pursuit of economic orthodoxy and market liberalization. The general argument was that, at least in the long run, sound and successful integration in the international economy would provide the stability and resources that are essential if the inherited "social deficit" attributable to past decades of economic mismanagement was eventually to be cleared. If that seems to rely too heavily on "trickle down" or economic determinist forms of reasoning it can be bolstered by the argument that successful economic reforms may go hand in hand with "reform of the state," and that a more effective and accountable state can not only make better economic policy but also better social policy. But how solid are the links in that argument and how does it relate to processes of democratization?

The fundamental source of potential instability is the persisting imbalance between the normative promise associated with modern democracy (citizenship for all, self-realization within a permissive framework of order), and "really existing" inequities and disorder. So long as the electorate is persuaded that this imbalance can be diminished over time by living within the constraints of minimalism, and/or that breaking with those constraints will only make matters worse, then redistributive reversals can be averted. But at existing levels of inequality, neither of these propositions is beyond challenge.[6] However, external observers who believe that more can and must be done to overcome Latin America's tradition of extreme social inequality need to temper their judgments with the consideration that under prevailing conditions of democratic rule, it is the electorate and the chosen political authorities who must strike the balance between competing priorities and determine the speed and content of any justice-enhancing reforms. There are some kinds of poverty and inequality that are socially and politically accepted by a majority, and there are others that are completely illegitimate from the point of view of the citizenry. It is necessary to differentiate between the various dimensions of poverty and inequality—such as between acceptance of certain contrasts in minimum living conditions in the countryside and in the cities—as opposed to others that are less acceptable, like exclusion from primary education.

In light of these conceptual and empirical observations, the technocratic illusion of a "targeted" social policy that is neutral, precise, and depoliticized must be questioned. Poverty is a condition that afflicts extended families and whole communities, and not just isolated individuals: poverty is a collective as much as a personal experience. There is a sizeable majority of the electorates of the region that experiences the reality of economic vulnerability and social insecurity on a daily basis. Anthropological studies of the poor show that many make the transition from average to marginal worker status (living on less than US$2 a day) within the space of a year, and that they do so not only once, but repeatedly. Their condition is not necessarily one of permanent poverty, but rather one of permanent risk and fear of falling into poverty. This is the reality of the informal labor market. It is also a political and conceptual mistake drastically to separate the phenomenon of generalized poverty and that of acute inequality. They are not the same and differentiated treatment for each is appropriate. However, they are very closely linked, particularly in competitive electoral systems, and they often interact—specially in a Latin America that is fragmented and socially unjust—and so they cannot be oversimplified either.

As a result of the multidimensionality of and the interpenetration between poverty and inequality, durable and effective social policies have to be managed in a participatory and not just technocratic way. One should not think of the poor as an isolated and stable entity that can be dealt with bureaucratically through "targeted" policies. If democratic political systems fail to recognize the fact that it is the "ordinary majority" that faces poverty, this inattention will tend to generate disenchantment and even despair among voters, who will then see their apparently indifferent political leaders and party systems as elitist and exclusionary. Another weakness of a technocratic approach is that while it advocates "targeted" policies that are based on supposedly accurate and reliable statistical data identifying the beneficiaries of "pro-poor" policies, the data often fail to provide a basis for such confidence.[7] In some cases, like that of the Brazilian *bolsa escolar* (school grant), this approach is defensible, but technical tools are generally not as precise or trustworthy. A recent study, for example, concluded that the global quantity of poverty in Latin America in 1996 could reasonably be estimated at 50.7 percent (or 243.5 million people), but a shift in technical criteria within reasonable margins can produce a figure as high as 66 percent, while other similarly acceptable shifts in technical criteria can bring the figure down to only 20 percent. When looking at the relative ranking of each of the seventeen countries surveyed, it is not difficult to identify Bolivia as among the poorest countries and Costa Rica among the wealthiest. But only 30 percent of rankings do not vary whatever the measurement techniques adopted. In any case, the various social groups have points of reference and comparison that are far from homogenous. Poor people with family ties in the United States have another yardstick for normal consumption compared with those who are barred access to that labor market. Further, as Amartya Sen demonstrates in the 2004 UNDP Development Report, not all individuals have the same income needs to meet essential living expenses. For example, around 10 percent of the population can be said to be incapacitated, and is more needy and less able to earn a minimum wage.

Democracy, Technocracy, and Injustice

All of this does not mean going back to a costly, irrational social policy that fails to reach the poorest, but in the 1990s there was undeniably a tendency to exaggerate the possibilities of an entirely technical policy of targeting. In a democracy that is populated by mostly poor and vulnerable people, it is hard to persuade the majority to believe in the fairness of a social policy that does not demonstrably and directly reach those they know personally to be in need. An intelligible and legitimate system can generate popular support and galvanize the will to generate resources dedicated to social solidarity. A system of this kind cannot be overly bureaucratic or insulated from public debate. It must arise from and be based on the kind of broad political debate and dialogue that characterize a democratic society. If technocrats succeed in excluding the issue from popular debate, they may undermine the support that is necessary to sustain a social policy, and thereby provoke disenchantment with the political system in general. So, in a democratic Latin America that has so far proved no more capable than before of reducing flagrant inequalities and promoting a real shift toward greater social justice, it is only to be expected that the region's long-standing problems of social integration will persist, and that they will continue to generate intermittent popular protest and resistance against policies seen as imposed from above. Whereas previous authoritarian regimes were quick to respond to such expressions of dissent with repression, the new democracies cannot afford to condone such unnecessary coercion. They will have to tolerate significant levels of social conflict. This acceptance of what Charles Tilly has labeled "contentious politics" runs counter to the rhetoric of democratic consolidation, and to the notion of procedural democracy as "the only game in town."[8] It also clashes with the aspirations of the region's outward-oriented elites and with international market demands to shore up investor confidence. But it is nonetheless an integral part of Latin America's distinctive sociopolitical reality, and it seems unlikely that either democratization or economic liberalization can work so powerfully as to wholly overcome these embedded characteristics.

If combating poverty and inequality is not an exclusively technical project, if it does involve political negotiation and management, then its potential for conflict cannot be denied, nor indeed suppressed. Admitting and recognizing the inevitability of a clash of interests does not mean falling into populist ungovernability. On the contrary, democracy offers the potential to process underlying conflicts in a healthy way. Suppressed resentments can potentially become responsible public demands if the democratization of very unequal societies, with long traditions of injustice, brings with it the possibility of all social sectors expressing their interests, and of mobilizing previously atomized groups to participate in the political process. In this way, latent and negative zero sum conflicts can be transformed into creative, sum positive conflicts. It is possible to disseminate an ethic of responsibility, a sense of shared participation in the benefits of what is publicly owned. Democratic governability can be promoted through tolerance and with the intelligent management of social conflict, and there are encouraging examples, such as the gradual evolution and learning process of the Uruguayan *Frente Amplio*. The potential is there and should be encouraged, and democrats cannot remain fearful of demands emanating "from below" for too long without risking the loss of what they most value: stable democracy. But if the conflictive tendencies inherent in the democratization of an unequal society are to be intelligently managed and contained, then it is not just chronic injustice that must be addressed. It is also severe citizen insecurity. Unfortunately, that too is a prominent component in the configuration of contemporary Latin America's most salient characteristics.

III. Democracy and Insecurity

Profoundly unequal and poorly integrated societies can be subjected to successive cycles of modernizing reform from above, but these transformations may each remain incomplete and contestable because the underlying requirements for a societal consensus do not exist. In Latin America, this was traditionally viewed as a key explanation for intermittent episodes of authoritarian rule (often by the military as the ultimate guarantor or order within the state) sometimes more personalist or more populist. Regardless of form, the basis for this recurring pattern was a widely perceived need to impose order and to define the boundaries within which actors could enjoy security in a context where social divisions might otherwise run out of control. In contrast with the relatively stable and durable despotisms that have arisen in other parts of the world, however, the authoritarian regimes of Latin America mostly neither lasted very long nor succeeded in justifying their existence beyond a more or less prolonged period of "emergency" rule. They were capable of inspiring fear and of generating acquiescence for limited periods of time, when the trauma of previous disorders was still most vivid in the collective memory, but their initial unity and rationale faded rather fast, and the underlying lack of consensus eventually turned against them.[9]

By the early 1980s, many Latin Americans had come to associate the latest cycle of authoritarian regimes not with the provision of a needed social order, but with gross human rights abuses and other forms of misgovernment, including the imposition of undemocratic projects of reform. The ensuing region-wide shift to civilian constitutional governments with competitive elections and freedom of expression reflected a widespread negative consensus (against abusive authoritarian rule) even if there was sometimes less positive agreement about how order was to be maintained in the absence of state coercion. Democracy was the internationally approved—and locally desired—solution to this problem: even Portugal and Spain had proved surprisingly capable of moving away from their dictatorial straitjackets. To some extent it has also provided Latin Americans with the opportunity to bridge some social divisions and to generate more consensus, but as compared with Southern Europe, or with the standard assumptions of liberal democratic theory, twenty years after most of Latin America's transitions to democracy, the region still displays many of the distinctive characteristics of weak social integration and lack of public security that used to provide the backdrop for episodes of emergency rule. In Guillermo O'Donnell's lexicon, "ours are democracies of truncated or low intensity citizenship."[10]

Thus, despite democratization, citizenship in most of contemporary Latin America confers uncertain real rights. For a large proportion of the population, rights remain precarious and susceptible to being withdrawn. It is not that there are no rights—even under authoritarian rule the situation was rarely that clear cut. Rather, and more typically, people have theoretical entitlements that are not translatable into real rights because of an array of institutional, political, economic, and even cultural blockages: in short, because of the distance between juridical and political theory and local configurations. As Panizza and Barahona de Brito argue for the case of Brazil, "the persistence of human rights violations is a product of four interrelated factors. First, at a socio-economic level, because of extreme levels of poverty and inequality, which in urban areas are linked with increased criminality and violence connected with drug-trading and in rural areas are expressed in land struggles resulting in violent conflict. Second, at a political, institutional, and cultural level, because of the survival and re-adaptation of "traditional" non-democratic forms of social and political power mediation which permeate the state and society and which co-exist with "modern" democratic modes of state-society relations. Third, and related to the above, because of ambiguous attitudes towards the "modern" concepts of rule of law, equality before the law and citizenship, among political and economic elites and within society as a whole, as a result of the survival and proliferation of an alternative view of justice and rights, whereby "the force of the law" is overwhelmed by "the law of force," which predominates in relations between the forces of law and order and sectors of the political class, on the one hand, and the "marginalized" or most under-privileged sectors of society on the other. Both of the dynamics or realities above pre-date the period of authoritarian military rule; however, the inheritance of "authoritarian enclaves", mentalities and practises from that period have reinforced the non-democratic character both of form of power mediation and attitudes towards the fundamental principles of citizenship and the rule of law. Fourth, on a more institutional level, the dynamic of violence occurs in an extremely fragmented and heterogeneous universe which limits the central state's capacity to implement effective strategies to improve the human rights situation." [11]

Asserting legally established rights requires activity and vigilance, not just by individuals but also by groups and communities, and such vigilance is often absent or not sustained. The state is always liable to default unless pressurized, and extra-legal power groups continue to constrain the unorganized majority from expressing and pursuing the "public good." Thus, what characterizes Latin American democracy is not just stark social inequality, but also the associated prevalence of multiple forms of citizen insecurity. This affects collective perceptions of the real consequences of top-down reform initiatives, however attractive they may sound in principle, and generates waves of protest and resistance from below, prompted by the fear of being cheated or excluded by elites that are better organized. It gives rise to what some have called "praetorian" patterns of political pressure and inter-group confrontation that exceed the boundaries of conventional liberal democratic practice, and that can easily destabilize whatever reform projects may currently be in vogue. In helps to explain what I have typified as a characteristically Latin American lack of institutional integration and social consensus, a recurring tendency found not only under authoritarian rule but also in many of the region's new democracies. Of course, not all of Latin America is affected to an equal extent, and nor is the region the only part of the world to experience bouts of praetorian instability within a loosely democratic institutional framework. Nevertheless, the precarious citizenship rights and the associated insecurities affecting much of the electorate are pronounced features of this region and go far to explaining why its experience with democratization differs both from the standard assumptions of democratic theory and from the template of "democratic consolidation."

"Citizen security" refers broadly to all the concerns related to criminality and the rule of law and, in principle, to other aspects of public policy that can affect the physical integrity of the population, ranging from the regulation of traffic accidents, protection from domestic, street, and school or college violence or intimidation (for every criminal act reported, many more may be threatened), to public health provisions, and collective protection against natural disasters such as earthquakes, hurricanes, or volcanic eruptions, all of which require public policy responses.[12] Contemporary notions of citizenship rights are more extensive. It has been argued that in democratic Central America "the concept of citizen security is expanding as governments and security officials recognize that crime and social violence are linked to broader social and economic issues, such as the lack of education, health, and economic opportunities," and that "citizen security needs to be perceived as a condition to wider political and economic development, and not an end in itself. Improved security on the streets and in the home is a joint responsibility of the local government and the citizens themselves and should not be viewed as a service to be provided by the government alone."[13] These are strong arguments in favor of an expansive concept of citizen security, but there are problems with such ambitions in settings where the reach of the state is often uncertain, and where traditionally neither "citizenship" nor "security" have been promoted or respected, and where the monopoly over the legitimate use of force by the state remains in dispute due to the legacy of attacks by state agents on the physical integrity of citizens and continuing severe social inequality. From a democratic perspective, all these sources of insecurity come together to the extent that voters hold authorities responsible for failure to respond effectively in such situations. Modern governments have more responsibility for technology and control over nature than was the case in the early days of democracy, and so citizen security is expected to extend to coping with disasters as well as regulating conflicts between citizens.

An Illustration from El Salvador

A brief sketch of citizen insecurity in post conflict El Salvador serves to illustrate these general points. This example is not typical of the region as a whole but it presents in stark form tendencies that are present throughout the region to a greater or lesser degree. El Salvador is frequently—and plausibly—presented as a demonstration of the changes that democratization can bring, but it also shows how resistant some practices are to regime change, how deeply entrenched social characteristics or traditions shape and constrain patterns of political and social behavior, and thus how important is the explanatory power of the contextual factors highlighted in this volume. The Salvadoran democratization process took place after more than a decade of extremely destructive internal conflict, during which time between 1 and 2 percent of the population were killed, and nearly one-fifth were driven to emigrate, mostly to the United States. The causes of the conflict were multiple and remain a matter of controversy, but the repressive and partisan conduct of the old forces of order—including various police agencies all ultimately subordinate to the armed forces—was undoubtedly a major contributory factor. Once both domestic and international opinion had come to a shared understanding that the old forces of order had contributed to create and aggravate the civil conflict, it followed that an externally monitored compromise peace settlement could provide for a far-reaching restructuring of the country's system of law and order. This was a key element of the January 1992 peace agreement, and constituted a central pillar of the democratization process in the 1990s.

Given this background, the provision of citizen security as an explicit political aim has figured more prominently in the Salvadoran process than in most other parallel processes in Latin America and more generally. Indeed, as most democracies failed to radically reshape police forces or remove from positions of command officials associated with previous episodes of repression, El Salvador became something of a model of post-conflict democratization in which a reformed police force plays a new and more positive role as a guarantor of citizen security. Peace was the overwhelming aim of a society subjected to a decade-long civil war, and it was assumed that peace would mean personal security, including freedom from the fear of sudden violence. However, this kind of security has failed to emerge, and the driving force behind ongoing efforts to improve citizen security is a result of this unmet demand. Indeed, as amply documented in the literature, citizen insecurity remains a severe and generalized problem in El Salvador.

Some survey results suffice to illustrate the gravity of the problem. In May 2000, 49 percent of the adult population rated crime and delinquency as the main national problem. This reality feeds perceptions that are liable to stimulate authoritarian and antidemocratic reflexes among significant sectors of the electorate, which means that the public institutions reshaped during democratization processes are the beneficiaries of no more than provisional or conditional popular approval. Their continued authority depends on delivering expected benefits, which is presently far from assured.[14] This point comes across in a 1999 survey, which found that whereas 40 percent of those with university degrees had reported being victimized over the previous twelve months, only 10 percent of illiterates had done so.[15] There was a similar gradient according to income levels, and also by size of municipality. If crimes affect mostly the better off and more educated in the urban centers, then collective perceptions of the gravity of the situation may be more alarmist than if the reverse is the case. On the one hand, the concerns of the educated can generate public pressure to tackle the problem more effectively through greater resources allocation or prioritizing crime-fighting over other problems, and on the other, it appears in this case that the more educated apparently tend to favor more reformist and less authoritarian strategies of crime control than the uneducated. This contrast emerged clearly when respondents were asked to choose between *mano dura* policing and "participation by all." Among those with no education 53 percent favored the first, compared to 39 percent preferring the second. Of those with higher education only 28 percent endorsed authoritarian alternatives compared to 66 percent favoring participatory responses.[16]

El Salvador's very high indices of criminal violence and absence of security are far from new and will not be easily improved. Guatemala, and to a lesser extent Honduras and Nicaragua, face similar problems, which indicates their rooted nature. There is evidence of widespread and severe disenchantment with the quality of public life in Latin America in general. Prominent causes are corruption, impunity, lack of accountability, and failure to deliver on election promises. Alarm over the often apparently uncontrollable expansion of common, organized, and petty crime, and distress over weak police forces and judiciaries feature recurrently as major aspects of citizen discontent. Survey data, crime statistics, victim reports, and press coverage all tend to underscore the gravity of the phenomenon, particularly in post-conflict new democracies such as El Salvador, but also more generally. The material, psychological, and institutional legacies of prolonged civil war clearly aggravate these problems of insecurity, even after almost a decade of peace. In El Salvador the situation is worsened by the fact that violence and justice system failings were already unusually high long before the armed conflict began.[17] Indeed, these factors materially contributed both to its genesis and severity. The 1932 *matanza* in which the government condoned the killing of about 1 percent of the population in a week, underlines the historically rooted nature of these traditions, which can be partially explained by reference to such features as high population density, the conflictive land tenure system, and repressive and oligarchic features of traditional state organization.

Post-conflict El Salvador is a predominantly urban society with a now quite well-developed set of democratic institutions, however, so whatever the historical and regional roots of citizen insecurity there are now countervailing tendencies and with time and appropriate strategies substantial improvements are possible, as the positive case of Costa Rica illustrates. Under democratic conditions the demand for security can be challenged through the electoral process (incumbents who are seen to make insufficient efforts to improve governmental performance risk being rebuffed by voters, even when they doubt that the opposition can do much better), the media (which can damage the reputation and even destroy the careers of public officials who are held to have failed in their duties), and local democracy (town hall meetings, local petitions, and related activism at the municipal and community levels). In other words, under democracy the public at large gains access to a variety of means of pressing for more effective public security policies. It can also exert negative pressure by stepping outside democratic restraints. Where the authorities are seen to fail them, citizens may resort to extra-legal direct action as dramatized by vigilantism in Guatemala and elsewhere on the continent, or they may shift their allegiance to leaders who are willing to use more ruthless methods to impose public order.

In addition to these political avenues of expression there are also other powerful—economically based—pressures for effective reform. Businessmen and foreign investors are less likely to invest in El Salvador if they feel vulnerable to kidnapping. Livestock farmers will be unable to maintain and improve their holdings if they cannot protect themselves from rustlers. Vehicle retailers will find their business hampered if car theft is rampant. Hotels and restaurants serving tourist attractions will founder if potential visitors are warned off by travel advisories. These and other harmful economic effects of citizen insecurity reduce tax revenues and job opportunities, and therefore make it harder for the authorities to deliver on any policy promises. One attempt to estimate the economic costs attributable to violence in Latin America concluded that El Salvador was the worst-affected country under study in 1998: 24.9 percent of GDP was the estimated loss. Next came Colombia (24.7 percent), Mexico (12.3 percent), Venezuela (11.8 percent), and then Brazil (10.5 percent).[18] If the calculation is even approximately correct, then all Salvadorans with an interest in economic recovery and development have the strongest possible incentive to press for effective reform policies in the area of security. This is not a narrow concern of the business community; on the contrary, one of the sectors best placed to reap the economic benefits of curbing such losses is the million strong Salvadoran émigré community. They are currently repatriating over US$1,500 million in remittances annually—about one quarter of the GDP—sending funds as far as the remotest corners and to the poorest sectors of Salvadoran society. These remittances involve heavy sacrifices from some of the most hard-working and lowly paid members of the U.S. labor force. If the Salvadoran economy can be made more secure, these remittances could be used with much greater effect.

The construction of a new democracy has profoundly changed the structure and the procedures of the country's law and order institutions, and created new expectations and channels of public expression on citizen security issues. Given the intensity of public concerns over this problem, a new democracy can gain in strength or become more fragile, depending on how well or badly these new arrangements operate or are believed to operate. In the presidential election campaign of 2004, twelve years after the signing of the peace accords, one of the issues most strongly emphasized by the winning candidate was his commitment to extremely harsh policies of crime control. Thus, in the Latin American republic that has gone the furthest in reorganizing its police and justice system to reflect the requirements of a working democracy, the persistence of an acute sense of citizen insecurity continues to overshadow the new regime.

El Salvador is certainly an extreme case, but this example is far from being just an aberration. In different guises the issue of citizen insecurity can be found shaping popular expectations of democracy in Colombia (where it may lead to the first presidential re-election in half a century), in Argentina (where strong passions are stirred by the *piquetero* movement), in Brazil (because of violence over land issues, for example), and in Bolivia (where road blockades brought down one president in 2003, and then another in 2005), to give just some examples. In Mexico and the Caribbean an additional source of tension arises from the role of transnational crime in trafficking drugs, arms, people, and illegal migrants across international borders and in laundering the huge monetary flows produced by such activities.[19] It has not been possible in the compass of this brief section to describe and classify all these diverse manifestations of citizen vulnerability and indeed their near defenselessness in so many of the new democracies of Latin America. But, as with the recurrent patterns of acute inequality traced in the previous section of this chapter, twenty years or more after the establishment of formally democratic political regimes throughout the subcontinent it is not clear that insecurity is in the process of being diminished or overcome. Indeed, where transnational sources of insecurity are concerned, it can be argued that if states as highly integrated and relatively well equipped to deal with such phenomena as those of the EU face tremendous difficulties in curbing transnational organized crime and its national manifestations, then the relatively less well-equipped and fragmented states of Latin America are likely to be far less able to exercise effective authority and, indeed, sovereignty in this domain. Insofar as this is true, the sources and manifestations of citizen insecurity are likely to increase in intensity rather than diminish in the foreseeable future. So the distinctive configuration of regional characteristics highlighted in this volume may well continue to include a paradoxical combination of democracy, inequality, and insecurity for decades to come. If so, what those who are interested in this region will need to analyze is not so much each of these traits in isolation, but rather the manner in which they all fit together and persist over time.

IV. Conclusions

According to liberal political theory, in a democracy all citizens should have a say about public affairs. Although they are not obliged to participate, if something concerns them they have the right to be heard by those in authority and they can even change their rulers at predetermined intervals to ensure that their concerns are taken seriously. There is a counterpart to this right to be heard, however: citizens are also subject to constraints. The theory of citizenship views them as individual agents, with some consequent equality of rights and responsibilities before the law. The rule of law protects critical aspects of personal and collective security, and in return citizens are obliged to abide by its provisions. If certain provisions of law are objectionable to them they may seek to change them by democratic means, but until such time good citizens must observe them anyway. Citizenship therefore involves an exchange—more security in return for less freedom of action. But this presupposes the existence of an effective and impartial justice system, of course, one that is capable of interpreting legal principles as they apply to the messy particulars of individual cases. It is hard to find any justice system that begins to approach these conditions in contemporary Latin America.[20] It may be that in due course and in favorable conditions this gulf can gradually be bridged, but this large region's long-standing and distinctive tradition of unstable/precarious citizenship rights and chronic insecurity is proving remarkably resilient. If so, this will constrain the effectiveness and credibility of current democratic regimes, just as it undermined their authoritarian predecessors.

During the Cold War, it was possible to view Latin America's inequalities, social conflicts, and lack of cohesion through the lens of a global ideological conflict. Two rival totalizing projects were on offer and attempts to stabilize an intermediate position kept breaking down, subverted either from the Left or from the Right. Political violence, insecure citizenship rights, and inoperative rule of law protections could all be explained as by-products of this unresolved foundational dispute. But since the dismantling of the Berlin Wall in 1989—at least until September 11, 2001—Latin America has ceased to debate such opposed alternative external images of modernity. Throughout the 1990s the region was subjected to a much more univocal liberal message. Outward-looking market democracy was presented as the externally sanctioned, final "end of history" version of modernity, and if the region was at last to occupy its proper place in the modern western first world, it would have to embrace the "Washington Consensus" as an economic model, and competitive electoral democracy as its standard political form. But the region still displayed some stubbornly distinctive configurative characteristics. As we saw in the previous chapter, when it embraced the "privatization" component of the economic model, the results turned out other than expected because despite strong liberal foundations the standard prescription was poorly adjusted to the regional context and outlook. Similarly with democratization, this chapter has underscored the paradox that arises when this abstract political formula is universalized without concomitant improvements in social equity and citizen security. The majority of ordinary voters in Latin America may be entirely receptive to a model of liberal market democracy that grants them consumer sovereignty, personal security, and stable political-civil rights. But what they experience is not this ideal, however compatible with their cultural traditions it may be. Instead they find that this version of modernity, like the many alternative projects that have preceded it, brings nothing like "end of history" closure, but rather something far more precarious and contested. Therefore market democracy has yet to generate the social cohesion that would reshape and create a new version of Latin America's configurative distinctiveness, one that would be more hospitable to the prescriptions and expected results of universal liberal theory.

From this standpoint of the region's median voter or typical citizen, three features of the current configuration can be highlighted as contrasts with the standard liberal template. First, as stressed throughout this chapter, rights that are supposed to be guaranteed as secure background conditions for the pursuit of individual objectives are experienced as precarious, unstable, subject to abrupt expansion and then contraction. The consequence of this is that it would be foolhardy to trust in formal institutions: from the point of view of the *indivíduo*, to use da Matta's term, they are not there so much to protect them, but rather to serve the interests of the elite. Thus, to the ordinary person it seems that the only way to convert ostensible rights and entitlements into cashable benefits is to practise vigilance (to instinctively mistrust rather than to instinctively assume good faith on the part of authorities); to seek powerful protectors (who by virtue of their influence and position can do the *favor* of "trickling down" to their preferred *protégés* the rights that are formally entitled to but can only obtain through such *favores*, to act in groups (which act self-defensively against the state rather than engaging with it as a part of the solution, and which tend, in the absence of widespread social trust or good faith, to withdraw from "national" action, and to prefer mobilization with people who can be trusted because they are not part of the system, such as families, local communities, or grievance-specific groups such as the landless, pensioners whose savings have been depleted by fiscally troubled and predatory states); and perhaps to protest before harm is done. This helps to explain the "direct action" or even "praetorian" component of collective action in the context of "contentious politics." This is the, often defensive, mobilization of those who do not trust the state and elites to act *de boa fé*.

Second, and related to the above, distrust of the state and of experts and elites is not just an expression of weak cohesion and the debility of traditional authority at the societal level. It is also a learned response to entrenched experiences of patrimonialism and partiality at the top of the social hierarchy. For the *indivíduo*, unless you are well connected it may be risky to report a crime to the police, as instead of serving the public good of combating crime you may be inviting the unwelcome and potentially life-threatening attention of criminal circles tied into the security apparatus. Similarly, only the naïve or foreigners would imagine that an anticorruption campaign could be aimed at fighting corruption in general. The entrenched popular assumption, reinforced by constantly renewed examples, will be that in general the elites enjoy impunity, and that when an exception arises this represents some settling of scores at the top rather than a genuine shift toward equality before the law.[21] And third, even if the liberal state were to develop a more impartial and rights-enforcing stance, this would not necessarily do much to promote increased social cohesion, given the strengthening of transnational forces that accompany liberalization and globalization. The citizen rights and protections that have been promised but not delivered by market democracy are responsibilities that accrue to the nation state. But ordinary people in Latin America are under few illusions about the margin of maneuver available to their respective state organizations in catering for a mass public while also retaining international confidence and the goodwill of the developed west. Remittances from the north often exceed the welfare budgets now available to many national administrations (budgets that are in any case subject to many forms of conditionality and external supervision); and estimates of the proceeds from transnational criminal activities, although hard to quantify with precision, are estimated to far outstrip the entire state budgets of most Latin American republics.[22]

Since September 2001, Washington's demands for border and security cooperation, the extradition of externally designated malefactors, and the privileged protection of U.S. assets overseas has swamped any more balanced approach to the strengthening of the rule of law for all in the region. More generally, the transnational forces unleashed by liberalization are often seen as generating more insecurity for ordinary people than can be handled by the rights protecting institutions of the democratic state. So although regional elites may still attempt to transmit modernizing reforms from "above and without," what many citizens observe from below and within is that the old boundaries between *lo nacional* (within) and *lo externo* (without) are breaking down as the centrality of state organization, and thereby sovereign capabilities, erode.

This chapter has sketched a synthetic interpretation of Latin America's distinctive—and in theoretical terms paradoxical—combination of democracy, extreme inequality, and insecurity. The brief treatment was required to counterbalance other chapters that have an elite or top-down focus. But the standard caveats are even more necessary here. Not all of Latin America is uniformly as described here, and not only in Latin America is such a paradoxical condition observed. Although these tendencies seem powerfully recurrent there should be no assumption that they are necessarily immutable. Over time, and in favorable circumstances, it must be possible to overcome popular distrust and strengthen social cohesion, and thereby to improve the "quality of democracy." But the region-wide liberal democratic convergence of the 1990s did not prove strong enough to overwhelm the distinctive patterns of expectations and response traced throughout this volume. Until those inherited reflexes and configurative patterns are dissolved, models that would obey one logic when applied in a "first world" context are likely to continue to produce unexpected forms of adaptation, resistance, and even reversal, when transposed to this large region. If this is so, then, as the conclusion to this book argues, there is a case for methodologically self-conscious "area studies" in general, and for explicit attempts to "characterize" large regions in particular.

Conclusion: On Characterizing Latin America

In this volume, I have attempted to "characterize Latin America," to formulate a personal interpretation of the most important features distinguishing this large region from the rest of the world, as well as those features it shares, or at least appears to share with other large regions, and most notably with Europe. This is a "configurative" enterprise, in that it involves the identification of a series of interrelated features that taken together differentiate one region from another. Such configurative assessments of large communities usually invoke some basic features of the long-run history, culture, and geographical context of the collectivity postulated as shaping its outlook and behavior. This is in contrast to the more one-dimensional yardsticks commonly used to rank and classify countries and regions (such as by per capita income, homicide rates, or human development indicators).[1]

Thus, just as we recognize a face or characterize an individual on the basis of multiple overlapping and loosely integrated pieces of partly subjective information, so too we formulate synthetic assessments about large regions and social collectivities, characterizing them by the attribution of recurring distinctive traits. Such generalizations are often highly impressionistic, and can easily lapse into stereotyping (where group solidarity prevails over the balanced appraisal of differences). In consequence, the general characterization of nations or regions has fallen very much out of favor with mainstream social scientists professionally trained to rely on objective indicators and to eschew all subjective interpretations. From the other side of the academic spectrum, cultural studies and postmodern scholars (who may be entirely untroubled by subjectivity) also steer away from such characterizations on the grounds that they are "totalizing" and represent attempts to impose grand narratives that do not respect the diversity of identities and the contested nature of all social labeling.

That still leaves some academics schooled in the tradition of area studies, and perhaps most importantly, regional historians, who may be warily disposed to venture into this tricky terrain, but usually with considerable trepidation and without much systematic consideration of the status of the claims that can defensibly be made in this area. The few who go further, such as Samuel Huntington, Howard Wiarda, and Octavio Paz, to name just a few, easily stray into the error of "essentializing" their claims, implying that they have identified some necessary and permanent underlying structure that clearly and permanently differentiates one country region or civilization from another and that therefore has clear predictive consequences when the most that can ever be established in this area is a relative disposition, a broad set of mentalities, or habitual tendencies that may be more marked in one setting than in another, but that are neither exclusive to any single collectivity, nor immutable in the face of external developments.

So, just as our ability to recognize an individual through his pattern of facial characteristics does not preclude us from recognizing strong family resemblances, or changes over time, and only generates the most weakly predictive of expectations about his or her behavior, so the characterization of a large region need not be either exclusivist or strongly predictive. When analysts go beyond this and attempt to isolate attributes that they suppose to be inherently and necessarily different in one society from another, they can be justly suspected of stirring up emotional reactions by projection of an alien "Other," this may be done either to intensify group solidarity in their own society, or to slight the collective claims of the alternative community.[2] Although in Latin America it has also been customary to highlight supposed inherent regional deficiencies—sometimes supposedly attributable to ethnic traits.

In view of such dangers, and the unfashionable nature of the enterprise, this attempt to characterize Latin America configuratively requires some justification. First, if such categories and assumptions are in any case going to be deployed, it is best to submit them to explicit scrutiny and evaluation. Second, the currently most fashionable social science alternative strategies of analysis risk creating a self-referring virtual world that can obscure more than it illuminates if not exposed to external reality checks. Third, September 11, 2001 has highlighted the practical consequences of losing the ability to characterize large regions carefully and without resorting to misleading stereotypes of an alien "Other." Let us consider these three points in turn.

The media and official discourse are replete with casual references to Latin America as a whole, to its supposed peculiarities and to its ambiguous location in international hierarchies of merit and approbation. This is a commonplace of public debate not only in North America and Europe, but also throughout the region. "Latin America" exists as much in the mind of outside observers as it does in the minds of Latin Americans themselves—both among elites and within popular culture. Brazilians anxiously debate why their country's position has been confused with that of less "serious" Spanish republics (Argentina in particular). Mexicans ironize about official claims that their country has left Latin America and joined the "first world," with membership of the North America Free Trade Agreement (NAFTA). Bolivians worry that all the most negative attributes of "Latin American-ness" are being delegated to themselves. Some Cubans and Venezuelans still try to champion a version of Latin American identity that proudly defies the onslaught of globalization, deploying an autonomous nationalist rhetoric that projects that mythical Latin American identity onto a homogenized global stage. Thus, stereotypical assumptions about regional characteristics and their distribution, appropriation, or rejection suffuse collective deliberations and sway public policy choices. This is so whether or not these assumptions are well founded or explicitly stated. So the first argument for scholarly work on this topic is that in its absence the subject will not disappear, but our understanding of it will be worse. There has to be some benefit in drawing attention to the relevant evidence and to what can and cannot credibly be claimed about regional characteristics. As this is not a consensual field of expertise, there may be no unambiguously correct answer, but it may nevertheless be useful to promote serious dialogue and encourage reasoned refutation of misguided claims.

At present, the main antidote to unsubstantiated claims about collective characteristics is the rigor of standard social scientific procedures of testing and measurement. This volume is not intended to slight such procedures. But it does rest on the assumption that they are often ill suited to capture all the interconnected dimensions that can be detected through a "configurative" characterization of a whole society. They are designed to impose a check on the subjectivity of the analyst by imposing precise impersonal definitions of all variables, and by assembling replicable quantitative indicators as proxies for each item of explanation. But the very strengths of such methods mean they are very narrowly focused on specific (and presumably universal) characteristics that can be readily observed and calibrated. While this may work well in a number of important social domains (electoral behavior, market interactions, or demography, for example) it is not so well adapted to the task of characterizing large-scale long-run configurative patterns of self-understanding and collective behavior.

This is like a pedometer that can accurately track how we run, but that has no counterpart to explain what we dream. Precision measurements can convey the realities of general income distribution, but they cannot show us how people experience time and space; they can show us how votes are distributed, but not the shape and color of political hopes. Such methods cannot make sense of Neruda's view that "Latin America is very fond of the word "hope." We like to be called the "continent of hope." Candidates for deputy, senator, president, call themselves "candidates of hope." This hope is really something like a promise of heaven, an IOU whose payment is always being put off. It is put off until the next legislative campaign, until next year, until the next century."[3] Any "Latin Americanist" will immediately recognize the "truth" of this portrayal of a certain kind of "mentality," and his or her "tacit knowledge" will tell them, even though it cannot be submitted to scientific testing, that it is a nuance that helps to explain certain kinds of political behavior. In effect, much standard social science technique therefore excludes from measurement most of what (from an area studies perspective) one might consider to be crucial for the understanding of large region differences and similarities. With the help of what they would regard as "tacit knowledge" social scientists can be encouraged to develop indicators that come closer to reflecting the practices they purport to measure. But in the absence of broader guidance, the blindly objective quantifier risks constructing a parallel universe of statistical abstractions that can autocorrelate without ever connecting to any external social reality. So this attempt to characterize large regional configurations that lie beyond the reach of most standard indicators is not so much a rejection of social science as an effort to ground it by systematizing some of the tacit knowledge it disregards.

In the current international climate, following the atrocity of September 11, and the reactions it provoked, there are additional reasons for concern over the dangers that can arise from an incapacity or unwillingness to recognize the historical and discursive subtleties that can separate one large region of the world from the rest. During the Cold War the makers of western policy did at least recognize the value of area studies, if not as an end in itself, than at least as a means to formulate more effective and appropriate strategies to counter the appeal of Communism. Whatever the distortions to understanding introduced by this motivation, it did at least validate the study of foreign languages and of the perceptions and belief systems of other peoples. In current conditions the alternative western security standpoint seems to be that sensitivity to regional and cultural distinctiveness becomes hard to distinguish from disloyalty to liberal values that are on the one hand assumed to be universal (such that, for instance, the exact content of the terms liberty and justice are similarly understood everywhere), but that on the other hand are also above all "Ours."

From this standpoint, such values both can and must be supported, and if necessary imposed on others, an enterprise that could be thwarted if too much attention were paid to the supposed differences of perspective attributed to some other regions and cultures. Within this framework Latin America's best interest would be best served by highlighting its commitment to western liberal traditions, and by downplaying any distinctive characteristics that would complicate the manichaeaneism of the "war on terror." Those in Latin America who persist in invoking "Bolivarian" traditions, or the anti-imperialist discourse of Martí, or indeed any structured alternative to a single unified "end of history" vision of modernity, are therefore readily reclassified at best as "fossils" of a lost era. Worse still, they risk being labeled as apologists for terrorism or fellow travelers of international crime, whose protestations of regional distinctiveness can then be dismissed as no more than ideology or self-deception. This increasingly prevalent justification for disregarding regional differences tends to reinforce the marginalization of area studies as an academic field, and further discourages scholarly enquiry into large region characteristics and differences.

Whether such militant disinterest in the belief systems and collective experiences of other peoples will really contribute to effective western security policies remains highly questionable. From a hard-nosed realist perspective it could be argued that the firm and consistent application of western power is all that is needed to bring "waverers" into line, and thus to isolate true security threats. Vague appeals for "understanding" the outlook of other peoples can thus be dismissed as distractions. However, even so-called realists who insist on the primacy of "hard power" have traditionally accepted the dictum that it is advantageous to attempt to "know your enemies." This is all the more crucial if security is to be promoted by the deployment of "soft" power (which appeals to common values, for example), as must be the case when relying on the supposed universality of liberal individualist aspirations. Further, whether or not western security can be furthered through the development of area studies, the main case for learning how to characterize other nations and regions is not so narrowly instrumental. By achieving a more nuanced understanding of the differences between societies and culture zones the West can arguably defuse various sources of conflict, and reduce the risk of frightening itself with distorted images of their peoples.

More generally, the case for this kind of area studies perspective extends far beyond the current preoccupations of Western security managers. By better characterizing our neighbors we can identify imaginatively with larger communities of interest, and we can thus construct broader collective identities to address shared problems. Characterizing other societies also helps us to see ourselves through the mirror of their perceptions—a critical step toward the extension of tolerance and civilization. Appreciating rather than fearing human diversity is also, in principle, a key feature of the liberal standpoint that western policy-makers claim to champion. So, on these three arguments, even if explicitly characterizing large regions is a difficult and unfashionable enterprise it is also analytically better than leaving the issue unaddressed, and it may even have the potential to help us construct a more tolerant and therefore a safer world.

This volume has concentrated on only one large region, and is exploratory in tone. Its intent has been to serve as an antidote to the current social science fashion for embracing universal models that by assumption screen out regional particularisms, and that generate over-confidence in the uniformity and predictive reliability of causal mechanisms in social explanation. The alternative to universal models is not to construct tightly specified predictive models that apply to only one region. On the contrary: nearly all the explanatory variables used to characterize Latin America (such as state organization or constitutional traditions) are present outside the region as well as within it. They are present, but not uniform, insofar as the way in which each variable operates depends upon its interaction with a constellation of other factors, some of which may be regionally specific. For example, state organization operates distinctively in a zone of peace, where states were precocious, have an unbroken tradition of autonomy, and have long exerted very uneven territorial control. So it is not the operation of any single causal variable that provides the explanatory thrust, rather it is *the way in which a variety of such factors are configured in a particular context*. Such local "configurative" features may go far to explaining why any general model operates in a specific way in one setting, but not in another (why "presidentialism" operates differently in Latin America and in the United States to take one example). This involves constructing what Max Weber referred to as "ideal types" more applicable in some contexts then in others. Thus, claims about a "bias toward modernity" among Latin American elites are *relative*. They do not exclude the possibility of finding similar biases elsewhere. Nor do they require that the same degree of bias always be present throughout the region. Since this strategy of explanation is both relative and configurative, it should not be expected to generate highly predictive conclusions. The ideal type highlights a tendency that can then be sought for when evaluating specific historical processes. It can be checked against relevant evidence (as in my inventory of Latin

America's "littered landscape" of superseded modernizing projects) but it should not be judged by the standard of mono-causal regularity.

This attempt to identify what distinguishes Latin America from the rest of the world is, of course, only the most recent in a long line of efforts to define a regional identity. There is no space here to review the vast torrent of Latin American literary and cultural output concerning every aspect of this issue (from Sarmiento on *Civilization and Barbarism* to Neruda's *Canto General*). Although such works certainly touch on the issues of concern to this volume they do so from a very different perspective. Their basic objective is to construct a regional self-understanding, to promote one or other identity-based claim, with its associated heroes and demons, and its prescriptive implications. This volume, by contrast, is addressed to a contemporary area studies and social science community, and comes from the United Kingdom. It is not prescriptive in intent, and one of its purposes has been to draw on recent scholarly work that adds precision and detail about historical topics that were hitherto subject to schematic polemics. Undoubtedly, the current generation of Latin American authorities on the theme of regional distinctiveness, including authors like Néstor García Canclini and Jorge Larraín,[4] are considerably more international and comparative in outlook, and more questioning of grand narratives. Some of their insights could surely enrich any attempt to characterize modern Latin America. But this volume is limited by my competences, which are in comparative politics and comparative historical analysis. It has therefore focused on specifying how and why contemporary Latin America resembles—or differs from—other large world regions, and what its distinctive regional configurations imply for universalistic models, and for theories of international convergence. Unlike most writing on Latin America, this contribution also takes the characterization of other large world regions seriously, and defends an in-depth global comparative approach.

So the closest counterparts to this undertaking can probably be found in the scattered work of analysts from various historical and social science disciplines, many of whom, like me, have studied the subcontinent sympathetically, but from the outside. For example, in the field of comparative economic history Stanley Engermann and Kenneth Sokoloff have stressed the crucial influence of the "factor endowment and attitudes towards it reflected in policy" in explaining the long-term divergence between the Spanish colonies of Mexico and Peru and the northern colonies of the North American mainland. While eschewing "path dependence" they accept "path influence" when they attribute the early history of extreme inequality in the

Spanish colonies, at least in part to their factor endowments: "In these cases, the extensive existing populations of indigenous peoples and the Spanish practices of awarding claims on land, native labor, and rich mineral resources to members of the elite encouraged the formation of highly concentrated landholdings and extreme inequality. In contrast, small family farms were the rule in the northern colonies of the North American mainland, where climatic conditions favored a regime of mixed farming centered on grain and livestock, which exhibited no economies of scale in production. The circumstances in these latter regions encouraged the evolution of more equal distributions of wealth, more democratic political institutions, more extensive domestic markets, and the pursuit of more growth-oriented policies than did those in the former. We suggest further that there are reasons for expecting regions with more equal circumstances and rights to be more likely to realize sustained economic growth and the breadth of evidence provided by the experiences of the New World colonies supports this view."[5]

A somewhat parallel attempt to characterize Latin America's historical distinctiveness, this time from the perspective of political ideas and institutions, can be found in the work of Richard Morse: "[. . .] surely we may assume that Latin America was from the start invaded, if not saturated, by a European economy that rationalized human dealings. If, however, we trace the unfolding of ideology, we find that only after 1760 did Latin Americans begin selectively to mesh Enlightenment precepts to received neo-Scholastic doctrine. And finally in our own era we discover that rationalization is still problematical, whether we speak of economic "development" or governance or social outlook." He goes on to cite with approval Roberto da Matta who "argues that citizenship in the industrial West is indeed the political corollary to the triumph of market relationships" and while cautioning against crude dichotomies he ventures the judgment that in Latin America "the aspiration to citizenship soared high with the achievement of nationhood. Yet it has made uncertain advance in a "relational" society. While merit criteria and individual rights became public doctrine, the laws of the state may even today recognize occupational hierarchies. Average citizens fear blind application of universal law that ignores buffers of connections or personal ties. If the social nucleus is relationship, not the individual, persons feel naked and apprehensive when addressed as citizens [. . .] We evoke Latin America's neo-Scholastic past to prove the persistence not of doctrines and institutions, but of a social ethic that remains congenial to many types of doctrines and institutions [. . .] First, "the natural order looms larger than the human community, and the community larger than the sum of its associations. The venerable tradition of 'natural law' has not atrophied, as in the United States"; second, "Latin American peoples still appear willing to alienate power to their chosen or accepted leaders, rather than delegate it to them"; third, "law-making and law-applying in Latin America are not in the last instance sanctioned by systematic referendum, by constitutions, by the bureaucratic ideal of 'service,' by tyrannical power, by custom, or by scientific or dialectical laws [. . .] in a patrimonial state the propriety of command is determined by the legitimacy of the authority that wields it. Hence the importance of sheer legalism in Latin American administration as constant certification for the legitimacy, not of the act, but of him who executes it [. . .]"; fourth, "the innate sense of the Latin American people for natural law is matched by a more casual attitude to man-made law. Human laws are frequently seen as harsh or unenforceable or as simply inapplicable to the specific case. Hence the difficulty of collecting taxes [. . .] the apathy of the police toward theft and delinquency; the thriving contraband trade at border towns [. . .] Finally, it seems scarcely less true now than in colonial times that the larger society is perceived in Latin America as composed of parts that relate through a patrimonial centre rather than directly to one another [. . .]."[6]

A third attempt of this kind illustrates the various styles of characterization that have preceded this volume. Here is Charles W. Anderson's approach (in the 1960s) to the task of generalizing about the distinctive regional context within which certain types of political change—often surprising and far reaching—may come to fruition (it is of particular interest in this volume because of the way it parallels some of the observations in chapter one): "[. . .] imperfect consensus on the nature of political regime is not a problem of politics peculiar to Latin America, nor does it account for the distinctiveness of Latin American politics. Rather, it is on a further dimension of the problem of political legitimacy that we must concentrate. For, in Latin America, no particular techniques of mobilizing political power, no specific political resources, are deemed more appropriate to political activity than others. No specific sources of political power are legitimate for all contenders for power [. . .] New contenders are admitted to the political arena of reciprocally recognizing elites in Latin America when they demonstrate a significant power capability, and when they provide assurances that they will not jeopardize the ability of any existing power contender to similarly participate in political activity. Thus, with the exception of 'real revolutionary' situations, the normal rule of Latin American political change is that new power contenders may be added to the system, but old ones may not be eliminated. It is this characteristic of the system that gives Latin American politics its distinctive flavour. While, in the history of the West, revolutionary experiences or secular change have sequentially eliminated various forms of power capability, contemporary Latin American politics is something of a 'living museum' in which all the forms of political authority of the western historic experience continue to exist and operate, interacting one with another in a pageant that seems to violate all the rules of sequence and change involved in our understanding of the growth of Western civilization."[7]

Forty years later some of Anderson's suggestions have been over-taken by events, in particular by the convergence on democratic procedures, which restrict alternative sources of legitimacy and elimi-nate power contenders who lack electoral support. Nevertheless, enough regional distinctiveness persists for his propositions to shed some light on how these particular democracies deviate from the stan-dard model. There is no space here for a review of the many attempts by political scientists writing after Anderson to improve on, or super-sede his proposal. But one effort in particular deserves mention here, because it deals with a very large theme not addressed in this volume. Ruth and David Collier constructed a model of political change and regime dynamics in Latin America that identified the entry of organized labor into the political arena as a vital "critical conjunc-ture," specific to the region. They did not claim that labor politics and state–labor relations could—of themselves—explain broader patterns of political change. But they did argue for its inclusion in what I am calling a "configurative" assessment of the region's political distinctiveness.[8]

Finally, this brief survey would be incomplete if it did not acknowl-edge my debt to S. N. Eisenstadt, whose efforts to differentiate Latin America's underlying characteristics from those of other large world regions include the following four suggestions. First, "one of the most important differences which characterise the Latin Americas and which they shared to some extent with other Americas, and which distinguish them from both the European and later the Asian societies was the relative weakness of primordial criteria in the definitions of their collective identities. In initial phases, the primordial attachments of the settlers were rooted in the European countries of origin and to a lesser extent in the new environment. With the passing of time and the consolidation of the new colonies, strong attachments developed to the new territory, but these attachments were defined in different terms from those that had crystallised progressively in Europe. In parallel there developed a much weaker combination of territorial, historical and linguistic elements as components of collective identity.

By sharing the respective hegemonic language with their countries of origin, and by sharing it among themselves, the very definition of primordial distinctiveness was unrelated to it in most Spanish American areas [. . .] From the beginning of the Hispanic as well as the Portuguese colonization, territoriality was defined above all in administrative terms, with important implications for the later development of 'natural' boundaries."

Second, "The orientation to the 'mother' country, and to the centres of Western culture, constituted continual models and reference points, to an extent probably unprecedented in any other society, including the later Asian ones in their encounter with the West. One of the most important differences between the various American civilisations and the Asian ones from the middle and end of the nineteenth century was that the confrontation with modernity, with the 'West,' did not entail, for the settlers in the Americas, a confrontation with an alien culture, imposed from the outside, but rather with their own other origins. Such encounters often became combined with a search to find their own distinctive place within the broader framework of European, or Western, civilisation. Accordingly, the relations between their own modernity, and those of other countries, constituted a continual concern about being at the margins of modernity. The possibility to develop from within these margins, possibly in conjunction with autochthonous traditions of the indigenous population also constituted a continual concern of many, especially *mestizo* groups and intellectuals in these countries."

Third, a strong statist orientation "developed in colonial times and persisted after independence, with states and political classes playing a central role in constructing the nations and national identities. At the same time, the strong hierarchical statist orientation was not, significantly enough, connected with the development of a parallel commitment to the political realm as a major focus of collective consciousness. Hence, side by side with the formal hierarchical principles, multiple social spaces developed, structured according to a variety of principles and identities, such as local identities, with relatively shifting boundaries and with the possibility of the incorporation of many of these identities into the central arena."

Fourth, "in contrast with North America, a very far-reaching 'de-autonomisation' of major elites occurred in Latin America. In place of aristocracy, with some autonomous rights of access to the centre, different oligarchies, dependent in principle on the state for both official, legitimate access to 'material' resources and to prestige and centres of power, became predominant. The major elites were internally weak, as evident in a relatively low degree of internal solidarity and in the symbolic and sometimes also organizational autonomy of the centres, and broader groups of the society, and of the major elites themselves. Few fully autonomous political, professional or cultural elites developed here. Most such elites tended to be strongly embedded, especially in mundane affairs, in broader ascriptive groups with little autonomous self-definition and orientation, even when they were already very specialized (e.g. professors or administrative echelons). It is in this context that the relations between conceptions of modernity, patterns of political representation and premises of religious authority and institutions should be analyzed as a continual perspective of political discourse in Latin America, especially in the discourse of modernity."[9]

Any attempt to characterize a large region of the world needs to consider not only its local traditions and practices but also its mode of interaction with other regions. Some regions, like Europe and North America, may be accustomed to acting from a position of strength and even assumed superiority *vis-à-vis* the rest of the world. Others may consider themselves great powers preoccupied with a need to "catch up" or perhaps to redress past injustices (consider Russia, China and earlier Japan). Still others may be resigned to a position of subordination in international hierarchies of power, or indeed to a state of aid dependence or external vulnerability. None of these possibilities accurately reflects the pattern of Latin America's external orientation.

This volume has drawn attention to the region's long tradition of importing population from elsewhere, and in particular its receptiveness to European immigration. Another crucial feature has been its physical separation from other regions, so that wars on the Eurasian landmass have not fundamentally threatened its sense of autonomy and relative security since independence—although proximity to the United States has been experienced as quite threatening in various past instances, and even today. The abundance of space and national resources, and the relative separation from centers of metropolitan control have also contributed to the region's distinctive orientation toward the rest of the world (an orientation particularly displayed by some elites, and not uniformly disseminated throughout heterogeneous and unequal societies). This relatively strong and recurrent disposition to emulate admired foreign models, and to compete over which variant should be introduced from without, helps distinguish Latin America from say, North America (which considers itself ahead of all others) or from the newly industrializing countries of East Asia (which aim to borrow selectively from the west in order to outperform it).

There may be some resemblance between this interpretation of Latin America and some of the ideas associated with the so-called dependency school of thought of the 1970s, in that both highlight the region's subordinate insertion in an unequal international system. But the two should not be conflated. Whereas the dependency perspective emphasized the dominant role of external constraints in determining local outcomes (barring a profound upheaval to break away from such linkages), and created a deterministic straightjacket that portrayed local elites as mere transmitters or agents of a perhaps involuntary but nonetheless structurally inescapable "class/imperial" struggle, this perspective highlights the subjective orientation, and relative autonomy, of Latin American elites (and to a less extent of Latin American societies in their entirety). It therefore sidesteps one of the crucial arguments used to discredit dependency theory—namely that if East Asia was able to overcome these external constraints they could not be as determining as the Latin American school liked to claim. In short, this perspective should be understood as a heuristic device, always to be checked against experience in successive domains, rather than as an encompassing theory of necessity. The external orientation sketched here is always open to revision and contestation. It is also a relative disposition (as compared to other parts of the world), rather than an absolute condition. To sum up the argument, the configurative interpretation of Latin America's distinctive characteristics can be reduced to four interrelated points stated baldly as follows.

First, Latin America's rival elites (including many of their supporting constituencies) are usually open to what they perceive to be "modern" external influences emanating from the metropolitan centers of Europe and North America. Indeed, insofar as being Latin American is another way of being European, models are as much imported as they are locally owned and contested: this is, after all, the "Far West."[10] Their region is sufficiently distant and autonomous from these latter centers for such influences to be appropriated selectively and interpreted locally (so there is always a degree of hybridity, rather than just straight emulation of foreign models). Long-established state organizations nurture successive and competing clusters of expertise, and offer considerable scope for the experts currently in power to implement far-reaching reforms, legitimized in the name of modern best practice. But there is no unique single model sustained to the very end. Different perceptions of alternative externally legitimized possibilities jostle against each other. The state may host a succession of authoritarian expert groups, each intolerant of the other. Reform projects therefore typically run out of steam and are replaced before they are finished. Lacking consensus they may never be stabilized.

Second, like other areas of new settlement, cut off from previous indigenous traditions and perceptions, Latin America also tends to look to the future rather than the past to evaluate the present. It has a "bias toward modernity." But unlike other areas of new settlement, this desired future is perceived as existing elsewhere, and as lacking at home: as Neruda says, it is like an IOU whose payment is always being put off. (During the Cold War a significant current of thought, particularly among the intelligentsia, imagined that communism could be the blueprint for this future. Since 1970, the options have narrowed to U.S. and European variants of market democracy, or perhaps to the sketchy hopes offered by the "World Social Forum".) This negative view of local conditions is neither stable nor absolute. There are partial achievements that can be built on, and there are always local experts available to promote further innovation and reform. But experience has taught most citizens to be skeptical. There is more agreement about what is wrong with the present than about which alternative would be either desirable or most feasible in the future. Consequently there are "multiple modernities" in contention, and fragmented perceptions of the desired better future.

Third, the region is very heterogeneous, with quite different experiences separating say Argentina from Brazil, or Buenos Aires from Jujuy. It is also suffers from marked social inequalities, by the compartmentalization of different subgroups, and by broader problems of social cohesion (exemplified, for example, by the absence of a reliable justice system, or a stable set of rights accessible to all). Some of this reality is captured by the many comparative social science databases that have proliferated since authoritarian rule was displaced by processes of democratization. But what these sources mainly convey is the dissatisfaction expressed by much of the population concerning the performance of their public institutions. This method helps establish where Latin American attitudes and perceptions are located in an international continuum of rankings, but it is less helpful in conveying how the various separate dimensions of dissatisfaction are configured, or what their consequences are for collective self-understanding and behavior. What emerges from this characterization of the region is a distinctive lack of conviction in the durability of each project of reform. This reflects the social heterogeneity and lack of consensus in most of these societies, and their long-established experiences of partial and reversible transformations. Survey data and behavioral rankings are insufficient on their own to convey this climate of opinion, which also needs to be tracked though cycles of progress and contentious political debate. The derogatory term "populism" is often involved to refer to all these irritating impediments to the stabilization of what some observers consider to be obviously desirable reforms. But this does not do justice to the complexity and rootedness of these popular traditions of resistance or to their configurative logic, so characteristic of the history of this region.

Fourth, as reiterated above, this characterization of Latin America's regional distinctiveness is intended as an aid to interpretation. This is a book of critical essays that make great use of a long accumulated "tacit knowledge," and which offer glimpses into a reality or a series of realities that can only be grasped and felt through a critical narrative exposition. The characterization is not meant to be predictive, nor is it intended primarily as a criticism. Rather, it is based on the view that a better understanding of how existing tendencies fit together and are reproduced can serve the cause of those who wish to modify unsatisfactory patterns. This exercise in large region characterization is only intended to address some neglected area of explanation. It is tentative and exploratory, and not intended to generate prescriptions.

In conclusion, Latin America is worth characterizing and distinguishing from other large regions, even if the exercise is difficult and wide open to debate. The idea that we can best analyze complex social realities by suppressing the names of countries and regions,[11] replacing them with abstract universal variables is both dangerous and foolhardy. It ignores "tacit knowledge," and suppresses the rich stock of implicit assumptions that always guide and structure practical human understanding of the social world. It seeks to banish this contextual richness, caricaturing it as mere "noise," unscientific prejudice, or ideology. But what actually results from this procedure is that its practitioners cut themselves off from the cognitive maps and collective discourses that we all need in order to make sense of our place in the social world around us. By dismissing as purely subjective the attributes widely associated with countries and regions, these analysts try to smuggle in by the backdoor an assumption that is highly questionable, and that for scientific purposes ought to be stated and defended up front— namely that explanatory variables are always universal and predictive, and that therefore particular national or regional contexts (configurations) either have no important effects, or if they do, they operate in ways that are impossible to specify with any rigor. Rather than making this assertion an article of scientific faith it needs to be tested against alternative strategies of explanation that *do* invoke contextual and configurative knowledge.

This is partly a question of good practice in generating social analysis, but it is more than just a question of method, and it extends beyond the domain of area studies that is our concern in this volume. Dangerous consequences can flow from a learned incapacity to evaluate social and political realities with the necessary attention to context, and to the tacit knowledge embodied in the descriptive language used by those involved. Such misplaced scientism can blind policy-makers, and public opinion in the more powerful nations, and prevent them from acknowledging the possibility that their assumedly universal laws and predictive models may trample on the susceptibilities of other peoples. It can therefore encourage arrogance and intolerance, emphasizing knowledge as an instrument of control, rather than as an aid to dialogue and mutual understanding. Even on its own terms it can therefore prove unsound as a strategy of prediction. Those who have rendered themselves incapable of understanding the configuratively structured differences of outlook that separate the various nations and large regions of the world will be poorly placed to appraise their own actions as they are perceived by other societies. If so, those actions are unlikely to produce the responses anticipated by supposedly more scientific and predictive methods of analysis.

So that is my case for area studies in general, and for contextual, configurative, and interpretative appreciations of regional specificities in particular. In this volume, I have provided one example by attempting a new characterization of Latin America as a large region to be compared and contrasted with other such entities. It is probable that this characterization is inadequate, but if so best practice will be for others to improve upon the enterprise, not to eschew it.

Notes

Introduction: Latin America in Comparative Perspective

1. See Samuel P. Huntington, *The Third Wave: Democratization in the Late Twentieth Century* (Norman, OH: Oklahoma University Press, 1993).
2. See Howard J. Wiarda (ed.), *Politics and Social Change in Latin America: Still a Distinct Tradition?* (Boulder, CO: Westview Press, 1992).
3. See, for example, Víctor Raúl Haya de la Torre, *La defensa continental* (Buenos Aires: Ediciones de Problemas de América, 1942).
4. Samuel P. Huntington, *Who Are We: The Challenges to America's National Identity* (New York: Simon & Schuster, 2004).
5. Harold Lasswell used to underscore the importance of what he called "configurative analysis." He introduced this term in 1938: "The configurative method of analysis requires of the analyst that he explore every mode of orientation which will increase the probability of success in his quest for the correct characterization of the relevant aspects of the totality." Immediately before the Second World War, he was highlighting the "restrictive processes of partial incorporation, geographical differentiation, and functional differentiation" that were likely to prevent the universal embrace of any single value system. See: *World Politics and Personal Insecurity* (New York: Free Press, 1965), p. 5 and p. 12, respectively. By the time this was taken up in the United States in the Cold War—his main concern was to argue against the Soviet aspiration to leadership of a world Socialist revolution, but the same arguments can also be directed against current U.S. aspirations to lead a world "democratic" revolution. I have therefore borrowed and adapted his "configurative" terminology for use in defence of contemporary area studies (the way in which different components of complex political, social, and economic processes are configured in a specific historical, cultural, and geographical setting). This is not the same as "essentializing" any given culture because it allows for reflexivity, learning from elsewhere, and adaptation; indeed, the configurative approach emphasizes that all developments have to be understood in terms of the

specific and holistic configurations of any given region. If this insight is lost, then area studies are deprived of their basic rationale. Anthropologists used to evoke a similar idea with their use of the term "culture," but that can also be criticized for "essentializing" reality. Elsewhere, I have argued for the use of the idea of "context" rather than "culture," particularly when explaining differences between large regions such as Asia and the West. See: Laurence Whitehead, "Afterword on Cultures and Contexts," in: Hans Antlov and Tak-Wing Ngo (eds.), *The Cultural Construction of Politics in Asia* (New York: St. Martins Press, 2000): 223–240.

6. For discussion of modernity in Latin America see: Néstor García Canclini, *Hybrid Cultures: Strategies for Entering and Leaving Modernity* (Minneapolis, MN: University of Minnesota Press, 1995), and Jorge Larraín, *Identity and Modernity in Latin America* (Oxford: Polity Press, 2000). More generally, see Reinhard Bendix, "Tradition and Modernity Reconsidered," *Comparative Studies in Society and History* 9 (3), April 1967: 293–346.

7. The focus here is on the Spanish American republics, and Brazil. The rest of the Caribbean is neither highlighted nor excluded. Those who view Los Angeles and Miami as among the great cities of Latin American can decide which of these generalizations also apply there.

8. For this purpose one might consult Malise Ruthven, *Islam: A Very Short Introduction* (Oxford: Oxford University Press, 1997), and for a more severe judgement Bernard Lewis, *The Crisis of Islam: Holy War and Unholy Terror* (New York: Random House, 2003).

9. Alain Rouquié, *Amérique Latine: Introduction à l'extrême-occident* (Paris: Seuil, 1987).

10. For one example see Jeremy Adelman, *Frontier Development: Land, Labor and Capital on the Wheatlands of Argentina and Canada, 1890–1914* (Oxford: Oxford University Press, 1994).

11. One striking new suggestion is that a Chinese fleet may have reached the Americas 71 years before Columbus, but this hypothesis has still to be confirmed. See Gavin Menzies, *1421: The Year China Discovered the World* (London: Bantam Press, 2002).

12. R. G. Collingwood, *The Idea of History* (Oxford: Oxford University Press, 1956), p. 305.

13. On Latin America's distinctive heritage see Richard M. Morse, "The Heritage of Latin America," in: Louis Hartz et al., (eds.), *The Founding of New Societies: Studies in the History of the US, Latin America, South Africa, Canada and Australia* (New York: Harcourt, Brace & Jovanovich, 1964):123–169.

14. Elinor G. K. Melville, *A Plague of Sheep: Environmental Consequences of the Conquest of Mexico* (Cambridge: Cambridge University Press, 1994).

15. Eduardo Lourenço, *América Latina entre natureza e cultura* (Lisbon: Edições Anteriores, 1999–2000). Compare this to Alexander von

Humbolt's introduction to his *Personal Narrative of Travels in the Equinocital Regions of America* (London: Penguin, 1995), in which he says that "in the New World, man and his productions disappear, so to speak, in the midst of a wild and outsized nature" (p. 12).

16. Salvador Osvaldo Brand, *El origen latinoamericano de las teorías de la moneda y de la inflación* (Bogota: Plaza y Janes, 1987).

17. José Antonio Aguilar Rivera, *En pos de la quimera: Reflexiones sobre el experimento constitucional Atlántico* (Mexico City: Fondo de Cultura Económica, 2000).

18. R. G. Collingwood, *The Idea of History*, op. cit.

19. See Eric Wolf, *Europe and the People Without History* (Berkeley, CA: University of California Press, 1997).

Chapter 1   Latin America as a "Mausoleum of Modernities"

* This chapter is a re-elaboration of my work: "Latin America as a Mausoleum of Modernities" in: Luis Roniger and Carlos Waisman (eds.), *Globality and Multiple Modernities. Comparative North American and Latin American Perspectives* (Brighton: Sussex Academic Press, 2002): 29–65.

1. Charles Taylor, "Nationalism and Modernity" in: John A. Hall (ed.), *The State of the Nation: Ernest Gellner and the Theory of Nationalism* (Cambridge: Cambridge University Press, 1998), p. 205. There are "failed states" and parasitic economies that may not immediately be taken over, or forced to undergo appropriate modernizing changes, but this is not a fatal objection to Taylor's basic position. See also: Shmuel Eisenstadt, N. F. Bonner, Robert Kahane, and B. Seibzehner (eds.), *Social Change in Latin American Societies: A Comparative Perspective* (Jerusalem: Magnes Press/Hebrew University, 1986).

2. Charles Taylor, ibid., p. 205.

3. Two illustrations serve to demonstrate the elasticity of the terminology. Plantation slavery acquired a distinctively "modern" form in the Americas after the Conquest, but Abolitionism was also a hallmark of modernity in the nineteenth century. In the twentieth, liberalism began and ended the century as the most modern of doctrines, but in between nationalism, fascism, and communism occupied much of that space for most of the period. All these diverse practices were promoted from above and without, and were said to follow the most up-to-date global trends.

4. This chapter focuses more on economic and political aspects of modernity than on the cultural dimension but culture and the collective imagination become central when discussing architecture for example. Beyond the technical aspects of modernizing initiatives there are acts of imagination and cultural construction that are inherently eclectic and at least partially self-referring. Strict mimetism or unilinear

progress toward a single "modernity" are therefore rather atypical and misleading constructs for our purposes.

5. For the most recent summary effort of this kind see: Shmuel N. Eisenstadt, "The Construction of Collective Identities in Latin America: Beyond the European State Model" in: Luis Roniger and Mario Sznajder (eds.), *Constructing Collective Identities and Shaping Public Spheres: Latin American Paths* (Brighton: Sussex Academic Press, 1998): 245–263.

6. See the exchanges between John Goldthorpe and his critics all in *Comparative Social Research* 16 (1997): 1–132.

7. This is not to deny the discursive power of idealized images of pre-Conquest social roots, which could be used to de-legitimize the existing order and to validate transformative alternatives. Thus the "socialist empire" of the Incas was somewhat implausibly invoked by mid-twentieth century Marxists, and the "Andean utopia" was used to mobilize insurgency in highland Peru in the 1980s. See for example, Anthony Pagden, *The Fall of Natural Man: The American Indian and the Origins of Comparative Ethnology* (Cambridge: Cambridge University Press, 1982).

8. As O'Gorman says: "If we examine the principles guiding Iberian colonisation [. . .] we find that the norm consisted in transplanting to American soil European, and more concretely Iberian, ways of life," and notably "the conscious intention to perpetuate these ways understood and lived as an 'entelechy' (or closed system) validated by divine will. This objective is apparent not only in the vigorous and intolerant implantation of Spanish Catholicism and Spanish social and political institutions but also in a whole rich range of artistic, cultural and urban expressions." Edmundo O'Gorman, *La invención de América*, (Mexico City: Fondo de Cultura Económica, 1958) pp. 153–154. See also Anthony Pagden, *Spanish Imperialism and the Political Imagination* (New Haven, CT: Yale University Press, 1990). On the crucial and distinctive theme of Latin American urban culture (a reflection of the preeminent role of the city in medieval Castile) Mark D. Szuchman expands on O'Gorman's basic insight, in "The City as Vision: The Development of Urban Culture in Latin America" in: Gilbert M. Joseph and Mark D. Szuchman (eds.), *I Saw A City Invisible: Urban Portraits of Latin America* (Washington DC: Scholarly Resources, Inc., 1996): 1–31. For a wide-ranging analysis of "modernity" in the Latin American context see also the various chapters in the volume by Roniger and Waisman, op. cit., by Roniger and Waisman (pp. 1–6), Smuel N. Eisenstadt (pp. 66–78), Roniger (pp. 79–105), and Waisman (pp. 106–116), in which the first version of this chapter was published.

9. The slave revolt in Haiti constitutes a notable exception, but even here no pre-European return path was possible.

10. The Tupac Amaru rebellion of 1780 has been interpreted in such terms, as indeed have more recent manifestations of an "Andean

utopia." There have been antimodern movements in Latin American history (more obviously in the 'New Jerusalem' at Canudos in Bahia, which was destroyed by the Brazilian army in 1897), but such rare and exceptional episodes do not negate the overall reality. On Canudos see: Euclídes da Cunha, *Os Sertões* (São Paulo: Três, 1984).

11. Edmundo O'Gorman, op. cit., pp. 154–6. José Rabasa recently criticized the "colonial discourse" and Eurocentrism often associated with the notion of 'inventing' America but his postmodern explorations treat O'Gorman's epistemology with wary respect. José Rabasa, *Inventing America: Spanish Historiography and the Formation of Eurocentrism* (Norman, OK: Oklahoma University Press, 1993).

12. Benedict Anderson, *Imagined Communities: Reflections on the Origin and Spread of Nationalism* (London: Verso, 1991).

13. David Brading, *The First Americans: The Spanish Monarchy, Creole Patriots, and the Liberal State 1492–1867* (Cambridge: Cambridge University Press, 1991); François-Xavier Guerra, "Les avatars de la représéntation en Amérique Laune au XIX sièclé," in: Georges Couffignal (ed.), *Réinventer la démocratie* (Paris: Presses de la Foundation Nationale des Sciences Polítíques, 1992): 1–65.

14. See chapter two, a condensed version of my "State Organisation in Latin America" in: Leslie Bethell (ed.), *The Cambridge History of Latin America*. Volume VI, Part II. (Cambridge: Cambridge University Press, 1994): 3–98.

15. On the vast topic of political representation in the Latin American republics a few recent authors offer interpretations pitched at this level of generality. See François-Xavier Guerra, "The Spanish American Tradition of Representation and its European Roots," *Journal of Latin American Studies* 26 (1), February 1994: 1–35; Elias José Palti, "Órden político y ciudadanía: Problemas e debates en el liberalismo argentino en el siglo XIX," *Estudios Interdisciplinares de América Latina y el Caribe* 5 (2), July–December 1994: 95–124; and Gabriel L. Negretto and José Antonio Aguilar-Rivera, "Rethinking the Legacy of the Liberal State," *Journal of Latin American Studies* 32 (2), May 2000: 361–397.

16. For one specific but telling illustration see Guy Thompson's case study of a remote Nahuatl speaking *municipio* in the mountains of Puebla in his "Bulwarks of Patriotic Liberalism: the National Guard, Philharmonic Corps and Patriotic Juntas in Mexico, 1847–88," *Journal of Latin American Studies* 22 (1), February 1990: 31–68.

17. Eisenstadt, op. cit. p. 256. Eisenstadt also argues in contradistinction to Benedict Anderson that Latin America's collective identities were not merely "imagined," but constructed on the three codes of primordiality, civility, and sacredness. Eisenstadt, ibid., p. 248 and p. 255. See the concluding chapter of this book for more details.

18. Here techniques should be understood broadly to include, for example, popular suffrage (not necessarily accompanied by a culture of citizenship) or individualistic entitlements (not necessarily accompanied by

social norms of universalism and subordination to an impersonal rule of law).

19. Pre-1870 Paraguay provided one eloquent exception, as did Papa Doc's Haiti.
20. Alain Rouquié, *Amérique latine: Introduction à l'extrême-occident* (Paris: Seuil, 1987).
21. From Albert O. Hirschman, *A Bias for Hope: Essays on Development and Latin America* (New Haven, CT: Yale University Press, 1971).
22. See the chapter in this book on expertise.
23. One rather neat illustration of this theme is provided by Anton Rosenthal, "The Arrival of the Electric Streetcar and the Conflict over Progress in Early Twentieth-century Montevideo," *Journal of Latin American Studies* 27 (2), May 1994: 319–341. The inauguration of this service in 1906 set off an intense debate between the city's elite and its anarchist workers over the nature of progress. The streetcar became a "contested symbol of modernity." The "trolley never became the clean, ordered conveyance which the rich had imagined [. . .] the result [. . .] was a stalemate between the elite, the middle-class and the workers [. . .] Foreign entrepreneurs were not given *carte blanche* to develop the city [. . .] They were unable to expand the network much [. . .] thus limiting the growth of Montevideo." Ibid., p. 319 and p. 340, respectively.
24. See: Jeffrey Needell, "The *Revolta Contra a Vacina* of 1904: The Revolt Against 'Modernisation' in Belle Époque Rio de Janeiro," *Hispanic American Historical Review* 67 (2), May 1987: 233–270.
25. David McCullough, *The Path Between the Seas; The Creation of the Panama Canal, 1870–1914* (Simon & Schuster: New York, 1977), p. 11 and p. 545.
26. Walter LaFeber, *The Panama Canal: The Crisis in Historical Perspective* (New York: Simon & Schuster, 1977), pp. 221–223.
27. See, for example: Simon Schama, *Landscape and Memory* (New York: Vintage Books, 1995).
28. U.S. travellers to Latin America brought their market logic within them from the earliest days. Thus, when John Lloyd Stephens first saw the volcano at Masaya in 1839 he was quick to observe that, "at home this volcano would be worth a fortune [. . .] with a good hotel on top, a zigzag staircase down the sides, and a glass of lemonade at the bottom." John Lloyd Stephens, *Incidents of Travel in Central America, Chiapas, and Yucatan* (New York: Dover Publications, 1969—originally published in London in 1841).
29. Even the Aztecs built over the temples of their predecessors and during the Spanish Conquest the Catholic Church followed this practice in relation to their pagan predecessors. Under the "Red Bishop" of Cuernavaca Marxist symbols decorated the sanctified walls.
30. A team of architects led by Frank Gehry (famed for the Guggenheim Museum in Bilbao) are working on a master plan for the whole Canal Zone. They are focusing on transforming the abandoned U.S. military

bases, constructing a bridge over the canal, and preserving a Spanish fort on a bluff overlooking the Chagres River on the Caribbean. There are also plans to turn the former American naval base into a theme park, and the long abandoned Panama Railroad has been recently reopened, now carrying tourist excursions to visit the old machinery and facilities lining the banks of the canal. So, even here some "heritage" marketing may be possible, although tourism in Panama is still incipient and the magnitude of the work makes the more visionary schemes hugely expensive.

31. See note 15 in the Introduction. Eduardo Lourenço has taken up Humboldt's idea of a continent where an excess of nature has reduced the scope for culture—and has therefore inspired many Latin Americans to think of their distinctiveness in terms of deficiency—a self-perception guided by an external preexisting European imaginary, which had to incorporate the discovery of an unexpectedly unmediated nature just when European Modernity began to emerge as a mental construct. Lourenço recognizes that in the twentieth century Latin Americans reacted against this negative view, celebrating the "telluric" foundations of their identity. Eduardo Lourenço, *América Latina: Entre Natureza e Cultura* (Lisbon: Edições Anteriores, 1999–2000).

32. Mauricio Tenorio Trillo, "1910 Mexico City: Space and Nation in the City of the Centenario," *Journal of Latin American Studies* 28 (1), February 1996, p. 77.

33. Ibid., pp. 78–79. The Paseo de la República had already been developed on the model of the Champs Elysées. Buenos Aires also celebrated a centenary in 1910 and also underwent a Haussmann-like transformation.

34. Ibid., p. 86.

35. Ibid., pp. 88–89.

36. Ibid., p. 91.

37. Adrián Gorelik, *La grilla y el parque: Espacio público y cultura urbana en Buenos Aires, 1887–1936* (Quilmes: Universidad Nacional de Quilmes, 1998). See also Beatriz Sarlo, *Una modernidad periférica: Buenos Aires 1920–1930* (Buenos Aires: Editorial Nueva Visión); and Emanuela Guano, "Spectacles of Modernity: Transnational Imagination and Local Hegemonies in Neo-Liberal Buenos Aires," *Cultural Anthropology* 17 (2), 2002: 181–209.

38. Jeffrey D. Needell, "Optimism and Melancholy: Elite Response to the Fin de Siècle Bonaerense," *Journal of Latin American Studies* 31(3), October 1999, p. 557.

39. Ibid., p. 557.

40. Gorelik, op. cit., p. 202.

41. On Lúcio Costa see "Brasilia is Orphan," at: http://www.brazil-brasil.com/p11jul98.htm.

42. James Holston, *The Modernist City: An Anthropological Critique of Brasilia* (Chicago, IL: Chicago University Press, 1989), especially

chapter 3 on the plan's hidden agenda, and part three of that chapter on the recovery of history.

43. James C. Scott, *Seeing Like a State* (New Haven CT: Yale University Press, 1998), chapter 4.

44. See: Michael Tsin, "Canton Remapped" in: Joseph W. Esherick (ed.), *Remaking the Chinese City: Modernity and National Identity, 1900–1950* (Honolulu: University of Hawaii Press, 1999): 19–29. The Canton Tramways Syndicate provided the finance to demolish the city walls and replace them with a new network of avenues ("Haussman-isation") and a new downtown. Following Foucault, Tsin suggests "that a new spatial order, such as that envisaged by Mayor Sun Fo and his associates, was an intrinsic part of the institution of a new political rationality, a political rationality that is central to the culture of modernity of our time [and] allowed the government to re-imagine Canton as a discrete entity, with clear boundaries and its own social and economic regularities, which could be uncovered with 'scientific' knowledge and were thus subject to systematic manipulation and intervention." Ibid., p. 29.

45. See: Michael Tsin, *Nation Governance, and Modernity in China: Canton 1900–1927* (Stanford, CA: Stanford University Press, 1998).

46. Gilberto Freyre, *Order and Progress: Brazil from Monarch to Republic* (Berkeley, CA: California University Press, 1986) p. 256. For the intellectual background to this outlook, and the absence of a rigid racism in Brazil see: Dain Borges, "Puffy Ugly, Slothful and Inert: Degeneration in Brazilian Social Thought, 1880–1940," *Journal of Latin American Studies* 25 (2), May 1993: 235–256.

47. This is a highly impressionistic list but serves to provide additional adornments to our prospective mausoleum.

48. W. B. Gallie, "Essentially Contested Concepts," 56 *Proceedings of the Aristotelian Society* 1956: 167.

49. José Guilherme Merquior wrote a powerful synthesis of the western liberal tradition serving as Brazilian ambassador to Mexico, *O liberalismo: antigo e moderno* (Rio de Janeiro: Nova Fronteira, 1991).

50. Ibid.

51. At the theoretical level this incoherence can be disguised (but not overcome) by resorting to a dichotomous distinction between "the right" and "the good." So long as these two components of "ought" are kept rigorously separate it is possible to segregate technique (trade liberalization becomes the technically right and necessary way to organize trade) from preference (individual voters do not consider it good to be "swamped by immigrants"). But if liberalism is about the promotion of liberty, the realm of freedom lies precisely in between technical necessity and revealed preference, both of which become illiberal when reified.

52. Who, for example, would have foreseen in 1990 that despite the collapse of the Russian economy and the disintegration of Russian society under the impact of liberalizing reforms in the ensuing decade,

Western liberals would still persist in claiming that their doctrine could be vindicated by this experience?

53. Ideology requires a mention, but much of the orientation toward modernity discussed in this chapter operates at the level of mentalities rather than ideology. Latin American elites knew they were in a new world and their countries' economies, societies, and institutions were still under construction. They claimed territories that still needed to be explored/occupied/understood. Nature could be mastered through reason, but scientific knowledge would have to be brought in from the outside. All this contributed to what might be called a basically "progressive mentality" in contrast to elsewhere.

54. R. G. Collingwood, *The Idea of History* (Oxford: Oxford University Press, 1956), p. 248.

55. In Foucault's rather opaque formulation, "governmentality" replaced "government" in the eighteenth century, when "the art of government found fresh outlets through the emergence of the problem of population." Thus, "the latter [. . .] disappears as the model of government, except for a certain number of residual themes of a religious or moral nature" and what emerged "into prominence is the family considered as an element internal to population, and as a fundamental instrument in its government." Michel Foucault, "Governmentality" in: Graham Burchell, Colin Gordon, and Peter Miller (eds.), *The Foucault Effect* (New York, NY: Harvester Wheatsheaf, 1991), pp. 98–99.

56. Xiaoqun Xu, " 'National Essence' US 'Science': Chinese Native Physicians Fight for Legitimacy, 1912–1937," *Modern Asian Studies* 31 (4), 1997: 847–877.

57. Sudipta Kaviraj stresses the modern constructivism of Indian-ness, which has parallels in Latin America. But he also describes India as "a society still knowing only one legitimising criterion—tradition," which is where the fundamental contrast with Latin America's orientation to modernity may lie. See his: "Modernity and Politics in India," *Daedalus* 129 (1), 2000: 137–162.

58. Sudipta Kaviraj, "Filth and the 'Public Sphere': Concepts and Practices about Space in the City of Calcutta," *Public Culture* 10 (1), 1997: 44.

59. Eisenstadt, op. cit., p. 259.

60. See, for example: Roberto González Echeverría, *La gloria de Cuba: Historia del beisbol en la isla* (Santiago: Editorial Colibrí, 2004); and Thomas Tufte, *Living with the Rubbish Queen: Telenovelas, Culture and Modernity in Brazil* (Luton: University of Luton Press, 2003).

Chapter 2   Latin American State Organization

* This chapter is a condensed and slightly updated version of my "State Organisation in Latin America" in: Leslie Bethell (ed.), *The Cambridge History of Latin America*. Volume VI. Part 2. (Cambridge: Cambridge University Press, 1994): 3–98.

1. This excludes Puerto Rico and the former British and Dutch colonies. For a more detailed examination of the subject of state organization, see my "State Organisation in Latin America" in: Leslie Bethell (ed.), *The Cambridge History of Latin America*. Volume VI. Part 2. (Cambridge: Cambridge University Press, 1994): 3–98, in which the footnotes offer a wealth of detail and suggested readings.

2. Benedict Anderson, *Imagined Communities: Reflections on the Origin and Spread of Nationalism* (London: Verso, 1991), p. 47.

3. François-Xavier Guerra, "Les avatars de la représentation en Amérique Hispanique au XIX Siècle" in: Georges Couffignal (ed.), *Réinventer la démocratie* (Paris: Presses de la FNSP, 1992): 1–65.

4. Brian Loveman, *The Constitution of Tyranny: Regimes of Exception in South America*. (Pittsburgh, PA: University of Pittsburgh Press, 1993), p. 5. Barahona de Brito and Panizza on Brazil note: "This was a [. . .] context of duality, where liberalism co-existed with the practice of *o favor* (the 'favour'), in which there were *indivíduos* ('individuals', who are subject to the full force of the law and usually most susceptible to ignorance of their rights and the legal institutions to which they could resort to safeguard those rights) and *pessoas* ('people', who can bypass the law by virtue of powerful personal connections)" and "laws apply only to individuals and never to people [. . .] the legal system that defines the so-called 'modern liberal state' is used in great part of semi-traditional societies [. . .] as another instrument of social exploitation, having a very different meaning to different segments of society [. . .]" Alexandra Barahona de Brito and Francisco Panizza, "The Politics of Human Rights in Democratic Brazil: '*A Lei Não Pega*,' " *Journal of Democratisation* 5 (4) Winter 1998, p. 39, citing Roberto da Matta, *Carnavais, maladros e heróis*. (Rio de Janeiro: Editora Guanabara, 1990), p. 193. As da Matta says: "Only individuals must go to police stations, are tried in court, stand in queues, use the public health and education facilities [or are] drafted into the military."

5. Loveman, op. cit., p. 4 and p. 5.

6. See, for example: William Canak, "The Peripheral State Debate," *Latin American Research Review* 19 (1), 1984: 3–36.

7. Oszlak's study of the formation of the Argentine state indicates that such a claim only became credible over half a century after the initial break from Spain, some time between 1862 and 1880. Oscar Oszlak, *La formación del estado argentino* (Buenos Aires: Editorial de Belgrano, 1990), chapter 3. But it is also notable that even before a "modern state" was fully constituted the Argentine Congress had already adopted certain laws like the abolition of slavery in 1853 and later to promote European immigration, which had very profound effects on the country's social structure.

8. For an illuminating contrast between the processes of state formation in Argentina and Brazil in the nineteenth century and Brazil and

Colombia see, respectively: Hélgio Trindade, "A construção do estado nacional na Argentina e no Brasil, 1800–1900: Esboço de uma análise comparativa," *Dados* 28 (1), Rio de Janeiro, 1985; and Fernando Uricoechea "Formação e expansão do estado burocrático-patrimonial na Colômbia e no Brasil," *Estudos CEBRAP* 21, July–September, 1977: 77–91; and *The Patrimonial Foundations of the Brazilian Bureaucratic State* (Berkeley, CA: University of California Press, 1980) by the same author.

9. Claudio Véliz, *The Centralist Tradition of Latin America* (Princeton NJ: Princeton University Press, 1980), especially chapter 7. Others describe the discontinuities more starkly. According to François Xavier Guerra, "We are not dealing with exotic countries that recently adopted European models with which they were unfamiliar [. . .] they adopted national sovereignty as the principle of legitimacy and the representative republic as their form of government. It is this political precocity that may explain their specific characteristics . . ." Ibid., pp. 49–50 and 53–54. Oszlak offers an alternative formulation of this precocity: "the great majority of Latin American countries acquired— as the first attribute of their condition as national states—formal external recognition of their sovereignty [which], however, preceded the institutionalization of a state power acknowledged within the national territory itself. This peculiar pattern, which in some cases persisted for several decades, contributed to the creation of the ambiguous image of a national state established in a society that failed to acknowledge fully its institutional presence." See: "The Historical Formation of the State in Latin America: Some Theoretical and Methodological Guidelines for its Study," *Latin American Research Review* 16 (2), 1981, p. 8.

10. Ibid, p. 20. On these issues see also: J. P. Deler and Y. Saint-Geours, *Estados y naciones en los Andes: Hacia una historia comparativa.* Volumes I and II (Lima: Instituto de Estudios Peruanos, 1986), and Sarah A. Radcliffe, "Imagining The State as a Space: Territoriality and the Formation of the State in Ecuador" in: Thomas Blom Hansen and Finn Stepputat (eds.), *States of Imagination: Ethnographic Explorations of the Post-Colonial State* (Durham, NC: Duke University Press, 2001): 123–145.

11. On the Sonora dynasty see: Héctor Aguilar Camín, *La frontera nómada: Sonora y la revolución mexicana* (Mexico City: Siglo XXI, 1977).

12. On Brazil and the distinctive organizational achievements of the state of São Paulo and Rio Grande do Sul see: Simon Schwartzman, *São Paulo e o estado nacional* (São Paulo: DIFEL, 1975).

13. Oszlak, "The Historical Formation," op. cit. p. 18.

14. Steve Topik, "The Economic Role of the State in Liberal Regimes: Brazil and Mexico Compared 1888–1910 in: Joseph L. Love and Nils Jacobsen (eds.), *Guiding The Invisible Hand: Economic Liberalism and the State in Latin America History* (New york Praeger, 1988), p. 139, which contrasts with the arguments of Trindade and Uricoechea

above. Chileans would certainly contest the claim that Brazil built the first "nation-state" in South America.

15. Nationalism in Latin America took a variety of forms and developed at a different pace in different places. Argentina, Chile, and Mexico certainly displayed strong currents of nationalism of all kinds before 1930. While it is hard to isolate any single causal factor, the linkage to the expansion of the educational system should not be underestimated.

16. This aspect of modern statehood is generally referred to as "legitimacy." Although this discussion focuses on state organization rather than "the state" as a moral community, the issue of legitimacy is briefly considered in the postscript below.

17. For a provocative overview that questions assumptions implicit in much of the democratization literature see: Marcelo Cavarrozzi, "Beyond Transitions to Democracy in Latin America," *Journal of Latin American Studies* 24 (3), October 1992: 665–684.

18. This is one area where a substantial amount of comparative and, in some cases, historically grounded work has been done. See my: "State Organisation," op. cit., for full bibliographical references.

19. See for example: John E. Hodge, "The Role of the Telegraph in the Consolidation and Expansion of the Argentine Republic," *Americas* 41, 1984; Richard Downes, "Autos over Rails: How US Business Supplanted the British in Brazil, 1910–28," *Journal of Latin American Studies* 24 (3), 1992: 551–584.

20. General Enrique Peñaranda, *Mensaje al H. Congreso Ordinario de 1943* (La Paz: Boletín del Congreso Nacional, 1942–1943), pp. 151–154.

21. The most extreme case arose earlier in the Dominican Republic, where direct rule from Washington centralized power and created an efficient system of administration, which was transferred after 1930 to US-*protegé* Trujillo who proceeded to act with great autonomy from external and internal restraints.

22. There were subsequent insurgencies—such as the urban guerrillas of the 1970s in Argentina and Uruguay and the Central American insurgencies of the 1970s and 1980s—but their basis was different.

23. Paradoxically, it was maritime Britain that first sacrificed the principle that a state's territorial waters should be limited to three nautical miles from the coast. In 1942, to obtain offshore oil needed for the war effort, London negotiated an extended boundary between Trinidad and Venezuela. Argentina followed in 1944, claiming the epicontinental sea as a temporary zone of mineral reserves, and in 1947 Peru and Chile, which saw that their continental shelf was too narrow to offer much advantage, laid claim to a 200 mile "patrimonial sea," including sea floor and water column. This claim was vindicated with the Montego Convention of 1980 that secured a 200-mile exclusive economic zone.

24. See, for example: Peter Sollis, "The Atlantic Coast of Nicaragua: Development and Autonomy," *Journal of Latin American Studies* 21 (3),

October 1989: 481–499. The first all-weather road from Managua to the northern coast was opened in 1981. Compare this to David C. Brooks, "US Marines, Miskitos, and the Hunt for Sandino: The Rio Coco Patrol in 1928," *Journal of Latin American Studies* 21 (2), May 1989: 311–330, which provides a vivid snapshot of the same region in the late 1920s, when it was extremely detached from the center.

25. Lawrence Herzog argues that after the 1950s there was a major shift in the function of international boundaries away from national security concerns and toward "more porous" cross-border social and economic interactions. Lawrence Herzog (ed.), *Changing Boundaries in the Americas* (La Jolla, CA: Centre for US-Mexican Studies, 1992), pp. 5–6. Central America and the Amazon basin provide notable instances where the retreat of the bureaucratic state is replaced not by the expansion of legal commerce and investment, but by enclaves of open lawlessness. See: Steve Bunker *Underdeveloping the Amazon: Extraction, Unequal Exchange, and the Failure of the Modern State* (Chicago, IL: Chicago University Press, 1985).

26. The figure is 153,000 out of a population of 16,553,000, of which 143,000 are male. *Dirección General de Estadística-Quinto Censo de Población. 15 de Mayo de 1930* (Mexico City 1934), p. 82.

27. ECLAC, "Structural Changes in Employment within the Context of Latin America's Economic Development," *Economic Bulletin for Latin America* 9 (2) October 1965 (Santiago), p. 167.

28. Adriana Marshall (ed.) *El empleo público frente a la crisis* (Geneva: ILO, 1990) p. 218. My reckoning, however, is that the total only reached 16 million (including 2.5 million Cuban workers in the state sector). Comparing like with like, I estimate that the ratio rose from 1.2 percent in 1960 to about 4 percent of total population in 1980—an extremely dramatic, and probably unsustainable shift in a twenty-year period. (Estimates of this ratio for individual countries in 1985 range from 8.1 percent in Uruguay to 2.5 percent in Chile.) Hugo Davrieux in Adriana Marshall, op. cit., calculated that the wage bill for this 4.8 percent of the population came to 11.0 percent of Latin America's GDP (in the OECD countries 9.0 percent of the population worked in the public sector, and received 13.4 percent of the GDP in wages).

29. John Lombardi, *Venezuela* (Oxford: Oxford University Press, 1982), p. 207. A detailed study of public finances and administration under Gómez somewhat qualifies this by underscoring the strengthening and centralization of power under his long administration: "Gomez understood the importance of the telegraph as an instrument of political and military control. Part of his daily routine consisted of reading the routine cables sent in by the various civil and military officials located all over the national territory, and those sent from abroad. The post of telegraphist became a position of political importance within the regime, and was assigned to those most trusted by Gomez and his

circle." Miriam Kornblith and Luken Quintana, "Gestión fiscal y centralización del poder en los gobiernos de Cipriano Castro y de Juan Vicente Gomez," *Politeia* 10, 1981 (Caracas), pp. 190–191. On the other hand, the economic interventionism of the period consisted basically of "the monopolisation of agricultural, commercial, and industrial activities, and the intermingling of the Public Treasury with the personal finances of the President and his cronies, practices which displayed lines of continuity with preceding administrations." Ibid., p. 199.

30. The Dominican dictatorship was exceptional, but also revealing, since various other rulers attempted what Trujillo achieved (from 1930 to 1961). On the "police state" established by Trujillo see Bernardo Vega, *Control y represión en la dictadura Trujillista* (Santo Domingo: Fundación Cultural Dominicana, 1986).

31. Kenneth Grieb, *Guatemalan Caudillo* (Athens, OH: Ohio University Press, 1979), p. 4 passim.

32. According to Alan Knight on Mexico: "As the Federal bureaucracy waxed [. . .] presidential power waned" although both trends were later reversed, as "state-shrinking" [accompanied] a reassertion of presidential power. As Salinas [. . .] declared: "The scale (dimension) of the state, of itself, is not sufficient to determine its greater or lesser capacity or effectiveness in meeting social demands Our problem has not been a small, weak, state, but a state which, by virtue of its burgeoning size, made itself weak." Alan Knight, "State and Civil Society in Mexico Since the Revolution," *Texas Papers on Mexico* 90-01, University of Texas at Austin, 1990.

33. Peter Flynn, *Brazil: A Political Analysis* (Boulder, CO: Westview Press, 1979), p. 105. The rollback of the Brazilian state in the late 1980s and early 1990s was much slower than elsewhere. For more details see my "State Organisation," op. cit.

34. Sergio Miceli, *Intelectuais e classe dirigente no Brasil, 1920–45* (Rio de Janeiro: DIFEL, 1979), especially chapter 3.

35. Lawrence Graham, *Civil Service Reform in Brazil: Principles Versus Practice* (Austin, TX: Texas University Press, 1968), pp. 27–28.

36. Maria do Carmo Campello de Souza, *Estado e partidos políticos no Brasil: 1930 a 1964*, (São Paulo: Alfa-Omega, 1983) p. 97.

37. In October 1945, the DASP lost its budgeting and specialist training functions. Liberals hailed this antibureaucracy drive, while nationalists denounced a plot to destroy the "organic machinery" of the Federal Administration. One indicator of the scale of the purge is that civil service employment fell from 0.7 percent of the population (2.2 percent of the labor force) in 1940 to only 0.5 percent and 1.5 percent in 1950. Vamireh Chacón, *Estado e povo no Brasil: As experiências do Estado Novo e da democracia populista: 1937–1964* (Rio de Janeiro: Livraria José Olympio, 1977), p. 150.

38. Ibid., p. 214.

39. Luciano Martins, *Estado capitalista e burocracia no Brasil pos-1964* (Rio de Janeiro: Paz e Terra, 1985), p. 43, and pp. 196–197.

40. Chacón, op. cit.

41. Guillermo O'Donnell, "On the State, Various Crises, and Problematic Democratisations," *CESDE Working Paper* (University of Bologna), 1992, pp. 9–10.

42. If there is a truly "predatory" state in the region, it is Haiti (see: Mats Lundahl, "Underdevelopment in Haiti: Some Recent Contributions," *Journal of Latin American Studies* 23 (2), May 1991: 411–429). On the predatory state see more generally see: Peter Evans, "Predatory, Developmental and Other Apparatus: A Comparative Analysis of the Third World State," *Sociological Forum* 4 (4), December 1989: 561–587.

43. The judgment of Ernesto Isuani, published by the Argentine Ministry of Health and Social Action, is representative. He highlights "the obsolescence of the technical equipment available to the public administration, and the ever more notorious deficiencies of the human resources in the service of the state. Public Service is ceasing to be a profession or way of life, above all for the well-qualified, for whom the State has ceased to offer attractive conditions of work and income." Ernesto Isuani and Emilio Tenti (eds.), *Estado democrático y política social* (Buenos Aires: EUDEBA, 1989), p. 23.

44. See: Paz y Justicia, *Urugauay Nunca Más: Human Rights Violations 1972–1985* (Philadelphia, PA: Temple University Press, 1992), p. 285.

45. This is well documented in *The UN Mission of Technical Assistance to Bolivia of 1951* (New York: United Nations, 1951), or Keenleyside Report. For example, rural land appraisal in Bolivia did not start until 1943, and by 1950 only part of the land in four out of nine departments had been appraised. All the rest was taxed on the basis of owners' self-assessment. The office for appraisal of rural taxes contained scarcely sixty employees in 1950. *The UN Mission Report*, p. 33.

46. See George Jackson Eder, *Inflation and Development in Latin America: A Case History of Inflation and Stabilisation in Bolivia* (Michigan, MI: Ann Arbor, 1968). Eder was the foreign adviser most involved in the 1956 reorganization and re-interpretation of Bolivia's public finances. Under the 1953 Agrarian Reform Law the state assumed enormous new responsibilities, but the President was required to personally read and sign the documentation on each land distribution. If President Siles had worked at this for 24 hours a day throughout his four-year term (1956–1960) he would have been unable to catch up with the paperwork. By contrast, in the mid-1960s President Barrientos used a USAID-designed management system that sped through the paperwork (he rarely set foot in his office), which conferred much popularity on his regime.

47. Admittedly such progress in Bolivia has been nonlinear and uneven. Symptomatically, in 1990, when after almost 40 years COMIBOL was finally instructed to undertake joint ventures with foreign investors, they found that it had "no clear idea of what mines it owns, where they are or what they are worth." As many as 800 of its mines were reportedly unexploited, and its resources were "virtually unmapped." *Financial Times* 15, March 1990. Nevertheless, a positive underlying trend can be documented, for example, by comparing the Keenleyside Report with Richard A. Musgrave's *Fiscal Reform in Bolivia: Final Report of the Bolivian Mission on Tax Reform* (Cambridge, MA: Harvard Law School, International Tax Programme, 1981). Further progress after 1985 derived partly from the implementation of some of Musgrave's ideas, and partly from "state shrinking" so that by the end of the 1980s Bolivia's public administration no longer lagged far behind that of, say, Brazil. See also: Manuel Contreras, "Debt, Taxes and War: The Political Economy of Bolivia 1920–1935," *Journal of Latin American Studies* 22 (2), May 1990: 265–288, and Carmenza Gallo, *Taxes and State Power: Political Instability in Bolivia, 1900–1950* (Philadelphia: Temple University Press, 1991).

48. This point is well illustrated for Porfirian Mexico by Robert H. Holden, "Priorities of the State in the Survey of the Public Land in Mexico, 1876–1911," *Hispanic American Historical Review*, November 1990: 70–74, who points out that although a survey of public lands was essential for modernization, rural proprietors would see it as an "act of aggression," and hence the rationality of delegating the job to private companies. See also: Raymond Craib, *Cartographic Mexico: A History of State Fixations and Fugitive Landscapes* (Durham, NC: Duke University Press, 2004).

49. António Carlos Roberto Moraes, "Notas sobre identidade nacional e institucionalização da geografia no Brasil," *15th Annual Congress of ANPOCS*, Caxambó, October 1991.

50. As reported in the *Jornal da Tarde* (Salvador), 29 July 1988 and the *Financial Times* 17 January 1992. In Argentina there is a relatively well-organized cadastral service in the Federal Capital, and the province of Buenos Aires, but "in the rest of the country the panorama is substantially different, with little information." *La Nación* (Buenos Aires), 9 July 1990. In La Paz in 1976 the tax register identified under 74,000 properties although planimetric studies indicated that 200,000 would be more accurate. Musgrave, op. cit., p. 404.

51. Those wishing to follow in Costa Rica's footsteps should consult Law 6545 establishing the *Cadastro Nacional* in April 1981. Similarly advanced is the Costa Rican civil register that provides every adult with an identity card, and thereby underpins the accuracy of the electoral register and the coverage of the tax and social security systems. Costa Rica actively "exports" its know-how to other countries of the

region. Rafael Villegas Antillón, *El Tribunal Supremo de Elecciones y El Registro Civil de Costa Rica* (San José: CAPEL, 1987).

52. Writing about Brazil in 1979, Anglade wrote: "until a special Secretariat for the Control of the State Companies (SEST) was created in that year, nobody—not even in the government—knew how many public firms there were, and much less how much they spent and how much they borrowed abroad." Christian Anglade and Carlos Fortín (eds.), *The State and Capital Accumulation in Latin America*. Volumes I and II. (Basingstoke: Macmillan Press, 1985 and 1990), p. 112. In the following decade this complaint remained pertinent, not only for Brazil but also for various other republics.

53. Merle Kling, "Taxes on the External Sector: An Index of Political Behaviour in Latin America," *Midwest Journal of Political Science* 3 (2), 1959: 127–150. For a seminal treatment of state command over resources and taxation see: Joseph A. Schumpter, "The Crisis of the Tax State," in: A. Peacock, et al., (eds.), *International Economic Papers: Translations Prepared for the International Economic Association* (New York: Macmillan Press, 1954): 5–38.

54. William McGreevey also notes that in 1985 SINPAS had 200,000 employees, financed a quarter of a billion physician consultations and 14 million hospitalizations annually, involving an annual expenditure of US$12 billion. In his view these payments were "not scrutinised with the same care by senior government officials as are the general tax revenues of the federal government." *Social Security in Latin America: Issues and Options for the World Bank* (Washington: World Bank, 1990), p. 11.

55. James M. Malloy, *The Politics of Social Security in Latin America* (Pittsburgh, PA: Pittsburgh University Press, 1979), p. 4. This principle was diluted toward the end of our period as some benefits were extended to noncontributing groups, and as the range of benefits proliferated. In its final form the system included pensions, unemployment insurance, disability and death benefits, occupational disease coverage, maternity leave, general health provision, family allowances, and profit-sharing. In some countries coverage became almost universal, and for Latin America as a whole coverage in 1980 was put at 61 percent of the population *and* workforce. In Malloy's words "the concept of social protection itself has been undergoing a fundamental change [. . .] to *segurança social*, a system which aims to protect citizens "not only from the consequence of events whose possible occurrence has been predicted, but from any event in any circumstance." Ibid., p. 141. This costly and impractical commitment underlay much of the 1988 Brazilian Constitution.

56. Circumstantial evidence for this can be found in McGreevey, who shows that state resources available for health and social security in Mexico fell from 4.7 percent of GDP in 1977 to 2.4 percent in 1986. Op. cit., p. 89. In Bolivia the fall was from 3.5 percent in 1979 to 1.7 percent in 1986. Ibid., p. 72.

57. Malloy, op. cit., p. 78.
58. For a clear and well-documented overview of the 1990s, highlighting the unresolved need to improve the quality of public policy after state shrinking see: Vito Tanzi, "The Role of the State and the Quality of the Public Sector," *CEPAL Review* 71, August 2000: 7–22.

Chapter 3   The Politics of Expertise

* This is an expanded and updated version of a paper first published in English as "The Politics of Expertise in Latin America," *Revista de Economia Política* (São Paulo) 20 (2), April–June 2000: 23–35.

1. Sheldon Wolin traces it back to Plato in *Politics and Vision: Continuity and Innovation in Western Political Thought* (Boston, MA: Little, Brown & Co., 1960), p. 60. See also: L. S. Feuer, "What is an Intellectual," in: Aleksander Gella (ed.), *The Intelligentsia and the Intellectuals: Theory, Method and Case Study* (London: International Sociological Association/Sage Studies in International Sociology 5, 1976).
2. The memoirs of Lucas Lopes, Treasury Minister to Kubitshek in 1958, give a revealing glimpse into that earlier period. Before joining the Federal cabinet engineer Lopes was charged with planning the electrification of the Sao Francisco valley. In 1988–1989 he looked back on his writings of the mid-1950s and he "discovered that at that time I had no idea of economic planning in the modern sense, using macro-economic and monetary decisions. When I was a planner it was the planning of Roosevelt, of Lilienthal, of construction that I worked. These categories were geographical rather than economic or political, building canals and dams to make the river navigable. My training was inspired by the New Deal and the Russian electrification plan." Lucas Lopes, *Memórias do desenvolvimento* (Rio de Janeiro: Centro da Memória da Electricidade no Brasil, 1991), p. 114.
3. For a vivid illustration of how the medical profession might link up with the modern state to impose highly authoritarian projects of health reform see: Carl J. Murdock, "Physicians, the State and Public Health in Chile, 1881–1891," *Journal of Latin American Studies* 27 (3), October 1995: 551–569. See also: Sidney Chalhoub, "The Politics of Disease Control: Yellow Fever and Race in Nineteenth Century Rio de Janeiro," *Journal of Latin American Studies* 25 (3), October 1993: 441–465.
4. There is a paradox inherent in this behavior. To be "true" standard bearers of "modern rationality" in "open societies," such experts would have had to comply with the rules of modern scientific rationality in the sense that they would have to accept the Popperian claim that the "truth" established by science is always subject to falsification, and the only way to make progress in knowledge, and to know if "expertise" is correct is to subject it to critical tests. This would mean that true "experts" would have to take on board the opposition and engage with their critics, rather than dismiss them as ignorant. The latter attitude is then more in

keeping with the Platonic "philosopher king," whose knowledge and wisdom puts him above the common man and gives him the right (and duty) to impose the "correct order." Insofar as this is true, Latin American experts fail to act in accordance with the rules of scientific discovery that is a vital aspect of the dynamics present in the external communities from whence they derive their domestic authority.

5. The complex interweaving of Domingo Cavallo's multiple personas between 1980 and 2001 would merit close analysis in this context. The remarkable international reputation he established during most of the 1990s was not based on a deep evaluation of his real place in Argentine public life. His ruthlessness both at the launch of the Convertibility Plan and during its last weeks was a logical reflection of his internal trajectory, but was far removed from the expectations of his foreign backers. What both this example and the various Brazilian stabilization plans of the 1980s and 1990s demonstrate is that experts with international credentials can be very much their own masters, balancing between multiple audiences, but captive to none.

6. For the latter see: Rudiger Dornbusch and Sebastian Edwards (eds.), *The Macroeconomics of Populism in Latin America* (Chicago, IL: University of Chicago Press, 1991); and for a particularly enlightening study of an archetypical case of the latter see: Carlos Huneeus, "Technocrats and Politicians in an Authoritarian Regime: The 'ODE-PLAN Boys', and the Gremialists in Pinochet's Chile," *Journal of Latin American Studies* 32 (2), May 2000: 461–502.

7. For one recent and instructive case of "bureaucratic patrimonialism" see: Victor Uribe "The Lawyers and New Granada's Late Colonial State," *Journal of Latin American Studies* 27 (3), October 1995: 517–550. Such studies usually highlight the contrast between administrative theory and local social realities, dominated by family clans and informal favors. The bald statements in the first paragraph fail to convey any of this, but instead draw attention to the underlying regulative framework.

8. See: David Brading, *The First Americans: The Spanish Monarchy, Creole Patriots, and the Liberal State: 1492–1867* (Cambridge: Cambridge University Press, 1991).

9. See: Sérgio Adorno, *Os aprendizes do poder: O bacharelismo liberal na política brasileira* (Rio de Janeiro: Paz e Terra, 1988). See also: Daniel Pécaut, *Entre le peuple et la nation: Intellectuels et la politique au Brésil* (Paris: Maison des Sciences de l'Homme, 1989).

10. On the case of Mexico see: Peter Cleaves, *Professions and the State: The Mexican Case* (Tucson, AZ: University of Arizona Press, 1987). For more details on the Mexican case see the following chapter in this volume. On the case of Bolivia see Manuel Contreras, who has traced the evolving fortunes of Bolivia's legal, medical, and engineering professions through to 1950, demonstrating the broad applicability of mainstream ideas about the sociology of the professions, even in this isolated and precarious setting. Manuel E. Contreras, *Tecnología*

moderna en los Andes: ingeniería y minería en Bolivia en el siglo XX (La Paz: ILDIS, 1994). See also: Marcos Cueto (ed.), *Saberes andinos: ciencia y tecnología en Bolivia, Ecuador y Perú* (Lima: Instituto de Estudios Peruanos, 1995). For a more general analysis see: Benno Galjart and Patricio Silva (eds.), *Designers of Development: Intellectuals and Technocrats in the Third World* (Leiden: CNWS Research School, 1995). See also: Veronica Montecinos, "Economic Policy Elites and Democratisation," *Studies in Comparative International Development* 28 (1), Spring 1993: 25–53; and Miguel Ángel Centeno and Sylvia Maxfield, "The Marriage of Finance and Order: Changes in the Mexican Political Elite," *Journal of Latin American Studies* 24 (1), February 1992: 57–85.

11. Alain Touraine, *La parole et le sang: politique et societé en Amérique Latine*, (Paris: Éditions Odile Jacob, 1988), pp. 138–139. Author's translation. Compare Jean Franco's, "Latin American Intellectuals and Collective Identity" in: Luis Roniger and Mario Sznadjer (eds.), *Constructing Collective Identities and Shaping Public Spheres: Latin American Paths* (Brighton: Sussex Academic Press, 1998): 230–241.

12. Albert O. Hirschman, *Journeys Towards Progress* (New York: W. W. Norton & Co., 1963), pp. 291–293.

13. *A República*, February 10, 1912.

14. In order to be fair to the argument I have spoken about "civil society" as a whole, although on a more critical reading the same case could be stated in terms of the requirements of an increasingly autonomous and hegemonic private business community or capitalist class.

15. Laurence Whitehead, "Bolivia Since 1930," in: Leslie Bethell (ed.), *The Cambridge History of Latin America*. Volume VIII (Cambridge: Cambridge University Press, 1991), p. 512.

16. Kathryn Sikkink, *Ideas and Institutions: Developmentalism in Brazil and Argentina* (Ithaca, NY: Cornell University Press, 1991), and Joseph Hodara B., *Prebisch y la CEPAL: Sustancia, trayectoria y contexto institucional* (Mexico: Colegio de México, 1987). See also by the same author: *América Latina: El fin de los intelectuales?* (Lima: Universidad F. Villareal, 1973).

17. See the recent José Ramón López Portillo, *Economic Thought and Economic Policymaking in Contemporary Mexico* (Oxford: Oxford University D.Phil., 1995).

18. Kathryn Sikkink, op. cit.

Chapter 4   Economics in Mexico: The Power of Ideas and Ideas of Power

* An earlier version was presented at the Colloquium, *Europa en México: La aportación de las Ciencias Sociales*, held at the Centro de Estudios de México of the University of Turin, Italy, on 23–24 September 1996, and published in *Europa en México: Por una colaboración en ciencias sociales*

(Turin, Italy: Centro de Estudios de México, 1997). This version has benefited from the comments of Victor Bulmer-Thomas, Enrique Cárdenas, Miguel Ángel Centeno, Valpy Fitzgerald, Joseph Hodara, Adrián Lajous, José Ramón López Portillo, Jaime Ros, Frances Stewart, and Victor Urquidi.

1. Octavio Paz, *The Labyrinth of Solitude* (New York: Grove Press, 1961), pp. 157–158.
2. Sarah Babb, *Managing Mexico: Economists from Nationalism to Neoliberalism* (Princeton, NJ: Princeton University Press, 2001), p. 12. She correctly presents her study of how economic expertise was constructed in Mexico over the twentieth century as both a prototype and an ideal type—rather extreme—instantiation of Latin American experience, including the more recent experience of "coercive isomorphism" (when organizations conform to the standards of powerful external actors, under the pressure of resource dependence). Ibid., p. 18. Where she is less convincing is in portraying Mexican economists as representative of economists in developing countries more generally. It seems unlikely that this generalization really works for, say, India, Nigeria, or South Africa.
3. In 1979, Gabriel Zaid, a disciple of Octavio Paz, updated the critique, asking himself how much difference it made to the quality of Mexican government that over 30 years civilians had been in charge. He concluded that it made "muchíssima diferencia," adding that "una especialista en ciencias sociales, distinguido politólogo, brillante ex-alumno de la Universidad Nacional, sabio investigador del Colegio de México y doctorado en la Sorbona, pudo estar a cargo de la administración nacional de los fraudes electorales. No un palurdo cualquiera. Ahora, para ser un perfecto bandido, ya no basta el talento, las oportunidades, la experiencia. Hay que tener un título universitario." Gabriel Zaid, *El progreso improductivo* (Mexico City: Siglo XXI, 1979), p. 260.
4. Sarab Babb, op. cit., p. 17.
5. This paragraph is heavily based on Roderic A. Camp, *Mexico's Leaders: Their Education and Recruitment* (Tucson, AZ: Arizona University Press, 1980), pp. 159–163. Referring to Mexico in the 1950s, Charles Anderson noted that skill in economic analysis was "a commodity which is vital to policy formulation in a complex economy, yet is in scarce supply." He added that, "few decentralised agencies or government ministers can rival the banks" in bidding for this scarce resource. Hence, "much of the outstanding professional economic talent in Mexico" was concentrated "in the leading banks—the Bank of Mexico, *Nacional Financiera*, the Foreign Commerce Bank to a lesser extent, the Public Works bank." Apart from their prestige, the "salary policies of these leading banks not bound by the chaotic civil service requirements permits that bank often outbid the government ministries for the first-rate talent. There is a feeling that one's achievements will not be so much limited by the demands of "politics" in the banks. Yet the door is not closed to

political success [. . .] for there is considerable exchange of personnel between top bank administrative posts and political positions." Quoted from Anderson's essay, "Bankers as Revolutionaries" in: William P. Glade and Charles W. Anderson (eds.), *The Political Economy of Mexico* (Madison, WI: Wisconsin University Press, 1963), pp. 159–160.

6. This paragraph is heavily based on Roderic A. Camp, *Mexico's Leaders: Their Education and Recruitment* (Tucson, AZ: Arizona University Press, 1980), pp. 159–163.

7. Raymond Vernon, *The Dilemma of Mexico's Development: The Roles of the Private and Public Sectors* (Cambridge, MA: Harvard University Press, 1963), p. 136. On the face of it, Vernon's argument would also imply that the U.S. economy should no longer be left to the "rough-and-ready ministrations of the politician," although the US Congress has been more reluctant to relinquish its constitutional prerogatives than its Mexican counterpart.

8. In addition to Vernon, Roderic Camp has also contributed usefully to this literature. See, for example: *The Role of Economists in Policy-Making* (Tucson, AZ: Arizona University Press, 1977); "El tecnócrata en Mexico," *Revista Mexicana de Sociología* 45 (2), April–June 1983: 579–599; "The Technocrat in Mexico and the Survival of the Political System," *Latin American Research Review* 20 (1), 1985: 97–118; *Intellectuals and the State in Twentieth Century Mexico* (Austin, TX: Texas University Press, 1985). Peter Smith's contributions include *Labyrinths of Power: Political Recruitment in Twentieth-Century Mexico* (Princeton, NJ: Princeton University Press, 1979); "Leadership and Change: Intellectuals and Technocrats in Mexico," in: Roderic A. Camp (ed.), *Mexico's Stability: The Next Five Years* (Boulder, CO: Westview Press, 1986) pp. 101–117. Miguel Ángel Centeno and Sylvia Maxfield provide a thorough literature review and new data in "The Marriage of Finance and Order: Changes in the Mexican Political Elite," *Journal of Latin American Studies* 24 (1), February 1992: 57–85.

9. Peter Smith, *Labyrinths of Power*, op. cit.

10. See: Peter A. Hall (ed.), *The Political Power of Economic Ideas: Keynesianism Across Nations* (Princeton, NJ: Princeton University Press, 1989), which contains a chapter by Albert O. Hirschman on the rise and decline of Keynesianism in Latin America. See also: Peter A. Hall, "Policy Paradigms, Social Learning and the State," *Comparative Politics* 25 (3), April 1993: 275–296.

11. Peter A. Hall, *The Political Power of Economic Ideas*, op. cit.

12. Miguel Ángel Centeno, *Democracy within Reason: Technocratic Revolution in Mexico* (University Park, PA: Penn State University Press, 1994), p. 137. Another professional qualification that does not receive separate consideration in his tables is the career of *contador*. This is particularly important in the growing financial sector. Economists and *contadores* in SPP proceeded to control and colonize other state agencies and ministries. See: Rogelio Hernández

Rodríguez, "La división de la elite política mexicana" in: Carlos Bazdresch, Nisso Bucay, Soledad Loaeza and Nora Lustig (eds.) *México: Auge, crisis y ajuste*. Lecturas del Trimestre Económico 73 (1), 1992 (Mexico City: Fondo de Cultura Económica).

13. Miguel Ángel Centeno, *Democracy within Reason*, op. cit., pp. 121–122.

14. The question of how far these alternative sources of foreign training mattered is considered in Section VI.

15. See also: Luiz Carlos Bresser-Pereira, "Seis interpretações sobre o Brasil," *Dados-Revista de Ciências Social* 5 (3), 1982: 269–306.

16. For a further discussion of this type of comparison see Laurence Whitehead, "Political Explanations of Macro-Economic Management: A Survey," *World Development* 18 (8), 1990: 1133–1146.

17. The Economic Research Corporation for Latin America (CIEPLAN). See Patricio Silva, "Technocrats and Politics in Chile: From the Chicago Boys to the CIEPLAN Monks," *Journal of Latin American Studies* 32 (2), May 1991: 385–410.

18. Compare Robert Dahl's presentation of the case for and against "guardianship" as an alternative to democracy: "In comparison with the judgments of ordinary people, which reflect all the uncertainties of mere opinion, the guardians can acquire knowledge of what is best for the community that approaches something like rational certainty" (or so they believe). But this ignores the inherently risky nature of policy decisions, and the fact that "experts often utterly fail to comprehend how the real world may stubbornly refuse to play by their rules." In any case, to rule well requires moral competence as well as instrumental expertise. These objections in principle are quite apart from the practical difficulty that guardians have often become corrupt and self-serving. Robert A. Dahl, *Democracy and its Critics* (New Haven, CT: Yale University Press, 1989), p. 75 and p. 70.

19. This section is derived from personal impressions accumulated from intermittent contact with Mexican economists, policy-makers, and students since my first visit in 1968. Victor Urquidi presented a first-hand memoir to the Turin Colloquium that covers similar ground with far more authority. My account is reinforced by discussions with José Ramón López Portillo whose 1995 Oxford doctoral thesis, *Economic Thought and Economic Policy-Making in Contemporary Mexico*, I supervised.

20. See *Trimestre Económico* 113 (249) 1995 for a useful retrospective on the journal's 62-year history.

21. Perhaps the most famous were Juan Noyola, one of the founders of "structuralism." See: Carlos Bazdresch, *El Pensamiento de Juan Noyola* (Mexico City: Fondo de Cultura Económica, 1984). However, Noyola's early influence declined after he enthusiastically embraced the Cuban revolution. Ifigenia Navarrete became well known for her work on Mexican income distribution, and her husband, Alfredo, published influential work on underemployment. On a

more parochial level Ángel Bassols Batalla promoted regional economics. See his *Treinta años de investigación económica regional en México* (Mexico City: Colección Nuestros Maestros, UNAM 1990).

22. According to Adrián Lajous, the crucial issue was whether the Colegio should offer an undergraduate degree in economics. Against his advice only a Masters course was provided. The best students were converts from other disciplines who needed catch-up training, including Jesús Seade (from Chemical Engineering) and Jaime Serra Puche (from politics), but they were too few to shape the discipline.

23. Sarah Babb, op. cit., p. 207.

24. This brief discussion relies heavily on the doctoral thesis by José López-Portillo, and material from Centeno and Maxfield, op. cit. See also: Judith Teichman, *The Politics of Freeing Markets in Latin America: Chile, Argentina, and Mexico* (Durham, NC: University of North Carolina Press, 2001).

25. Sarah Babb, op. cit., pp. 218–219.

26. Miguel Ángel Centeno, *Democracy within Reason*, op. cit., pp. 211–212.

27. Ibid., op. cit., pp. 211–212.

28. Ibid., p. 219.

29. Ibid., p. 228.

30. Enrique Cárdenas supplied this information in his commentary on the paper on which this chapter is based.

31. Although the potential exists, there are many good reasons to fear that it may not be realized. A vigorous survey can be found in Miguel Ángel Centeno, "Has Mexico's Technocratic Revolution Failed?," Paper presented at the *CEDLA Workshop on Technocrats and the Politics of Expertise in Latin America*, Amsterdam 14–15 September 1995. Compare my more open-ended and *longue durée* perspective in the chapter on expertise in this volume.

32. For a good example of David Ibarra's efforts to promote serious debate about Mexico's economic options see his "Mexico: The Plan and the Current Situation," *CEPAL Review* 58, April 1996: 115–128. Of particular relevance for the purposes of this chapter is the following assessment: "In the economic and social sphere it is often counterproductive to pursue isolated goals while neglecting others with which they are interconnected or, even worse, interdependent. Thus, at the beginning of the 1980s, there was an obsessive effort to achieve specified growth targets, with little thought for their inflationary repercussions, while during the last Administration, the fixation was on reducing inflation to single-digit levels, regardless of such a policy's devastating impact on the balance of payments and companies' microeconomic variables. Neither of these very different structural reform strategies went far enough or was sufficiently thought though, and the country was therefore exposed to severely destabilizing processes" (Ibid., p. 118). Ibarra was outside the circuits of power long enough to see that pluralist debate and democratic guarantees could be useful defences against the

repetition of such one-sided strategies. In response to his arguments, President Zedillo chose to launch a public attack upon him. Subsequently, *Reforma* alleged that Ibarra had received money from drugs-related sources when serving as finance minister, a charge that was eventually retracted. In mid-1996 he resigned from the PRI.

33. On June 23, 1996 President Zedillo observed to a group of journalists in Zacatecas that, "Lo que nos ha faltado en México durante varios años es debatir políticamente cuál es el camino económico para que nuestro país se desarrolle. Ha habido muchas críticas, muchas posiciones rígidas por parte del Estado, y creo que lo que tenemos que hacer, entre la crítica y la posición rígida, es dialogar, debatir y todos poner nuestro mejor acuerdo [. . .]." On September 29, in a television interview with the economist Rolando Cordera, the president was asked why the debate he wanted was not progressing better. Zedillo replied: "[. . .] he visto que realmente el nivel de análisis y de crítica no corresponde con la gravedad e importancia de los temas que se discuten [. . .] en realidad estoy observando una suerte de oscurantismo," and he called for "un mínimo de rigor intelectual" from his critics. This produced the following observation about Zedillo and his economic advisers from PRD economic adviser, former director of the UNAM Economics Faculty and former Senator Ifigenia Martínez: "lo único que ven y saben es la literatura que se produce en Estados Unidos, para problemas que son totalmente distintos a los nuestros. Yo creo que el presidente no lee nunca—sus asesores tampoco—lo que se produce en nuestras universidades." *Proceso* 1040, 6 October 1996, p. 9.

34. Sarah Babb, op. cit., p. 22.

Chapter 5   Privatization and the Public Interest: Partial Theories, Lopsided Outcomes

* This chapter is a reworked and updated version of my work "Privatisation and the Public Interest: Partial Theories, Lopsided Outcomes," in: Werner Baer and Joseph L. Love (eds.), *Liberalization and its Consequences: A Comparative Perspective on Latin America and Eastern Europe* (Northampton, MA: Edward Elgar Publishing, 2000).

1. This is the central thesis of the comparative study by Hector Schamis, *Re-Forming the State: The Politics of Privatisation in Latin America and Europe* (Ann Arbor, MI: University of Michigan Press, 2002).

2. Although this chapter focuses on Latin America, it contains some cross-references to post-Communist Eastern Europe, and some of the lessons are perhaps of more general applicability. However, post-Communist privatization arose from very different initial conditions, so that their trajectories and consequences are unlikely to be that similar.

3. Leslie Elliott Armijo, "Balance Sheet or Ballot Box? Incentives to Privatise in Emerging Democracies," in: Philip Oxhorn and Pamela K. Starr (eds.), *Markets and Democracy in Latin America: Conflict or Convergence?* (Boulder, CO: Lynne Rienner, 1998), p. 23.

4. William Glade "Privatisation: Pictures of a Process" in: William Glade (ed.), *Bigger Economies, Smaller Governments: The Role of Privatisation in Latin America* (Boulder, CO: Westview Press, 1996), p. 23.

5. Dieter Helm "The Economic Borders of the State" in: Dieter Helm (ed.), *The Economic Borders of the State* (Oxford: Oxford University Press, 1989) pp. 32–33. The section concludes thus: "despite the apparent consistency and coherence of the theory behind the general policy approach, the programme has frequently resorted to *ad hoc* pragmatism [. . .] it has often been plagiarised to meet political necessity. The result is frequently a mishmash of ideas, influences and values." Ibid., p. 36. The author then extends the analysis to include legislation against trade union "monopoly" and in favor of the private provision of health care, and education, and the disposal of the social housing stock.

6. The Bolivian Supreme Court upheld a presidential interpretation that the Congress could rewrite the law guaranteeing the new *Bono Solidario* (BONOSOL) pension rights. Subsequently, this precedent has served to destabilize the rights of the oil companies as well, and to pave the way for arguably confiscatory taxes, together with the effective recreation of the dismantled state oil company. The result provides no legal security, either for pensioners or foreign investors. Similarly, in Argentina, the finance ministry under Domingo Cavallo ended a cycle of liberalization by shamelessly raiding the privatized pensions funds.

7. Glade, op. cit., p. 23. Just what kind of behavioral constraints have motivated the managers of PDVSA is not a topic closely examined by Glade, since it could undermine his overall enthusiasm for market disciplines. Juan Carlos Boué examined this case in considerable detail in his 1996 Oxford D.Phil. The Chávez administration is now attempting to curb such antistate managerialism but risks lurching to the opposite extreme.

8. See: Carmelo Mesa-Lago and Katharina Muller, "The Politics of Pension Reform in Latin America," *Journal of Latin American Studies* 34(3), August 2002: 687–715.

9. Anthony Hall, "Privatising the Commons: Liberalisation, Land and Livelihoods in Latin America," in: Werner Baer and Joseph L. Love (eds.), *Liberalisation and its Consequences: A Comparative Perspective on Latin America and Eastern Europe* (Cheltenham: Edward Elgar, 2000), 232–258.

10. Carl J. Bauer, *Against the Current: Privatisation, Water Markets, and the State in Chile* (Boston, MA: Kluwer Academic Publishers, 1998), p. 121.

11. The Chilean case is among a series evaluated by Raquel Alfaro, Ralph Bradburd, and John Brisco "Reforming Former Public Monopolies: Water Supply" in: Nancy Birdsall, Carol Graham, and Richard H. Sabot (eds.), *Beyond Trade-Offs: Market Reforms and Equitable Growth in Latin America* (Washington, DC: Brookings, 1998): 273–304.

The Valparaiso municipal water and sewage system was privatized at the end of 1998, but within a fairly strong regulatory framework. The public sector retains a "golden" share (to control possible takeovers), horizontal integration is forbidden, and vertical integration is restricted. This set the precedent for a subsequent, larger privatization of the municipal water and sewage utility in Santiago.

12. TPSA similarly accounts for about 40 percent of capitalization on the Warsaw stock market and telecoms also head the list in the Czech Republic and Hungary.

13. See: Michael Heller, *The Politics of Telecommunications Policy in Mexico* (University of Sussex, unpublished doctoral thesis, 1990).

14. Eli M. Noam (ed.), *Telecommunications in Latin America* (New York, NY: Oxford University Press, 1998), p. xv.

15. Ibid., p. xvi.

16. Ibid., p. xxiii. This provides something of an antidote to the optimism expressed by Glade concerning Argentine telecoms. Op. cit., pp. 17–18.

17. Ibid., pp. xv–xvi and p. xxviii. Again this judgment runs counter to the positive evaluation given by Glade, but corresponds to my own observations in Bolivia.

18. Noam, op. cit., p. xxvi.

19. Ibid., p. xxvi.

20. Ibid., p. xv.

21. Argentina's 1995 Insolvency Statute shifted power from the Labor Court to the Bankruptcy Court, and to committees of creditors and receivers. However, analysts express doubt over how they work. Brazil's new bankruptcy law comes into force for the first time in 2005.

22. The Chilean case suggests that a well-ordered hierarchy of ministries staffed with competent personnel is key, as this kind of hierarchy limits and orders points of access, thus favoring policy coherence. However, extremely insulated, rigidly ideological policy-makers in contact with a narrow coalition of conglomerates may contribute to "skewed reform measures and inflexible policy-making styles." Eduardo Silva, *The State and Capital in Chile: Business Elites, Technocrats, and Market Economics* (Boulder, CO: Westview Press, 1996), p. 9.

23. See: Lourdes Sola and Laurence Whitehead (eds.), *State-Crafting Monetary Authority: Brazilian Comparative Perspective* (Oxford: Centre for Brazilian Studies, Oxford University, forthcoming, 2005).

24. For a revealing case study of this see: Marukh Doctor, "Institutional Modernisation and the Legacy of Corporatism: The Case of Port Reform in Brazil," *Journal of Latin American Studies* 35(2), May 2003: 341–366.

25. Although this seems a fairly solid generalization, initial reactions within the Mexican political class to President Zedillo's February 1999 proposal to privatize the CFE suggest that this may not be a universal law.

26. In Puerto Rico, for example, the government earmarked some of the US $2.1 billion proceeds from the telecom privatization to finance overdue infrastructure spending that would overcome the island's problems of water shortage, in association with *General des Eaux* and Thames Water.

27. Idilko Taksz, *Economic Policy Implementation in East Central Europe: Industrial Privatisation in Hungary in the Early 1990s* (Oxford: D.Phil Dissertation, 1997).

28. Indeed, John Welch made a fair comment on a draft of this chapter at the 1999 conference that preceded the publication of the volume by Werner Baer and Joseph L. Love (eds.), *Liberalisation and its Consequences: A Comparative Perspective on Latin America and Eastern Europe* (Northampton, MA: Edward Elgar Publishing, 2000), when he referred to "wave observations" rather than "wave theories."

29. To some extent this may be driven by the increased value of the real estate assets that would be released in comparison to the residual transport services still provided. Idilko Taksz, op. cit.

30. It would be highly speculative to suggest that later on, when this industry matures, it might become more of a candidate for state ownership, although the current Justice Department case charging Microsoft with monopolistic practices is intriguing.

Chapter 6   Democracy, Inequality, and Insecurity: A Paradoxical Configuration

* In contrast with the rest of the chapters in this volume, this one is not a modified version of a single text previously published elsewhere. Instead it is a composite derived from several different essays and works in progress. The most substantial precursor was my "Chronic Fiscal Stress and the Reproduction of Poverty and Inequality in Latin America" in: Victor Bulmer-Thomas (ed.), *The New Economic Model in Latin America and its Impact on Income Distribution and Poverty* (Basingstoke: Macmillan Press, 1996): 53–77, although the focus here is much broader, and the supporting evidence has been omitted. The subsection on El Salvador uses unpublished material from a 2001–2002 collaborative study.

1. This chapter does not recapitulate the already abundant literature on the "quality" of democracy in Latin America, as compared to elsewhere, focusing instead on the two specific areas of inequality and insecurity.

2. United National Development Programme, *UNDP Human Development Report* (Oxford: Oxford University Press, 1998) p. 206.

3. See: C. Binetti and F. Carrillo (eds.), *Democracia con desigualdad?* (Washington, DC: Inter American Development Bank, 2004).

4. On global poverty and inequality see: Richard Kohl (ed.), *Globalisation, Poverty and Inequality* (Paris: OECD Development Centre, 2003). For the Arab world see: "Arab Development: Self-Doomed to

Failure," *The Economist*, 4 July 2002; and the UNDP 2002 Arab Human Development Report at: *www.undp.org/rbas/ ahdr*. For a wider discussion of poverty, inequality, and politics see: Amartya Sen, *Commodities and Capabilities* (Amsterdam: North-Holland, 1985), and *Development as Freedom* (Oxford: Oxford University Press, 1999), by the same author.

5. As O'Donnell says: "the [. . .] hard fact is that the poor are politically weak. Their permanent struggle for survival is not conducive, excepting very specific [and usually short lived] situations and some remarkable individuals, to their organisation and mobilisation. Furthermore, this weakness opens ample opportunity for manifold tactics of cooptation, selective repression and political isolation." Guillermo O'Donnell, "Poverty and Inequality in Latin America: Some Political Reflections," in: Victor E. Tokman and Guillermo O'Donnell (eds.), *Poverty and Inequality in Latin America: Issues and Challenges* (Notre Dame, NC: Notre Dame University Press, 1998), p. 51.

6. See: Carol Graham and Sandip Sukhtankar, "Does Economic Crisis Reduce Support for Markets and Democracy in Latin America?" *Journal of Latin American Studies* 36(2), May 2004: 349–377.

7. See discussion in: Miguel Szekely, Nora Lustig, Martín Cumpa, and José Antonio Mejía, "Do We Know How Much Poverty There Is?" *Oxford Development Studies* 32(4), December 2004: 523–558.

8. Charles Tilly (ed.), *Formation of National States in Western Europe* (Princeton, NJ: Princeton University Press, 1975). See also his *The Politics of Collective Violence* (Cambridge: Cambridge University Press, 2003), and *Dynamics of Contention* (Cambridge: Cambridge University Press, 2001), edited by Tilly, and authored by Douglas McAdam and Sidney Tarrow.

9. There are literally hundreds of case studies and monographs tracing variants of this dynamic. To select one vivid illustration almost at random, see: José Matos Mar, *Crisis del estado y desborde popular* (Lima: Instituto de Estudios Peruanos, 1984). For a more recent compilation with many relevant examples, see: Douglas A. Chalmers, Carlos M. Vilas, Katherine Hite, Scott B. Martin, Kerianne Piester, and Monique Segarra, *The New Politics of Inequality in Latin America* (Oxford: Oxford University Press, 1997).

10. O'Donnell, op. cit., p. 58. He adds that "effective citizenship is not only uncoerced voting: it is also a mode of relationship between citizens and the state and among citizens themselves. It is a continuing mode of relationship, during, before, and after elections, among individuals protected and empowered by their citizenship. Citizenship is no less encroached upon when voting is coerced than when a battered woman or a peasant cannot hope to obtain redress in court, or when the home of a poor family is illegally invaded by the police." Ibid., p. 58.

11. Alexandra Barahona de Brito and Francisco Panizza, "The Politics of Human Rights in Democratic Brazil: 'A Lei Não Pega,' *Journal of Democratization* 5(4) Winter 1998: 20–51.

12. This was before the catastrophic earthquake (registering 7.9 on the Richter scale) that struck El Salvador on January 13, 2001, and underscores the absolute centrality of this aspect of public policy.

13. Juan L. Londoño and Rodrigo Guerrero, *Violencia en América Latina: Epidemiología y Costos* (Washington, DC: Inter-American Development Bank, 1999).

14. However, although opinion and victim surveys reveal a very bad objective situation, there are also encouraging signs from those interested in crafting a democratic strategy of crime prevention.

15. According to a 1998 IUDOP survey about 60 percent of the population has experienced some form of violent delinquency at some point in the past decade. IUDOP, *Normas Culturales y Actitudes Sobre La Violencia: Estudio Activo* (San Salvador: IUDOP, May 1999), p. 13. Londoño and Guerrero suggest that even though current rates of violence might decline, the stock of those ever exposed to it can continue to increase, producing progressively more adverse perceptions of the overall security situation. Londoño and Guerrero, op. cit.

16. Democrats should not underestimate the gravity of the fact that 44 percent of respondents to our survey (including 40 percent of FMLN supporters) endorsed the *mano dura* option. An earlier IUDOP survey on norms and attitudes toward violence provides more detail: 27 percent of respondents believed the police should be enabled to detain people on the basis of their appearance; 24 percent thought it acceptable to take justice into one's own hands; 16 percent thought the police should be allowed to torture suspects in order to obtain information; and 15 percent would approve of "social cleansing." Such severe attitudes can better be understood when considering that 20 percent claimed to have been victims of at least one armed robbery in the previous twelve months; 6.2 percent said they had received death threats; 3.0 percent said they had been mistreated by the police; 1.2 percent said they had been kidnapped; and 1.4 percent had been injured in an assault (0.8 percent by firearms). IUDOP, op. cit., p. 13.

17. Although statistics must be treated with great caution, it is worth noting that before the Civil War, in 1974–1977, the official homicide rate in El Salvador was 33 per hundred thousand, as compared to 22 per hundred thousand in Colombia and 17 in Mexico. If the data can be trusted, the Salvadorian rate was comparatively high already, although far lower than at present.

18. Juan Londoño and Rodrigo Guerrero, op. cit.

19. There is a large and growing body of literature on the impact of transnational crime in Latin America. To take just two examples see: Tom Farer (ed.), *Transnational Crime in the Americas* (New York: Routledge, 1999); Mats Berdal and Monica Serrano (eds.), *Transnational Organised Crime and International Security: Business and Usual?* (Boulder, CO: Lynne Rienner, 2002), particularly the chapter by Monica Serrano and María Celia Toro, "From Drug

Trafficking to Transnational Organised Crime in Latin America" (pp. 155–182).

20. See: Juan E. Méndez, Guillermo O'Donnell, and Paulo Sérgio Pinheiro (eds.), *The (Un)Rule of Law and the Underprivileged in Latin America* (Notre Dame, NC: Notre Dame University Press, 1999); Fernando Gonzalbo Escalante, *Ciudadanos imaginarios* (Mexico City: Colégio de México, 1992); José Álvaro Moisés, *A cidadania que não temos* (São Paulo: Ática, 1994); and James Holston and Teresa Caldeira, "Democracy, Law and Violence: Disjunctives on Brazilian Citizenship" in: Felipe Aguero and Jeffrey Stark (eds.), *Fault Lines of Democracy in Post-Transition Latin America* (Miami, FL: North-South Centre Press, 1988): 263–289.

21. Although Stanislav Andreski overgeneralized on this issue, his *Parasitism and Subversion: The Case of Latin America* (London: Weidenfeld & Nicolson, 1966), does contain some vivid insights on regional characteristics not studied elsewhere.

22. In 2002, CNN reported that "money laundering activities already account for between two to five percent of world GDP, while the United Nations has said that people smuggling is the world's fastest growing criminal business, raking in up to $10 billion a year." See "Asian Police Need to 'Act Like Triads,'" 21 March 2002 at: http://archives.cnn.com/2002/WORLD/asiapcf/east/03/21/asia.crime/index.html.

Conclusion: On Characterizing Latin America

1. See endnote five in the introduction to this volume.

2. Pierre Bordieu, *Practical Reason: On The Theory of Action* (Stanford, CA: Stanford University Press, 1988).

3. Pablo Neruda, *Memoirs* (New York: Farrar, Strauss and Giroux, 2001).

4. Néstor García Canclini, *Hybrid Cultures: Strategies for Entering and Leaving Modernity* (Minneapolis, MN: University of Minnesota Press, 1995); Jorge Larraín, *Identity and Modernity in Latin America* (Oxford: Polity Press, 2000).

5. Stanley L. Engermann and Kenneth L. Sokoloff, "Factor Endowments, Institutions, and Differential Growth Paths Among New World Economies," in: Stephen Haber (ed.), *How Latin America Fell Behind* (Stanford, CA: Stanford University Press, 1997), p. 262. This passage is quoted to illustrate one approach to comparing large regions, rather than as the last word on the subject, especially considering the problem of accommodating the peculiar institution of African slavery within this framework. Other related general contributions include: Stanley J. Stein and Barbara H. Stein, *The Colonial Heritage of Latin America: Essays on Economic Dependence in Perspective* (New York: Oxford University Press, 1987), and John Sheahan, *Patterns of Development in Latin America: Poverty,*

Repression and Economic Strategy (Princeton, NJ: Princeton University Press, 1987).

6. Richard M. Morse, *New World Soundings: Culture and Ideology in the Americas* (Baltimore, MD: Johns Hopkins University Press, 1989), pp. 100–103. Again this passage is quoted as another serious effort to characterize Latin America by a leading U.S. scholar, rather than as a definitive verdict. Compare Fernando Escalante Gonzalbo, *Ciudadanos imaginarios* (Mexico City: Colegio de México, 1992), on Mexico.

7. Charles W. Anderson, "Toward a Theory of Latin American Politics," in: Howard J. Wiarda (ed.), *Politics and Social Change in Latin America: Still a Distinct Tradition?* (Boulder, CO: Westview Press, 1992), p. 241 and p. 245.

8. Ruth Berins Collier and David Collier, *Shaping the Political Arena: Critical Junctures, the Labour Movement, and Regime Dynamics in Latin America* (Notre Dame, NC: University of Notre Dame Press, 2002).

9. Shmuel N. Eisenstadt "The Construction of Collective Identities in Latin America: Beyond the European State Model," in: Luis Roniger and Mario Sznadjer (eds.), *Constructing Collective Identities and Shaping Public Spheres: Latin American Paths* (Brighton: Sussex Academic Press, 1998), pp. 255–258.

10. One might add: what is being Latin American except an extension of what "we" are, and what are we but a reflection of what "they" are. Thus, to take one example, September 11 is an event that belongs as much to a Brazilian *cordel* poet, as it is the privileged site of mourning of New York and London City workers and families. See the *cordel* by Azulão in: Candace Slater, "Terror in the Twin Towers: The Events of September 11 in the Brazilian *Literatura de Cordel*," *Latin American Research Review* 38 (3) October 2003: 37–59.

11. See: Adam Przeworksi and Henry Teune, *Logic of Comparative Social Enquiry* (Melbourne, FL: Krieger Publishing Company, 1982). For another view on this see: Charles Tilly, *Big Structures, Large Processes, Huge Comparisons* (New York: Russell Sage Foundation, 1989).

Bibliography

Abreu, Marcelo I. P. and Werneck, Rogério L.F., "Privatization and Regulation in Brazil: The 1990–2 Policies and the Challenges Ahead," *Paper presented at the Property Rights, Privatization and Regulation in Latin America Conference*, University of Illinois, Champaign-Urbana, 19–20 November 1992.

Adelman, Jeremy, *Frontier Development: Land, Labour and Capital on the Wheatlands of Argentina and Canada, 1890–1914* (Oxford: Oxford University Press, 1994).

Adorno, Sérgio, *Os aprendizes do poder: O bacharelismo liberal na política brasileira* (Rio de Janeiro: Paz e Terra, 1988).

Aguilar Camín, Héctor, *La frontera nómada: Sonora y la revolución mexicana* (Mexico City: Siglo XXI, 1977).

Aguilar Rivera, José Antonio, *En pos de la quimera: Reflexiones sobre el experimento constitucional Atlántico* (Mexico City: Fondo de Cultura Económica, 2000).

Alfaro, Raquel, Bradburd, Ralph, and Brisco, John, "Reforming Former Public Monopolies: Water Supply" in: Nancy Birdsall, Carol Graham, and Richard H. Sabot (eds.), *Beyond Trade-Offs: Market Reforms and Equitable Growth in Latin America* (Washington, DC: Brooking Institute Press/Inter-American Development Bank, 1998): 273–304.

Anderson, Benedict, *Imagined Communities: Reflections on the Origin and Spread of Nationalism* (London: Verso, 1991).

Anderson, Charles W., "Bankers as Revolutionaries" in: William P. Glade and Charles W. Anderson (eds.), *The Political Economy of Mexico: Two Studies* (Madison, WI: Wisconsin University Press, 1963): 103–191.

—— "Toward a Theory of Latin American Politics" reprinted in: Howard J. Wiarda (ed.), *Politics and Social Change in Latin America: Still a Distinct Tradition?* (Boulder, CO: Westview Press, 1992): 238–254.

Andreski, Stanislav, *Parasitism and Subversion: The Case of Latin America* (London: Weidenfeld & Nicolson, 1966).

Anglade, Christian and Fortín, Carlos (eds.), *The State and Capital Accumulation in Latin America*. Volumes I–II (Basingstoke: Macmillan Press, 1985/1990).

Antillón, Rafael Villegas, *El Tribunal Supremo de Elecciones y El Registro Civil de Costa Rica* (San José: CAPEL, 1987).

Armijo, Leslie Elliott, "Balance Sheet or Ballot Box? Incentives to Privatise in Emerging Democracies," in: Philip Oxhorn and Pamela K Starr (eds.), *Markets and Democracy in Latin America: Conflict or Convergence?* (Boulder, CO: Lynne Rienner, 1998).

Babb, Sarah, *Managing Mexico: Economists from Nationalism to Neoliberalism* (Princeton, NJ: Princeton University Press, 2001).

Barahona de Brito, Alexandra and Panizza, Francisco, "The Politics of Human Rights in Democratic Brazil: 'A Lei Não Pega' ", *Journal of Democratisation* 5(4), Winter 1998: 20–51.

Bassols Batalla, Ángel, *Treinta años de investigación económica regional en México* (Mexico City: Colección Nuestros Maestros, UNAM 1990).

Bauer, Carl J., *Against the Current: Privatisation, Water Markets, and the State in Chile* (Boston, MA: Kluwer Academic Publishers, 1998).

Bazdresch, Carlos, *El pensamiento de Juan Noyola* (Mexico City: Fondo de Cultura Económica, 1984).

Bendix, Reinhard, "Tradition and Modernity Reconsidered," *Comparative Studies in Society and History* 9(3), April 1967: 293–346.

Beozzo, José Oscar, "A Igreja entre a Revolução de 1930, o Estado Novo e a redemocratização" in: Boris Fausto (ed.), *História geral da civilização brasileira.* Volume III: O Brasil Republicano—Economia e cultura, 1930–1964 (São Paulo: DIFEL, 1984): 273–341.

Berdal, Mats and Serrano, Monica (eds.), *Transnational Organised Crime and International Security: Business and Usual?* (Boulder, CO: Lynne Rienner, 2002).

Bordieu, Pierre, *Practical Reason: On The Theory of Action* (Stanford, CA: Stanford University Press, 1988).

Borges, Dain, "Puffy Ugly, Slothful and Inert: Degeneration in Brazilian Social Thought, 1880–1940," *Journal of Latin American Studies* 25(2), May 1993: 235–256.

Brading, David, *The First Americans: The Spanish Monarchy, Creole Patriots, and the Liberal State 1492–1867* (Cambridge: Cambridge University Press, 1991).

Brand, Salvador Osvaldo, *El origen latinoamericano de las teorías de la moneda y de la inflación* (Bogotá: Plaza y Janes, 1987).

Brooks, David C., "US Marines, Miskitos, and the Hunt for Sandino: The Rio Coco Patrol in 1928," *Journal of Latin American Studies* 21(2), May 1989: 311–330.

Bunker, Steve, *Underdeveloping the Amazon: Extraction, Unequal Exchange and the Failure of the Modern State* (Chicago, IL: Chicago University Press, 1985).

Burchell, Graham, Gordon, Colin, and Miller, Peter (eds.), *The Foucault Effect: Studies in Governmentality* (Hertfordshire: Harvester Wheatsheaf, 1991).

Camp, Roderic A., "The Technocrat in Mexico and the Survival of the Political System," *Latin American Research Review* 20(1), 1985: 97–118.

—— *Intellectuals and the State in Twentieth Century Mexico* (Austin, TX: Texas University Press, 1985).

—— "El tecnócrata en México," *Revista Mexicana de Sociología* 45(2), April–June 1983: 579–599.

—— *Mexico's Leaders: Their Education and Recruitment* (Tucson, AZ: Arizona University Press, 1980).

—— *The Role of Economists in Policy-Making* (Tucson, AZ: Arizona University Press, 1977).

Campello de Souza, Maria do Carmo, *Estado e partidos políticos no Brasil: 1930 a 1964* (São Paulo: Alfa-Omega, 1983).

Canak, William, "The Peripheral State Debate," *Latin American Research Review* 19(1), 1984: 3–36.

Cavarozzi, Marcelo, "Beyond Transitions to Democracy in Latin America," *Journal of Latin American Studies* 24(34), October 1992: 665–684.

Centeno, Miguel Ángel, "Has Mexico's Technocratic Revolution Failed?," Paper presented at the CEDLA *Workshop on Technocrats and the Politics of Expertise in Latin America*, Amsterdam 14–15 September 1995.

—— *Democracy within Reason: Technocratic Revolution in Mexico* (University Park, PA: Penn State University Press, 1994).

Centeno, Miguel Ángel and Maxfield, Sylvia, "The Marriage of Finance and Order: Changes in the Mexican Political Elite," *Journal of Latin American Studies* 24(1), February 1992: 57–85.

Chacón, Vamireh, *Estado e povo no Brasil: As experiências de Estado Novo e da democracia populista: 1937–1964* (Rio de Janeiro: Livraria José Olympio, 1977).

Chalhoub, Sidney, "The Politics of Disease Control: Yellow Fever and Race in Nineteenth Century Rio de Janeiro," *Journal of Latin American Studies* 25(3), October 1993: 441–465.

Chalmers, Douglas A., Vilas, Carlos M., Hite, Katherine, Martin, Scott B., Piester, Kerianne, and Segarra, Monique, *The New Politics of Inequality in Latin America* (Oxford: Oxford University Press, 1997).

Cleaves, Peter, *Professions and the State: The Mexican Case* (Tucson, AZ: University of Arizona Press, 1987).

Collier, Ruth Berins and Collier, David, *Shaping the Political Arena: Critical Junctures, the Labor Movement, and Regime Dynamics in Latin America* (Notre Dame, IN: University of Notre Dame Press, 2002).

Collingwood, R. G., *The Idea of History* (Oxford: Oxford University Press, 1956).

Contreras, Manuel. E., *Tecnología moderna en los Andes: ingeniería y minería en Bolivia en el siglo XX* (La Paz: ILDIS, 1994).

—— "Debt, Taxes and War: The Political Economy of Bolivia 1920–1935," *Journal of Latin American Studies* 22(2), 1990: 265–287.

Craib, Raymond, *Cartographic Mexico: A History of State Fixations and Fugitive Landscapes* (Durham, NC: Duke University Press, 2004).

Cueto, Marcos, (ed.), *Saberes andinos: ciencia y tecnología en Bolivia, Ecuador y Perú* (Lima: Instituto de Estudios Peruanos, 1995).

Cunha, Euclídes da, *Os Sertões* (São Paulo: Três, 1984).

Dahl, Robert A., *Democracy and its Critics* (New Haven, CT: Yale University Press, 1989).

Dain, Sulamis, *Empresa estatal e capitalismo contemporâneo* (Campinas: Editora UNICAMP, 1986).

Deler, J. P. and Saint-Geours, Y., *Estados y naciones en los Andes: Hacia una historia comparativa.* Volumes I and II (Lima: Instituto de Estudios Peruanos, 1986).

Doctor, Marukh, "Institutional Modernisation and the Legacy of Corporatism: The Case of Port Reform in Brazil," *Journal of Latin American Studies* 35(2), May 2003: 341–366.

Dornbusch, Rudiger and Sebastian Edwards, (eds.), The *Macroeconomics of Populism in Latin America* (Chicago, IL: University of Chicago Press, 1991).

Downes, Richard, "Autos over Rails: How US Business Supplanted the British in Brazil, 1910–28," *Journal of Latin American Studies* 24(3), 1992: 551–584.

Draibe, Sônia Miriam, *Rumos e metamorfoses: Estado e industrialização no Brasil* 1930–60 (Rio de Janeiro, 1985).

Eder, George Jackson, *Inflation and Development in Latin America: A Case History of Inflation and Stabilisation in Bolivia* (Ann Arbor, MI: University of Michigan Press, 1968).

Eisenstadt, Shmuel. N., F. Bonner, R. Kahane, and B. Siebzehner (eds.), *Social Change in Latin American Societies: A Comparative Perspective* (Jerusalem: The Magnes Press/Hebrew University, 1986).

Eisenstadt, Shmuel, "The Construction of Collective Identities in Latin America: Beyond the European State Model" in: Luis Roniger and Mario Sznajder (eds.), *Constructing Collective Identities and Shaping Public Spheres: Latin American Paths* (Brighton: Sussex Academic Press, 1998): 245–263.

—— "The First Multiple Modernities: Collective Identity, Public Spheres and Political Order in the Americas," in: Luis Roniger and Carlos H. Waisman (eds.) *Globality and Multiple Modernities: Comparative North American and Latin American Perspectives* (Brighton: Sussex Academic Press, 2002): 66–78.

Engermann, Stanley L. and Sokoloff, Kenneth L., "Factor Endowments, Institutions, and Differential Growth Paths Among New World Economies," in: Stephen Haber (ed.), *How Latin America Fell Behind* (Stanford, CA: Stanford University Press, 1997): 261–304.

Escalante Gonzalbo, Fernando, *Ciudadanos imaginarios* (Mexico City: Colegio de México, 1992).

Escudé, Carlos, "Contenido nacionalista de la enseñanza de la geografía en la República Argentina, 1879–1986," *Ideas en Ciencias Sociales* 9, 1988 (Buenos Aires: Universidad de Belgrano).

Evans, Peter, "Predatory, Developmental, and Other Apparatus: A Comparative Analysis of the Third World State," *Sociological Forum* 4(4), December 1989: 561–587.

Farer, Tom (ed.), *Transnational Crime in the Americas* (New York: Routledge, 1999).

Feuer, Lewis S., "What is an Intellectual?" in: Aleksander Gella, (ed.), *The Intelligentsia and the Intellectuals: Theory, Method and Case Study* (London: Sage Publications, 1976): 47–58.

Flynn, Peter, *Brazil: A Political Analysis* (Boulder, CO: Westview Press, 1979).

Foucault, Michel, "Governmentality" in: Graham Burchell, Colin Gordon, and Peter Miller (eds.), *The Foucault Effect. Studies in Governamentality* (Chicago, IL: University of Chicago Press-Harvester, 1991): 87–104.

Franco, Jean, "Latin American Intellectuals and Collective Identity" in: Luis Roniger and Mario Sznadjer (eds.), *Constructing Collective Identities and Shaping Public Spheres: Latin American Paths* (Brighton: Sussex Academic Press, 1998): 230–241.

Freyre, Gilberto, *Order and Progress: Brazil from Monarchy to Republic* (Berkeley, CA: University of California Press, 1986).

Galjart, Benno and Silva, Patricio (eds.), *Designers of Development: Intellectuals and Technocrats in the Third World* (Leiden: CNWS Research School, 1995).

Gallie, W.B., "Essentially Contested Contents," 56 *Proceedings of the Aristotelian Society* 167, 1956.

Gallo, Carmenza, *Taxes and State Power: Political Instability in Bolivia, 1900–1950* (Philadelphia, PA: Temple University Press, 1991).

García Canclini, Néstor, *Hybrid Cultures: Strategies for Entering and Leaving Modernity* (Minneapolis, MN: University of Minnesota Press, 1995).

Geddes, Barbara, "Building 'State' Autonomy in Brazil, 1930–64," *Comparative Politics* 22(2), 1990: 217–235.

Glade, William, "Privatisation: Pictures of a Process" in: William Glade (ed.), *Bigger Economies, Smaller Governments: The Role of Privatisation in Latin America* (Boulder, CO: Westview Press, 1996): 3–24.

Gliejeses, Piero, "The Agrarian Reform of Jacobo Arbenz," *Journal of Latin American Studies* 21(3), October 1989: 450–467.

Goldthorpe, John, "Current Issues in Comparative Macrosociology," *Comparative Social Research.* 16 (1997): 1–26.

—— "A Response to the Commentaries," *Comparative Social Research* 16 (1997): 121–132.

González Echeverría, Roberto, *La Gloria de Cuba: Historia del beisbol en la isla* (Santiago: Editorial Colibrí, 2004).

Gorelik, Adrián, *La grilla y el parque: espacio público y cultura urbana en Buenos Aires 1887–1936* (Quilmes: Universidad Nacional de Quilmes, 1998).

Graham, Carol and Sukhtankar, Sandip, "Does Economic Crisis Reduce Support for Markets and Democracy in Latin America?" *Journal of Latin American Studies* 36(2), May 2004: 349–377.

Graham, Lawrence S., *Civil Service Reform in Brazil: Principles Versus Practice* (Austin, TX: University of Texas Press, 1968).

Greib, Kenneth, *Guatemalan Caudillo* (Athens, OH: Ohio University Press, 1979).

Guano, Emanuela, "Spectacles of Modernity: Transnational Imagination and Local Hegemonies in Neo-Liberal Buenos Aires," *Cultural Anthropology* 17(2), 2002: 181–209.

Guerra, François-Xavier, "The Spanish American Tradition of Representation and its European Roots," *Journal of Latin American Studies* 26(1), February 1994: 1–35.

Guerra, François-Xavier, "Les Avatars de la représentation en Amérique Hispanique au XIX siècle" in: Georges Couffignal (ed.), *Réinventer la démocratie* (Paris: Presses de la Fondation Nationale des Sciences Politiques, 1992): 1–65.

Hall, Anthony, "Privatising the Commons: Liberalisation, Land and Livelihoods in Latin America," in: Werner Baer and Joseph L. Love (eds.), *Liberalisation and its Consequences: A Comparative Perspective on Latin America and Eastern Europe* (Cheltenham: Edward Elgar, 2000): 232–258.

Hall, John A. (ed.), *States in History* (Oxford: Oxford University Press, 1988).

Hall, Peter A., "Policy Paradigms, Social Learning and the State," *Comparative Politics* 25(3), April 1993: 275–296.

—— (ed.), *The Political Power of Economic Ideas: Keynesianism Across Nations* (Princeton, NJ: Princeton University Press, 1989).

Haya de la Torre, Víctor Raúl, *La defensa continental* (Buenos Aires: Ediciones de Problemas de América, 1942).

Heller, Michael, *The Politics of Telecommunications Policy in Mexico*, University of Sussex unpublished Doctoral Thesis, 1990.

Helm, Dieter, "The Economic Borders of the State" in: Dieter Helm (ed.), *The Economic Borders of the State* (Oxford: Oxford University Press, 1989).

Hernández Rodríguez, Rogelio, "La división de la elite política mexicana" in: Carlos Bazdresch, Nisso Bucay, Soledad Loaeza, and Nora Lustig (eds.), *México: Auge, Crisis y Ajuste*. Lecturas del Trimestre Económico 73(1), 1992 (Mexico City: Fondo de Cultura Económica, 1992).

Herzog, Lawrence (ed.), *Changing Boundaries in the Americas* (La Jolla, CA: Centre for US-Mexican Studies, 1992).

Hirschman, Albert O., *A Bias for Hope: Essays on Development and Latin America* (New Haven, CT: Yale University Press, 1971).

—— *Journeys Towards Progress* (New York: W. W. Norton & Co., 1963).

Hodara, Joseph B., *Prebisch y la CEPAL: Sustancia, trayectoria y contexto institucional* (Mexico City: Colegio de México, 1987).

—— *América Latina ¿El fin de los intelectuales?* (Lima: Universidad F. Villareal, 1973).

Hodge, John E., "The Role of the Telegraph in the Consolidation and Expansion of the Argentine Republic," *Americas* 41, 1984.

Holden, Robert H., "Priorities of the State in the Survey of the Public Land in Mexico, 1876–1911," *Hispanic American Historical Review*, November 1990.

Holston, James, *The Modernist City: An Anthropological Critique of Brasilia* (Chicago, IL: Chicago University Press, 1989).

Holston, James and Caldeira, Teresa, "Democracy Law, and Violence: Disjunctives on Brazilian Citizenship" in: Felipe Agüero and Jeffrey Stark (eds.), *Fault Lines of Democracy in Post-Transition Latin America* (Miami, FL: North-South Center Press, 1998): 263–298.

Humbolt, Alexander von, *Personal Narrative of Travels in the Equinocital Regions of America* (London: Penguin, 1995).

Humphreys, R. A., *Latin America and the Second World War: 1942–45* (London: Athlone, 1982).

Huneeus, Carlos, "Technocrats and Politicians in an Authoritarian Regime: The 'ODEPLAN Boys,' and the Gremialists in Pinochet's Chile," *Journal of Latin American Studies* 32(2), May 2000: 461–502.

Huntington, Samuel P., *Who Are We: The Challenges to America's National Identity* (New York: Simon & Schuster, 2004).

—— *The Third Wave: Democratisation in the Late Twentieth Century* (Norman, OH: Oklahoma University Press, 1993).

Ibarra, David, "Mexico: The Plan and the Current Situation," *CEPAL Review 58, April 1996: 115–128.*

Isuani, Ernesto and Tenti, Emilio (eds.), *Estado democrático y política social* (Buenos Aires: EUDEBA, 1989).

IUDOP, *Normas culturales y actitudes sobre la violencia: estudio activo* (San Salvador: IUDOP, May 1999).

Joseph, Gilbert M., *Revolution from Without: Yucatan, Mexico and the United States, 1880–1924* (Cambridge: Cambridge University Press, 1982).

Kaviraj, Sudipta, "Modernity and Politics in India," *Daedalus* 129(1), 2000: 137–162.

—— "Filth and the Public Sphere: Concepts and Practices about Space in Calcutta," *Public Culture* 10(1), 1997: 83–113.

—— "The Imaginary Institution of India," *Subaltern Studies 7*, 1993: 1–39.

Kling, Merle, "Taxes on the External Sector: An Index of Political Behaviour in Latin America," *Midwest Journal of Political Science* 3(2), 1959: 127–150.

Knight, Alan, "State and Civil Society in Mexico Since the Revolution," *Texas Papers on Mexico* 90–01, University of Texas at Austin, 1990.

—— "Mexico: 1930–1946" in: Leslie Bethell (ed.), *Cambridge History of Latin America*. Volume VII (Cambridge: Cambridge University Press, 1990): 3–82.

Kohl, Richard (ed.), *Globalization, Poverty and Inequality* (Paris: OECD Development Centre, 2003).

Kornblith, Miriam and Quintana, Luken, "Gestión fiscal y centralización del poder en los gobiernos de Cipriano Castro y de Juan Vicente Gómez," *Politeia* 10, 1981 (Caracas): 143–219.

LaFeber, Walter, *The Panama Canal: The Crisis in Historical Perspective* (Oxford: Oxford University Press, 1977).

Larraín, Jorge, *Identity and Modernity in Latin America* (Oxford: Polity Press, 2000).

Lasswell, Harold, *World Politics and Personal Insecurity* (New York: Free Press, 1965).

Lewis, Bernard, *The Crisis of Islam: Holy War and Unholy Terror* (New York: Random House, 2003).

Lloyd Stephens, John (with Frederick Catherwood), *Incidents of Travel in Central America, Chiapas, and Yucatan* Volumes I–II (New York: Dover Publications 1843).

Lombardi, John, *Venezuela* (Oxford: Oxford University Press, 1982).

Londoño, Juan L. and Guerrero, Rodrigo, *Violencia en América Latina: Epidemiologia y Costos* (Washington, DC: Inter-American Development Bank, 1999).

Lópes, Lucas, *Memórias do desenvolvimento* (Rio de Janeiro: Centro da Memória da Electricidade no Brasil, 1991).

López Portillo, José Ramón, *Economic Thought and Economic Policymaking in Contemporary Mexico* (Oxford: Oxford University D.Phil., 1995).

Lourenço, Eduardo, *América Latina entre natureza e cultura* (Lisbon: Edições Anteriores, 1999–2000).

Loveman, Brian, *The Constitution of Tyranny: Regimes of Exception in South America* (Pittsburgh, PA: University of Pittsburgh Press, 1993).

Lundahl, Mats, "Underdevelopment in Haiti: Some Recent Contributions," *Journal of Latin American Studies* 23(2), 1991: 411–429.

Malloy, James M., *The Politics of Social Security in Brazil* (Pittsburgh, PA: Pittsburgh University Press, 1979).

Marshall, Adriana, *El empleo público frente a la crisis: estudios sobre América Latina* (Geneva: IIEL, 1990).

Martins, Luciano, *Estado capitalista e burocracia no Brasil pos-1964* (Rio de Janeiro: Paz e Terra, 1985).

Matos Mar, José, *Crisis del estado y desborde popular* (Lima: Instituto de Estudios Peruanos, 1984).

Matta, Roberto da, *Carnavais, maladros e heróis* (Rio de Janeiro: Editora Guanabara, 1990).

McCullough, David, *The Path Between the Seas: The Creation of the Panama Canal, 1870–1914* (New York: Simon and Schuster: New York, 1977).

McGreevey, William, *Social Security in Latin America: Issues and Options for the World Bank* (Washington, DC: World Bank, 1990).

Melville, Elinor G.K., *A Plague of Sheep: Environmental Consequences of the Conquest of Mexico* (Cambridge: Cambridge University Press, 1994).

Méndez, Juan E., O'Donnell, Guillermo, and Pinheiro, Paulo Sérgio (eds.), *The (Un) Rule of Law and the Underprivileged in Latin America* (Notre Dame, IN: University of Notre Dame Press, 1999).

Menzies, Gavin, *1421: The Year China Discovered the World* (London: Bantam Press, 2002).

Merquior, José Guilherme, *O liberalismo: antigo e moderno* (Rio de Janeiro: Nova Fronteira, 1991).

Mesa-Lago, Carmelo and Muller, Katharina, "The Politics of Pension Reform in Latin America," *Journal of Latin American Studies* 34(3), August 2002: 687–715.

Meyer, Lorenzo, *Historia de la revolución mexicana 1928–34* (Mexico City: Colegio de México, 1978).

Miceli, Sergio, *Les intellectuels et le pouvoir au Brésil 1920–1945* (Paris: MSH, 1981).

—— *Intelectuais e classe dirigente no Brasil, 1920–45* (Rio de Janeiro: DIFEL, 1979).

Moisés, José Álvaro, *A cidadania que não temos* (São Paulo: Ática, 1994).

Montecinos, Veronica, "Economic Policy Elites and Democratisation," *Studies in Comparative International Development* 28(1), Spring 1993: 25–53.

Moraes, António Carlos Roberto, "Notas sobre identidade nacional e institucionalização da geografia no Brasil," *Paper presented at the 15th Annual Congress of ANPOCS*, Caxambó, October 1991.

Morse, Richard M., *New World Soundings: Culture and Ideology in the Americas* (Baltimore, MD: Johns Hopkins University Press, 1989).

—— "The Heritage of Latin America" in: Louis Hartz et al., (eds.), *The Founding of New Societies: Studies in the History of the US, Latin American, South Africa, Canada and Australia* (New York: Harcourt, Brace & Jovanovich, 1964): 123–169.

Murdock, Carl J., "Physicians, the State and Public Health in Chile, 1881–1891," *Journal of Latin American Studies* 27(3), October 1995: 551–569.

Musgrave, Richard A., *Fiscal Reform in Bolivia: Final Report of the Bolivian Mission on Tax Reform* (Cambridge MA: Harvard Law School, International Tax Programme, 1981).

Needell, Jeffrey D., "Optimism and Melancholy: Elite Response to the Fin de Siècle Bonaerense," *Journal of Latin American Studies* 31(3), October 1999: 551–588.

—— "The *Revolta Contra a Vacina* of 1904: The Revolt Against 'Modernisation' in Belle Époque Rio de Janeiro," *Hispanic American Historical Review* 67(2), May 1987: 233–270.

Negretto, Gabriel L. and Aguilar-Rivera, José Antonio, "Rethinking the Legacy of the Liberal State in Latin America: The Cases of Argentina (1853–1916) and Mexico (1857–1910)," *Journal of Latin American Studies* 32(2), May 2000: 361–397.

Neruda, Pablo, *Memoirs* (New York: Farrar, Straus and Giroux, 2001).

Nettl, J.P., "The State as a Conceptual Variable," *World Politics* 20(4), July (1968): 559–592.

Noam, Eli M., (ed.), *Telecommunications in Latin America* (New York: Oxford University Press, 1998).

O'Donnell, Guillermo, "Poverty and Inequality in Latin America: Some Political Reflections," in: Victor E. Tokman and Guillermo O'Donnell (eds.), *Poverty and Inequality in Latin America: Issues and Challenges* (Notre Dame, IN: Notre Dame University Press, 1998): 49–71.

—— "On the State, Various Crises, and Problematic Democratisations," *CESDE Working Paper* (University of Bologna), 1992.

O'Gorman, Edmundo, *La invención de América* (Mexico City: Fondo de Cultura Económica, 1958).

Oliveira Nunes, Edson de and Geddes, Barbara, "Dilemmas of State-Led Modernization in Brazil," in: John Wirth et al., (eds.), *State and Society in Brazil: Continuity and Change* (Boulder, CO: Westview Press, 1987): 103–145.

Osvaldo Brand, Salvador, *El origen latinoamericano de las teorías de la moneda y de la inflación* (Bogotá: Plaza y Janes, 1987).

Oszlak, Oscar, *La formación del estado argentino* (Buenos Aires: Editorial de Belgrano, 1990).

—— "The Historical Formation of the State in Latin America: Some Theoretical and Methodological Guidelines for its Study," *Latin American Research Review* 16(2), 1981: 3–32.

Pagden, Anthony, *Spanish Imperialism and the Political Imagination* (New Haven, CT: Yale University Press, 1990).

Pagden, Anthony, *The Fall of Natural Man: The American Indian and the Origins of Comparative Ethnology* (Cambridge: Cambridge University Press, 1982).

Palti, Elías José, "Orden político y ciudadanía: problemas y debates en el liberalismo argentino en el Siglo XIX," *Estudios Interdisciplinarios de América Latina y el Caribe* 5(2), July–December 1994: 95–124.

Paz, Octavio, *The Labyrinth of Solitude* (New York: Grove Press, 1961).

Pécaut, Daniel, *Entre le peuple et la nation: intellectuels et la politique au Brésil* (Paris: Maison des Sciences de l'Homme, 1989).

Peñaranda, General Enrique, *Mensaje al H. Congreso Ordinario de 1943* (La Paz: Boletín del Congreso Nacional, Code 4548, Year 1942–1943, Redactor del Honorable Congreso Nacional de 1942–1943).

Pérez Díaz, Víctor, *Sueño y razón de América Latina* (Madrid: Taurus, 2005).

Petrecolla, Alberto, Porto, Alberto, and Gerchunoff, Pablo, "Privatisation in Argentina," *Paper presented at the Property Rights, Privatisation and Regulation in Latin America Conference*, University of Illinois, Champaign-Urbana, 19–20 November 1992.

Przeworski, Adam and Teune, Henry, *Logic of Comparative Social Enquiry* (Melbourne, FL: Krieger Publishing Company, 1982).

Rabasa, José, *Inventing America: Spanish Historiography and the Formation of Eurocentrism* (Norman, OK: Oklahoma University Press, 1993).

Radcliffe, Sarah A., "Imagining The State as a Space: Territoriality and the Formation of the State in Ecuador" in: Thomas Blom Hansen and Finn Stepputat (eds.), *States of Imagination: Ethnographic Explorations of the Post-Colonial State* (Durham, NC: Duke University Press, 2001): 123–145.

Roniger, Luis, "Global Immersion: Latin America and its Multiple Modernities", in: Luis Roniger and Carlos H. Waisman (eds.) *Globality and Multiple Modernities: Comparative North American and Latin American Perspectives* (Brighton: Sussex Academic Press, 2002): 79–105.

Roniger, Luis and Mario Sznajder (eds.), *Collective Identities and Shaping Public Spheres: Latin American Paths* (Brighton: Sussex Academic Press, 1998).

Roniger, Luis, and Waisman, Carlos H. (eds.) *Globality and Multiple Modernities: Comparative North American and Latin American Perspectives* (Brighton: Sussex Academic Press, 2002).

Roniger, Luis, and Waisman, Carlos H., "Approaching Multiple Modernities in Latin America," in: Luis Roniger and Carlos H. Waisman (eds.), *Globality and Multiple Modernities: Comparative North American and Latin American Perspectives* (Brighton: Sussex Academic Press, 2002): 1–6.

Rosenthal, Anton, "The Arrival of the Electric Streetcar and the Conflict over Progress in Early Twentieth-century Montevideo," *Journal of Latin American Studies* 27(2) May 1995: 319–341.

Rouquié, Alain, *Amérique latine: Introduction à l'extrême-occident* (Paris: Seuil, 1987).

Ruthven, Malise, *Islam: A Very Short Introduction* (Oxford: Oxford University Press, 1997).

Sarlo, Beatriz, *Una modernidad periférica: Buenos Aires 1920–1930* (Buenos Aires: Editorial Nueva Visión, 1988).

Schama, Simon, *Landscape and Memory*, (New York: Vintage Books, 1995).

Schamis, Hector E., *Re-forming the State: The Politics of Privatisation in Europe and Latin America* (Ann Arbor, MI: University of Michigan Press, 2002).

Schumpeter, Joseph A., "The Crisis of the Tax State" in: A. Peacock, et al., (eds.), *International Economic Papers: Translations Prepared for the International Economic Association* (New York: Macmillan, 1954): 5–38.

Schwartzman, Simon, *São Paulo e o estado nacional* (São Paulo: DIFEL, 1975).

—— "Regional Contrasts within a Continental-Scale State: Brazil" in: S. N. Eisenstadt and Stein Rokkan (eds.), *Building States and Nations*, Volume II (New York: Sage Publications, 1974): 209–231.

Schwarz, Roberto, *Misplaced Ideas: Essays on Brazilian Culture* (London: Verso, 1992).

Scott, James C., *Seeing Like a State* (New Haven, CT: Yale University Press, 1998).

Sen, Amartya, *Development as Freedom* (Oxford: Oxford University Press, 1999).

—— *Commodities and Capabilities* (Amsterdam: North-Holland, 1985).

SERPAJ (Servicio Paz y Justicia), *Urugauay Nunca Más: Human Rights Violations 1972–85* (Philadelphia, PA: Temple University Press, 1992).

Sheahan, John, *Patterns of Development in Latin America: Poverty, Repression and Economic Strategy* (Princeton, NJ: Princeton University Press, 1987).

Sikkink, Kathryn, *Ideas and Institutions: Developmentalism in Brazil and Argentina* (Ithaca, NY: Cornell University Press, 1991).

Silva, Eduardo, *The State and Capital in Chile: Business Elites, Technocrats, and Market Economics* (Boulder, CO: Westview Press, 1996).

Silva, Patricio, "Technocrats and Politics in Chile: From the Chicago Boys to the CIEPLAN Monks," *Journal of Latin American Studies* 32(2), May 1991: 385–410.

Skocpol, Theda, "Bringing the State Back In: Strategies of Analysis in Current Research" in: Skocpol, Theda, Evans, Peter B., Rueschemeyer, Dietriech, et al., *Bringing the State Back In* (Cambridge: Cambridge University Press, 1985): 3–43.

Slater, Candace, "Terror in the Twin Towers: The Events of September 11 in the Brazilian Literatura de Cordel," *Latin American Research Review* 38(3), October 2003: 37–59.

Smith, Peter, "Leadership and Change: Intellectuals and Technocrats in Mexico" in Roderic A. Camp (ed.), *Mexico's Stability: The Next Five Years* (Boulder, CO: Westview Press, 1986): 101–117.

—— *Labyrinths of Power: Political Recruitment in Twentieth-Century Mexico* (Princeton, NJ: Princeton University Press, 1979).

Sola, Lourdes and Whitehead, Laurence, (eds.), *State-Crafting Monetary Authority: Brazil in a Comparative Perspective* (Oxford: Centre for Brazilian Studies, Oxford University, forthcoming, 2005).

Sollis, Peter, "The Atlantic Coast of Nicaragua: Development and Autonomy," *Journal of Latin American Studies* 21(3), October 1989: 481–499.

Stein, Stanley J. and Stein, Barbara H., *The Colonial Heritage of Latin America: Essays on Economic Dependence in Perspective* (New York: Oxford University Press, 1987).

Stephens, John Lloyd, *Incidents of Travel in Central America, Chiapas, and Yucatan* (New York: Dover Publications, 1969—originally published in London in 1841).

Szekely, Miguel, Lustig, Nora, Cumpa, Martín, and Mejía, José Antonio, "Do We Know How Much Poverty There Is?" *Oxford Development Studies* 32(4), December 2004: 523–558.

Szuchman, Mark D., "The City as Vision: The Development of Urban Culture in Latin America" in: Gilbert M. Joseph and Mark D. Szuchman (eds.), *I Saw A City Invisible: Urban Portraits of Latin America* (Wilmington, DE: Scholarly Resources, Inc., 1996): 1–31.

Taksz, Idilko, *Economic Policy Implementation in East Central Europe: Industrial Privatisation in Hungary in the Early 1990s* (Oxford: D.Phil Dissertation, 1997).

Tanzi, Vito, "The Role of the State and the Quality of the Public Sector," *CEPAL Review* 71, August 2000: 7–22.

Taylor, Charles, "Nationalism and Modernity" in: John A. Hall (ed.), *The State of the Nation: Ernest Gellner and the Theory of Nationalism* (Cambridge: Cambridge University Press, 1998): 191–218.

Teichman, Judith, *The Politics of Freeing Markets in Latin America: Chile, Argentina, and Mexico* (Durham, NC: University of North Carolina Press, 2001).

Tenorio Trillo, Mauricio, "1910 Mexico City: Space and Nation in the City of the *Centenario*," *Journal of Latin American Studies* 28(1), February 1996: 75–104.

Thomas, Hugh, *Cuba or the Pursuit of Freedom* (London: Eyre & Spottiswoode, 1971).

Thompson, Guy, "Bulwarks of Patriotic Liberalism: the National Guard, Philharmonic Corps and Patriotic Juntas in Mexico, 1847–88," *Journal of Latin American Studies* 22(1), February 1990: 31–68.

Tilly, Charles (ed.), *Formation of National States in Western Europe* (Princeton, NJ: Princeton University Press, 1975).

—— *Big Structures, Large Processes, Huge Comparisons* (New York: Russell Sage Foundation, 1989).

—— (ed.), *Dynamics of Contention* (Cambridge: Cambridge University Press, 2001).

—— *The Politics of Collective Violence* (Cambridge: Cambridge University Press, 2003).

Topik, Steven, "The Economic Role of the State in Liberal Regimes: Brazil and Mexico Compared 1888–1910" in: Joseph L. Love and Nils Jacobsen (eds.), *Guiding The Invisible Hand: Economic Liberalism and the State in Latin American History* (New York: Praeger, 1988).

—— *The Political Economy of the Brazilian State* 1889–1930 (Austin, TX: University of Texas Press, 1987).

Touraine, Alain, *La parole et le sang: politique et société en l'Amérique Latine* (Paris: Éditions Odile Jacob, 1988).

Trindade, Hélgio, "A construção do estado nacional na Argentina e no Brasil, 1800–1900: Esboço de uma análise comparativa," *Dados* 28(1), Rio de Janeiro, 1985: 61–87.

Tsin, Michael, "Canton Remapped" in: Joseph W. Esherick (ed.), *Remaking the Chinese City: Modernity and National Identity, 1900–1950* (Honolulu, HW: University of Hawaii Press, 1999): 19–29.

—— *Nation Governance, and Modernity in China: Canton 1900–1927* (Palo Alto, CA: Stanford University Press, 1998).

Tufte, Thomas, *Living with the Rubbish Queen: Telenovelas, Culture and Modernity in Brazil* (Luton: University of Luton Press, 2003).

Uribe, Victor, "The Lawyers and New Granada's Late Colonial State," *Journal of Latin American Studies* 27(3) October 1995: 517–550.

Uricoechea, Fernando, *The Patrimonial Foundations of the Brazilian Bureaucratic State* (Berkeley, CA: University of California Press, 1980).

—— "Formação e expansão do estado burocrático-patrimonial na Colômbia e no Brasil," *Estudos CEBRAP* 21, July–September, 1977: 77–91.

United Nations, *The UN Mission of Technical Assistance to Bolivia of 1951— Keenleyside Report* (New York: United Nations, 1951).

United Nations Development Programme, *UNDP Human Development Report* (Oxford: Oxford University Press, 1998).

Vega, Bernardo, *Control y represión en la dictadura Truiillista* (Santo Domingo: Fundación Cultural Dominicana, 1986).

Véliz, Claudio, *The Centralist Tradition of Latin America* (Princeton, NJ: Princeton University Press, 1980).

Vernon, Raymond, *The Dilemma of Mexico's Development: The Roles of the Private and Public Sectors* (Cambridge, MA: Harvard University Press, 1963).

Villegas Antillón, Rafael, *El Tribunal Supremo de Elecciones y El Registro Civil de Costa Rica* (San José: CAPEL, 1987).

Waisman, Carlos H., "The Multiple Modernities Argument and Societies in the Americas," in: Luis Roniger and Carlos H. Waisman (eds.) *Globality and Multiple Modernities: Comparative North American and Latin American Perspectives* (Brighton: Sussex Academic Press, 2002): 106–116.

Whitehead, Laurence, "Latin America as a Mausoleum of Modernities" in: Luis Roniger and Carlos H. Waisman (eds.), *Globality and Multiple Modernities. Comparative North American and Latin American Perspectives* (Brighton: Sussex Academic Press, 2002): 29–65.

—— "Privatization and the Public Interest: Partial Theories, Lopsided Outcomes" in: Werner Baer and Joseph L. Love (eds.), *Liberalisation and its Consequences: A Comparative Perspective on Latin America and Eastern Europe* (Northampton, MA: Edward Elgar Publishing, 2000): 262–289.

—— "The Politics of Expertise in Latin America," *Revista de Economia Política* (São Paulo), 20(2), April–June 2000: 23–35.

Whitehead, Laurence, "After Word on Cultures and Contexts" in: Hans Antlov and Tak-Wing Ngo (eds.), *The Cultural Construction of Politics in Asia* (New York: St. Martins Press, 2000): 223–240.

—— "La economía en México: El poder de las ideas e ideas de poder" in: *Europa en México: Por una colaboración en ciencias sociales* (Turin: Centro de Estudios de México, 1997): 129–172.

—— "Chronic Fiscal Stress and the Reproduction of Poverty and Inequality in Latin America" in: Victor Bulmer-Thomas (ed.), *The New Economic Model in Latin America and Its Impact on Income Distribution and Poverty* (Basingstoke: Macmillan Press, 1996): 53–77.

—— "State Organisation in Latin America" in: Leslie Bethell (ed.), *The Cambridge History of Latin America*, Volume VI, Part 2 (Cambridge: Cambridge University Press, 1994): 3–98.

—— "Bolivia Since 1930" in: Leslie Bethell (ed.), *The Cambridge History of Latin America*, Volume VIII (Cambridge: Cambridge University Press, 1991): 5509–5585.

—— "Political Explanations of Macro-Economic Management: A Survey," *World Development* 18(8), 1990: 1133–1146.

Wiarda, Howard J. (ed.), *Politics and Social Change in Latin America: Still a Distinct Tradition?* (Boulder, CO: Westview Press, 1992).

Wolf, Eric, *Europe and the People Without History* (Berkeley, CA: University of California Press, 1997).

Wolin, Sheldon, *Politics and Vision: Continuity and Innovation in Western Political Thought* (Boston, MA: Little, Brown & Co., 1960).

Xu, Xiaoqun, " 'National Essence' US 'Science': Chinese Native Physicians Fight for Legitimacy, 1912–1937," *Modern Asian Studies* 31(4), 1997: 847–877.

Zaid, Gabriel, *El progreso improductivo* (Mexico City: Siglo XXI, 1979).

Index

cartography, *see* mapmaking
Castro, Fidel, 60, 88, 128, 131, 156
catch-up theories, 24, 33, 34, 60,
 189–90, 192, 232
Catholic Church/Catholicism, 1,
 28, 33, 56, 59–60, 71, 76, 123,
 124, 126, 240, 242
Cavallo, Domingo, 122, 132, 133,
 146, 255, 262
census data, 98, 99, 101
Centeno, Miguel Ángel, 142, 155–6,
 158, 256, 257, 258, 259, 260
Central America, 78, 89, 211, 249
central banks, 108, 109, 110,
 129, 150
central planning, 164
centralization, 17, 63, 74, 75, 76,
 88–9, 93, 96, 100, 115, 116
*Centro de Investigación y Docencia
 Económica* (CIDE), 151, 152,
 153, 157
cepalista tradition, 157
Chaco War, 71, 84
Chávez, Colonel Hugo, 60, 131,
 177, 179, 181, 262
Chiapas, 63
Chicago School, 145, 146, 153,
 169, 188, 259
children, rights of, 200
Chile
 banks, 185
 economy, 157, 189
 expertise, 128, 133, 144, 145,
  146, 155, 255, 259, 263
 inequality, 7, 31, 198, 204
 liberalism, 72, 183
 liberalization, 63
 nationalism, 248
 nationalization, 109, 187, 249
 neoliberalism, 150, 260
 organization, 77, 98, 111–12
 plebiscite, 1989, 86
 pre-1973, 204
 privatisation, 152, 169–70, 172,
  174–5, 176, 177, 185, 188
 Socialist Party, 60, 71
 territorial control, 84, 86

Chilean Water Code, 169
China, 12, 50, 152, 159, 201, 232,
 244
Christian Democratic Party of Chile,
 (PDC), 152
Christian Democrats, 8
Christianization, 27
Church and state, separation
 of, 4
citizenship, 19, 20, 80, 81, 110,
 113–14, 209, 210, 216, 228,
 265, 267
civic rights, 202, 211, 234
civil service, 93, 98
civil society, 58, 64, 74, 76, 115,
 116–17, 130, 195, 256
civil war, 211–13
Civilization and Barbarism, 227
civilizations distinctive to region, 2
class system, 51, 68
 conflict, 82
 fragmentation, 72
 struggle, 233
clericalism, 126
coca leaf, 15
Cochabamba, 43
coffee plantations, Guatemala, 52
"cognitive" capacity, 96–103,
 115, 120
cohesion, social, 7, 14, 196, 216,
 218, 219, 234
Colbún-Machicura dams, 175
Cold War, 89, 107, 116, 128, 130,
 216, 224, 234, 237
 post-cold-war period, 55, 120,
  122, 128, 129, 133, 134,
  216–17
Colegio de Economistas, 143
Colegio de México, 148, 157
collective identity, 7, 9, 231, 256
collective imagination, 7, 10, 15–16,
 25, 30, 50, 239
Collingwood, R. G., 8, 17, 65, 238,
 239, 245
Colombia, 41, 44, 63, 77, 83, 84,
 87, 116, 125, 126, 214, 215,
 246, 266